"This magisterial conclusion to Poe's three-volume biography of Lewis is dispositive and compelling. Here the reader meets the man, finally: C. S. Lewis in full. Required reading (including the notes!) for anyone interested in the ironies, tribulations, joys, and triumphs of a major figure of twentieth-century world literature."

James Como, author, *Mystical Perelandra*; Founding Member, New York C. S. Lewis Society

"With *The Completion of C. S. Lewis*, Harry Lee Poe brings to conclusion his discerning and comprehensive three-volume biography. To read it is to walk side by side with Lewis through day-to-day life as well as through the life-changing events of his latter decades. The publication of this book is an event worth celebrating, and all three volumes are a must-read for Lewis admirers, scholars, and critics alike."

Carol Zaleski, Professor of World Religions, Smith College; coauthor, *The Fellowship: The Literary Lives of the Inklings: J. R. R. Tolkien, C. S. Lewis, Owen Barfield, Charles Williams*

"In this third and final book of his entrancing biography, Harry Lee Poe covers an extraordinary continuity of unfolding events and realities—moving from the effects of Lewis's coming of age to outstanding maturity, marked by ongoing clarity, a gripping imagination, and fresh expression. Poe's trilogy captures Lewis's creativity and his seemingly effortless portrayal of the relevance of Christian faith, whether to children and laypeople or scholars and friends. Here Poe's in-depth and vivid study ranges from the end of World War II to Lewis's passing. Prior elements of what made the man are fully brought together as concluding elements emerge, such as the grief of losing his wife and deep friend, Joy Davidman, not long before his own death. What Lewis said of his late friend Dorothy L. Sayers also applies well to him: 'let us thank the Author who invented' this extraordinary person."

Colin Duriez, author, *C. S. Lewis: A Biography of Friendship* and *Tolkien and C. S. Lewis: The Gift of Friendship*

"Select any event in C. S. Lewis's life from 1945 to his death in 1963 in Harry Lee Poe's *The Completion of C. S. Lewis*—from the Elizabeth Anscombe Socratic Club brouhaha, to Lewis's tumultuous relations with J. R. R. Tolkien and T. S. Eliot, to his marriage to Joy and grieving her death—and you will encounter meticulously detailed accounts that will not only richly enhance your previous understanding of the twentieth century's most prominent English apologist, but also prompt you to reassess previously accepted interpretations. A bonus: when Poe discusses Lewis's *Studies in Words*, he also provides what could be a thesis sentence for a college apologetics course: 'How to think as a Christian in a universe made coherent by its Creator.'"

W. Andrew Hoffecker, Professor of Church History Emeritus, Reformed Theological Seminary; author, *Revolutions in Worldview* and *Charles Hodge: The Pride of Princeton*

"Go into virtually any bookstore in the English-speaking world and you will find a volume or two (or more) of the works of C. S. Lewis. It really is amazing: the reading public seems to never tire of his works of fiction and powerful prose. This fact alone warrants new studies of Lewis's thought. In this masterful conclusion to his biographical trilogy of Lewis's life, Poe provides such a study, replete with fresh insights drawn from a lifetime of reflection upon Lewis's literary corpus. A must-read for all who wish to profit from a remarkable Christian author. In fact, make sure to buy the two preceding volumes, which provide the background for this concluding volume in Poe's rich biography!"

Michael A. G. Haykin, Chair and Professor of Church History, The Southern Baptist Theological Seminary

THE COMPLETION
OF C. S. LEWIS

Other Crossway Books by Harry Lee Poe

Becoming C. S. Lewis: A Biography of Young Jack Lewis (1898–1918)

The Making of C. S. Lewis: From Atheist to Apologist (1918–1945)

THE COMPLETION OF C. S. LEWIS

From War to Joy
(1945–1963)

HARRY LEE POE

WHEATON, ILLINOIS

Library of Congress Cataloging-in-Publication Data

Names: Poe, Harry Lee, 1950– author.
Title: The completion of C.S. Lewis : from war to joy (1945–1963) / Harry Lee Poe.
Description: Wheaton, Illinois : Crossway, [2022] | Includes bibliographical references and index.
Identifiers: LCCN 2021061432 (print) | LCCN 2021061433 (ebook) | ISBN 9781433571022 (hardcover) | ISBN 9781433571039 (pdf) | ISBN 9781433571046 (mobi) | ISBN 9781433571053 (epub)
Subjects: LCSH: Lewis, C. S. (Clive Staples), 1898–1963. | Authors, English—20th century—Biography. | LCGFT: Biographies.
Classification: LCC PR6023.E926 Z8393 2022 (print) | LCC PR6023.E926 (ebook) | DDC 823/.912 [B]—dc23/eng/20220113
LC record available at https://lccn.loc.gov/2021061432
LC ebook record available at https://lccn.loc.gov/2021061433

To
Jimmy H. Davis,
colleague and friend in teaching and writing about the science
and faith conversation, which meant so much to C. S. Lewis

Contents

Acknowledgments

As a freshly minted PhD forty years ago, I began writing reviews in academic journals. My first review was of Walter Hooper's *Through Joy and Beyond*, which I continue to regard as the best short biography of Lewis, especially with its rich display of photographs, easily unmatched by any other biography. I followed that review with one of *Brothers and Friends*, the outstanding edition of the diaries of Warren Lewis edited by Marjorie Lamp Mead and Clyde Kilby. These were followed later by reviews of Michael D. Aeschliman's *The Restitution of Man: C. S. Lewis and the Case against Scientism*, James Brabazon's *Dorothy L. Sayers*, and *G. K. Chesterton and C. S. Lewis*, edited by Michael H. Macdonald and Andrew A. Tadie.

By 1990, I was too busy with my own writing projects to undertake many book reviews, but I realized that Lewis kept popping up in everything I wrote, whether I was dealing with the Holy Spirit, the nature of the gospel, science and religion, evangelism, thinking from a Christian perspective, youth ministry, or religion and art. Though I wrote only a dozen or so articles specifically about Lewis, he was affecting my thought in many ways. After I led a two-week seminar titled "Apologetics in a Postmodern World" for the C. S. Lewis Summer Institute in Oxford and Cambridge in 1998, Stan Mattson invited me to become the Program Director for the summer institute for the triennial gatherings in 2002, 2005, and 2008. Chuck Colson, who was on the program for that summer institute in Cambridge, sat in on my seminar, which led to his funding of my professorship at Union University, the Charles Colson Chair of Faith and Culture. In 2002 I began teaching my course on C. S. Lewis at Union.

During this period, I was also working on science and faith issues with my colleague Jimmy H. Davis, who holds an endowed chair as a chemistry professor at Union, and with whom I have published four books. I found Lewis extremely helpful in my thinking through the issues related to science and faith, particularly in clarifying that most of the conflict involves philosophy rather than science or faith. Lewis also offered a window on how Christians in the academy might go about thinking of their disciplines from a faith perspective when so many evangelical schools were abandoning the faith and learning project simply because they did not know how to do it. Furthermore, Lewis provided a model for how ordinary people can share their faith through their testimonies at a time when the standard personal evangelism model had moved toward a salesmanship approach that involved "closing the sale." Finally, Lewis helped me think about how the stories we tell can reflect the culture in which we live or undermine that culture. His stress on how stories "work on" people reflects the choice of Jesus to use parables, but it also provides a basis for a Christian understanding of art.

With this volume, I have now written five books about C. S. Lewis, but Lewis informed all of my other fifteen books. For me, his great value is not as someone who made a splash a long time ago but as someone who can help us think about issues that had not even arisen during his lifetime. Of course, he anticipated many issues that would later arise, such as the ethical questions surrounding genetic engineering, the failure of values, and the diminished role of rational judgment.

With the writing of this third volume of the biography, I developed something of a personal connection with Lewis, because I came to know so many people who knew or studied with Lewis during this last period of his life and who generously extended to me their time and, in some cases, their friendship. Walter Hooper died while I was writing this book, but this project would not have been possible without him, because of his long labors in making the letters, diaries, and uncollected essays and articles available to the world. He was always available to untold thousands of people who made their way to Oxford on the trail of C. S. Lewis. He encouraged so many and always seemed to have that one bit of information at hand to fill in the missing piece of the Lewis puzzle.

Basil Mitchell served as vice president of the Socratic Club with Lewis, succeeding him as president when Lewis moved to Cambridge. One of the great Christian philosophers of the twentieth century, Mitchell had a deep appreciation for Lewis and always invited me to tea in his home when I was in Oxford, where we talked about Lewis and the Socratic Club. Derek Brewer invited me and my daughter Rebecca to dine with him at Emmanuel College, Cambridge, where he had served as master when we were editing *C. S. Lewis Remembered*, to which he contributed a chapter. Brewer belonged to the small supper club with Lewis and Hugo Dyson that met a few days after Lewis's encounter with Elizabeth Anscombe, and his experiences as a pupil of Lewis gave flesh to the accounts of Lewis as tutor. Barbara Reynolds invited me to tea whenever I was in Cambridge. A friend and collaborator with Dorothy L. Sayers in translating Dante, Reynolds had gone to hear Lewis's inaugural lecture as Professor of Medieval and Renaissance Literature at Sayers's request. Reynolds extended herself to me in an unusual way from our first meeting when she realized that I was related to Edgar Allan Poe. Sayers was a great admirer of Poe, and Reynolds had been nominated for a prestigious Edgar Award by the Mystery Writers of America for her biography of Sayers, one of the greatest English mystery writers.

George Watson, who taught for his entire career at St John's College, Cambridge, invited me into his rooms at St John's on several occasions when he learned of my interest in Lewis. Watson was not a religious man, but he had a profound appreciation for Lewis as a scholar and an interest in why his academic contribution continues to be important. Bishop Simon Barrington-Ward was the chaplain at Magdalene College, Cambridge, when Lewis was in residence there. He gave me a tour of Magdalene and wrote the preface to *C. S. Lewis Remembered*. Alastair Fowler was a doctoral student of Lewis in the early 1950s and went on to have an illustrious career at the University of Edinburgh, where we met. We carried on a lengthy correspondence about Lewis for many years. Francis Warner served as Lewis's research assistant in Cambridge when he collaborated with T. S. Eliot on the revision of the Psalter. I have appreciated his kind support and many courtesies over the years. Much closer to home, I have enjoyed the friendship of Brown Patterson, for many years the dean of the University of the South in Sewanee, Tennessee, who studied as a Rhodes scholar with Lewis just before he left Oxford for Cambridge.

Lawrence Harwood, the son of Cecil Harwood, was one of Lewis's godchildren. We corresponded before we ever met in Oxford in 2005, but that correspondence was the encouragement he needed to publish his own memoir of Lewis. He gave me a glimpse of how Lewis behaved toward children. Though I have no formal acquaintance with Douglas Gresham, I have heard him speak a number of times over the last quarter century and am grateful for the way he has worked to preserve the legacy of Lewis and for how he has provided a picture of life at the Kilns.

Writing a book is only the tip of the iceberg in the book's publication. So many people are involved after the author has typed the last period. Samuel James, acquisitions editor at Crossway, took an interest in this project when it was planned as only a one-volume biography of Lewis the teenager. All decent authors rewrite their work, either after they have finished a first draft or as they go. The thought of having to go through another editing can be dispiriting, but it must be done. Mistakes are always there. What seemed as clear as day in the writing can actually be as confusing as Bedlam in the reading. Thom Notaro undertook the editing of this volume, and he has been a pleasure to work with in making the book better than it would have been. Once the manuscript was scrubbed and polished, many other skilled hands pitched in to design the interior and cover, plan a marketing strategy, set up interviews and appearances, interest journals and magazines in reviewing the book, and much, much more. I am grateful to Jill Carter, Claire Cook, Josh Dennis, Darcy Difino, Amy Kruis, Edward LaRow, Lauren Milkowski, Cory Smith, Lauren Susanto, and Matt Tully for all they did in the publication process.

Even with the enormous amount of material that Hooper has edited, much remains unpublished at the Marion E. Wade Center of Wheaton College and in the Bodleian Library of Oxford University. I am indebted to the Wade Center and its staff for their great kindness, generosity of spirit, encouragement, and helpfulness during several trips for extended periods of research into the primary documents related to Lewis during his last years. Marjorie Lamp Mead has always been gracious to me and all those who come to use the resources of the Wade. Laura Schmidt and Elaine Hooker went out of their way to find things that I did not know existed. Most of this volume was written during the COVID-19 pandemic, when the Wade Center was closed to visitors, but the staff went to extraordinary lengths to help me utilize resources held by the center. This book could not have been completed without their help. David and Crystal Downing have been encouraging and supportive of this biography, as they are of so many other Lewis and Inklings research projects that make use of the materials at the center. Their creativity and energy have expanded the work of the Wade Center, and I appreciate the opportunity to take part in their podcast and describe my work. I am delighted that they will be leading this important research library into the future.

I also appreciate the help and courtesy given me by Rachel Churchill of the C. S. Lewis Company in securing permission to quote Lewis. The C. S. Lewis Company has safeguarded the work of Lewis, preserving his legacy for future generations, for which many are grateful.

I have had the pleasure of dialogue with many colleagues over the years with whom I have shared an interest in Lewis. Insights often come in undocumented conversations long forgotten. I am particularly indebted to Don King, Colin Duriez, Rebecca Hays, Paul Fiddes, William O'Flaherty, Dennis Beets, Barry Anderson, Malissa and Russ Kilpatrick, Stan Shelley, Nigel Goodwin, Joseph Pearce, Jerry Root, Holly Ordway, and James Como.

For a number of years, I have taught a course on C. S. Lewis at Union University. My students have sparked my imagination with their questions, and I have found that new insights often come in the process of answering questions on my feet before the students. Connections are made that would otherwise have gone unnoticed. I have long believed that some of the best scholarship emerges from the classroom experience. My work has been enhanced this year by my interaction with Lucy Baker, Nicholas Bitterling, J Bryan, Cameron Burgin, Ally Cochran, Grace Evans, Elliot Garrett, Sullivan Hogan, Meagan Jaeger, Devon Koepsell, William Lewis, J. V. Martinez, Christian Meyers, Jackson Millner, Anna Moss, Abigail Orwig, Adren Pearce, Ilsa Person, Aleah Petty, Matthew Piqué, Daniel Potts, John Putman, Samuel Sadler, David Sheilley, Caleb Simpson, Natalie Stookey, Caroline Summar, Nicholas Terra, Daniel Thomas, Matthew Van Neste, Jake Vaughan, Hunter Walker, Jack Waters, Anna Williams, and Cameron Woodard.

I could not undertake projects of this sort without the support of Union University, particularly our president, Samuel W. ("Dub") Oliver; the provost, John Netland; and the dean of the school of theology and Missions, Ray Van Neste. My wife, Mary Anne Poe, has long supported my interest in Lewis and has been a great encouragement in the writing of this book. Finally, to the many friends who have participated in the retreats sponsored by the Inklings Fellowship over the past twenty years through the annual Inklings Weekend in Montreat and the triennial Inklings Week in Oxford, I am grateful for your support and interest in the life and work of C. S. Lewis.

I

The Dreary Aftermath of War

1945–1949

As the Allied armies closed in on Berlin in the spring of 1945, the inevitable defeat of Germany loomed ahead. Just as inevitably, C. S. Lewis anticipated the departure of Charles Williams from Oxford when victory finally came. The Oxford University Press would return to its London office, and the friendship that had meant so much to Lewis seemed likely to enter a new phase, like his friendship with Owen Barfield or Arthur Greeves. They would see each other once or twice a year and write every six months or so, but the days of vital energy would soon end with the coming separation.

Rather than sink into depression over the loss of Williams, Lewis decided to seize the moment and publish a *Festschrift* in honor of his friend. He enlisted Barfield and J. R. R. Tolkien in the plan. It was a thoughtful and generous thing to do. A *Festschrift* is normally an honor bestowed on only the most accomplished scholars of a great university. Before Lewis could fully develop his plans for the volume, however, Williams suddenly died the week after the German surrender.

With the end of World War II and the death of Charles Williams, one major phase of the life of C. S. Lewis came to an end, and the last phase of his life began. Lewis had been remarkably productive during the war. He produced the books that would earn him an international reputation as a Christian apologist. He bolstered his reputation as a major scholar with his treatment of Milton. He wrote science fiction, fantasy, literary criticism, and philosophical apologetics. He gained fame, if not notoriety, for his broadcast talks. He delivered prestigious academic lectures at several different universities and scholarly societies. He spoke to common airmen across the length and breadth of Britain. He worked himself to the limits of physical and mental endurance. For his efforts, he earned the envy and jealousy of many of his English faculty colleagues. With the end of the war, however, his war work came to an end. He could return to his own work. He could write what he wanted to write. He had fulfilled his duty.

With the death of Williams, however, Lewis felt a new duty. He must complete the work he had started as a tribute and celebration of his friend. What a party they would have had upon the book's completion and presentation to Williams were he still alive! But Williams would not be there to receive the toast or the praise. His wife and son would be there without a husband and father to provide for them. So Lewis turned his attention to publishing the collection of essays as a means of providing some income for Florence Williams.

Essays Presented to Charles Williams

Two days after Williams died, Lewis wrote to Dorothy L. Sayers to enlist her help in the volume of essays. He explained that it would be a memorial volume with the proceeds to benefit Mrs. Williams. Since the book had no common theme, Lewis left it to Sayers to decide the subject of her essay. The only common feature of the essays would be that all would be written by friends of Williams.[1] Then Lewis did what might seem a surprising thing. He asked T. S.

Eliot to contribute a chapter. Eliot had known Williams longer
than Lewis, and Eliot's firm of Faber and Faber had published
several of Williams's books. Despite Lewis's feelings about Eliot
and his poetry and criticism, he knew that Williams had always
highly regarded Eliot. Lewis asked him to write an essay evaluat-
ing Williams's poetry or giving a sketch of Williams, but assured
Eliot that almost anything would be fine. Then he got around to
the main point: Would Faber and Faber publish the volume? He
thought that Oxford University Press would probably be willing
to publish it, given Williams's long association with OUP, but he
thought that Faber and Faber would do a better job of marketing
the book. In the end, this was a case of being in it for the money—
for Mrs. Williams.[2]

Sayers questioned whether anyone would actually buy the kind
of book Lewis had in mind, which was not about anything in
particular, but she agreed to participate. Tolkien would contribute
"On Fairy-Stories," a paper he had presented as the Andrew Lang
Lecture at the University of St Andrews in 1939.[3] Lewis would
contribute a paper on popular romance, which he finally named
"On Stories."[4] He had suggested that Sayers might want to do
something on Williams's novels, but his novels were not what
had attracted Sayers to Williams, as they had attracted Lewis.
Her friendship with Williams truly began with the publication of
his *The Figure of Beatrice* from Dante. They corresponded about
Dante and his *Divine Comedy*, which led to Sayers undertaking
a translation of the entire work. She decided she could work up
an appropriate essay based on her correspondence with Williams,
and that is what she did.[5] Her essay was "'. . . And Telling You a
Story': A Note on *The Divine Comedy*." Her greatest reservation
was that she was not, nor did she pretend to be, a Dante scholar.
Yet it was precisely her fresh look at Dante that Williams had encouraged. Her interest was the narrative itself, rather than all the
"theology-politics-scholarship" and the "who-was-the-Veltro?"
aspect of formal Dante scholarship.[6]

Lewis responded that all the scholars would need what Sayers had to say, more than anyone else, since "the last thing they ever dream of noticing in a great narrative poem is the *narrative*." Lewis thought that what she had in mind would actually fit nicely with what he and Tolkien were doing with their essays related to story.[7] The book would accidentally have some unity. In a follow-up note to Sayers, he explained that a formidable group of modern scholars have disdain for a strong narrative because it tends to make literature entertaining. Since great art involves more than entertainment, this company of "prigs" committed the logical fallacy of concluding that "entertainment has no place in great art," a view akin to the modern prejudice against classical music having a "catchy tune."[8] Lewis would incorporate these thoughts and others like them in *An Experiment in Criticism* almost twenty years later.

In his negotiations with T. S. Eliot, Lewis stressed that the essays by Tolkien, Sayers, and him all dealt, in some way, not just with *story* but with "*mythopoeia*," the one element of literature that critics from Aristotle to Maud Bodkin had left "entirely alone." The connection with Williams was that this kind of literature was his strong suit. Having gotten nowhere with the suggestion that Eliot write an essay on Williams's poetry, perhaps having forgotten that Eliot thought the poetry as obscure and difficult as he did, Lewis suggested that Eliot write about the novels or plays.[9] In any event, he wanted Eliot's professional opinion as a book editor about whether such a *Festschrift*, whether published by Faber and Faber or by someone else, would be marketable.[10] A *Festschrift* is not the sort of book that Faber and Faber published for its general audience, but Eliot suggested that Lewis contact Sir Humphrey Milford at Oxford University Press, for whom Williams had worked his entire career. Within a few weeks, Milford replied that he would be happy to publish the book. He told Lewis that as soon as the OUP had the full manuscript, they could make estimates and offer "a suggestion of terms and prices." Lewis was horrified! He wrote to Eliot with the news of what sounded to him like the expectation that the OUP would publish the book only if Lewis paid the expenses.[11] He had an earlier experience with a required subvention fee when he and some friends had tried to publish an anthology of their poetry during his undergraduate days at Oxford.

Lewis also wrote to Sayers to let her know what Milford had proposed and at the same time wrote to Milford explaining that he and the other contributors expected no remuneration. They intended for all proceeds to go to Mrs. Williams. He explained to Sayers that by this means he hoped to "shame" Milford into making a better offer.[12] She was outraged, as only Dorothy L. Sayers was capable of being, and wrote to Lewis:

> Good God Almighty! And Charles served that firm faithfully for nearly all his life!
>
> And (if an invocation to Our Father Below is more effective, as it sometimes is in this world) Proh Lucifer! Does that comic little man expect ME to pay for the privilege of being published by him? *Pay*? PAY?—Or, if it comes to that, YOU? Most publishers would be pretty glad to have our names on their lists at any price.[13]

Having made herself clear, Sayers, who had a much better head for business and figures than did Lewis after her years of working at an advertising firm, informed Lewis that her agent would be contacting him with forms for him to sign that allowed Sayers to retain the copyright on her essay.

Unfortunately, poor Lewis had misunderstood Sir Humphrey Milford's publishing language. Milford had been doing his business for many decades, and he knew better than Lewis that *Festschrifts* make no money for the contributors or publishers. A *Festschrift* is one of those things publishers do from time to time for the academy as public relations. By "terms and prices," Milford explained in a letter to Lewis, he had meant the royalty and the publication price.[14] In humiliation, Lewis wrote to Sayers with the clarification. He sent her a copy of Milford's letter and a brief notice:

Best quality Sackcloth & Ashes
in sealed packets
delivered in plain vans at
moderate charges
Messrs M. Cato and R. E. Morse.[15]

Sayers replied characteristically that her menu for supper that night would be

HUMBLE PIE
IPSISSIMA VERBA
with sharp sauce
FRUITS
Meet for Repentance

and added that she took everything back that she had written, including "comic little man."[16] Lewis also sent a copy of Milford's letter to Eliot, but without the added advertisement of his humiliation.[17]

By December 1945, Sayers had finished sixty handwritten pages, which she turned over to her secretary to type.[18] While working on this project, she had also undertaken the writing of a play to commemorate the 750th anniversary of Lichfield Cathedral. It would be named *The Just Vengeance* and would be performed in June 1946.[19] She advised Lewis that she could send to him what she had completed, but that she was willing to edit it down to a manageable size if it was too out of proportion with the other essays.[20] Lewis urged her to send the manuscript as written.[21] They corresponded on what might be cut from her manuscript and what changes should be made. Among other things, Lewis asked Sayers to translate her many quotations of Dante from Italian into English.[22] Lewis had learned a hard lesson about foreign-language quotations in the 1930s. By the first week of January 1946, Lewis had edited Sayers's

Dorothy L. Sayers, spring of 1950. Used by permission of the
Marion E. Wade Center, Wheaton College, Wheaton, IL.

essay and she had approved the changes.[23] Apparently he did not
share her concern about any disproportion among the essays. In
the published volume, Sayers's essay, the first in the collection, ran
thirty-seven pages. Tolkien's essay came next with fifty-two pages.
Lewis's essay came third with only sixteen. Owen Barfield's essay
followed with twenty-one pages. Next came Gervase Mathew's
essay at only eight. Warren Lewis's essay came last with ten pages.
It was a highly uneven book. Missing was Eliot's essay.

By February 1946, Eliot had sent nothing to Lewis, who had
hoped to have all the contributions by the previous Christmas.
He remarked to Dorothy L. Sayers that Eliot was not a writer in
the same sense that she was. Instead, he was "one of these poets
(in the worst sense of the word)."[24] He complained to her that
Shakespeare, Dryden, and Pindar could all meet their deadlines,

but not Eliot.[25] Sayers suggested a tone in which Lewis might write to Eliot. In his letter to him of February 28, Lewis had praise for Sayers's essay on Dante and relayed the news that he had almost all the manuscripts ready to go to press. To this brief message, he added the question "When may I expect yours?"[26]

Eliot put Lewis off and suggested a distant date by which he could submit a contribution. Lewis stressed that he wanted to release the book before everyone had forgotten about Williams's death, and Eliot's suggested date was when Lewis had hoped to go to press. If Eliot could not write anything sooner, Lewis suggested that he might submit an unpublished poem instead of an essay. He even added that the poem need have no connection with Williams.[27] Lewis seems to have recognized that even though he did not care for Eliot, many people did. His primary concern at this point was to publish a book that would honor Williams and bring Mrs. Williams some ready cash. Eliot responded on March 26 that he would send Lewis something.[28] By the end of May, however, Eliot had written again to say he could not send anything yet. After consulting with others (presumably his brother, Warren, and Tolkien and perhaps others), Lewis wrote to Eliot to say that they would feel the loss of his contribution, which would have made the book stronger, but that they feared a further delay would be disastrous. He ended by suggesting that Eliot might find his own way of honoring their friend.[29]

In the end, Gervase Mathew supplied an essay to fill the gap left by Eliot. It was an unfortunate ending to Eliot's involvement in Lewis's plans to honor Williams, especially in light of Lewis's long-standing attitude toward Eliot, of which Eliot was aware. Williams had hoped they might become friends. Eliot's failure to contribute anything to the *Festschrift* is difficult to explain, especially since he had already published an article titled "The Significance of Charles Williams" in the December 19, 1946, issue of *The Listener*. Tolkien's contribution was a recycled paper nearly ten years old, so Eliot might have submitted his piece from *The*

Listener, except it would have been the same sort of article that Lewis would need to write as an introduction. Eliot clearly wanted to honor Williams and help Mrs. Williams, but perhaps he also wanted to keep his distance from Lewis. In the end, Eliot did find a way to honor his friend, and in a much more profitable way for Mrs. Williams than *Essays Presented to Charles Williams*. At Eliot's initiative, Faber and Faber issued a second edition of all of Williams's novels between 1946 and 1948, which also were published in the United States by Pellegrini & Cudahy. For *All Hallows' Eve*, Eliot wrote a lengthy, glowing introduction.

Essays Presented to Charles Williams was finally published in December 1947. It was not a publishing success. Since *Out of the Silent Planet*, Lewis had grown accustomed to major attention in the form of reviews whenever he released a book. The *Festschrift* received only two reviews, and these were unflattering.[30] The hostile review in *Theology* was so egregious that Sayers and Lewis both took the unusual step of writing letters to the editor to rebut the false assumptions and allegations in the review.[31] By July 1948, he had to admit to Sayers that they had not had "much luck" with their efforts.[32]

In terms of honoring the legacy of Charles Williams, Lewis had another project that brought attention to Williams's poetry. In one of his early exchanges with Eliot, Lewis had mentioned that he might lecture on Williams's poetry or even write a book about it.[33] In November 1946, long before the completion of *Essays Presented to Charles Williams*, Lewis sent a manuscript to Gerard Hopkins at the Oxford University Press that included his critique of Williams's King Arthur poems and the prose fragment of "The Figure of Arthur" by Williams. He named it *Arthurian Torso*. Williams had a relationship with the literary agents of Pearn, Pollinger & Higham, and Lewis instructed Hopkins to negotiate terms and royalties with them on behalf of Mrs. Williams. Hopkins and Williams had been not only colleagues but good friends who had moved from London to Oxford together during the war. Hopkins was even known warmly by the Inklings, so Lewis made clear that he relied upon him to help the widow by publishing the book.[34] Not until March 1947, however, did it occur to Lewis that he should ask Florence Williams's permission and authorization to publish the book, since she owned the rights. In writing to her, he made clear that all proceeds would go to her, and he asked if he might dedicate the book to her.[35] The Oxford University Press published *Arthurian Torso* in October 1948.[36]

With the republication of Williams's novels, which generated new interest in Williams, the BBC approached Lewis about giving a talk about Williams's novels over the radio. Lewis wrote to Ronald Levin that Eliot or Sayers would do a better job and would bring more prestige to the task. He agreed to do it if no one else would, but he asked to be excused, since he was very busy and unwell. Nonetheless, he repeated that he would do it in order to help the sales of Williams's books.[37] Levin responded that if Lewis could not do the talk, the BBC would postpone the idea. Lewis immediately replied that he would do the talk. In fact, he had already written a draft on the off chance that Eliot or Sayers declined.[38] With this talk, Lewis had done his duty to his friend, and he appears to have been ready to move on with his life. Before he reached that point, however, Lewis had many other issues with which to deal.

Years of Austerity

On August 6, 1945, the United States Army Air Corps dropped an atomic bomb on Hiroshima, which effectively wiped the city from the face of the earth. Three days later, a second atomic bomb was dropped on Nagasaki with a similar result. On August 10, the Japanese government informed the Allies of its intention to surrender, and Emperor Hirohito made the announcement of surrender by radio to the Japanese people on August 15, which became known as V-J Day, for victory over Japan. From India to Burma to Singapore and the very edges of Australia and New Zealand, the British

Empire had been involved in a desperate struggle with Japan even as it fought Nazi Germany in Europe. Finally, it was over.

Britain had not had a general election for ten years. In May 1945, Winston Churchill had a popularity rating of 83 percent. With the defeat of Germany, Churchill had called for a general election, and the king dissolved Parliament in June ahead of the election in July. When the votes were counted on July 26, Churchill failed to win a majority for his Conservative Party. The Labour Party, under the leadership of Clement Attlee, who had served with Churchill in a coalition government during the war, won a stunning victory. Labour had an overwhelming majority in Parliament of 393 seats to the Conservative Party's 197 seats, and this allowed it to implement its agenda of major reform of the nation. The reforms included the nationalization of the coal and railroad industries (among others), economic planning, full employment, a National Health Service, and a system of social security. With the promises of Labour, Britain expected sunny days ahead.

Labour succeeded in implementing most of its proposals, but postwar Britain was far from sunny. One expects privations and sacrifice during war, but one also expects that to the victor go the spoils. Britain found, however, that rationing did not end with the war. Lewis never complained about shortages during the war, though he would joke about it from time to time. Shortages during a time of peace, however, galled him beyond measure. During the five years following the war, Britain found itself suffering from food shortages at times worse than during the war. Britain found itself in the humiliating position of needing the same kind of relief that the Marshall Plan provided to war-ravaged Europe. One of the most important relief programs developed in the United States, to which millions of Americans contributed, was the Cooperative for American Remittances to Europe (CARE), which was founded in November 1945 to relieve hunger and starvation. Households all over Britain benefited from the CARE packages that arrived from the United States. C. S. Lewis, his family, and his friends numbered among the beneficiaries in Britain. I recall the CARE advertisements on television as late as the mid-1950s.

By reading Lewis's letters, we can gain a glimpse of what he was thinking and concerned about during important phases of his life. We have seen pronounced phases in his letters from 1914 through 1918, 1919 through 1930, 1931 through 1939, and 1939 through 1945. If the letters tell the tale, then Lewis's thoughts focused on his domestic life from 1945 through 1950. The easiest concern to follow is food, both its scarcity and its provision. As it turns out, Lewis did not starve or do without. Relief came to him from an unlikely source—the abominable Americans.

Among the oppressive flood of letters that Lewis began to receive from Americans during the war was one in April 1945 from Dr. Warfield Firor, an eminent surgeon on the faculty of Johns Hopkins School of Medicine in Baltimore. Firor had liked *Perelandra*, and Lewis sent him the customary brief acknowledgment that normally went to Americans.[39] Then in January 1946, Firor sent Lewis a package of paper. Lewis had grown accustomed to letters from Americans who asked long and involved questions on the most intimate of subjects, but he had not grown accustomed to Americans sending gifts with invitations to spend a vacation in the Rocky Mountains.[40] He thanked Firor for the paper, an essential item for his work and a necessity if he was to answer all the letters he received. Paper was just one of many items in short supply in Britain, and the supply would grow scarcer. While declining the invitation to visit the United States, Lewis did something quite remarkable for him. He told the total stranger that he could not leave Oxford because he was caring for "an aged and ailing mother" without the help of servants.[41] What we know of how Lewis felt about his domestic life in the years following the war comes from the seemingly endless stream of thank-you notes he wrote to Firor and his other American benefactors.

In October 1946, Firor sent another package of stationery and a box of dried fruit. In expressing his thanks, Lewis remarked that fruit was very scarce in England, like so many other things.[42] More parcels followed in July and September 1947 with more stationery and more food that would supplement "the monotonous and scant rations" at the Kilns.[43] In October, the floodgates opened and Lewis received a ham and a block of cheese from Firor. Lewis said that it lifted him into the millionaire class! Such things could only be found on the black market at an exorbitant price.[44] In January 1948, several packages arrived from Firor that contained plum pudding, chocolates, jelly, chicken, sardines, lard, syrup, butter, and another ham.[45] In March, Lewis received a third ham. Henceforth, Firor would be known for sending Lewis hams on a regular basis. Lewis remarked that if it became known that he had a ham, it would be a greater attraction to burglars than gold plate.[46]

The third ham prompted a famous dinner at Magdalen College for many, but not all, of the Inklings. The company included Lewis and Warren ("Warnie"), Tolkien, Dyson, Lord David Cecil, Christopher Tolkien, Colin Hardie, and Dr. Robert "Humphrey" Havard.[47] The kitchen staff at Magdalen cooked the ham and provided a soup, filet of sole, and a pâté savory. Tolkien and Dyson each brought two bottles of burgundy from the stores of Merton College. Cecil brought two bottles of port. Warnie observed that Colin Hardie "covered himself with glory in the ungrateful role of carver."[48] With his thank-you note, Lewis included a sheet with the heading "The undersigned, having just partaken of your ham, have drunk your health." Each of the companions in the ham feast signed his name and gave his honor.[49]

With April came another ham and a cake, which Lewis cut at the Inklings meeting when it arrived.[50] By now, it might have been obvious to Firor that Lewis was sharing his food packages with his friends. As rare as such things were during the hard period of austerity, Lewis did not hoard his bounty. Lewis let Firor know that the Inklings were preparing for another ham banquet, but each man had to bring his own bread, since bread was rationed strictly.[51] Other parcels arrived, and in July Firor sent two more

Ham dinner appreciation note to Dr. Warfield Firor, March 11, 1948. Used by permission of the Bodleian Libraries, University of Oxford, MS. Eng. Lett. C. 220/1, fol. 86.

hams; and for the first time, Lewis kept one ham for the Kilns.[52] He admitted to Firor that he loved to eat, and the rationing of food in England came with the consolation that he had recovered a pleasure at fifty years of age that he had enjoyed when he was thirteen. In September, Firor sent two more hams in addition to a string of parcels of canned goods, a common item that had almost disappeared from the shops.[53] When Lewis thanked Firor for the hams he sent in November, he mentioned signs of improvement in the food supply. The ration for shortening was to rise from one ounce per week to two ounces.[54] Life was truly grim. Just in time for Christmas, yet another ham arrived.[55]

In February 1949, three more parcels arrived from Firor, one of which contained another ham.[56] More parcels arrived through the winter, and in April, two more hams came.[57] Firor had invited Lewis regularly for four years to visit the United States, but the answer was always the same. He had an invalid mother to care for and no reliable servants to help. Lewis, in turn, regularly invited Firor to visit Oxford. In April, Lewis received the news that Firor would visit Belfast in July and planned to come over to Oxford to meet Lewis. When the time came, Firor stayed in Lewis's rooms in Magdalen. Lewis treated him to dinner in the hall of Magdalen College, which was a grand affair even under rationing, after which they attended an Inklings meeting back in Lewis's rooms.[58]

With so many benefactors, Lewis accumulated an enormous store of food that would have made Janie "Minto" Moore's hoarding days during the war seem amateurish by comparison. Though Lewis amassed the rare bounty of food, he did not hoard it, nor did he take it to the Kilns. He turned a corner of his rooms at Magdalen into a warehouse from which he distributed what he had to his friends and those whose need was greater than his. He did not confess to Dr. Firor what he was doing until the winter of 1949, almost four years after the war.[59] To appreciate the considerable size of Lewis's larder, however, it is helpful to know that Firor was not his only benefactor. It is impossible to say how many people from the United States and Canada were sending food and other rarities to Lewis before rationing finally ended in the 1950s. Besides letters of thanks to Warfield Firor, letters to Edward Allen, Vera Mathews, Mr. and Mrs. E. L. Baxter, Walden Howard, Chad Walsh, Frank Lombar and the National Association of Evangelicals, Kathleen Andrews, and Edward Dell survive.[60]

The things that his benefactors sent to Lewis suggest just how desperate life had grown in the years of privation after the war. Firor and Allen regularly sent Lewis stationery, something we take for granted, but paper was in short supply, and Lewis needed it every day.[61] The shortage goes a long way toward explaining why so many of Lewis's typed letters are written on strips of paper rather than on full sheets. The paper shortage also affected the publishing industry, and Lewis found that *The Allegory of Love* was temporarily out of print by 1949.[62]

The things he missed most by the end of 1947 were meat, tea, and washing powder for the laundry. He could not understand why there would be a shortage of laundry soap but not hand soap.[63] What dismayed Warnie Lewis at the end of 1947 was the government announcement that potatoes would be rationed at the rate of three pounds of potatoes a week. He never dreamed that the time would come when he would go to bed hungry.[64] Clothing also continued to be in short supply for years. He marveled at the large supply of butter—eight week's rations—and a large slab of bacon from Vera Mathews, along with a quantity of eggs.[65] One of the items in shortest supply was lard/shortening/cooking fat.[66] Thus, Lewis was particularly grateful to receive a can of Crisco.[67]

While Firor could be relied upon for a steady supply of hams, Mathews kept Lewis supplied with bacon, tea, and shortening.[68] To her, Lewis made so bold as to confess that tobacco would be gratefully received, for it was still "short and dear." Lewis, who began smoking by the time he first went to Wynyard School, preferred Golden Flake cigarettes, but during the years of austerity, he was happy to smoke anything.[69] By Christmas of 1948, Lewis felt the greatest shortage to his own comfort in sugar and tea.[70] And he assured Edward Allen that the American bacon, which is mostly fat, could not be "too fat" for him, since England was "permanently short of fats."[71] As 1949 began, Lewis told Firor that the government was instituting further austerity![72]

While the average British home experienced food shortages, somehow Magdalen College managed to survive. Fellows were allowed to invite no more than one guest at a time to dinner. Warnie commented on an excellent meal in Magdalen in October 1947 that included lobster salad, partridges, and peach Melba. Though they managed to survive on such rations, the discussion at the Inklings that evening focused on whether cannibalism might ever be justified![73]

The fact that Lewis kept the food and other supplies in his rooms at Magdalen rather than his much larger house suggests the state of domestic affairs at the Kilns after the war. Lewis had seen how Minto managed the food there during the war. If the food had entered the house, it would have fallen under her superintendence. By keeping the food in his rooms, he could bring food home that had come as a gift without placing the burden of management on Minto. An example of his benevolence appears in a letter to Vera Mathews on October 1, 1949.[74] She had sent Lewis a package of fresh beef, a true rarity in England. Just a week earlier, he had received a painted tray from his friend the poet Ruth Pitter. He had been to London several times to eat lunch with Pitter and their mutual friend Owen Barfield. In his letter to Mathews, Lewis confessed that he had sent the beef to a lady in London who had trouble making ends meet. Pitter supported herself by painting flowers on wooden or paper-mache trays. We can only speculate that she was the recipient of the beef. In explaining what he had done, however, Lewis wrote to Mathews that though he liked beef very much, he liked "to share the good things" her generosity had supplied him even more.[75] When Edward Allen sent him a dinner jacket that did not fit, he had a raffle for it among the Inklings. Colin Hardie won the jacket, but it did not fit him either. He gave it to Christopher Tolkien, J. R. R. Tolkien's son who had become a regular Inkling after the war, who Warnie thought "looked admirable in it."[76] Lewis explained to Allen that the dinner jacket was worth an entire year's clothing ration. Several months later, a second dinner jacket arrived to benefit Lewis's "younger & slighter friends."[77] He also informed Allen that he sent a parcel on to Tolkien rather than keeping it for himself, because his old friend "has no Mr. Allen."[78]

Grown-Up Talk

The great shortages of food and other basic commodities for nine years beyond the end of World War II led to something that Lewis had successfully avoided throughout his life—grown-up talk. As a teenager, Lewis had despised the endless discussions of politics by Albert Lewis and his family and friends. The Irish question, war, civil war, national strikes, the abdication of the king, and numerous other political questions had never tempted Lewis as topics of discussion in his letters except in the most casual fashion. When politicians began to meddle with his table, however, Lewis drew the line. He admitted to Arthur Greeves that he had begun to grumble "about 'this rotten government'" the same way their fathers had done.[79] He regularly made disparaging remarks about the government throughout the years of austerity. By 1947, he resented the "monotonous and scanty ration" of food that the government allowed.[80] He referred to the planning and policies of the Labour government as "Mr. Attlee's Iron Curtain."[81] By 1948, he began to face the fact that shortages were getting worse.[82] He began to pin his hopes for the well-being of England on the Marshall Plan. After a lifetime of looking down on beastly Americans, he found himself the recipient of American generosity, not unlike Paul's collection among the Gentile churches of Macedonia, Greece, and Asia Minor for the poor Jewish Christians in Jerusalem.[83] Lewis marveled that Edward Allen continued his generous parcels even after he had a temporary cut in his own income of 50 percent.[84] The American government, rather than the British government, was dealing with the shortages in Britain and Europe.

When Americans began sending packages of food by the millions to the people of England, the British government introduced the policy of decreasing the rations of those who received parcels that weighed more than five pounds. As a result, Lewis found that his benefactors began sending him three or more parcels under the weight limit, rather than one large package, so that he did not lose his meager ration.[85] And as for the paper shortage, Lewis complained that if the government would only print "fewer forms, appeals, posters, pamphlets etc.," the country would be better off and could have stationery.[86] By March 1948, the government reduced the cheese ration from two ounces to one and a half ounces a week, so that life became "very drab" without the food parcels.[87] He wrote to Edward Allen in May 1948 that if it were not for the Americans, England "would starve through sheer incompetence."[88] He noted that the clothing warehouses were overflowing, but the country had a clothing shortage. When England had a beautiful May for the first time in many years, Lewis cynically remarked that the government had not yet found a way to ration the sunlight.[89] At the end of 1948, the government promised an increase in the sugar ration, and the shortening ration was to go from one ounce of shortening per week to two ounces.[90]

Lewis regularly asked his American benefactors about the American political scene, which seemed most confusing in 1948 when Mr. Dewey had been expected to win the presidential election, and war loomed in Asia and possibly other points around the globe. Lewis appears to have begun reading the newspapers again, so dire was the situation. He told Edward Allen that the "Socialist press" in England hailed the Truman victory as a sign that the United States was about to become a modern democracy, which Lewis cynically interpreted as "state ownership, beaurocracy [sic], and all the joys of present day English life."[91] He had a dim view of the Labour Party government under Clement Attlee, which he described as "a government elected by a majority which is really a minority."[92] Lewis lamented to Allen in early 1949 that something was terribly wrong with the distribution system of the new order, in which it was easy to get champagne and gin but hard to get envelopes.[93] By February 1949, the average English family ate fish as its main meal five days a week, and the meat shortage began to intensify in the face of the Labour government's new conflict with Argentina, a primary source of meat for the British Isles.[94] A month later, the government cut the meat ration again.[95]

One of the themes of Lewis's life, which has many examples, was the way he managed to change his mind not simply about ideas but in attitude. Throughout the privations of the postwar years, he grew profoundly grateful and deeply touched by the almost careless generosity of so many Americans not only to him but to millions of other Britons. His increasing irritation with the government centered on his own changing opinion of Americans, which had never been very high before. The government seemed determined not to acknowledge the debt owed to the American public. He read in the papers a remark that "every third meal we eat is 'on America'."[96] Lewis wrote to Vera Mathews, almost with a sense of shame, that the government could not bring itself to admit that the recovery from the war was due to anything but "the Socialist government."[97] He repeated this apologetic observation to Edward Allen, and denigrated the "half hinted expressions of gratitude" to America when they finally began to come.[98]

Lewis grew more outspoken in his criticism of the government in his letters to his American benefactors as the Argentine crisis grew and meat became even more scarce. He chaffed against government interference of the most paternalistic style. In the face of severe food shortages, one government minister insisted that things were much better under government rationing. Whereas families once bought the kinds of foods they liked, under rationing they were forced to eat "a properly balanced diet" by government standards.[99] He commented to Mathews that it might do the country good to see a few government ministers "dangling from a lamp post in Whitehall."[100] When the government realized that people were ordering groceries from Ireland, the Customs officials stopped the practice.[101]

Lewis's remarks on politics all centered on the same subject about which he had spoken in his wartime broadcast to the people of Iceland. In that talk, he had expounded the English disdain for self-important bureaucrats, who sought to exceed their authority in an attempt to exercise power over others. He had traced this feeling of contempt for the unworthy official throughout English literature as a legacy of the Norse influence. His argument might have been a slight stretch to aid the war effort, but he certainly felt the sentiment strongly during Britain's experiment with socialism and a regulated economy in the postwar period.

Life at the Kilns

The food situation might not have bothered Lewis as much as it did if he had not also had an increased burden with his care of Mrs. Moore. In the last year of the war, Lewis had the help of June Flewett at the Kilns, which made it possible for him to be away from time to time. After the war, however, he had little help. Minto's health and mental state continued to deteriorate so that the maids only aggravated her disposition. He had expressed an interest in doing something again for the BBC after the war, but the increased workload at Magdalen with so many men return- ing from the war as undergraduates, on top of his obligations at the Kilns, pushed the BBC further away.[102] He did not mention anything about his domestic situation in letters to Owen Barfield, but to Arthur Greeves he confided that Minto's health was only "so-so" and, perhaps worse, she was often "unhappy in mind."[103] Her routine called for her to remain in bed until lunch time. The only consolation Lewis found with her condition was that she had started to read books! By Christmas 1945, she had read *War and Peace*, a novel Lewis had been praising lately. Though he and Arthur had not seen each other since before the war, he explained to Arthur that it would likely be impossible for him to visit Ireland again as long as Minto was still alive.[104]

Lewis did not mention his domestic situation with most of his regular personal and professional correspondents, with the exception of June Flewett and Sister Penelope, with whom he had been confiding for years. Perhaps surprisingly, he did mention it to most of the Americans who sent him food and other things. He told Sister Penelope in early 1946 that "Jane" had her ups and downs, alternating between "miserable and jealous" and "gentle and even jolly."[105] At Easter 1946, he told June that Minto was doing "pretty poorly."[106] They had two maids, Queenie and Flora, of whom Lewis could only say that the household could be much worse off. June would have understood. To the Americans—beginning with Warfield Firor, bestower of many hams—Lewis explained that he had "an aged and ailing mother" whom he could not leave, due to the absence of any domestic help.[107]

When invitations came his way, Lewis inevitably explained to people he barely knew about the restrictions that the care for Mrs. Moore placed on him. To Thomas Wilkinson Riddle, a Baptist minister and editor of a Baptist paper, who had asked Lewis to write and speak on several occasions, Lewis explained that he was behind in his professional work and that his domestic difficulties included the care of an invalid without servants to help. He said that he felt like the prisoner in Poe's "The Pit and the Pendulum."[108] He described his situation to Laurence Whistler, who had written to Lewis to enlist his help in founding a new journal that presented a moral point of view, as being "tied to the bedside of an elderly invalid."[109] He used the same expression when he explained to Nathan Comfort Starr, an American who had written to compliment his work, why he could not visit the United States.[110] George Rostrevor Hamilton urged Lewis to take part in Whistler's scheme, but Lewis said they should not expect him, since he was a "tethered man."[111] When the Marquess of Salisbury, elder brother of Lord David Cecil, asked him to take part in a meeting, Lewis declined, pleading "duties as a nurse and domestic servant" for his mother, who was "old & infirm."[112]

To make matters worse, he explained that her difficulties were mental as well as physical. In their biography of Lewis, however, Roger Lancelyn Green, a former student of Lewis, and Walter Hooper suggested that Lewis managed to attend the meeting in the end.[113] Green knew the strain under which Lewis labored at the time, for he had made a request that Lewis could not grant, since he was "in a sad pickle at home" taking care of someone ill while the college kept him busy with tutorials and interviews.[114] He could not join his former student Dom Bede Griffiths for lunch in early 1948 because he was a "prisoner" during the middle of the day when he had to go back to the Kilns to check on Minto.[115]

By 1947, Arthur Greeves, who had always had a series of serious health conditions, had a "nurse companion." Lewis began to think that a nurse companion for Minto might be the best solution to his domestic stress, but he feared that "the mere suggestion would almost kill her."[116] Lewis was not exaggerating, because by early March 1947, Minto lay at death's door. Warnie thought that she would die and even felt sorry for her. He prayed for her recovery, but reverted to his usual assessment of her once the crisis had passed and her temperament returned to normal.[117] In the aftermath of Minto's illness, her daughter, Maureen Blake, came up from Malvern to assess her mother's condition and the overall situation at the Kilns. She determined that Jack had to have a break from her mother and contrived a plan by which she would come to stay at the Kilns during Easter, while Jack and Warnie would stay in her house in Malvern. Warnie was mightily impressed by Maureen's skill in making her mother believe that she had come up with the idea, which approach stood in stark contrast to the old arguments between mother and daughter.[118]

On Good Friday, April 4, Jack and Warnie left the Kilns by car and motored to Malvern, where they settled into number 4, the Lees, in time for lunch. At the Lees, they were looked after by Bernard Le Varlet, whom Warnie described as Maureen's French factotum. He attended to whatever needed attending to and proved to be an excellent cook, as well as good company. In the evenings, Bernard and Jack read French and English to each other, correcting each other's accents. From Good Friday to Easter Sunday, the weather was too cold and windy to do anything but stay in their newfound pub and drink cider, but after Easter, the weather warmed and spring burst upon them for the remainder of their twelve-day vacation. They took to the Malvern Hills and walked for miles.

On Saturday, Hugo Dyson joined them. Normally, Dyson's war wounds prevented him from taking part in the long walks that Lewis loved, but on Monday, he felt well enough to walk the four miles with the brothers to the British Camp, an Iron Age hill fort. That evening, they dined at the County, where they enjoyed two bottles of Algerian wine followed by several gins at the Foley Arms, where Dyson, always exuberant, broke into a rousing chorus of "The Red Flag," the anthem of the Labour Party, much to the horror of Warnie. It was all in the spirit of the last night of the vacation and managed to keep Jack in high spirits even after they returned to Maureen's house, where Dyson sang and danced "Ta-ra-ra-boom-dy-ay" for the benefit of Bernard. The next day, however, they had to leave the beauty and freedom of the Malvern Hills to return to the Kilns and Minto.[119]

From August 4 through 18, Maureen once again provided a reprieve and traded houses with Jack and Warnie. This time, Ronald Tolkien joined the holiday for the first week, and Warnie did the cooking.[120] George Sayer, Lewis's former pupil who had taken a teaching post in English at Malvern College, joined them on several days when they tromped the Malvern Hills. It struck Warnie that he actually enjoyed his housework now that he was left to his own and not ordered about.[121]

By October 1947, Lewis told June Flewett that Minto had grown "feeble."[122] He explained to Sister Penelope in November that his "mother" continued to decline and that he was "tighter tied every month," but at least for the moment he had a reliable maid to help.[123] Not until the middle of December did he finally mention to Owen Barfield that life at the Kilns was "never worse."[124] Caring for Minto had affected him in a terrible way— "self-pity, rage, envy, terror, horror and general bilge."[125] In a second letter to Barfield during Christmas, he explained that he could not leave "an old semi-paralysed lady" alone in a house for any length of time. He had a duty to look after his "people," a duty he may have felt he had failed to perform for his father. Yet he felt rage over the interruption of his life that prevented him from doing the things he wanted to do. On reflection, he had regarded Minto's illness as an interruption of his chosen vocation, when, actually, caring for her was the vocation that belonged to him at that moment.[126] Maureen intervened again, and Jack and Warnie spent Christmas of 1947 in Malvern with Leonard Blake and his son, Richard, while Maureen went to be with her mother at the Kilns.[127]

Lewis had been writing for some time in Latin to Don Giovanni Calabria, an Italian priest who was interested in Christian unity. These letters focused on the relations between the branches of Christianity, but at Easter 1948, Lewis mentioned that he had come to realize that Christ is present in the person who comes knocking at his door and in his ailing mother.[128] Every day during term, Lewis spent from one o'clock until five at the Kilns in order to check on Minto. During the weekends, when the maids were not on duty, Lewis was never off duty.[129]

Maureen once again traded places with Jack and Warnie in 1948 for two weeks at the end of the summer, from August 16 through 31. Again, Leonard and Richard Blake remained in Malvern. Maureen did not seem eager for her son to be around his grandmother. In January 1949, Maureen came to the rescue again. This time Jack and Warnie were joined for eight days by Humphrey Havard. In a letter to Dr. Warfield Firor, Lewis described the trip as a "rest." They ate well, for they carried along one of Firor's gift hams for Warnie to cook.[130] In Havard's estimation, Warnie was a good cook.[131]

Warnie

Warnie had always enjoyed a drink or two, or five, or ten. The extent of his problem drinking is difficult to judge until the end of the war and the days of austerity. In a letter to June Flewett the day after Easter 1946, Jack remarked that Warnie had "one of his turns" but that he was better.[132] After his vacation with Jack over Easter 1947, Warnie left Jack at the Kilns on June 11 and went off to Ireland for a holiday away from Minto by himself. He felt guilty about leaving his brother, and the guilt soon yielded to depression. The depression quickly accelerated his drinking. Unfortunately, he was drinking gin that his Irish supplier had mixed with methyl alcohol, and it almost killed him. On June 20, he was admitted to the Convent Hospital of Our Lady of Lourdes in Drogheda, where the Sisters of the Medical Mission of Mary cared for him. The sisters succeeded in exploding Warnie's long-nurtured prejudice against Catholicism in all its manifestations. Rather than the sinister, gray, sad picture he had of nuns, Warnie found them to be happy, valiant Christians. To this enclave of love and mercy C. S. Lewis rushed when he heard of his brother's brush with death. Jack stayed with Warnie until he was released from the hospital and snuggly installed at the White Horse pub in Drogheda, where he continued his holiday. Awash with depression at saying goodbye to his brother again, he settled in with his Guinness and sherry.[133]

Warnie's drinking was not always a problem. From time to time, however, he went on binges for days on end. In the course of a week, he might go out drinking every morning with Tolkien or Dyson and remain sober.[134] He might drink just one glass of wine at an Inklings meeting without being set off.[135] On his holidays to Malvern with his brother, he did not get drunk. He could drink with the Inklings every Tuesday morning without losing control. Yet Jack must have grown concerned about his brother's exposure to alcohol. After years of enjoying an occasional bottle of wine at an Inklings gathering, Jack announced to the other Inklings in November 1947 that they would no longer drink wine at their meetings.[136] For their Christmas dinner in Malvern, however, Jack produced two bottles of burgundy and one of Commandaria for the three men to share, in addition to a half bottle of gin, which suggests that Jack was not overly concerned about Warnie's consumption of alcohol. For his part, Warnie cooked a turkey, along

Jack and Warren at Annagassan, Ireland, ca. 1949. Used by permission of the Marion E. Wade Center, Wheaton College, Wheaton, IL.

with soup, boiled potatoes, brussels sprouts, and a pudding![137] The restriction on drinking wine at the Inklings meetings was also relaxed by late January 1948, when they enjoyed a bottle and a Kentucky brandied fruitcake.[138]

In spite of several holidays with Jack in Malvern, Warnie's situation at the Kilns continued to deteriorate. He had an ally in Vera Henry, a friend of Minto from Ireland who stayed at the Kilns from time to time and who took on many of the domestic duties after World War II. Vera shared Warnie's exasperation with Minto and her treatment of Jack, but she proved to be no real solution or release for Warnie. By February 1949, he was in the Acland Hospital after a prolonged downward spiral. He described the cycle as proceeding through insomnia, drugs, depression, spirits, to illness. Jack, on the other hand, thought the cycle began with spirits. They were probably both wrong. From Warnie's description of his homecoming after the Acland stay, depression seems to be the driving force of his binges:

> The contrast between the warm cosy Acland and this cold dreary house was disastrous; went in to make my bow to Minto and was given a lecture on the extreme coal shortage, the iniquities of Betty, and an enquiry as to how long I proposed to stay cured this time? Went down to the refrigerated study feeling that I was indeed "home" again. Whether from cold, temper, depression, or all three, I had a shocking night, and when I tried to pray I found the line "dead".[139]

With such a welcome home, Warnie did not stay cured for long.

At the end of April, Jack had five more days in Malvern during the Easter vacation. He reveled in the beauty of the Malvern Hills: "larks singing in a blue sky, lambs bleating, the wind rustling in the grass."[140] At the end of his stay, however, he returned to Oxford in a "very disgruntled" mood to face the beginning of Trinity term and all of life's stress. For Warnie, returning to the Kilns meant a return to depression. A return to depression meant a return to heavy drinking. A return to heavy drinking meant a return to the Acland Hospital, where he found himself again in May.[141]

With the enormous number of letters that C. S. Lewis had received the last few years, Warnie had provided his brother with a valuable service as his secretary. Warnie had become a proficient typist, and he managed much of his brother's correspondence that did not require a personal response.[142] Some of the letters Lewis would have dictated, as he did when Walter Hooper helped with his correspondence in 1963.[143] When Warnie went on a binge, however, Jack was left with all the letters to answer on his own. Inevitably, he got behind as the mail piled up. He had to begin his letters with an apology for his slow response owing to his secretary's "illness."[144] In addition to the stress of Minto and Warnie, his large workload, and his correspondence, Lewis received a letter from Owen and Maud Barfield complaining about the children's book that he wanted to dedicate to their daughter, Lucy. It was called *The Lion, the Witch and the Wardrobe*. They objected to fur coats. Lewis seemed to be endorsing the fur trade based on the killing of innocent animals. They also objected to children being trapped inside a wardrobe. It was all too horrible. Tolkien had also objected to the story in the strongest and bitterest terms. Under the weight of so much stress, Lewis collapsed.

When Warnie returned from a weekend in Malvern on Monday, June 13, 1949, he found an ambulance at the Kilns preparing to take Jack to the Acland Hospital. He had a high temperature, severe headache, sore throat, and swollen glands.[145] On Tuesday, Jack was delirious. Dr. Havard injected him with penicillin every three hours. He remained in the hospital from Monday until Friday. The diagnosis was streptococcus throat, but Havard said the real problem was exhaustion, which would have weakened his immune system, and he insisted that Jack get away from the Kilns, and presumably Mrs. Moore, for a long holiday.[146] Strep throat can lead to inflammation of the kidneys and to rheumatic fever, which can affect the heart and joints. Based on Lewis's medical complaints later, it is possible that this attack had some long-lasting implications for him. The first obvious lingering symptom was an impairment of his hand muscles, which made it difficult for him to write.[147]

Upon Havard's insistence that Jack have a long holiday, Warnie left the bedside of his brother and returned to the Kilns "sick with fright and savage with anger."[148] A fierce argument ensued in which Warnie confronted "her ladyship" with the facts of Jack's situation. One of Warnie's great fears was that Jack would die before him and leave him alone. His best friend and only real friend from the army, Major Herbert Denis Parkin, was thinking of moving to Mauritius, an island in the Indian Ocean, where his small pension would stretch further. The prospect of losing Jack was overpowering. He made his point, and Minto relented. Jack would have his long vacation in Ireland.

As it turned out, however, Jack did not have his vacation. Warnie went instead, and Jack remained at the Kilns. On Thursday, June 23, Lewis wrote to Arthur Greeves with the good news that he was coming home to Ireland and would stay from July 4 until August 4.[149] The concrete plans set off a new binge for Warnie, who could only look forward to a month alone with Minto in the Kilns. By Sunday, Warnie was in such bad shape that Jack and Humphrey Havard begged him to go back to the Acland, but he refused. Not until Friday, July 1, did Warnie finally agree to go for help, but by then it was too late. The hospital kept him one night and then expelled him for being completely out of control. Even as Lewis was writing with the bad news, he was expecting a "mental specialist" from a local asylum, the Warneford Hospital, to assess Warnie for admission.[150] Lewis explained to Arthur that he could not leave Warnie and Minto together at the Kilns. To all his other friends, Lewis explained that Warnie suffered from "nervous insomnia," but to Arthur he confided—for his ears only—that Warnie's problem was alcohol. As long as that was the case, Jack could not leave the Kilns for more than a day or two.[151]

It seemed a shame that no one should go to Ireland, so Warnie left the Kilns on August 14 and remained in Ireland until September 26.[152] It hardly seems fair, but with one less source of stress in his life, Lewis at least had some mild relief. Warnie was on his best behavior after his stay in the asylum, and life went on as usual at the Kilns until April 29, 1950, when Minto fell out of bed three times during the night. In the morning, she was taken to Restholme, a nursing home nearby, where she would spend the last year of her life.[153] Lewis would visit her almost every day he was in Oxford. He confided to Arthur Greeves that her confinement was an "enormous liberation" for him.[154]

As for Minto, Warnie noted that the nurses objected to her strong language, and she wanted to know how soon she could escape "this hell on earth."[155] Jack, in turn, confessed to Warnie that she had never gotten on very well with her son, Paddy. The idyllic relationship between mother and son was all make-believe.[156] Lewis told Arthur that on her best days, Minto grouched a good deal, and he did not think she was any more discontented at Restholme than she had been at the Kilns. Jack could not bring himself to leave her in the nursing home without his daily visits, so he could not allow himself the longed-for vacation to Ireland. On the other hand, with Minto in the nursing home, the Kilns was a "less horrible" house so that Arthur might come for a visit to Oxford.[157] Life was taking on a new glow.

Lewis explained to Don Giovanni Calabria that in the context of the horrors of the Kilns, both Jack's zeal and his talent for writing had decreased. The Kilns by 1949 was a house "devastated by women's quarrels."[158] He did not think his writing pleased the public the way it once did, and he did not know if he would write any more books. It was a troubling time for him under the pressures of home. On reflection, he wondered if it might not be a good thing to lose fame and talent in order to protect himself from his long-dreaded temptation of vainglory.[159]

2

Work, Work, Work

1945–1949

With the beginning of the first new academic year after the war in October 1945, Harry Weldon returned to Magdalen College after his war duty. Lewis had dreaded his return and the ironic resumption of hostilities that peacetime would bring. No sooner had Weldon returned than he urged the wartime president, Sir Henry Tizard, to appoint Weldon's friend and bridge partner David Hunt as the new dean. Lewis opposed the move strenuously in the meeting of the faculty, insuring continuing hostility between him and Weldon's faction within the Magdalen faculty. Lewis would have seen Weldon's initiative as the worst sort of cronyism, typified by the "inner ring" represented in *That Hideous Strength*. It is possible that Weldon recognized himself in Devine, the master manipulator and academic politician; or in Weston, with the striking similarity between the names of Weldon and Weston.

While Lewis began a phase of his life in which he would suffer one academic political defeat after another, Tolkien continued to thrive in the give-and-take of academic politics. The academic year began with Tolkien taking his new place as Merton Professor of English Language and Literature.[1] His election involved leaving Pembroke College, where he had been a fellow since 1925, and moving to Merton College, which housed the professorship. Within the world of Oxford colleges, Merton was a more wealthy, and therefore prestigious, college than Pembroke. Tolkien was by far the better academic politician than Lewis, who never showed any aptitude for politics. Tolkien came to Oxford with a professorship and within twenty years acquired a second, more prestigious and more lucrative professorship. Though Tolkien had never produced any significant scholarship like *The Allegory of Love* or *A Preface to Paradise Lost*, he had done something much more important in the academic game. He had not offended anyone, and he had given no one cause to feel jealous of him. He was every bit the Christian that Lewis was, but he kept it to himself. Tolkien, like so many of their colleagues, had not approved of Lewis's dabbling in theology during the war, when he had no academic or ecclesiastical credentials in theology.

For Lewis, Michaelmas term 1945 came with a heavier-than-usual load. In addition to his tutorials with more pupils than had been normal before the war, he also delivered three sets of public lectures. On Tuesdays at five in the afternoon, the subject was "The Poetry of Charles Williams." On Wednesdays at five, "Principles of Textual Criticism," for BLitt students. On Thursdays and Saturdays at ten in the morning, "Milton."[2] Whereas Lewis's war duties, such as lecturing at RAF bases, had come to an end, his responsibilities with the Socratic Club had not. The club still met each Monday evening at eight fifteen, and Lewis was expected to respond without preparation to whatever the guest speaker might have to say. Lewis knew the topic ahead of time, since he took part in planning the programs. He would have known the general issues at stake in the discussion. He would even have known the general way the speakers would handle the issues in their writings. Nonetheless, he had to respond to whatever each speaker might actually say. Fortunately, this need for an immediate response to remarks was the stuff of an Inklings meeting. Lewis did it all the time. Still, the Socratic Club meant one more demand upon his time and an entire evening lost every week, term after term.

During Hilary term, after Christmas, Lewis lectured every Wednesday and Saturday at noon, his subject, "Prolegomena to the Study of Medieval Poetry."[3] Fortunately, he had just this one set of lectures to deliver during the term. He had done it many times before, and they were among the most popular lectures at Oxford. Hilary term presented other challenges in 1946—some good, some bad.

Lewis took part in a "Brains Trust" program for the BBC at Liverpool in March. This obligation meant being away from Oxford and the Kilns from Monday morning, March 18, until Friday, March 22. Being away in the middle of term meant missing the Socratic Club and the Inklings, all of the tutorials, one lecture, and his duty to Mrs. Moore. Yet off he went with Warnie and Hugo Dyson, who also would have missed his tutorials, for a wonderful holiday. Dyson could be exasperating with his antics, but the Lewis brothers often turned to him for company. On this trip, he was late to meet the brothers for lunch before getting lost at the station while catching their train. Then he got separated from them when they changed trains at Rugby and was lost again. Jack remarked that Hugo should always wear a "collar and lead" when they travel with him.

Dyson shared Warnie's love of trains and ships, and he provided most of the entertainment with an unending stream of stories and songs. Warnie, who hated philosophy, inadvertently started a debate about the difference between art and philosophy that raged for an hour between Jack and Hugo before they realized they were talking about two different subjects. Rather than stay in Liverpool proper, they stayed in a hotel across the River Mersey, which meant they took the ferry every time they went into Liverpool to see the town. Dyson developed a love of ferries, so they made the trip over and over. Jack fulfilled his "Brains Trust" duties on Wednesday, while Hugo continued to enjoy the ferry and Warnie walked about Birkenhead, which he thought captured the description of hell in the first chapter of *The Great Divorce*.[4]

Even though Lewis had learned somewhat to say no to invitations, he still felt obliged to accept some. A week after the trip to Liverpool on March 31, he preached at his own church, Holy Trinity in Headington Quarry, for Evensong. He addressed what many people, including his brother, took to be a problem in the Book of Common Prayer. During the time of confession before Communion, the congregation declares about their sins, "The burden of them is intolerable." Lewis reasoned that the phrase does not refer to how people feel about their sins, but refers to the reality of the enormity of sin that people cannot deal with.[5] Joel Heck has suggested that this Evensong sermon may be a version of "Miserable Offenders," a sermon he would preach on April 7 at St Matthew's Church in Northampton, an hour north of Oxford.[6] This sermon was published later that year in *Five Sermons by Laymen*. In the meantime, Lewis had to be in Manchester on Tuesday, April 2, but this time, Warnie let Jack ("poor devil") go to Manchester by himself.[7]

During Trinity term, after Easter in 1946, Lewis again delivered his lecture series "Prolegomena to the Study of Medieval Poetry" on Thursdays and Saturdays at noon.[8] After the war, he was giving these lectures at Magdalen College, which did not have a large lecture hall like the one in the Examination Schools that Lewis would famously fill with standing room only within a few more terms.

Tutorials

We know a great deal about what happened in a tutorial with C. S. Lewis because so many of his former pupils have written about their experiences with him. Still, the experience of Lewis as a tutor in 1925 was considerably different from what a pupil might experience after World War II. The young Lewis was still an arrogant, aspiring poet with something to prove. He knew what he had been like in his tutorials with his tutors, and he expected the same of his pupils. All things considered, this was an unreasonable expectation. His diary from his early years as a tutor has little nice to say about the pupils who sat before him each week and read their essays while he tried to listen attentively and give constructive criticism, followed by a mini-lecture to supplement what the pupil should have discovered.

First impressions often remain fixed in the mind, and Lewis's pupils tended to recall their first impressions of him. Derek Brewer recalled meeting a "plump cheerful man with a large, red countryman's face and a loud voice, who rolled his *r*'s."[9] Brown Patterson saw Lewis before he knew who he was.

> He was out for a walk along the college "water walks" by the Cherwell River. He was wearing baggy trousers—corduroy, I think—and a shapeless tweed jacket over a loosely fitting sweater. On his head was an old tweed hat with its brim turned down. His shoes were heavy brogues. I identified him—to myself, of course—as one of the gardeners.[10]

This was the second mistake of the day for Patterson, who thought the neatly dressed head porter was Magdalen's president. Upon Paul Piehler's first meeting with him, Lewis left this impression: "A plump-ish, red-faced Ulsterman with a confident, jovial Ulster rasp to his voice, at first sight he could have been taken for a cheerful and prosperous ineluctable butcher rather than one of the great minds of the age."[11] Twelve years earlier, when Peter Bayley went up to Oxford in 1940, he recalled a younger but similar Lewis dressed in a brown, "slightly too small Harris tweed jacket," with all three buttons buttoned, and unpressed, baggy, gray flannel trousers.[12] Bayley thought Lewis seemed older than his nearly forty-two years.

After his conversion in 1931, Lewis grew more relaxed with his pupils. In his letters, he remarked that he enjoyed the way they became new friends. While he tended to enjoy the people, he probably never came to enjoy the drudgery of tutoring. A tutorial was not true conversation with a well-informed companion. For five hours a day, Lewis had to focus his attention on listening to a pupil read a paper that was probably dashed off the night before, if not the morning of, the tutorial. He had to comment on the quality of writing, the choice of words, the content of the paper, and the strength of the argument. He would interrupt the pupil to comment on something that could not wait until the end, but some of the criticism required taking in the whole of the paper so as to discuss its merits as well as demerits. He had to ask pointed questions about why a pupil might have taken one approach rather than another. He might ask why he had relied on one source more than others. In all of this, Lewis strived to train the minds of his pupils as W. T. Kirkpatrick had trained his mind.

Peter Bailey, an American pupil of Lewis after the war, has noted an important benefit of reading the essay aloud. He said that this method forced the undergraduate to write to be heard.[13] Spoken language precedes written language, and spoken language must be understood immediately. Spoken language has an audience. The danger of written language is that it happens in isolation, within the mind of the writer, without consideration of the reader's hearing. Unspoken ideas can have a half-baked quality to them. When I say that I have an idea, but I can't quite express it, what I mean is that I almost have an idea, but I have not developed it. Errors in grammar and syntax, as well as logic, leap to the fore when we must read aloud something we have written. After writing sixty to seventy-two term papers over the course of a three-year program of study, an Oxford graduate has learned to write and to speak in a logical, persuasive, coherent manner.

To make matters worse, and tutoring less enjoyable, in his early years, Lewis had to teach outside his area of interest. In

1936, Magdalen College had only two freshmen reading English. When he first began teaching, he had taken philosophy pupils to fill out his load, but he had lost professional interest in philosophy by the 1930s. In addition to his few English pupils, Lewis taught political science to Magdalen undergraduates reading history and "Modern Greats."[14] Never mind that he loathed talking about politics. Even when concentrating on English, Lewis taught the entire English syllabus, from Anglo-Saxon to 1830.[15] Whereas in an American university, an English professor might teach the Victorian novel or Shakespeare or Chaucer, Lewis had to teach them all, even though his area of interest was medieval poetry to Spenser. After the war, however, all of that had changed with the huge influx of undergraduates. With the changing times, English also became a more popular course of study. Though he had a heavy tutorial load, Lewis found that his pupils tended to be more interested in the subject.

This kind of teaching is markedly different from the lecture method of the United States, in which the student is the passive receptacle of what the teacher has to say. Better teachers will punctuate their lectures with questions aimed at the students, but this approach lacks the focus on the development of the individual student. Students in the United States may write a term paper for a course, or maybe even several short papers, but they rarely receive more than a grade and a few odd comments in the margins. The American system on the whole involves the retention, if not the mastery, of information as determined by doing well on a test. Lewis's tutorials were as far from the lecture method as one might get.

One of Lewis's first pupils was Alan Griffiths who took the name Dom Bede Griffiths when he took Holy Orders. Griffiths had studied classics but switched to English in 1927. He would have been one of the more conscientious pupils, who had something interesting to say. At the end of the formal critique of his tutorials, Griffiths continued to stay and talk with Lewis, who was only a few years Griffiths's senior at the time.[16] In stark contrast to Griffiths, John Betjeman annoyed Lewis by his inattention to his studies and his unjustified arrogance. On his side, Betjeman had frequently baited Lewis. He might have thought such a young tutor beneath his dignity, for such a gifted poet on the way to fame certainly deserved more. In the end, Betjeman achieved the fame as a poet that Lewis failed to achieve. His poetry not only was critically acclaimed but also sold in the tens of thousands of volumes. He was knighted in 1969 and named poet laureate of the United Kingdom in 1972. Yet Lewis was not the only don who found Betjeman lacking in the requisite conscientiousness to succeed in Oxford. He failed to earn his degree.

George Sayer was another of Lewis's pupils who went on to become a close friend. He took his degree in 1938, so he would have been a pupil when Lewis published *The Allegory of Love* and *Out of the Silent Planet*. Lewis had gained strong self-confidence by this time and was engaged in his "Personal Heresy" literary dispute with Eustace M. W. Tillyard. When pupils complete their writing of PhD dissertations, each must then give an oral defense of his or her work before an examining committee, which asks difficult and embarrassing questions. Lewis's pupils had to give oral defense of their papers every week. Sayer recalled that Lewis might ask, "What exactly do you mean by the word 'sentimental,' Mr. Sayer?" Lewis would then give a history of the word and how its meaning had changed and been used in different ways through the centuries. If Sayer could not rise to the occasion and give Lewis a strong answer, he might say, "Well, Mr. Sayer, if you are not sure what the word means or what you mean by it, wouldn't it be very much better if you ceased to use it at all?"[17] Lewis regularly corrected pupils who used the wrong words or used them in the wrong ways. Brown Patterson once used *fortuitously* instead of *fortunately*. Lewis reminded him that *fortuitously* means "by chance," and that there is no reason to change its meaning when there is already a perfectly good word meaning "fortunately."[18]

Lewis avoided the technical language that literary criticism developed as it sought a respectable place in the academy alongside the old disciplines. When Sayer used the current and quickly changing jargon, Lewis would say: "I am not quite sure what you mean by this term. Perhaps you would be so good as to translate it for me into plain English."[19] Years later, when Sayer rose to the rank of friend and taught English at Malvern College, he and Lewis discussed the proliferation of technical jargon that tended toward the pseudoscientific within the discipline of English literature. Lewis thought it might be because the average person looked on literature as recreation, and the English faculty sought to improve its status by sounding scientific. This may account for the tendency among some literary critics to speak of literature in terms of sociology, psychology, philosophy, economics, or some other discipline in which they are not trained.

John Lawlor, who began his studies with Lewis in 1936, described Lewis's habitual manner in a tutorial. The pupil appeared at the appointed hour and knocked on the door while dressed in the traditional black, undergraduate sleeveless gown that falls to just below the waste. By tradition, the gown is always worn to tutorials. Lewis settled into his armchair while the pupil sat opposite on the couch and read his essay of some three thousand words—about ten to twelve pages. Lewis always smoked either cigarettes or a pipe, and he did not stop for a tutorial.[20] He drew pictures, doodled, and made notes while the pupil read for twenty minutes or so. Then Lewis commenced the examination on what the pupil had said and not said. Over the three-year period in which Lawlor had tutorials with Lewis, he made the transition "from dislike and hostility to stubborn affection, and then to gratitude for the weekly bout in which no quarter was asked or given."[21] Lawlor went on to describe tutorials with Lewis as warfare. Lewis was a howitzer against Lawlor's peashooter, but Lewis allowed Lawlor "choice of weapons." In tutorials, they "joined battle."[22]

After World War II, however, George Watson said that Lewis's engagement with his pupils was more "politely merciless."[23] By the late 1940s and early 1950s, Lewis's manner had calmed to the point that some of his pupils nicknamed him "Papa Lewis."[24] Others called him "Uncle Lewis."[25] The demanding nature of the tutorial had not changed, but Lewis's patience had grown. In his biography of Lewis, while discussing John Betjeman, A. N. Wilson suggested that Lewis was prone to bullying his pupils.[26] The judgment of his former pupils, however, exonerates him from this charge and pleads that he acted sternly only when pupils were lazy and did not do their work.[27]

George Bailey, who went up in 1946, said that Lewis had three stock responses to the essays he heard from his pupils after the war. If the essay was very good, he would remark, "There is a good deal in what you say." If the essay was acceptable but nothing to shout about, Lewis would remark, "There is something in what you say." If the essay fell far short of the mark, Lewis would remark, "There *may* be something in what you say." Bailey, who went on to have a distinguished career as a journalist, recalled that Lewis did not pay compliments lightly and that the highest praise he heard was, "Much of that was very well said."[28]

Derek Brewer, who began Oxford for the 1941–1942 year before serving as a young infantry officer during the war and returning in 1945 to complete his degree, dismissed the suggestion that Lewis bullied his pupils. Brewer recalled that Lewis treated him not like a schoolboy but like a man who had come to read with him.[29] Brewer felt "a sense of fundamental equality" with Lewis based on their common pursuit of English literature, even though Brewer was always aware of a difference in rank. Whereas Lawlor's essays might take twenty minutes to read, Brewer's essays rarely took more than ten. Whereas Lewis doodled through most of Lawlor's essays and made few notes, he rarely doodled during Brewer's essays and made many notes. Without reference to Lawlor, Brewer explained that Lewis doodled only when bored.[30]

Lewis listened to the essays most attentively, according to Brewer, not because they were fascinating but because it was his duty. It was the job he was paid to do. On one occasion, Lewis demonstrated just how closely he listened when the phone rang in Lewis's other room, and he left for five minutes to take the call. Upon returning, he quoted Brewer's last sentence verbatim before asking him to carry on.[31] Brown Patterson, who served for many years as dean of the University of the South in Sewanee, Tennessee, studied with Lewis in the early 1950s as a Rhodes scholar. He recalled that in his tutorials, during the critique Lewis regularly quoted back to him sentences that Patterson had read aloud.[32]

Although Lewis's pupils had varying experiences with him in the tutorials, they all seemed to believe that his aim was to teach them how to think. He cared about their ability to develop their own ideas and to express them convincingly. Unlike the American system, in which great attention is given to the opinions of scholars in secondary sources, Lewis had no interest in secondary sources and discouraged his pupils from consulting them. His emphasis on studying the primary texts differed sharply from the practice at Cambridge at that time, which emphasized a study of what the critics had said about the texts.[33] Lewis wanted his pupils to grapple with the great texts and draw their own conclusions. He wanted them to develop confidence enough to draw reasoned conclusions that could stand up to debate. In order to do this, he asked questions. He prodded. He exposed weakness in logic or in evidence. In his early years, he did it ruthlessly, but by the postwar period, with food and coal scarce and with all the misery of the Kilns, Lewis grew more gentle in his treatment of his pupils while never relaxing the relentless battery of questions. Another dynamic might also have been at work. Many of Lewis's pupils after the war had served in combat and came up to Oxford in their mid-twenties. Lewis once remarked to Derek Brewer that it was as though he were teaching his own generation, whose college years had been interrupted by the First World War.[34]

Lewis rarely expressed his own opinions about literature in tutorials. If his students wanted to know his opinions, they had to attend his lectures, which were entirely voluntary. His efforts in tutorials aimed at helping his pupils develop their own opinions.[35] Perhaps his experience with W. T. Kirkpatrick convinced him of the impressionability of young minds and the need to avoid imposing his own views on his charges. Avoiding imposing his views on his pupils also extended to his faith. Lewis did not sprinkle his tutorials with religion. Paul Piehler, an atheist at the time, "discerned no hint of evangelism" from Lewis in his tutorials.[36] When Brown Patterson asked to have his tutorials with Lewis, he said that he wanted to study with the author of *The Allegory of Love*, but in his heart, he wanted to study with someone who shared his views on religion and morality.[37] Patterson wanted to discuss the kinds of issues Lewis had raised in *Christian Behavior* and *Beyond Personality*, which had not yet been published together as *Mere Christianity*. Lewis allowed such questions if they pertained to the subject under study.[38] In this sense, he helped those who were interested to see the faith issues present in the subject without artificially imposing Christianity upon the subject from the outside. This sounds as though he avoided faith in his teaching. To the contrary, for those who were interested, it became apparent that faith issues permeate virtually every literary text. George Watson, on the other hand, was neither a Christian nor a conservative, and he found that Lewis never tried to make him a disciple.[39] Compulsion and manipulation do not lead to faith.

Lecturing

For Lewis, lecturing two to four times a week came with a certain pleasure. After the first few awkward years, he got better at it. For most good lecturers, lecturing has an element of the theatrical about it. Good lecturing demands self-confidence, but also a desire that students will come to love the subject and not merely acquire information about it. Lecturing has cognitive and emotional dimensions to it. The student must be informed about something, but retention requires that the student care about the information. If the lecturer appears to be bored by his or her own subject, students will follow the lead.

When the new academic year began in October 1946, Lewis once again had lectures to deliver each week. He gave his "Prolegomena to Renaissance Poetry" at noon on Wednesdays and Saturdays at Magdalen College.[40] This series of lectures would play a vital part in the writing of his massive project for the Oxford History of the English Language (OHEL) series, for they allowed him to do double duty. In preparing a series of lectures on Renaissance poetry, he was developing the material he would use in writing *English Literature in the Sixteenth Century*. This action represents a classic strategy of successful scholars in the humanities who manage to publish regularly. Their publications tend to come from the overflow of their teaching, and their teaching is informed by their publishing. Lewis was a master at moving lectures to books. For Hilary and Trinity terms, however, he did not have the same lecturing load.

For Michaelmas term in 1947, Lewis lectured once again on Milton each Wednesday and Saturday at noon.[41] This year, however, he delivered his lectures at the Examination Schools building, where the large hall upstairs could accommodate the growing crowds that came to hear him speak. The North Writing School room holds 330 seats, while the South Writing School room holds 440. Lewis felt compelled to ask that visitors please make way for students due to the large numbers who came to hear him.

George Watson, who for many years was a fellow in English literature at St John's College, Cambridge, first encountered Lewis at his lectures in the Examination Schools in 1948. He went to hear Lewis because his tutor told him *not* to go. His tutor was one of the many new, young fellows at Oxford who resented or even despised Lewis for a variety of reasons. Some regarded his popular introductory lectures to medieval and Renaissance literature too European and too wide-ranging. Also, the postwar spirit in Britain appeared not only in the form of the socialist agenda of the Attlee government but also in a new radical direction within the faculties of many universities. Lewis was conservative in most of his views.

Older members of the English faculty continued to nurture resentment of Lewis for the part he played in the election of Adam Fox as professor of poetry, and for writing popular books outside his teaching area. Though Tolkien played as big a part, and probably a bigger part, than Lewis in organizing Fox's election, no one had seemed to blame him. Tolkien had the political skill to mastermind the election, just as he had masterminded the revision of the English syllabus, and the skill to avoid any taint. Lewis did not. Younger members of the faculty could resent him simply for himself. Watson's young tutor told him, "If I hear you are going to Lewis . . . I shall have serious doubts about you."[42]

Watson went to the lectures and took careful notes, which he kept throughout his career.[43] When Lewis gave his lectures in the Examinations Schools, he had to push his way through the milling crowd of several hundred to make his way to the raised podium. Watson said that his short, stocky figure gave Lewis the appearance of a butcher, though Piehler insisted that even with his "roly-poly" figure, Lewis entered the room with "magisterial authority."[44] Everyone agreed that Lewis then spoke with a slow, booming voice, unlike the soft-spoken but fast-paced lectures that were the norm in Oxford at the time.[45]

In contrast to his extemporaneous remarks at the Socratic Club, Lewis prepared his lectures with meticulous care. Despite his prodigious memory and knowledge of texts, and his habit of quoting great portions of literature in conversation or tutorials, Lewis wrote out the quotations in full that he recited in his lectures. The main body of a lecture, however, only had a skeleton outline. A few words in an outline provided the memory prompt for Lewis to expound a lengthy explanation from his vast knowledge. The discussion unfolded in formal, logical order, along an outline of points and sub-points.[46] Alastair Fowler used the notes he took at Lewis's lectures to edit Lewis's notes on *The Faerie Queene* and publish them as *Spenser's Images of Life* after Lewis died. Fowler could do this because the lectures had such a clear, logical development for the benefit of those taking notes, and Lewis's slow, clear speech allowed Fowler to record dictation. Ironically, Fowler's notes from hearing the lectures were more extensive than Lewis's notes for delivering them, for Lewis kept most of the lectures tucked away in his mind.

Lewis even had small prompts for the standard jokes he always told, as if spontaneously.[47] The humor formed a strategic element of Lewis's lectures. Derek Brewer heard Lewis's lectures before he went away to war and again when he returned to Oxford to complete his degree. The order, the clarity, the illustrations, the quotations all combined to make the lectures memorable. They had not changed much between the two hearings, but Lewis continually added to them over the years, which forced him to condense them when he finally prepared them for publication as *The Discarded Image* just before his death. One of the things that struck Brewer about the lectures was the timing of the humor. Having heard the lectures before and remembered them so well, Brewer recognized how Lewis planned the humor without the audience realizing it. Brewer remarked that "the fuse might be lit several minutes before the actual, yet unexpected, explosion."[48]

Lewis's lecture style struck Fowler as "avuncular informality."[49] His style was conversational but with a heightened degree of drama. His dramatic performance was so well executed that he seemed to be exploring thoughts with the undergraduates for the first time instead of delivering the conclusions from decades of study. Though he always wore his plain black lecture gown, his manner was informal as he began speaking while making his way to the podium and continued speaking as he left the podium while heading for the door. In summation, Fowler, one of the lions of the British critical world when he wrote his memoir, remarked:

> He was a popular and (not at all the same thing) *good* lecturer—lecturing sometimes to an audience of three hundred or more. He towered above his colleagues in the English faculty—at a time, admittedly, when lecturing standards were not high. His resonant voice suited the rostrum; he was always easily audible (something that could not be said of Tolkien).[50]

It takes a great deal of work to be prepared each day to give such lectures with apparent effortless ease.

Doctor of Divinity

While Lewis went about his weekly routine generally unnoticed by his colleagues, far to the north the University of St Andrews had decided to confer the doctor of divinity degree on him. The honorary doctoral degree in the United Kingdom differs from an honorary doctoral degree in the United States. In the States, it usually means that money has changed hands or someone has done something that will result eventually in money changing hands. In the United Kingdom, an honorary doctoral degree recognizes major achievement. That was even more the case in 1946. Lewis did not have a high regard for the research doctoral degree (the PhD in the United States and the DPhil in Oxford). When I was doing research in Oxford in 1979, the senior fellows still referred to it as "the American degree." Lewis had thought about doing a research degree when he finished his BA and no jobs were available, but he quickly rejected the idea. An honorary degree, however, which recognized the work he had done, was quite another matter. He would accept it with pleasure, and he would pay for his brother to go with him.

On Wednesday, June 26, 1946, Jack and Warnie left Oxford for London on their way to St Andrews. Upon arriving at Paddington Station, they traveled by underground to King's Cross Station, where they had dinner at the Great Northern Hotel. After dinner, they walked through the area south of Euston Road to survey the serious bomb damage still evident after the war. (When I first visited London over Christmas 1971, signs of the bombing could still be seen.) At quarter past ten that evening, they caught the night train, on which each had his private compartment, perhaps to make up for all the wartime trains in which Jack had traveled under the most uncomfortable circumstances.[51] Even with the luxury of his own private compartment, Warnie noted that sleeping in a "sleeper" is an "acquired habit."[52]

In the midst of the food shortage in England, the brothers discovered that the shortage did not extend to Scotland and passengers on the Great Northern. They luxuriated over "real porridge . . . plenty of butter, edible sausages, toast, marmalade, coffee!"[53] After changing trains several times, they arrived in the "ancient," gray-stone town of St Andrews by the North Sea, acclaimed for its medieval university and its golf course. They spent the day touring the town before settling into their hotel for tea and reading before supper. In his diary, Warnie recorded his feelings of "all that 'northernness' which was my first love and will be my last."[54] C. S. Lewis made much of his experience of "northernness" in his own life, but Warnie had also tasted of this experience.

The degree ceremony took place on Friday. Jack had not thought to bring his white tie, the standard attire for formal academic occasions in Oxford. When he noticed the number of people dressed in black with a white tie, he rushed off to a clothier in time to dress properly for the ceremony. St Andrews went one step beyond Oxford, for their tradition included that candidates for the doctoral degree should wear black cassocks with scarlet buttons. Honorary degrees were conferred following the granting of the seventy or eighty earned degrees. Lewis was the last of twelve honorary degrees. The dean for each faculty presenting an honorary degree gave brief remarks about the recipient. The dean of the faculty of divinity, Professor D. M. Baillie, said of Lewis:

With his pen and with his voice on the radio Mr Lewis has succeeded in capturing the attention of many who will not readily listen to professional theologians, and has taught them many lessons concerning the deep things of God. . . . In recent years Mr Lewis has arranged a new kind of marriage between theological reflection and poetic imagination, and this fruitful union is now producing works which are difficult to classify in any literary genre: it can only be said in respectful admiration that he pursues 'things unattempted yet in prose or rhyme'.[55]

Warnie slipped out after the ceremony to go back to the hotel to get their bags while Jack attended a celebratory reception hosted by the vice chancellor.[56]

Warnie took a taxi to retrieve Jack, and then they headed to the station, where they planned to take another night train south. They changed trains at Dundee, where they had supper and made arrangements for their sleeping berths. They had planned on a quiet, pleasant trip, but they had not counted on the hordes of graduates and their parents who would also be leaving St Andrews after the graduation ceremony. To make up for the crowded trains back to London, they enjoyed what Warnie called the best meal he had since the war.[57] No doubt, C. S. Lewis believed that the trips to Liverpool and St Andrews with Warnie helped to keep his brother somewhat stable in the midst of the stress at the Kilns. Such trips, however, could not come often enough for Warnie.

When Lewis returned from St Andrews, he began a practice that would continue for several years: dining with Hugo Dyson and a group of four undergraduates at the end of term. The group included two of Lewis's pupils from Magdalen, Derek Brewer and Tom Stock; Philip Stibbe, a pupil of Dyson at Merton College; and Peter Bayley, from University College, who was also reading English.[58] The first time they dined, on June 30, 1946, Lewis was late because of a meeting of the Tutorial Committee of Magdalen College, which decided to increase the enrollment of the college. This dining club represents just one of many instances of how much Lewis valued Dyson. Though the impetus for Lewis's conversion following his experience on Addison's Walk in 1930 usually focuses on Tolkien because of his later fame, Dyson was there that night and stayed to talk with Lewis for several hours after Tolkien went home. Lewis credited Dyson with his conversion as much as he did Tolkien.

With the beginning of the academic year in October 1945, Dyson had left Reading University to take a fellowship at Merton College. His change of teaching post also involved moving from Reading to Oxford. On July 25, 1946, Hugo and Margaret Dyson invited Jack and Warnie to join them for dinner at their new home at 12 Holywell Street, across from New College. In spite of their shyness around women, the brothers enjoyed the evening and the excellent dinner, complete with polished silver and crisp table linen, in sterling contrast with the drabness of life at the Kilns, which Warnie probably regretted more than Jack, who had learned to do without.[59] Besides, Jack had all the silver, linen, and crystal he needed at the high table of Magdalen College.

The academic year began in October 1947 with a new president at Magdalen. Thomas Boase replaced Sir Henry Tizard. Boase would serve until 1968. Lewis thought that Boase was an improvement over Tizard.[60] With the decision of the Tutorial Committee to increase the number of undergraduates at Magdalen, the tutorial load only increased for Lewis. More pupils meant more preparation and more critical response to each pupil's weekly paper, the equivalent of an American term paper each week. As Lewis's health declined, as his domestic stress increased, and as the crushing load of five hours of intense critical interaction with pupils each day threatened to overwhelm him, Magdalen College added a new fellow to teach English. J. A. W. Bennett came to Oxford from New Zealand as an undergraduate on a scholarship. He gained a reputation for his hard work as a scholar, his saintliness, and his forgetfulness.[61] During the war, he worked with the British Information Service in America. Upon his arrival at Magdalen, he relieved Lewis of some of his tutorial load and took on the task of teaching Anglo-Saxon.[62] Lewis soon invited him to join the Inklings. Following the death of Lewis, Bennett was elected to the Lewis Chair of Medieval and Renaissance Literature at Cambridge.

The Merton Chair

The addition of Bennett was a great help to Lewis, but what the academy gave with one hand, it took away with the other. In 1947, a Merton Professorship came open with the retirement of David Nichol Smith. Oxford has two Merton Professors. Tolkien was elected as Merton Professor of English Language and Literature in 1945. Smith was Merton Professor of English Literature. Tolkien hoped to manage Lewis's election as Smith's replacement, which would provide Lewis with a comfortable income and a reduced workload. The added bonus would be that the two friends would belong to the same college and have rooms near each other. Unlike the professor of poetry, who was elected by all the members of the university, the Merton Professors were elected by a small group of four, including Tolkien, himself a Merton Professor. The other electors were H. W. Garrod, C. H. Wilkinson, and Helen Darbishire. When Tolkien proposed Lewis to the other electors, they all balked. None of them thought Lewis an appropriate candidate.

The reasons they gave for Lewis's unsuitability sound somewhat legitimate on the surface. He had not produced a significant body of scholarship for such an important professorship. His most successful work, they continued, had been novels and popular religious books rather than important critical work. To give Lewis a professorial chair on such thin terms would diminish the stature of the Merton Professorship and the English School of Oxford University. Lewis had also alienated them by his attitude toward the higher research degrees. He thought that most research theses tended to be obscure, trivial, dull, and lacking in merit. He took the view that if someone had something important to write, that person should go ahead and write it rather than wasting time securing certification to write. George Sayer reported that Lewis was fond of saying that Oxford had three kinds of literacy: the literate, the illiterate, and the B Litterate. Lewis preferred the first two to the latter.[63] The BLitt, or bachelor of letters, was a second undergraduate degree experiment in the journey toward research degrees. His friend Owen Barfield had spent years writing his BLitt thesis in hopes that it would establish his literary career, but it did not happen.

Still, Lewis did accept the supervision of some research students. In 1952, he accepted Alastair Fowler, but only after much intercession and prodding from others. Fowler went on to become one the great names in English Renaissance literary studies, but when he first appeared in Oxford, he wanted to study with Charles Williams, only to discover that Williams had been dead for seven years. At that point, he turned to Lewis, only to discover that Lewis rarely accepted research students. Upon coming to Oxford, Fowler belonged to Pembroke College, where R. B. McCallum was a fellow in history. McCallum had been a regular member of the Inklings for many years. When Lewis turned down Fowler, McCallum suggested that he would write to Lewis and that Fowler should also enlist the help of Hugo Dyson. Between the entreaties of McCallum and Dyson, Lewis relented and agreed to supervise Fowler.[64] Fowler's experience was typical of Lewis's attitude toward graduate degrees.

In 1947, the new discipline of English still struggled to find its way within the university. For instance, Garrod, who completed his undergraduate degree in 1902 in classics like Lewis, had no degree in English, unlike Lewis. Helen Darbishire wrote a book on Milton and may have disliked Lewis's treatment of Milton in *A Preface to Paradise Lost*. Though Garrod, the self-taught English literary figure, published a good deal, neither Wilkinson nor Darbishire had approached Lewis's critical literary accomplishments in 1947. The objections to Lewis's scholarship appear to fall in the face of the enormous importance of *The Allegory of Love* and *A Preface to Paradise Lost*. Peter Bailey observed that all of Oxford, dons and undergraduates, were still talking about these two books that had such an impact on their fields of study long after they were written, books still in print twenty-five years after Bailey's time at Oxford when he wrote his memoir. Lewis's colleagues recognized that these books were, in Bailey's words, "unquestionably among the finest examples of literary criticism" of the twentieth century.[65] Lewis had also given a number of important lectures that were published as books or in journals. His critical engagement with Tillyard, published as *The Personal Heresy*, challenged a major trend in criticism and probably played a part in a general reassessment of the problem Lewis identified. In the final analysis, the electors did not like Lewis's religious writings, and they particularly objected to the *success* of his religious writings. Passing over Lewis was simply an embarrassment to the English faculty that does not fade with time.

In the end, Tolkien changed horses in midstream and supported the election of Lord David Cecil, their fellow Inkling. The electors, however, rejected Cecil, again on the basis of a poor record of scholarship. It is remarkable that they used the same grounds with Cecil, who also had an impressive publication record. Not only did he publish books; his books had a significant impact on his field. Cecil brought attention to Jane Austen, Charles Dickens and the Victorian novelists, and Thomas Hardy. He may have also been faulted for writing biographies so popular that they went into many editions. His biography of Lord Melbourne was President John F. Kennedy's favorite book.

Cecil also accomplished something Lewis admired. He wrote little books on a variety of subjects with the Christianity latent. Cecil was actually better at this than Lewis. His masterful biography of Melbourne leaves one wondering how a man who lacked any convictions or moral compass could have succeeded so spectacularly at politics. Rather than attacking Melbourne for his shortcomings, Cecil laid Melbourne bare for the reader to draw the conclusions Cecil intended. He did the same with his scholarly treatment of Hardy, which he gave as a series of guest lectures at Cambridge before publishing them as a book. After masterfully describing and analyzing how and why Hardy wrote the kinds of stories he wrote, Cecil drew a powerful conclusion. He argued that Hardy wanted the values of Christ without Christ. He wanted the benefits of righteousness without God. Cecil then modestly suggested that Hardy may have been wrong, and he believed he was. This way of thinking and writing was why Lewis wanted Cecil's company and why the electors did not want him to hold a Merton Professorship. There may have been one more reason. While Lewis held forth in the South Writing School, Cecil was the other great lecturer, who occupied the North Writing School. Jealousy may have played a part in the electors' decision. It sometimes does.

In the end, the electors chose Lewis's English tutor F. P. Wilson for the Merton Chair. He was safe. He was reliable. He had no enemies. He was also a legitimate scholar, producing a number of books on Shakespeare and gaining a reputation as one of the most important Elizabethan scholars of his generation. In addition to his own work, he edited the OHEL series and was responsible for Lewis being condemned to work on his contribution for years. While Lewis would have been disappointed, the election of his former tutor would have been easier to take than the election of someone of his own generation of less ability and accomplishment.[66]

Probably to the horror of those who took exception to Lewis's growing popular fame, and possibly to his embarrassment, the September 8, 1947, issue of *Time* magazine featured Lewis on its cover with a feature story. The color image of Lewis captures perfectly the allegorical concept of the *bellum intestinum* (the internal war) between virtue and vice that figures so prominently in *The Allegory of Love*. In the cover portrait, a devil with pitchfork stands on Lewis's left shoulder, while just out of the frame

Time magazine, September 8, 1947

stands an angel with one wing and a bit of the halo protruding into the picture. The article, coming just when it did, would have confirmed the electors in their decision to pass over Lewis. Lewis thought the article was "ghastly" and hoped no one would believe how he was portrayed in print. He particularly protested against the claim that he disliked women. To Margaret Fuller he wrote: "Who said I disliked women? I never liked or disliked any *generalization*."[67]

In 1948, the Goldsmith Chair of English Literature fell vacant.[68] This time, Lewis was not even a contender. The professorship went to Lord David Cecil. It is not difficult to see why Lewis invited Cecil to the Inklings meetings. Like Lewis, he had no use for "the personal heresy," or for psychological, sociological, historical, socio-linguistic, philosophical, or methodological theories of interpretation. He cared no more for theories than Lewis did. He was also critical of the approaches of Edmund Wilson, F. R. Leavis, and I. A. Richards. Cecil wanted to deal with the text, like Lewis.[69] Lewis could have congratulated Cecil as a worthy recipient of the chair and an ally, but he was still left with a huge workload and little recognition from his peers. For his part, Cecil said that Lewis was the "most distinguished member of the English faculty" but was denied the professorship "because his forceful manner combined with his equally forceful piety to make him unpopular with a prim and agnostic electorate."[70] Not to be considered would have come as a disappointment to Lewis at a time in his life when he did not need more disappointment while stress from life at the Kilns mounted. Of these two episodes with professorships, Helen Gardner wrote:

> While undoubtedly there were a good many people in Oxford who disliked Christian apologetics *per se*, there were others who were uneasy at Lewis's particular kind of apologetic, disliking both its method and its manner. These last considerations were probably the strongest, and accounted for the fact that when, in the following year, a second Chair in English Literature was established his name was not put forward.[71]

Gardner observed that while Lewis "aroused warm affection, loyalty, and devotion in his friends," he also managed to arouse "strong antipathy, disapproval, and distaste among some of his colleagues and pupils." She thought, "It was impossible to be indifferent to him."[72]

The Anscombe "Debate"

In Hilary term, Lewis began 1948 with his lectures "Prolegomena to the Study of Medieval Poetry" at noon on Wednesdays and Saturdays at the Examinations Schools.[73] Soon after the beginning of term, on Monday evening, February 2, the Socratic Club met at St Hilda's College, with Elizabeth Anscombe as the guest speaker. Anscombe was a devout Catholic who held the post of philosophy tutor at Somerville College, where Helen Darbishire served as principal. In her talk, Anscombe proposed to give a reply to Lewis's book *Miracles*, which Geoffrey Bles had published in 1947. She was an analytical philosopher who had studied with Ludwig Wittgenstein, the creator of linguistic analysis, and she became recognized as his preeminent interpreter. Wittgenstein chose her to translate his *Philosophical Investigations* from German into English, and he named her one of his literary executors. No one could have given a more robust linguistic analysis of Lewis's argument in *Miracles* than Anscombe.

Anscombe's critique focused on chapter 3 of the book, "The Self-Contradiction of the Naturalist." In her criticism of Lewis's argument, she did not analyze the validity of his argument. Linguistic analysis represents a complete departure from traditional philosophical debate as it has been understood for the past 2,500 years. Rather than criticize the validity of Lewis's argument, she criticized his use of the word *validity*. In a very loose sense, the difference between Anscombe's approach and Lewis's approach might be seen as the difference between rhetoric and logic. Nonetheless, her criticism was not without good logic. Lewis had argued that rationality could not be the result of irrational causes; therefore, some rational cause other than irrational matter must lie behind the development of human rationality. Anscombe pointed out that in addition to rationality and irrationality, Lewis ought to have included nonrationality, since matter might be neither rational nor irrational.

Lewis had an earlier brush with linguistic analysis through some of his pupils who introduced him to the idea that all statements of value are actually expressions of personal feeling. He had addressed this view in *The Abolition of Man*. He had not, however, immersed himself in Wittgenstein's departure from traditional philosophy. Logical positivism had declared that only statements that can be known with the senses have any meaning. Since God cannot be known through the senses, the concept of God is meaningless or nonsense. Lewis had been influenced by positivism during his youthful days of atheism, and he had seen its flaws because of his growing awareness of the reality of values, even though they are immaterial. As a result of the failure of sense experience to explain all phenomena, positivism collapsed by the 1920s, but Wittgenstein developed linguistic analysis from its ruins. According to linguistic analysis, meaning is determined by usage. Religious language is meaningful within the religious community, but religious language has no cognitive or objective meaning. Under the rules of linguistic analysis, philosophy became an examination of how people use words rather than an attempt to establish objective truth.

In her response to chapter 3 of *Miracles*, Elizabeth Anscombe pointed out that Lewis had used the words *valid* and *validity* in a way that could be construed as ambiguous.[74] Accepted meanings and traditional understandings of words among philosophers no longer mattered, because Anscombe was playing a new game. Lewis was taken off guard by something that did not sound like philosophy or grammar. To add to the disorientation of her presentation, Anscombe came smoking a cigar with her hair cut short.[75] According to Basil Mitchell, vice president of the Socratic Club at the time and successor to Lewis as president when he went to Cambridge, Anscombe understood "gamesmanship" and Lewis did not.[76] With his longstanding awkwardness around women, Lewis grew uncharacteristically flustered and embarrassed. According to Mitchell, a major philosopher who held the Nolloth Chair of Philosophy of the Christian Religion at Oxford for many years, Lewis won the argument about the self-defeating nature of naturalism, but he lost the presentation in the face of Anscombe's tactics.

In fact, Lewis and Anscombe did not have a debate about *Miracles*, since Anscombe agreed with Lewis about naturalism.

She had merely pointed out the weak parts of Lewis's argument with suggestions for how he could strengthen them. She was unaware that they had a debate or that anyone thought Lewis had "lost." In a sense, the great Lewis-Anscombe debate did not take place on the evening of February 2, 1948, at St Hilda's College. It actually occurred years later in the retelling of events, such as this retelling. Antony Flew, one of the premiere atheist philosophers of the twentieth century, who advocated naturalism, was present that evening as a student but had no recollection of the discussion, since, to him, it was only a technical discussion of phrasing. Flew did recall, however, that as he followed Anscombe across Magdalen Bridge from St Hilda's, she seemed "exultant," while Lewis, on the other side of the bridge and a little ahead of them, hurried quickly back to his rooms.[77] Anscombe herself was unaware that a debate had taken place. The philosophers present who have spoken about the matter, both Christians and atheists, were unaware of a debate or that Lewis had lost the debate of which they were unaware. The idea of a debate mushroomed a few days later among English undergraduates who had not been present at the Socratic Club.

Two nights after the Socratic Club meeting, Lewis attended the dinner club with Dyson and the four undergraduates. In his diary, Brewer had written that Lewis was "deeply disturbed" because Anscombe "had disproved some of the central theory of his philosophy about Christianity."[78] Brewer was a great literary critic and went on to become the master of Emmanuel College in Cambridge, but he was not a philosopher and did not seem to understand the fine points under discussion that had dismayed Lewis at the meeting Brewer had not attended. For her part, Anscombe was surprised by the account of the evening given by those who were not there. She wrote:

> The fact that Lewis rewrote that chapter, and rewrote it so that it now has those qualities [to address the objections], shows his honesty and seriousness. The meeting of the Socratic Club

at which I read my paper has been described by several of his friends as a horrible and shocking experience which upset him very much. Neither Dr Havard (who had Lewis and me to dinner a few weeks later) nor Professor Jack Bennet remembered any such feelings on Lewis's part. . . . My own recollection is that it was an occasion of sober discussion of certain quite definite criticisms, which Lewis' rethinking and rewriting showed he thought was accurate. I am inclined to construe the odd accounts of the matter by some of his friends—who seem not to have been interested in the actual arguments or the subject-matter—as an interesting example of the phenomenon called "projection."[79]

Brewer probably records accurately how Lewis felt two nights after the event, but he probably did not understand what had upset Lewis so much.

Nearly two decades later, at the Socratic Club meeting on February 2, 1967, Basil Mitchell enlisted Elizabeth Anscombe to reenact the original meeting, with John Lucas standing in for Lewis, and with the title "Is Mechanism Self-Refuting?" Anscombe presented her critique to chapter 3 with forty-eight students in attendance, but this time Lucas responded.[80] Lucas was a fellow of Merton College and philosopher tutor who had wide-ranging research interests in various fields of philosophy, unlike Lewis. He and Mitchell were convinced that Lewis's essential argument about naturalism was sound but that he was caught off guard by Anscombe's "gamesmanship." Lucas, born in 1929, belonged to a different generation from Lewis and did not have Lewis's reserve around women. He had also not been affected by the stories of gallantry and chivalry in the service of a lady that had so affected Lewis. Without these constraints, Lucas did Anscombe the compliment of fighting her on her own ground. When Mitchell and Lucas told me this story in 2004, they claimed that Lucas won the debate with Lewis's argument.[81] Of course, more than fifty years after the reenactment, who is to say who won?

In 2004, John Lucas was corresponding with me and Jerry Walls about Lewis and Anscombe. Since we were asking the same questions, Lucas asked Walls to send me the succinct evaluation Lucas had sketched of the status of Lewis's argument in *Miracles*. He wrote:

Musing on the whole matter, I see the debate as a search for greater articulateness.

1. Lewis was not wrong in putting forward the original argument in *Miracles*. That he was onto something is borne out not only by passages cited from Haldane, but by many other thinkers, including Joseph, an eminently respectable Oxford logician. (I give some references in my *The Freedom of the Will*, p. 174.)

2. The argument given by Lewis [in chapter three] was not the centerpiece of *Miracles*, but a preliminary clearing away of objections which would rule out the whole enterprise. It needed to be brief.

3. Anscombe fastened on its brevity, and made a number of valid distinctions Lewis had slurred over. But the fact that Lewis had slurred over them did not invalidate his main argument. It is quite right to point out (as Aristotle had earlier) that there are different meanings to the words 'cause' and 'because', and different types of explanation in terms of them. But that does not show that the claim of the naturalist to give a *complete* deterministic explanation in terms of cause and effect, is compatible with the thesis that arguments can be adduced and assessed in their own terms. Lewis's examples of Marxist and Freudian explanations undercutting our ordinary commitment to rationality still stand.

4. Faced with Anscombe's attack, *and the fact that his argument against naturalism had been seen by many to be of great significance*, Lewis was quite right to go back

over it, and try to re-phrase it so as to meet Anscombe's objections.

5. Lewis's revised argument is still far from watertight, and open to further criticism.

6. This is standardly the case with all important philosophical arguments. Unlike mathematical proofs, which, if valid, are such that denial of the conclusion to them is self-contradictory, philosophical arguments do not close off the debate. Discussion goes on. New objections are raised, and sometimes successfully countered.

7. Anscombe was right to claim *at the time* that she had won, but wrong not to recognize that it was only a preliminary skirmish over a necessarily brief exposition of an important argument.

8. Anscombe was right and generous later to recognize that Lewis's revised argument was onto something.[82]

Having spoken with Mitchell, Brewer, and Flew sixty years after the night at the Socratic Club, I think it apparent that they reported different aspects of the same event. Mitchell and Flew reported the evening as philosophers concerned with ideas. Brewer, and later George Sayer in his biography of Lewis, reported how Lewis felt about the evening. To complicate matters, Sayer reported that several weeks later, Lewis told him that he would never write another book like *Miracles*.[83] The so-called "Lewis-Anscombe Debate," which involved only a brief response by Lewis to Anscombe's critique, has had a much more interesting afterlife than those attending the Socratic Club that night might have suspected.

At a meeting of the Oxford C. S. Lewis Society on November 12, 1985, Elizabeth Anscombe presented a paper on Lewis's revisions to chapter 3 in light of her critique. What often escapes notice is that Anscombe offered Lewis the kind of critique he had long sought from the Inklings. The purpose for the Inklings was to read one another's work and to provide helpful feedback for improvement. However Lewis might have felt about the performance that evening, he took Anscombe's remarks under consideration and revised the third chapter of *Miracles* significantly. Mitchell and Lucas attended the meeting of the C. S. Lewis Society that night, as did Walter Hooper.[84] Anscombe still did not believe Lewis had met her objections.[85]

In his 1990 biography of Lewis, A. N. Wilson described the encounter with Anscombe as a completely devastating moment in Lewis's life that created a psychological barrier to his ever taking up philosophical debate again.[86] Wilson suggested that Lewis turned to writing children's stories because he had proved to be a complete failure at apologetics, or at least felt himself to be.[87] Wilson asserted that *"The Lion, the Witch and the Wardrobe* grew out of Lewis's experience of being stung back into childhood by his defeat at the hands of Elizabeth Anscombe at the Socratic Club."[88] The problem with Wilson's attempt to assign cause and effect to Elizabeth Anscombe is the old problem of time. As has been seen in volume 2 of this biography, Lewis had decided by 1944 that he would never again write another book like *Miracles*. He told the BBC over and over that he had nothing more to say along the lines of the apologetics he had done during the war. The encounter with Anscombe came four years after he had tired of that sort of thing. It had never been his idea to take up that kind of writing in the first place. He had decided in the 1920s that his heart lay with literature instead of with philosophy.

Alister McGrath's 2013 biography follows a much more constructive approach. He takes Wilson to task for his unsubstantiated declarations about Lewis's feelings and motives while pointing out that Lewis continued to write essays that dealt with philosophical issues touching on faith.[89] Perhaps the greatest evidence that Lewis did not feel himself completely defeated and incapable of mounting a reasoned defense of his faith came the next Monday night after his encounter with Elizabeth Anscombe, and every succeeding Monday night during term for the next six years. He continued his work with the Socratic Club, in which, off the cuff as with Anscombe, he responded to intellectual objections to faith. He kept his hand in, but Lewis had other fish to fry. Antony Flew continued to attend the meetings as an atheist and remained unconvinced by Lewis's moral argument for God represented in *Mere Christianity.*

By one of those odd strokes of irony, Flew changed his mind and came to believe in God more than fifty years later, convinced by new insights from the Intelligent Design movement. Intelligent Design is a modern variation on the old teleological argument of Thomas Aquinas, which he borrowed from Aristotle. In summary form, the argument from design observes that the universe at all levels of organization shows evidence of design; therefore, a designer must exist. In contrast to Flew's experience, Lewis told Dom Bede Griffiths that the design argument is "the weakest possible ground for Theism."[90] In *Mere Christianity*, Lewis acknowledged that the universe shows evidence of an artist, but it gives us no clue to the character of the artist. For Lewis, the internal evidence of the moral law provides better evidence for what kind of God exists.[91] The different experiences of the two men demonstrates why only one approach to apologetics will not help everyone, and why Lewis experimented with a variety of approaches. In the end, apologetics does not involve mounting an argument but answering questions.

John Lucas was a great friend of Hugo Dyson, who told him that at their dinner club meeting two nights after the Socratic Club discussion with Anscombe, Lewis had lamented his loss in public and confessed, "It shows that I am no philosopher," to which Dyson replied, "We never thought you were, Jack: you are a literary man."[92]

The English Syllabus

With the leftward lean of politics in the United Kingdom after the war, and with the effort by the Soviet Union to infiltrate the universities, which had begun with some success by the 1930s (they were particularly successful in Cambridge), a climate developed which advanced the notion that the teaching of English might become a vehicle for social change.[93] It was not necessary to be a communist or a socialist to be swept up in the idea of reforming the English syllabus that Tolkien had engineered in 1931 with Lewis's support. Their reform, designed to make the study of Old English secure within the curriculum, ended with 1830. Jane Austen might be included, but not Dickens, Tennyson, Thackery, the Brownings, the Brontës, Morris, Trollope, or George Eliot. No less a conservative and champion of the Christian faith than Lord David Cecil urged the inclusion of Victorian literature in the syllabus. Cecil published an important study in 1934, *The Early Victorian Novelists*. What Lewis did for Milton, Cecil did for Jane Austen, Charles Dickens, and Thomas Hardy. The nineteenth-century novelists and poets had played a particularly important part in the development of Lewis's love of literature, especially Austen, Morris, MacDonald, and the Brontës. He continued to reread them. Nonetheless, Lewis opposed the effort to extend the syllabus to 1900.

Lewis, whose lectures focused on the background and culture of the medieval worldview, believed that the critical study of nineteenth-century literature would require too much reading in other areas to understand fully the context of what had been written at the height of the empire in the Industrial Revolution. A. N. Wilson describes a confrontation between Lewis and Helen Gardner at a heated meeting of the English faculty in which these issues were discussed in the late 1940s.[94] After Lewis expressed his view that too much material would have to be mastered for a legitimate study of Victorian literature, Gardner challenged him by asking how students of Renaissance literature could understand their period without reading Calvin's *Institutes*. Lewis immediately replied that all of his students had read Calvin. Wilson then stated: "His eyes met Miss Gardner's. He knew that she knew that he was lying."[95] In her memoir of Lewis in *The Proceedings of the British*

Academy following his death, Gardner simply remarked of his public style of argument that he tended to "exaggeration and extravagance."[96] By way of apology after the meeting, Lewis invited Gardner to one of his famous ham suppers with the Inklings. On this occasion, it took place at the Kilns, which must have looked like a run-down boarding house to Gardner according to how Warnie described it in those days. With Mrs. Moore upstairs in bed and Hugo Dyson in all probability carrying on his outrageous antics, it must have been a startling experience for Gardner.

In the end, the English faculty changed the syllabus that Tolkien had created. Though Lewis opposed the change, Tolkien did not. Ever the consummate politician, Tolkien appears to have seen nothing to gain by opposing changes in the study of literature. For him, language was the thing; as long as the study of Old English was preserved, it did not matter if the syllabus ended in 1830 or 1900. From a language perspective, it could have ended with Shakespeare. He preferred the old stories before the Norman Conquest, but he had less interest in the literature written after the Normans "Frenchified" the language.[97] Lewis was on his own.

3

A New Agenda and New Friends

1945–1950

After the war, with the influx of veterans who had delayed college, Lewis had an increased tutorial load. Before the war, he took his pupils one at a time, but after the war, he began taking two at a time.[1] His normal daily schedule during term began with correspondence from nine until ten in the morning, when his first pair of pupils came. Then tutorials followed until one o'clock, when he went home to spend the afternoon looking after Minto.[2] He resumed tutorials at five and continued the hour-long sessions until seven. During vacations, he tried to work in the Bodleian Library every morning from nine thirty until one.[3]

Compared with his enormous productivity between 1935 and 1945, Lewis wrote and published very little in the years between the end of the war and Mrs. Moore's confinement in the nursing home. He published *The Great Divorce* in 1946 and *Miracles* in 1947, but he had written them during the war. The other books he published between 1945 and 1950 were only edited volumes for which he wrote brief introductions, including *George*

87

MacDonald: An Anthology (1946), *Essays Presented to Charles Williams* (1947), *Transposition and Other Addresses* (1949—published in the United States as *The Weight of Glory and Other Addresses*)—and Charles Williams's *Arthurian Torso* (1948). Lewis also wrote short prefaces to several books by friends, including B. G. Sandhurst's *How Heathen Is Britain?* (1946), Eric Bentley's *The Cult of the Superman* (1947), and J. B. Phillips's *Letters to Young Churches* (1947). Although thoughtful and insightful, these short prefaces were not essays that Lewis would have undertaken except as a duty. Besides these pieces, he published twenty-eight very short pieces of a few pages each in a variety of journals and several short scholarly essays.[4] As we saw in the last chapter, Lewis was completely drained by his domestic life at the Kilns, which robbed him of time and emotional energy.

Meditations

The twenty-eight short pieces that Lewis published between 1945 and 1950 are interesting as a window on Lewis's frame of mind during this stressful period because, for the most part, they are meditations. Walter Hooper collected fifteen of these short meditations in *God in the Dock* (1970). He published the rest in *Christian Reflections* (1967), *Of This and Other Worlds* (1982), and *Present Concerns* (1986). Lewis published only two of these meditations in volumes of collected essays. He included one in *Transposition* (1949), which was published in the United States as *The Weight of Glory*, and one in *They Asked for a Paper* (1962), which was not published in the United States. In many ways, these meditations are not like Lewis's other writing.

Lewis enjoyed writing, and he always enjoyed publishing another book. Yet he made no apparent effort to make a book of these meditations that appeared in church newspapers and magazines. These meditations are not apologetics intended for a secular audience. They are his reflections on what it means to be a Christian, which for Lewis did not mean belonging to the organization but meant belonging to Christ. In these short meditations, he reflected on prayer, on the fallacy of trying to live "the good life" without Christ, on the essence of faith as connected with doctrine, on the paradox of caring for the ill while yearning for heaven, on the need we have for God to rid us of that bit of hell within us that we nurture, on the whole story of Jesus, and on much more.

While the radio broadcasts and *The Pilgrim's Regress* focused on the journey to faith and Christ, and the demonic tales (*The Screwtape Letters*, *The Great Divorce*, *Perelandra*, and *That Hideous Strength*) focused on the challenge of temptation, the meditations that Lewis wrote after World War II focus on growing in faith and living the life of faith in Christ. Perhaps the most well-known of these is "Meditation in a Tool Shed." It certainly illustrates what thoughts came to Lewis during the ordeals at work and at the Kilns after the war. Always a visual thinker, Lewis described being in his toolshed when he noticed a beam of sunlight shining down through a crack in the top of the door. The darkness of the shed made the light even more prominent. He moved toward the light and looked along the beam, through the crack, and out to the wide world beyond. He saw leaves, trees, and the Sun shining "90 odd million miles away."[5] In this meditation, Lewis reflected on the importance not only of looking *at* but also of looking *along*. From the outside, we may see and understand something in one way that makes perfect sense to us, but if we experience something from the inside, we may have an entirely different understanding of it. So it is with faith in Christ.

With these short meditations, we have a brief glimpse at the devotional life of C. S. Lewis. He said little about his devotional life except to note that he spent time in prayer every day and spent time reading the Bible. We also know from his letters that he read the Christian devotional classics of the past two thousand years. He had read *The Pilgrim's Progress* several times before he even became a Christian. He attended church each Sunday, just as he attended morning prayer in college during term, as a spiritual discipline. In the course of a year, the Book of Common Prayer goes through the entire Bible, so Lewis either read or heard the Bible as a daily, weekly, and yearly matter throughout his life. Thus, Lewis had a context and a reserve of spiritual resources on which to lean during the stressful years after World War II. The meditations, as reflections of his devotional life, demonstrate how Lewis pondered his life as a Christian. To some, these meditations might seem Lewis's least important work, but in many ways they represent how Christ was working on him, nurturing him, healing him, preserving him, and preparing him for the next stage of his life after the enormous work he performed during the war.

The Dreaded OHEL Volume

Dr. Robert Havard, one of the most faithful attendees of the Inklings meetings from about 1934, had a firsthand acquaintance with the many writing projects Lewis undertook. According to Havard, the one that gave him the most trouble, "at least the one he complained of most," was *English Literature in the Sixteenth Century Excluding Drama*, which formed part of the multivolume Oxford History of English Literature (OHEL).[6] Lewis had agreed to write the volume in 1935, though he would have preferred to write on the fourteenth century.[7] By 1938 he regretted his decision to take part. It was proving to be a tedious book to research, for it meant reading everything, whether good or bad, that anyone—talented or not—had published in England during the sixteenth century. Though it would include his beloved Spenser, it would also have to treat some pretty ordinary writing. He wrote to the general editor, F. P. Wilson, that "the O HELL lies like a nightmare on my chest," and henceforth referred to this volume as the "O HELL."[8]

With his increased workload at Magdalen, which bulged with ex-servicemen as well as the usual influx of "first years," and with the increasing demands on him at home with Minto's declining physical and mental health, Lewis had little time for writing, compared with his war years. The only time he had to work on the "O HELL" volume was during vacation, when he could spend only a few hours in the Duke Humphrey Library each day.[9] The Duke Humphrey is the original part of the great Bodleian Library of Oxford. It is situated on the upper floor of the original building of the Bodleian, which expanded round it. The lower floor, with its exquisite spiderweb, late-Gothic vaulting, contains the Divinity School. Lewis read the original editions of the sixteenth-century volumes in the room constructed by the university in the late fifteenth century to hold the library donated by Humphrey, Duke of Gloucester, a younger son of Henry IV.[10] By working in the Duke Humphrey Library, Lewis physically entered the world of the writers he examined.

Lewis's Personal Testimony

Lewis's personal testimony, or the account of his conversion, had been on his mind for several years when the war ended. He had declined the invitation to tell his story on the BBC, because he had already given the primary intellectual aspects of it in his earlier broadcasts and because he simply did not feel that he was the sort of person who could tell his own story. Once suggested, however, the idea continued to grow ever so slowly.

In his talk titled "Christian Apologetics," at the end of the war, Lewis declared:

> I am not sure that the ideal missionary team ought not to consist of one who argues and one who (in the fullest sense of the word) preaches. Put up your arguer first to undermine their intellectual prejudices; then let the evangelist proper launch his appeal. I have seen this done with great success.[11]

In fact, he had not *seen* it done; he actually had done it himself on a number of occasions during and after the war. During the war, while giving his RAF talks, Lewis teamed up with Chaplain A. W. Goodwin-Hudson, later Anglican bishop in Sydney, Australia, in evangelistic meetings. Their partnership had begun as a result of

Lewis departing from his usual program of dealing with obstacles to faith and instead speaking about his own struggles in following Christ and what it had cost him. At the close of the service, a number of men responded, and Goodwin-Hudson reported to his wife that "some of the cream of English manhood have come forward to talk to us and to confess Christ as Savior and Lord."[12]

After the war, Lewis became involved in the evangelistic ministry of Tom Rees. Rees conducted a series of evangelistic meetings in London at Methodist Central Hall Westminster, across the street from Westminster Abbey.[13] Its twenty-three hundred seats were sufficient for the weeknight crowds, but on the weekends, Rees rented the Royal Albert Hall and packed it with eight thousand people. Rees often invited Stephen Olford and several other young preachers to join him and share the preaching responsibilities. He also invited someone to give a testimony each evening. On one evening when Olford preached, C. S. Lewis gave his testimony. Heather Brown, who served as Rees's secretary and pianist for his meetings, said that Lewis surprised everyone by the way he dressed. He had not dressed in a fine suit but wore an old jacket and baggy trousers. She thought he looked like a farmer. Sixty years later, when she told me about Olford and Lewis working together, her memory of the evening was as fresh as if it had taken place only the evening before. Olford appears to have made the greater impression, for she married him a short while later.[14]

In the context of these evangelistic meetings, Lewis learned to give his testimony before thousands of people. These were much larger crowds than he spoke to in the largest lecture hall in Oxford. Furthermore, they were not university people. He was face-to-face finally with his vast radio audience. Fortunately, a testimony is nothing more than a story. Despite his earlier misgivings, he could tell a story. It was his story. He knew it well. He found that his testimony provided a way to talk about his intellectual obstacles to faith without using technical language. It was the same sort of thing he had done in his first radio broadcasts, when he talked about right and wrong as a clue to the meaning of the universe. Only, this time, he explained that these were his obstacles, and the answers led him to Christ.

On February 15, 1946, Lewis wrote a succinct letter to Mr. N. Fridama of Clifton, New Jersey, in which he presented his personal testimony in three brief paragraphs that form the basic outline of what would become *Surprised by Joy*. It deserves to be quoted in full to demonstrate that Lewis had a clear idea of the steps along the way of his conversion, pieces of which he had elaborated in his broadcast talks. He wrote:

> I was baptized in the Church of Ireland (same as Anglican). My parents were not notably pious but went regularly to church and took me. My mother died when I was a child.
>
> My Xian faith was first undermined by the attitude taken towards *Pagan* religion in the notes of modern editors of Latin & Greek poets at school. They always assumed that the ancient religion was pure error: hence, in my mind, the obvious question 'Why shouldn't ours be equally false?' A theosophical Matron at one school helped to break up my early beliefs, and after that a 'Rationalist' tutor to whom I went finished the job. I abandoned all belief in Xtianity at about the age of 14, tho' I pretended to believe for fear of my elders. I thus went thro' the ceremony of Confirmation in total hypocrisy. My beliefs continued to be agnostic, with fluctuation towards pantheism and various other sub-Xtian beliefs, till I was about 29.
>
> I was brought back (a.) By Philosophy. I still think Berkeley is unanswerable. (b.) By increasing knowledge of medieval literature. It became harder & harder to think that all those great poets & philosophers were wrong. (c.) By the strong influence of 2 writers, the Presbyterian George Macdonald & the R.C., G. K. Chesterton. (d.) By argument with an Anthroposophist. He failed to convert me to his own views (a kind of Gnosticism) but his attack on my own presuppositions smashed the ordinary pseudo-'scientific' world-picture forever.[15]

Lewis's letters from this period suggest the extent to which he began to think about his conversion experience. After the war, his letters to Arthur Greeves took on a nostalgic tone that approached the "sentimentality" of his father, which he had always ridiculed. He almost always included a passage about days gone by. He talked about the way they listened to gramophone records as boys, and the hope that he had grown less arrogant and dictatorial now that they were both "elderly."[16] In December 1946, Lewis confided to Dom Bede Griffiths:

> The early loss of my mother, great unhappiness at school, and the shadow of the last war and presently the experience of it, had given me a very pessimistic view of existence. My atheism was based on it: and it seems to me that [by] *far* the strongest card in our enemies' hand is the actual course of the world: and that, quite apart from particular evils like wars and revolutions.[17]

Yet, to Roy Harrington, who had written in January 1948 with a variety of personal questions, Lewis wrote: "My conversion was much too gradual and intellectual to be described briefly or even interestingly. I haven't got any hobbies."[18]

Lewis had also begun to reflect on his childhood with his brother. Jack and Warnie dined together at Magdalen College on Maundy Thursday, March 25, 1948. There being no Inklings that night, they walked home to the Kilns along Cuckoo Lane, a path that leads from the back of Magdalen College all the way through Headington, almost to the Kilns, but hidden away like a trail through the country. As they walked, they talked about their boyhood and their rejection of games. It was an important conversation because, despite what he had written to Harrington, Jack had begun working on what he was calling his autobiography.[19]

Lewis kept his benefactors during the food shortages apprised of his work. By September, he wrote Vera Mathews that he was busy working on his autobiography.[20] To Edward Dell, he wrote in March 1949 that he hoped someday to write an autobiography, which would explain *"what I know* (= the experience) of my own conversion."[21] He thought, however, that the real event of his conversion as known by God would differ from what he knew about his conversion as much as the total event of a decaying tooth differs from the pain. Lewis explained to Warfield Firor that he had begrudged the passing of his childhood when he was young because it meant going away to school, and he thought that being a schoolboy would not be as pleasant as childhood. He added, "And as it turned out, I was right."[22] All of these reflections on childhood found their way into his conversion story.

This first attempt at a straightforward account of his conversion, in contrast to his earlier allegorical account in *The Pilgrim's Regress*, exists in a notebook along with some other writing. Walter Hooper, who discovered it, named it "Early Prose Joy" and dated it to 1930 because it comes several pages after a poem in the notebook that Lewis dated August 1930.[23] At first blush, the date of the poem would seem to prove that Lewis wrote the early draft of his testimony in 1930 or thereabouts. This view, however, does not take into account Lewis's writing habits. By 1930, he had all but abandoned his plans to become a great poet. Not until after the war would he begin to write poetry again in earnest after writing so much of the prose for which he became famous. The notebook may have sat idle for over fifteen years when he picked it up again while looking for spare paper to write his testimony when paper was scarce. From his correspondence with his American benefactors during and after the war, we know that paper was in short supply and that Lewis made use of every scrap he had. He often wrote on the backs of letters and old manuscripts. Finding a notebook with empty pages after the war would have been a logical way for Lewis to begin.

The most compelling reason for a postwar date for "Early Prose Joy," however, comes from the internal evidence in which Lewis indicated the climate in England when he began his spiritual memoir. On the first page, he stated that he hoped his conversion story would fill a gap between the extremes in the current "religious revival" underway in Britain.[24] Britain did not undergo a religious revival in the period between the world wars. The religious revival came after World War II, and as we have seen, Lewis participated in evangelistic meetings. During this period, John Stott and Stephen Olford came to prominence as evangelists. Organizations like InterVarsity and the Navigators began. The trans-Atlantic revival is perhaps most associated with the ministry of Billy Graham, which began in the aftermath of the war. The early date is certainly possible, but from all that Lewis said about his reluctance to write a personal testimony earlier, and all he said about deciding to write it in the late 1940s, the fragment probably fits better during this period after the war.

While Lewis was recalling and reflecting on his experience of Joy from his early childhood, he may have also discussed these experiences with Warnie. Jack Lewis was not the only member of the family who experienced what he called "Joy." Warnie mentioned it from time to time in his diary. On April 2, 1946, Warnie wrote that he had been suffering

> from that restless melancholy discontent which fine spring weather always produces in me; it is one of my oldest feelings; I can remember feeling it in the days when I looked *up* into the delicious fragrant mass of a flowering currant at the old house. For years I thought it a materialist phenomenon—that the discontent would be instantly cured by a change of station, more money, more leave etc. But I begin to suspect that it is a spiritual, a subconscious longing for another world.[25]

In November 1947 he wrote:

> Seeing a birch tree with its russet leaves in the bright sunlight, I got that feeling—or rather that *vision* that comes like a flash of lightening [sic], and leaves a confused feeling that this is only a pale shadow of some unimaginable beauty which ei-

ther one used to know, or which is just round some invisible corner. I accept it with deep thankfulness whenever it comes as a promise of immortality. And am rather strengthened by the fact that it never bears analysis: even as I write, the feeling is fainter than when I opened this book.[26]

After his August 1948 holiday in Malvern, Warnie had the experience once again while waiting for the Communion service to begin at St Cross in Oxford, the church the Dysons attended, and where Charles Williams was buried. He called it a blinding flash of "exquisite happiness."[27]

During the same period that Jack began working on what would become *Surprised by Joy*, he also recovered his desire to write poetry. Whether writing poetry sparked an interest in writing about his youth, when he had planned to be a great poet, or writing about his youth and the long path to Christianity renewed his youthful interest in poetry is impossible to say. We do know, however, that the two arose together.

Poetry

If we view Lewis's publication history after the war only in terms of the sort of writing for which he is best known, he appears to have been in a slump, but we miss where his heart lay after the war. Between the end of the war and 1950, Lewis published thirty-two poems—half again as many as he had published in the preceding thirty years combined![28] After the war, he had returned to his first love, writing poetry. It was the only real writing he was doing besides the dreaded OHEL.[29] He experimented with different forms and seemed determined to make a new try at becoming a recognized poet. When he read his poem "Donkey's Delight" to the Inklings in October 1947, Warnie observed that it was his best effort "since he took the craze for playing about with metre."[30]

Lewis published in a variety of magazines and journals, but seventeen of the thirty-two poems from this period appeared in *Punch*, the sophisticated satirical magazine. In *Punch*, however, he did not write under his own name. As with his first two volumes of poetry, he assumed a nom de plume, signing with the initials N. W., which stand for Nat Whilk, an Anglo-Saxon phrase that means "I do not know."[31] He told Arthur Greeves and Sister Penelope that he signed his *Punch* poems this way to keep his authorship secret.[32] Few others knew of his return to poetry. Of course, the Inklings knew, for he read his poetry at their meetings, as Warnie recorded. Owen Barfield also knew.[33] For purposes of improving his poetry, Lewis also told a new friend all about what he was doing.

In July 1946, Lewis made the acquaintance of Ruth Pitter, an accomplished traditional poet who swam against the stream of trends in modern poetry. By the time Lewis met her, she had published many volumes of poetry, was well known among living British poets, and had won the Hawthornden Prize in 1937 for *A Trophy of Arms*. Herbert Palmer, a poet and critic a generation older than Lewis, had undertaken the project of bringing Pitter and Lewis together. He had taken the initiative to write and introduce himself and his poetry to Lewis in late 1945. In reply, Lewis disclosed an amazing amount of personal information for a supposedly private person, but the disclosures seem appropriate for a man who had begun to think about the long road he had traveled since childhood. Palmer may have been prompted to write to Lewis, by then a famous figure, after reading *The Pilgrim's Regress*, which included several of Lewis's short poems. Lewis told Palmer that he had sweated blood trying to become a poet between the ages of fifteen and thirty, but he had given up after his book of narrative poems failed to sell. His assessment of the poems in *The Pilgrim's Regress*, which he had written independently of that book several years earlier, was that they were not so much "the dawn of a talent coming but the twilight of a talent going."[34] He explained that he had not written much poetry since then.

Lewis and Palmer continued to correspond, and Lewis continued to reveal his private thoughts about poetry and his own efforts at writing. He lamented having wasted so much time fretting over T. S. Eliot and his followers. Palmer also told Lewis that Ruth Pitter admired his work. In his turn, Lewis told Palmer that he had admired the poetry of Pitter that he had seen.[35] By December, Lewis had begun to write poetry again. He sent copies of his new poem "The Atomic Bomb" to Barfield and Harwood.[36] Correspondence with Palmer about poetry continued, and Lewis invited him to dine and stay the night at Magdalen in May 1946.[37]

After spending the evening with Lewis, Palmer wrote to Pitter to tell her all about the visit. He had earlier written to tell her what Lewis had said about her poetry. More to the point, Lewis said that he would like to meet Pitter, despite the fact that she was a woman! With gratitude, she wrote to Palmer to say that she "would do any honest thing under the sun to know C. S. Lewis."[38]

Pitter had good reason to want to meet Lewis. He had played a central part in her conversion to Christianity. When the war broke out, Pitter and her friend Kathleen O'Hara had an arts and crafts business in decorative painting of household objects, which they had worked twenty years to build. The small business gave the two women financial independence, something Pitter's poetry could never do. The demand for such decorative items collapsed, however, in the face of war and privation, as did the little firm. Pitter went to work in a munitions factory and grew increasingly depressed. Her depression bordered on the suicidal as she contemplated jumping into the Thames from London's Battersea Bridge. Then she heard Lewis's broadcast talks, and everything began to change. Lewis spoke to both her heart and her mind.[39] She then read *The Screwtape Letters* and Lewis's science-fiction novels with great pleasure.

Pitter and Lewis might have gotten together sooner. Her poetry had come to the attention of Lord David Cecil, probably through the intercession of Lady Ottoline Morrell, whose famous literary gatherings had brought together so many of the major literary figures of England between the world wars. Cecil recommended

A Trophy of Arms to the Hawthornden Prize Committee.[40] When Cecil returned to Oxford as a fellow of New College in 1939, he soon made friends with Lewis and found himself part of the Inklings. In a letter to Pitter around the time of the first BBC broadcasts, he praised Lewis as by "far the most brilliant English Literature man in Oxford."[41] Cecil might have been the one to introduce Pitter and Lewis, except for the war. Everyone was too busy with war work. Thus, it fell to Herbert Palmer, a new acquaintance to Lewis, to effect the introductions.

Once she knew that Lewis was interested in knowing her, Pitter wrote to him in early July 1946 to ask if she might come to Oxford to meet him.[42] Lewis wrote a brief reply inviting Pitter to visit him on Wednesday morning, July 17. Thus began a primary relationship in Lewis's life that would not alter significantly until ten years later, when another lady took Pitter's place. It must have been a good meeting, for it initiated mutually complimentary correspondence that would continue for years as they exchanged poetry and commented on one another's work. Immediately upon returning home after their first meeting, Pitter sent Lewis three volumes of her poetry so that he would have a broader picture of her work.[43]

In acknowledging the gift, Lewis lavished Pitter with praise, but also mentioned the poem he did not like. This additional negative remark reflects a view Lewis had about reviews and letters of recommendation. He thought that negative remarks gave praise real credibility. He had explained this view to Derek Brewer upon writing a recommendation for him at a teaching post. Brewer thought Lewis was naive in this view, for in his experience, negative remarks from a recommender suggested serious issues. In the case of Pitter's poetry, Lewis struggled to find a believable reservation. He finally settled on the criticism that "The Flower Piece" was "just *too* well written."[44] Then, his note took a turn that did not appear in his letters over the previous forty years. He wrote like a nervous schoolboy:

Why wasn't I told you were as good as this? I expect I may have made a considerable ass of myself on Wednesday. Did I—did I—I hardly dare to put it into words—but I wasn't 'kind' was I? The dreadful suspicion will make me turn all hot on wakeful nights ten years hence. . . . By 'kind' I mean patronizing.[45]

An immediate reply from Pitter produced one of the longest letters by Lewis since before the war. In it, he gave a careful assessment of Pitter's work and then included three of his recent poems for her review. Lewis, who notoriously had a dim view of the intellect of women theretofore, wanted her opinion and critique. Specifically, he wanted to know from her if they were "real poems" or only prose in the form of poetry.[46]

Lewis continued to solicit Pitter's evaluation of his poetry over the next weeks and months. He sought from her what he had once found within the Inklings. His writing club had been a great help during the years when he wrote only prose, but once he returned to poetry, he probably realized that the Inklings could not help him as much as Ruth Pitter. He finally confessed as much to Pitter at the end of 1948.[47] Most of the Inklings wrote poems. Most of Tolkien's published work was poetry. But Tolkien was not a poet. He was not even a literary critic. Dyson was a critic who knew poetry, but he did not write poetry and could not make suggestions to improve what Lewis wrote. Pitter, however, was a fine poet with good judgment who could help him improve his writing in a way that Williams and Barfield never could. Barfield had grand ideas about poetry, but they did not translate into grand poetry. Williams was just obscure.[48] Besides, Lewis liked Pitter's company. In August 1946, he volunteered that he looked forward to her next visit to Oxford.[49]

Her first meeting with Lewis and their beginning correspondence marked the end of a long spiritual journey for Pitter. She had come to faith in Christ, but she had not yet made that faith public. In September she was confirmed as a member of the Church of

England at a country church service in East Anglia. She would later say that she had been driven to Christianity "by the pull of C. S. Lewis and the push of misery."[50]

When Pitter delayed a return trip to Oxford, Lewis resorted to extraordinary measures. He invited her to a luncheon with a few friends of his on Wednesday, October 9, at Magdalen College, in one of the private dining rooms. Lewis did not give luncheons for his friends and their wives. It was precisely the sort of thing that he and Warnie had ridiculed about their Belfast days and the social circle of their family. To entice her, he mentioned that David and Rachel Cecil would be there. He added that his friend Hugo Dyson, who had a deep appreciation for Pitter's poetry, wanted to meet her.[51] At the luncheon, Dyson flattered her by demanding as only Dyson could, "Can't we devise something that will get her here to Oxford?"[52] The luncheon seems all the more remarkable since the days of food shortage were fast upon them. A luncheon party would have been a special treat during this time of austerity.

Pitter loved Lewis's science-fiction trilogy, but she took particular delight in *Perelandra*. Inspired by *Paradise Lost*, it is the most poetic of the three books. She was so taken with *Perelandra* that she asked Lewis if she might adapt the ending into Spenserian stanzas.[53]

When she asked Lewis if David Lindsay had based *A Voyage to Arcturus* on *Perelandra*, he explained that the inverse was true. As diabolical as Lindsay's novel might be, it taught Lewis how a tale of space travel might be good for relating "*spiritual* adventures."[54] In the modern world, a space flight is the equivalent to the medieval journey to the end of the world that had so delighted Lewis. In terms of their form, if not their accessories, the three science-fiction novels are thoroughly medieval. Their plots involve journeys of great adventure through which the characters change and grow. In *That Hideous Strength*, the journeys involve only a few miles, but their life-changing consequences are as dramatic as Ransom's first trip beyond the Silent Planet.

How Stories Work

Lewis had also been learning something else about fiction. It portrays things that a mere lecture or essay cannot. A story affects a reader in a way that a lecture or rational argument does not. In his own experience, he had learned that stories "work on" a person. The story of the journey had created powerful feelings of longing within Lewis that would not let him go. He had been discussing this capacity and nature of stories with Tolkien for some time. It forms the central theme of Tolkien's lecture "On Fairy-Stories," which he delivered as the Andrew Lang Lecture at St Andrew's University in 1939 and later published in *Essay Presented to Charles Williams*. In the same Williams *Festschrift*, published in 1947, Lewis contributed "On Stories," in which he elaborated the ways stories might affect people through their power to "produce (at least in me) a feeling of awe." While acknowledging that not all stories do this and that not all people are moved by stories, Lewis noted the uncanny way some stories do affect many people. His friendships with Sister Penelope, Dorothy L. Sayers, and Ruth Pitter had all begun because his Ransom stories had a powerful effect on these ladies who wrote to Lewis.

What Lewis was learning about fiction had implications for nonfiction. He had undertaken the argumentation of apologetics at the request of other people. He was asked to write *The Problem of Pain*. He was asked to deliver the radio talks. He was asked to oversee the Socratic Club. He was instructed to write *Miracles*. When he wrote apologetics his way, however, he produced fiction in the form of *The Pilgrim's Regress*, *The Screwtape Letters*, *The Great Divorce*, *Perelandra*, and *Out of the Silent Planet*. By the end of the war, he had concluded that rational arguments for Christianity were not the best kind of apologetics. When asked to speak to a group of youth ministers at the end of the war on how to do apologetics, he gave a nice little talk on basic apologetic ideas and major issues of currency in Britain that needed addressing. When he got to the area of distinguishing science from philosophical ideas that people often confuse with science, Lewis said that rational argument is probably not the most effective way to address wrong patterns of thought now normative within a culture. He said that what we need are not more little books about Christianity but more little books on every subject with the Christianity latent.[55]

Instead of a book that attacked the materialist assumptions that many people intermingled with scientific ideas, Lewis argued that a more constructive approach would be to write books about science from a Christian point of view. He insisted that the science had to be perfectly honest. Lewis saw no conflict between science and faith, for science in itself only describes the way the universe works, and God made the universe. The conflict between science and faith has nothing to do with science or faith. The conflict comes when people mingle philosophical ideas with their science or with their faith, both of which happen all the time, though people rarely notice when it happens. Lewis then suggested looking at the matter the other way around.

Looking at matters from the other perspective was a technique he had first developed when trying to explain difficult ideas to Arthur Greeves when they were teenagers. It was the method he employed in *The Screwtape Letters*. He observed that few Christians would have their faith shaken by lectures on materialism. If every textbook or article a Christian read about science had materialistic assumptions, however, that might truly shake them. In fact, Lewis had seen this very thing happen with young people who came up to Oxford. He had not only seen it; he had lived it. He had experienced materialistic ideas slipped into his mind by W. T. Kirkpatrick. The issue of unexamined assumptions formed the theme of *The Abolition of Man*, in which he observed that all manner of ideas can be slipped into people's minds when they think they are merely doing their English homework. Now Lewis proposed that Christians should do the same thing. Perhaps unintentionally, he had done it in *The Allegory of Love* and in *A Preface to Paradise*

Lost. What is clear is that by 1944, Lewis had decided not to take up any more of his valuable time constructing logical arguments. He had written what he had to say. He had made his contribution. He had done his war work. He had fulfilled his duty. Once the war was over, he intended to get back to his own work.

Poetry, fiction, and the study of literature were his own work. Ruth Pitter helped Lewis return to his poetry and settle once and for all whether it was any good as poetry. From July 1946 to July 1947, Lewis sent Pitter a number of his new poems for her critique: "The Birth of Language," "To C. W.," "On Being Human," two versions of "Two Kinds of Memory," "Donkey's Delight," "Young King Cole," and "Vitrea Circe."[56] During this period, Lewis regularly wrote that he looked forward to Pitter's next visit to Oxford. They almost seemed to be inventing excuses to see each other. Pitter wrote that she wanted to bring Sir Ronald Storrs to Oxford to meet Lewis because Storrs took a first in classics at Cambridge and had been in the military and then civil governor of Jerusalem once it fell under British control from 1917 until 1926. Lewis invited them to lunch on May 31, 1947, but Sir Ronald proved difficult to pin down to a date that suited Lewis with his duties at the Kilns. As the proposed date drew near and Sir Ronald had still not confirmed, Lewis urged Pitter to "come without him."[57] Lewis proposed a new date of Wednesday, June 16, which Pitter pointed out did not occur. June 16 did not fall on a Wednesday. She assured Lewis that she would come with or without the illustrious knight, but she needed to know if Lewis meant Monday, June 16 or Wednesday, July 16.[58] The confusion of dates was classic Lewis. He confirmed their luncheon for Wednesday, *July* 16.[59]

In the end, Sir Ronald did join the luncheon party, and Pitter wrote to Laurence Whistler that the conversation between Lewis and Storrs was so good that she just listened. In the days of austerity, Lewis also managed to provide a "first rate lunch," no doubt out of the bounty from the United States.[60] Then silence. After a year of bright correspondence and several comfortable get-togethers, suddenly the correspondence ceased. Don King has speculated that Pitter might have hoped for a closer relationship than the comfortable friendship that had developed.[61] For Lewis, having a comfortable friendship with a woman was virtually a unique experience, a fact Pitter might not have realized owing to her near veneration of his reputation as a scholar and writer. She had also had a series of romantic relationships with men that had come to nothing, including an on-again, off-again relationship with George Orwell in the 1920s. Perhaps she was protecting herself from another disappointment.

Lewis and Pitter saw each other at a dinner party given by David and Rachel Cecil in January 1948. Pitter wrote to Herbert Palmer that Lewis had been "pretty chirpy" and that she would like to write to him again, but she had determined not to write again unless Lewis wrote to her first. Pitter did not go to university, so she carried with her a feeling that went with the British class system of being inferior to the university educated, and she referred to Lewis as her "betters," which suggests that she thought Lewis could never really take her seriously.[62] Lewis probably would have thought that way in 1920, but by 1948, after his friendship with Charles Williams, his views were changing. He would have viewed her with some awe as an accomplished poet, something he had not achieved in spite of his prodigious education. They both had their own sets of issues that would have worked against a continuing relationship. Their friendship might easily have ended through neglect, but Lewis broke the silence. At the end of August 1948, Pitter finally responded to a letter from Lewis just as he had determined he would write again to her. In his return letter he said: "On a railway platform this morning (I am just back from Malvern) I made a resolution. I said 'I will no longer be deterred by the fear of seeming to press for an opinion about my poems from writing to find out whether R. P. is dead, ill, in prison, emigrated, or simply never got my letter.' So it was with great pleasure that I found yours awaiting me."[63]

After that last exchange, they continued on with their correspondence. From time to time they met for lunch in Oxford, occasionally at other places with Owen Barfield, and at Pitter's flat in Chelsea. Barfield had written to Pitter on his own account and managed to become part of a threesome throughout 1949 on at least six occasions.[64] Lewis continued to be haunted by the idea that the poems he wrote were not really poetry at all, and Pitter was the one to whom he turned for an answer. Apparently, she never gave him a straight answer, but after he died, she reflected on the question.[65] In a note to Lewis's persistent question, she wrote:

> Now, I wonder. *Is* his poetry after all not? About how many poets or poems would readers agree 100% or even 50%? . . . Did his great learning, & really staggering skill in verse inhibit the poetry? . . . It is almost as though the adult disciplines, notably the techniques of verse, had largely inhibited his poetry, which is perhaps, after all, most evident in his prose. I think he wanted to be a poet more than anything. Time will show. But if it was *magic* he was after, he achieved this sufficiently elsewhere.[66]

Despite Pitter's reluctance to answer Lewis's question, he may have drawn his own conclusion. He never stopped writing poetry, but his production of it declined after 1950, even though his correspondence and regular lunches with Pitter would continue.

The Inklings in Transition

The Inklings waited until December 1945 to celebrate the end of the war with a victory holiday spent at the Bull Hotel in Fairford. Jack and Warnie scouted the area in September on the recommendation of Rev. Eric Bleiben, their vicar, that Fairford was a good place of refuge. Warnie judged Fairford one of the loveliest towns he had ever seen with its dominant Georgiana and Queen Anne architecture. On the second day, while out for a walk, the brothers were caught in a rain shower and took refuge in an

abandoned RAF barracks. Jack thought the country would benefit from having more deserted RAF camps scattered across the
countryside.[67]

As it turned out, the victory holiday was not a great success.
Only Tolkien and Havard joined Jack and Warnie in Fairford, and
even then, they did not all spend the whole time together. Lewis
had invited Barfield to join them, but he was sick. Warnie and
Tolkien went on the train on Tuesday morning, December 11, but
Jack did not come until Wednesday morning. Havard drove over
on Wednesday afternoon. Despite the low turnout, in some ways
it represented a return to the original Inklings, minus Dyson and
Coghill. The small band walked, talked, and enjoyed the courtesy
of the countryside, including homemade gingersnaps that their
landlady gave them with their beer.[68] The overall response to the
holiday suggests the changes that had come to the Inklings.

Throughout the 1930s and during the war years, Lewis's greatest encouragement in writing had come from the Inklings. Until
the war, the group included the Lewis brothers, Ronald Tolkien,
Nevill Coghill, Hugo Dyson, Robert Havard, Adam Fox, and
Charles Wrenn. It began as a writing club, but it had gradually
changed with the composition of its membership. People came and
went. The first great change had come with the war. Nevill Coghill
attended fewer Inklings meetings owing to the demands upon his
time in his efforts to save the Oxford Dramatic Society.[69] He came
often enough, however, to hear Charles Williams read *Taliessin
through Logres* with his "endearing cockney" and to hear him
declare, "Well, I don't know if that is *pow*-etry, but that's how it
comes to *me*!"[70] Upon completing his five-year term as professor
of poetry, Fox relocated to London during the war as a canon of
Westminster Abbey, where he wrote several volumes on Plato, the
Greek New Testament, and related matters.

While Coghill no longer had time for Inklings meetings, his
friendship with Lewis did not end. They continued to see each
other because they were friends as well as colleagues in the En-

glish faculty. At the end of May 1948, Princess Elizabeth made an official visit to Oxford, and Coghill wrote and produced a play in her honor. It was an allegory about Britannia's triumph over adversity during the war, which Coghill called "The Masque of Hope." Lewis was invited to the play and to the garden party for the princess, in all likelihood through the courtesy of Coghill.[71]

Even as old Inklings members left, new members came during the war. Charles Williams joined the group when Oxford University Press moved from its London office to Oxford at the outbreak of war. Colin Hardie, the brother of Lewis's old philosophy friend Frank Hardie and colleague of Lewis at Magdalen College, joined the group. Lord David Cecil, who had taught at Wadham College and left to pursue an independent writing career, returned to Oxford in 1939 as a fellow in English literature at New College. He began attending Inklings meetings during the war. Gervase Mathew, a Dominican at Blackfriars and a lecturer in modern history, entered the group. Commander James Dundas-Grant came to Magdalen in 1944 to command the University Naval Division, and Lewis eventually invited him to an evening in his rooms with his literary friends.[72]

After the war, a new group joined the Inklings. Hugo Dyson had been one of the original members, but he lived thirty miles away in Reading, where he taught at the University of Reading. In 1945, however, he was elected a fellow in English literature at Merton College, which made his presence easier. Christopher Tolkien, the youngest son of Ronald Tolkien, who had served with the RAF in South Africa during the war, returned and became a regular member. John Wain, who had been one of Lewis's brighter pupils during the war and who would eventually gain a reputation as a poet and novelist, was invited to the meetings. Ronald B. McCallum, a fellow with Tolkien at Pembroke College in modern history and politics, attended.[73] Lewis also invited J. A. W. Bennett, another colleague at Magdalen in English literature, whom Lewis called JAW.[74] Courtney "Tom" Stevens, who had been a fellow in ancient history at Magdalen with Lewis since 1934, was asked to join in 1947.[75]

In 1960, when he was thirty-five, John Wain included a description of an Inklings evening in his autobiography. Wain had attended in the days when he still thought of himself as a Christian.[76] Only twenty-one years old when Lewis invited him to attend the Thursday night meetings, Wain immediately took up pipe smoking to fit in.[77] Wain said of those postwar meetings during the dreary days of austerity:

> I can see that room so clearly now, the electric fire pumping heat into the dank air, the faded screen that broke some of the keener draughts, the enamel beer-jug on the table, the well-worn sofa and armchairs, and the men drifting in (those from distant colleges would be later), leaving overcoats and hats in any corner and coming over to warm their hands before finding a chair. There was no fixed etiquette, but the rudimentary honours would be done partly by Lewis and partly by his brother, W. H. Lewis, a man who stays in my memory as the most courteous I have ever met—not with mere politeness, but with a genial, self-forgetful considerateness that was as instinctive to him as breathing. Sometimes, when the less vital members of the circle were in a big majority, the evening would fall flat; but the best of them were as good as anything I shall live to see. This was the bleak period following a ruinous war, when every comfort (and some necessities) seemed to have vanished for ever; Lewis had American admirers who sent him parcels, and whenever one of these parcels had arrived the evening would begin with a distribution. His method was to scatter the tins and packets on his bed, cover them with the counterpane, and allow each of us to pick one of the unidentifiable humps; it was no use simply choosing the biggest, which might turn out to be prunes or something equally dreary. Another admirer used to send a succulent ham now and then; this, too, would be shared out. In winter we sat

round the electric fire; in summer, often, on the steps at the back of the 'New Building', looking on to the deer-haunted grove.[78]

One of the things all of the new members had in common was their lack of interest in myth and fantasy, which had always sparked the Inklings in the early days. Most of the new members were scholars who wrote books in their areas of teaching, but none of them wrote fiction like Lewis and Tolkien, or as Williams had done. Conversation continued to be spry and witty, erudite and clever, entertaining and engaging. Very little reading of works in progress took place after the war. Perhaps, most of the work did not lend itself to reading. For instance, Wrenn published *The English Language* in 1949. During 1947, Tolkien read some from *The Lord of the Rings*, which had been in progress for ten years, but he rarely had something new to read, and Dyson did not care to hear any more of elves.[79] Dyson exercised a veto over more readings from *The Lord of the Rings* when he attended an Inklings evening, but he did not attend very often once he lived in Oxford. Lewis had little of his work to read except for a poem from time to time.[80] Lord David Cecil read a section on Thomas Grey from his forthcoming *Two Quiet Lives* (1948), a comparative study of Grey and Dorothy Osborne.[81] Colin Hardie read what Warnie called "an interminable paper on an unintelligible point about Virgil." John Wain's assessment was less flattering: "To say I didn't understand it is a gross understatement."[82] As a writing club, the Inklings had deviated from their original purpose. The group was drifting.

It also began to fragment. Just as Dyson had grown tired of Tolkien's elves and the strong Catholic presence, relations between other members began to strain. Tolkien and Wrenn fell out. Wrenn spent the war years at King's College, London, but returned to Oxford to take up Tolkien's chair of Anglo-Saxon when Tolkien gained the Merton Chair in 1945. According to John Lawlor, who had Lewis as undergraduate tutor and Tolkien as graduate supervisor, Tolkien had viewed Wrenn's tireless devotion to his undergraduate pupils with a mixture of admiration and scorn: admiration because Wrenn had only partial sight and had to work with a magnifying glass in order to read and correct the many undergraduate papers, but scorn because of his unseemly industry. When Wrenn arrived at Pembroke College to take up his new post, Tolkien was moving from Pembroke to Merton with Lawlor's help. Wrenn managed to get a first-floor room in the front quad at Pembroke, while Tolkien was moving into smaller rooms at Merton. Tolkien derided Wrenn as the "room-getter" and his industry as mere "wheeling and dealing." As to how the two men used their time, Lawlor remarked: "Time loftily saved was not devoted to increasing an academic publication-list. We had to wait until 1936 for Tolkien's lively Academy lecture '*Beowulf*: the Monsters and the Critics', longer for Wrenn's little book on the English Language; and longer still for Wrenn's edition of *Beowulf*."[83]

Scorn and derision eventually led to hostility. When Wrenn organized the International Association of University Professors of English in 1950 with its first meeting at Magdalen College, he invited those who had helped arrange the meeting to sit at the high table in Magdalen's hall. In the middle of dinner, Tolkien burst into the hall and harangued Wrenn for using Magdalen's high table in such a way when there were Oxford professors in the hall. Lawlor observed: "Speechless at last, stammering as he subsided, Tolkien glared in outrage at the astonished company. Was this the time?, Wrenn murmured. Tolkien flung out and came no more to any Conference proceeding."[84]

Perhaps a deeper reason for a rift resulted from Wrenn's term as chair of the Examining Board. This group had the thankless responsibility for setting and overseeing the final examinations of pupils. John Lawlor was with Tolkien when the final examination results were posted publicly for anyone to see. Tolkien suggested that they stop in at the Examination Schools building to see the results for his son Christopher, who in years ahead would edit and publish much of his father's work. His son had not done as well as Tolkien expected, and with his hand clenched above his head and a contorted face, Tolkien lamented, "My poor Christopher, my poor Christopher." Lawlor attempted to make peace between Tolkien and Wrenn—whom Tolkien seemed to blame—but to no avail. Lawlor observed of Tolkien that he "mourned and would not be comforted: for his habitually mild and benevolently quizzical temper was capable of volcanic upheaval."[85] Whatever the depth and breadth of the rift may have been at the time, Wrenn would coedit the *Festschrift* for Tolkien's seventieth birthday in 1962.

On Thursday evening, October 27, 1949, Warnie recorded in his diary that "no one turned up after dinner" for the Inklings meeting. He made no further record of a Thursday evening Inklings gathering. The Tuesday morning gathering to drink and talk at the Eagle and Child continued to take place for years to come, but the writing club appears to have run its course. For the most part, the friends did not cease to be friends. They continued to meet to talk and to dine from time to time, but the group that began with an interest in writing was no longer a writing club.[86] Hugo Dyson, in particular, continued to make a threesome with Jack and Warnie, such as when he had gone with them to the movie theater to see Jill Flewett appear in her first film, *The Woman in the Hall*.[87] Dr. Havard also enjoyed regular sociability with the brothers apart from Tuesday mornings. The brothers would also dine with David and Rachel Cecil from time to time, but the Inklings had changed.

Lewis and Tolkien had invited visitors to the Inklings from the earliest days. The earliest clear mention of the group appears in a letter from Lewis to Charles Williams, inviting him to visit his club. Lewis also invited Owen Barfield and George Sayer from time to time, as well as Roy Campbell, though Barfield does not appear to have attended after the war.[88] Though Campbell was a recognized poet, Lewis thought he had "frittered away a real talent" by writing "too much poetry *about* poetry" and the current state of poetry.[89] None of the visitors could actually help Lewis become a better poet. John Wain recalled that "one of the founding members introduced a notorious bore into the circle and then stayed away on the grounds that the meeting was boring."[90] Since Lewis and Tolkien were the only ones who dared to bring new people to the meetings, Wain probably referred to Tolkien, the other founding member. He no doubt had hurt feelings as well over Dyson's reaction to his elves, a reaction similar to Tolkien's reception of Lewis's Narnia. A writing club, however, that ceased to be interested in his writing ceased to be a helpful writing club for Tolkien.

Not only did new members and visitors fail to contribute to the Inklings as a writing club; some new members aggravated some of the old members. From the beginning, the group had included both Catholics and members of the Church of England. The ecclesiastical differences did not seem to matter as long as the primary focus of the Inklings involved writing. As writing declined and talk increased, the subjects of conversation often tended to matters on which Anglicans and Catholics disagreed. The shift in the composition of the group away from writers appears to have created a deeper wedge along ecclesiastical lines. Hugo Dyson, after years of faithful attendance when living thirty miles away, attended less and less after the war when he moved to Oxford. Warnie noted that Dyson had threatened to resign if any more "Papists" joined the Inklings, but Dyson tended to have, as Warnie observed, a "puzzlingly strong view on the matter."[91]

After the war, the Catholic members included Ronald and Christopher Tolkien, Robert Havard, Colin Hardie, Jim Dundas-Grant, and Gervase Mathew. The Church of England members included Jack and Warnie Lewis, Hugo Dyson, David Cecil, and possibly John Wain, Tom Stevens, Charles Wrenn, Jaw Bennett, and R. B. McCallum. Jack and Warnie had no qualms with a

The Inklings at the Trout Inn, Godstow: Commander James Dundas-Grant, Colin Hardie, Dr. Robert E. Havard, C. S. Lewis, and Peter Havard, ca. 1955. Used by permission of the Marion E. Wade Center, Wheaton College, Wheaton, IL.

strong Catholic contingent, for Jack had invited most of the Catholics himself. Warnie felt particularly close to Humphrey Havard. It only meant that with a membership who no longer wrote and who tended to be divided on many questions under discussion, the Inklings simply were not what they once were. So, when no one turned up on October 27, 1949, Lewis appears to have allowed the group to end, apparently without protest. We do well to recall that at this point in his life, Lewis had already collapsed with exhaustion and had few emotional and physical resources to keep the club going.

The Zernov Group

Lewis always had more than one intellectual circle. He usually belonged to several circles at the same time over the years with some overlap of members. Austin Farrer had been one of those new friends who came as a result of involvement with the Socratic

Club. Lewis came to know Farrer in a new way when the Inklings ceased their regular Thursday night meetings just before Mrs. Moore went into the nursing home. Lewis and Farrer became part of a new group that met with Nicholas Zernov, a Russian Orthodox theologian, at his flat in North Oxford every Saturday night. Zernov had founded the Fellowship of Saint Alban and Saint Sergius as a vehicle to promote closer relations between the Church of England and Orthodoxy, a matter about which Lewis was deeply interested. Alban was the first Christian martyr in Roman Britain, and Sergius was a venerated Russian Orthodox monk. Hugo Dyson and Gervase Mathew from the Inklings and Basil Mitchell from the Socratic Club also joined the group. James Houston, founding principal and later chancellor of Regent College in Vancouver, shared an apartment with Zernov and his wife, Melitza, from 1947 until 1953, when Lewis was involved. In format, the group resembled others to which Lewis belonged over the years. Someone presented a paper at each meeting, and then everyone joined in discussion about it. As an added bonus, the evening also included a buffet supper.[92] Zernov, like Lewis, was interested in church unity. During these years, Lewis also carried on a lengthy correspondence with Don Giovanni Calabria about church unity.

Living in Oxford, Lewis and Zernov would have had little occasion to correspond, but the two letters we have say a great deal more than their content. Lewis tended to formality in his letters unless he felt particularly close to someone. Only when friendship had developed to a significant level could he address Ruth Pitter as Ruth and Dorothy L. Sayers as Dorothy. With men, he used the formal Mr. or Dr. or some other title before addressing them in the more familiar Edwardian style of last names only. He eventually moved from addressing his American benefactor as Dr. Firor to simply Firor. When Lewis wrote a brief note to Zernov on February 3, 1950, he already addressed him simply as Zernov. It was a thank-you note for the "splendid evening, as yours always are."[93]

The note tells us that Lewis already felt close to Zernov and that Saturday evenings had become a regular affair. Ten years later, a few months after Joy's death, Lewis sent another thank-you note to Zernov, this time addressed to "My dear Nicholas."[94] On a visit with Joy and Jack earlier that year when the Zernovs came to tea, Melitza had taken several photographs. After Joy's death, Zernov sent Jack the negatives so that he could have some prints made. Walter Hooper published these photographs of Jack and Joy in the "Common Room" of the Kilns in *Through Joy and Beyond.*[95]

What made this group different from all others to which Lewis belonged was that it included ladies. Of course, the Socratic Club included primarily female undergraduates, but that was not a group of equals. Lewis was never just one of the members. He stood apart. With Zernov's group, however, Lewis was just one of many extraordinary people, many of whom were female. He may have attended a Russian Orthodox Church service with Zernov. At least, he appears to have been aware of the service from his comments in a letter in 1956 in which he expounded the difference between doctrine and taste as they relate to judgments about different churches. He wrote:

> My model here is the behavior of the congregation at a 'Russian Orthodox' service, where some sit, some stand, some kneel, some lie on their faces, some walk about, and *no one takes the slightest notice of what anyone else is doing.* That is good sense, good manners, and good Christianity. 'Mind one's own business' is a good rule in religion as in other things.[96]

Lewis was not interested in ecclesiology or liturgy, but he had a profound interest in doctrine. Orthodoxy probably had an attraction for Lewis because it had not introduced new doctrines over the centuries but endeavored to cling to Patristic doctrine. His hesitancy to draw closer to Catholicism probably also involved, to some degree, the failure of Roman Catholicism and Eastern Orthodoxy to draw closer to each other.

A New Literary Friend

Lewis had always taken pleasure in the development of friendships with his former pupils. By 1945, the number had begun to mount. One of his new young friends was Roger Lancelyn Green, who had taken his BA in English literature in 1940 and remained in Oxford to complete the BLitt in 1944 with a thesis titled "Andrew Lang as a Writer of Fairy Stories and Romances," which Tolkien supervised.[97] In 1938, Green had attended Lewis's lectures "Prolegomena to Medieval and Renaissance Literature." Because Lewis did not carry a watch, he borrowed the watch of someone sitting at the front to keep track of the time, and during Michaelmas term 1938, that person was Green. At the end of the term, Green wrote a fan letter to Lewis about *Out of the Silent Planet*, and Lewis replied with suggestions for other science fiction Green might want to read.[98]

In 1945, Green took up the post of deputy librarian of Merton College and wrote *Andrew Lang: A Critical Biography*.[99] At the same time, his interest in mythology and fairy stories led him to write "The Wood That Time Forgot," his own effort at a fairy story, which he sent to Lewis for critique. Lewis gave helpful advice, including a warning not to put himself into the story. He explained that in his own case, only when he managed to extricate himself from his writing did he find that the "re-enchantment" began.[100] Green tried his hand at a new book, *From the World's End: A Fantasy*, which was accepted for publication by Edmund Ward in early 1947.[101] When the book came out the next year, Green sent a copy to Lewis as a Christmas present and received a glowing letter of thanks in return. The gift came at a particularly low time in Lewis's life at the Kilns, and his letter reflects the blessing that the gift meant to him just then. With this letter, Lewis made clear that Green should dispense with calling him "Mister." They would now be friends.[102]

On March 10, 1949, a few months after the last Inklings evening meeting, Roger Lancelyn Green dined with Lewis at Magdalen College. They talked in Lewis's rooms until midnight, during the course of which Lewis read two chapters from the manuscript of *The Lion, the Witch and the Wardrobe*. He had made an effort at writing a fairy story in about 1939, but that attempt had stalled, probably owing to his many wartime duties.[103] In a letter to Mary Neylan in 1940, Lewis spoke of children as "Adam's sons, Eve's daughters," terminology he would incorporate into *The Lion, the Witch and the Wardrobe*.[104] What he originally had written, however, the Inklings had not received well, so Lewis burned the manuscript.[105] He told Green that he had already read this new attempt to Tolkien.[106] When Chad Walsh visited Lewis during the summer of 1948, Lewis had already begun working on a children's story.[107] This was the period during which he was busy working on his autobiography and talking with Warnie about their childhood. It was a time when all the imaginary world that he loved when he was young came rushing back into his memory. He also mentioned to Ruth Pitter in September 1948 that when he had the flu, he had read *Wind in the Willows* again.[108] When, at age sixteen, he first went to live with W. T. Kirkpatrick in Great Bookham, Jack had the picture in his mind "of a Faun carrying an umbrella and parcels in a snowy wood."[109] Lewis's childhood memories and interests, stoked by his efforts at writing his conversion story, probably began to spark his imagination. With his health issues, Mrs. Moore, and Warnie to contend with on top of his teaching load at Magdalen, it was a difficult time to be creative, but somehow he managed to finish the story in less than a year.

Tolkien hated the story.[110] His criticism went beyond evaluation and suggestion to the level of insult. The idea of mixing Father Christmas with fauns repelled him, because these two figures come from different traditions separated by time and space. Tolkien was a purist on such matters. The Norsemen would never have included Father Christmas or fauns in their stories. When he heard that Lewis had shown the story to Green, Tolkien turned on Green with vehemence and declared: "It really won't do, you know!

I mean to say: '*Nymphs and their Ways, The Love-Life of a Faun*'. Doesn't he know what he's talking about?"[111] Lewis knew exactly what he was talking about, and Green was delighted. When Green published a short book about Lewis for the Bodley Head Monograph series of biographies of its own authors, he observed that Lewis had set aside his fairy story "owing to criticism from one of his older friends by then rather out of touch with children and their books, and wedded to different modes of thought where fairy-tale and fantasy were concerned."[112] Modestly, Green added that "by March 1949 he was working on it again, and reading the early chapters to another friend, who proved more encouraging—and perhaps saw more clearly that here was the beginning of a really new and exciting development in children's literature."[113]

Lewis deeply appreciated Green's support, and George Sayer reported that Lewis doubted he would have finished the book without Green's encouragement.[114] Other than from Green, he received little encouragement from his old friends in writing his Narnia stories. Griffiths did not read them until after Lewis died.[115] Lewis appears not to have told Dorothy L. Sayers, Ruth Pitter, or Sister Penelope about his children's story at first, but he did suggest to Sister Penelope the pen name of G. H. Pevensey for a science-fiction novel she was attempting.[116] Sister Penelope did not use the name, but Lewis changed the name to Pevensie and used it as the family name of the children in *The Lion, the Witch and the Wardrobe*.

Lewis was writing a fairy story for children who lived in Britain just after World War II. They lived with trains, airplanes, radios, and tourists. They read the tales of King Arthur and Hercules. Their culture had inherited the stories from around the world. Children are not professors of Anglo-Saxon. As much as Tolkien talked about the boundary between our world and the world of faerie, he did not write stories that involved crossing that boundary, but Lewis did. Tolkien worked hard at imitating a style of elevated language and duplicating a form of storytelling that predated the

Norman invasion of 1066. As monumental an achievement as *The Lord of the Rings* may be, it is not a fairy story. By contrast, *The Lion, the Witch and the Wardrobe* is a fairy story for children in 1950 who inherited the global collection of stories of the fading British Empire. For them, Santa Claus, or Father Christmas, was the magical figure who remained in the modern world and helped form a bridge to the world of imagination.

Lewis decided to dedicate his fairy story to Lucy Barfield, the daughter of Owen and Maud. He sent a copy of the manuscript to them in May 1949 for their approval. What seemed a routine matter met with two snags, as mentioned earlier: (1) Maud objected to the children wearing fur coats since it seemed an endorsement of the fur trade and the murder of all the innocent animals needed to make such a coat, and (2) Maud objected to the danger of children being shut inside a wardrobe. In addition, Owen did not like the Beavers. He wondered if they had been included so that no one would take the story too seriously. Lewis responded to Owen on May 30, but apparently his assurances were not strong enough. The matter was not settled. He wrote a second letter to Maud on June 4 in which he promised to add a warning to children not to shut themselves in a wardrobe.[117] Finally, the matter was settled and Lewis did a bit more rewriting before sending the manuscript to the publishers on July 29, no doubt delayed by his emergency adventure in the hospital a week after his stressful exchange with Maud Barfield.[118]

George Sayer has suggested that Geoffrey Bles, Lewis's publisher for all his popular works except his science fiction, expressed initial reluctance to publish *The Lion, the Witch and the Wardrobe*. A children's story coming from C. S. Lewis seemed a strange thing, and Bles doubted that it would sell. They had a good property in C. S. Lewis, whose works maintained brisk sales long after most books went out of print. Bles did not want Lewis to do anything that might damage his reputation and their sales. Sayer put forward the theory that Bles refused to publish *The*

Lion, the Witch and the Wardrobe unless Lewis agreed to make it part of a series.[119] In light of Lewis's decision to publish the last two books with The Bodley Head, Sayer's theory collapses. If Lewis had agreed to write seven stories in discussion with Geoffrey Bles, even if they did not have a contract, Lewis would have felt obligated by honor to publish all the books with Bles. In fact, Lewis did not envision a seven-book series at the beginning. Instead, he explained: "When I wrote *The Lion* I did not know I was going to write any more. Then I wrote *P. Caspian* as a sequel and still didn't think there would be any more, and when I had done the *Voyage* I felt quite sure it would be the last."[120]

No sooner had Lewis emerged from the Acland Hospital than he began writing his second children's book about Narnia and Aslan. Green visited Lewis at Magdalen College in June, probably to drop off the manuscript of his revised version of *The Wood That Time Forgot*, and found Lewis busy at work on a sequel. It involved two children named Digory and Polly. This story was intended to tell of the beginnings of Narnia. Digory had the ability to understand the speech of animals and trees until he cut an oak tree while helping Polly build a raft. The story stalled when Digory's godmother, Mrs. Lefay, who practiced magic, appeared on the scene.[121] Green agreed with Lewis that the story was not working, so he abandoned it for the time being, reworking it several years later into *The Magician's Nephew*. In June 1949, however, Lewis told Green he was interested in the idea of being drawn by magic into Narnia across time and space.[122] By the end of December, culminating a most difficult six-month period for Lewis, he sent to Green for his review the completed manuscript of a story in which the children are drawn by magic into Narnia across time and space—*Prince Caspian*.[123]

Even as he realized that his efforts to revive his career as a poet stood little chance of success, Lewis found that his creative imagination was drawing him forward the way something magical drew the children into Narnia. On September 17, 1949,

C. S. Lewis during interview, 1950. Photo by Hans Wild / The *Life* Picture Collection / Getty Images. Asar Studios / Alamy Stock Photo.

he wrote to Vera Mathews, one of his American benefactors, that he had a good idea for a children's story that morning. Since he was already working on *Prince Caspian*, the story idea may have been for *The Voyage of the Dawn Treader*.[124] The point is that important ideas for stories were coming to him. Though his stories often began with a picture, they sometimes began with an idea like being drawn into Narnia across time and space.[125] With The Chronicles of Narnia, Lewis experienced a renewal of his imaginative power that brought him out of the dismal and draining situation at the Kilns.

4

Narnia and Beyond

1949–1954

Geoffrey Bles offered Lewis a contract to publish *The Lion, the Witch and the Wardrobe*, which he signed on August 13, 1949. The first of his Narnia stories had taken Lewis almost a decade to write, but it had been a busy decade. Until September 6, 1945, when he renewed acquaintance with Roger Lancelyn Green at the wedding reception of the daughter of David Nichol Smith, then Merton Professor of English Literature, Lewis had no encouragement or inspiration to work on his children's story.[1] Green recalled that he and Lewis had been drinking champagne and withdrew into a window recess where the conversation soon drifted to George MacDonald, Rider Haggard, and E. Nesbit.[2] Green, a newly minted BLitt for his thesis "Andrew Lang and the Fairy Tale," then told Lewis he was working on a fairy story of his own. Lewis was delighted and agreed to read Green's manuscript and make suggestions. Ten days later, he sent Green a two-page review with recommendations and invited Green to dine at Magdalen so that they could discuss their common interest.[3]

Green's story, *The Wood That Time Forgot*, struggled to find a publisher, but Lewis saw in it Green's potential for storytelling. He would publish several dozen books, but his great talent lay in retelling the classical and Norse myths for a modern audience. Thus, Lewis's new, young friend shared with him what had formed the first friendship with Arthur Greeves and the friendship with Tolkien. In Green's story, three children and an Oxford undergraduate find themselves in a wood that is cut off from the rest of the world by time. The setting resembled Lewis's beginning of a story about four children evacuated from London at the beginning of World War II and appears to have inspired Lewis to ponder his own story again. Slowly, the pieces began to come together for him. Lewis said that the material simply bubbled up in his mind.[4] Somehow, between September 1945 and March 1949, Lewis's imagination formed Narnia in his mind. The writing had not begun as an effort to tell the Christian story in a fairy-tale form. Aslan had not been part of the original conception. Like Tolkien struggling with a plot for *The Lord of the Rings*, Lewis had no idea where his story was going, "But then suddenly Aslan came bounding into it."[5]

It had taken Lewis ten years to write one children's story, but the next six books wrote themselves rather quickly, with one exception. Lewis had begun writing a second Narnia book as soon as he finished *The Lion, the Witch and the Wardrobe*, but this one about Digory and Polly simply failed to come together, so Lewis quickly moved on to a third attempt, which became *Prince Caspian*. Roger Lancelyn Green provided Lewis with a name for the series. He called it The Chronicles of Narnia.[6] Lewis liked the name.

Lewis had finished *The Lion, the Witch and the Wardrobe* by May 1949, when he asked the Barfields for permission to dedicate the book to their adopted daughter, Lucy.[7] By December 1949, Lewis had finished *Prince Caspian* and sent a copy to Green to review for suggestions and revisions.[8] By February 21, 1950, Lewis had a completed manuscript of *The Voyage of the Dawn Treader* for Green to read when he came to dine with Lewis at Magdalen.[9]

C. S. Lewis at Magdalen College, 1950, as part of a photo essay in *Vogue* magazine. Photo © Norman Parkinson Archive / Iconic Images / Getty Images. Asar Studios / Alamy Stock Photo.

Green returned to visit Lewis at the end of February 1951, when he received the completed manuscript of *The Silver Chair*. He promptly read it and responded with suggestions by early March, when Lewis thanked him for his suggestions.[10] Lewis finished writing *The Last Battle* by March 2, 1953, but did not send a copy for Green to review until several months later.[11] Lewis submitted *The Horse and His Boy* to Geoffrey Bles on March 20, 1953, a full year after completing *The Silver Chair*.[12] By February 22, 1954, Green had approved the revised draft of *The Magician's Nephew*, the book Lewis had begun writing immediately after *The Lion, the Witch and the Wardrobe*, and Lewis sent it to his publisher by mid-March.[13] When Lewis enlisted Spencer Curtis Brown as his literary agent at the end of 1954, Curtis Brown negotiated a better contract with The Bodley Head to publish the last two books.[14]

The speed with which Lewis wrote the stories seems all the more remarkable when seen against the backdrop of his life circumstances. As Lewis wrote *The Lion, the Witch and the Wardrobe*, Warnie went on his first serious binge and landed in the Acland Hospital. With Warnie away, Jack had no one to help him with his enormous correspondence. As soon as he completed the story, he collapsed and spent a week in the hospital himself. While Lewis was writing *Prince Caspian*, Warnie spent six weeks in Ireland after another spell and internment in the local mental asylum. Having written *The Voyage of the Dawn Treader* at breakneck speed, essentially during the Christmas vacation of 1949–1950, he needed a year to finish *The Silver Chair*. No sooner had he begun writing it than Mrs. Moore's condition deteriorated to the degree that she had to be placed in a nursing home. Almost in competition for Jack's attention, Warnie resumed his drinking. Jack confided to Warfield Firor, his American ham benefactor, that "the old lady" whom he called "my mother" had always been of a "worrying and . . . a jealous, exacting, and angry disposition," but that her paralysis and dementia seemed to make her happier, or at least less unhappy.[15] Lewis had little free time to write.

Probably the greatest obstacle to fast progress on his Narnia stories during this period, however, lay with his OHEL volume. He told Firor that he spent most of his time reading back issues of academic journals for fear of missing something that ought to be included. It particularly annoyed him, because he regarded most of the journal articles as "rubbish" that attempted a pseudoscientific approach to literary criticism.[16] Helen Gardner observed Lewis from her nook in the Duke Humphrey Library of the Bodleian as he worked on this study. She wrote of his method: "To sit opposite him in Duke Humphrey when he was moving steadily through some huge double-columned folio in his reading for his Oxford History was to have an object lesson in what concentration meant. He seemed to create a wall of stillness around him."[17] To help him finish the OHEL volume, Magdalen College granted Lewis a sabbatical for the 1951–1952 academic year, during which he was relieved of all teaching responsibilities.[18]

The other momentous aid to his writing came when Mrs. Moore died on January 12, 1951.[19] Lewis does not appear to have grieved the death of Mrs. Moore after more than thirty years together. On the other hand, he did grieve the death of his confessor, Father Walter Adams, which came during his sabbatical on March 3, 1952.[20] With the sabbatical and the death of Mrs. Moore coinciding, one might have thought that Lewis would have more free time to finish his Narnia stories. A duty-bound Lewis, however, would have felt the obligation to honor the sabbatical and devote himself to completing the tiresome volume *English Literature in the Sixteenth Century*.

The Poetry Chair

The decision by Magdalen to grant Lewis a sabbatical may have come as the result of another disappointment in his life. Between the death of Mrs. Moore and the granting of the sabbatical, Lewis had been defeated in the election for a new professor of poetry on February 8, 1951.[21] Unlike the Merton Chair, the professor of poetry was elected by the entire Convocation rather than a small group of electors. Convocation includes all graduates of Oxford University. This time, Lewis enjoyed the support of almost all of the heads of the individual colleges of Oxford, and, surprisingly, most of the English faculty signed the nomination paper for Lewis.[22] Since Convocation voted for this position, however, the extent of Lewis's support within the ranks of the fellows of the university mattered little.

A movement sprang up to elect a practicing poet, and the name of Cecil Day Lewis gained attention. By 1951, he had seven volumes of poetry to his credit. Though C. S. Lewis had published two volumes of poetry and dozens of individual poems in a variety of magazines and journals, almost all of his poetry had been published under different pen names. Hardly anyone knew of him as a poet. Edmund Blunden was a third candidate. He had published more volumes of poetry than C. Day Lewis, but in the end, Blunden stood down to clear the field. The ballot offered two names: C. D. Lewis and C. S. Lewis, in that order. The vote came on a Thursday evening, the old meeting time for the Inklings. That night, Jack and Warnie dined at the Royal Oxford Hotel with Lord David Cecil, Humphrey Havard, J. A. W. Bennett, and Owen Barfield. There they received the news that Jack had lost to C. Day Lewis by a vote of 194 to 173.[23] Warnie speculated that Blunden and C. Day Lewis would have split the "Atheist-Communist" vote and given the election to Jack if Blunden had stayed in. Jack simply said that there were political issues on both sides.[24] Tolkien recorded that a few days later at the Eagle and Child, they found Lewis awaiting everyone at perfect ease and declaring: "Fill up! . . . and stop looking so glum. The only distressing thing about this affair is that my friends seem to be upset."[25] Both C. Day Lewis and Blunden went on to hold the post of national poet laureate after Betjeman.

Another factor that may have affected Lewis's work on the Narnia stories was the departure of Roger Lancelyn Green from Oxford in August 1950. Green had met with Lewis almost weekly, as Tolkien had done twenty years earlier, so his departure meant the loss of the kind of stimulating conversation that always helped to spark Lewis's imagination. With the death of his father in 1947, Green became the thirty-first Lord of Poulton and inherited Poulton Hall, an estate in Chesire that had been in the family for nine hundred years.[26] Still, they maintained a steady correspondence, and Green regularly visited Lewis in Oxford, filling the role of literary confidant once held in turn by Arthur Greeves, Owen Barfield, Ronald Tolkien, and Charles Williams.

Illustrations of Narnia

When Geoffrey Bles agreed to publish *The Lion, the Witch and the Wardrobe*, they decided that they wanted the book illustrated.

Like Tolkien, Lewis was capable of illustrating his own stories. He kept his drawing skill alive by sketching as he listened to boring papers from pupils during tutorials. With so much happening in his personal life in 1949, however, Lewis did not undertake the illustrations for his book. By a happy coincidence, Tolkien published his little book *Farmer Giles of Ham* in 1949. Set in the Island of Britain during the Saxon period, it demonstrated how *The Lion, the Witch and the Wardrobe* might be illustrated. Tolkien recommended Pauline Baynes, the artist who did the work for him. By one of those odd ironies of life, Tolkien would have a major indirect influence on the public reception of a story that he abominated. Lewis agreed to allow Baynes to draw the illustrations for his story.[27]

Lewis and Baynes did not have a close working relationship. They probably met just three times: once for luncheon at Magdalen, once in the offices of Geoffrey Bles, and once in a London train station between trains.[28] When Baynes came to lunch at Magdalen College on December 31, 1949, to meet Lewis, she joined several other special friends of Lewis: Ruth Pitter, Owen Barfield, and Barfield's friend Marjorie Milne.[29] Milne was a devout Anglo-Catholic nun, prone to excessive enthusiasm, who had undertaken the task of making Lewis a national figure, much to his embarrassment and against his inclinations. He instructed Barfield never again to tell her of any of his personal troubles lest it encourage more of her sympathy.[30] The dynamics at the luncheon table must have been strange indeed with so many people tangentially connected to Lewis but without connection to each other. Lewis later apologized to Baynes for appearing preoccupied when they met on the train platform, but he dreaded the thought of having a long wait for another train once she had left.[31]

Though he offered Baynes strong words of encouragement, Lewis was disappointed in her work and in her response to his suggestions. He wrote to I. O. Evans that Baynes was a "timid, shrinking young woman who, when criticised, [looks] as if you'd pulled [her] hair or given [her] a black eye," and that his "resolution was exhausted by the time [he'd] convinced her that rowers face aft not (as she thinks) forward."[32] Though Baynes lived fairly near Oxford, Lewis preferred going into London and reviewing the new illustrations with his publisher to meeting with Baynes.[33]

Lewis thought that Baynes's illustrations improved from one book to the next, but her ability to draw animals never rose to his expectations for Narnia. He facetiously suggested that Geoffrey Bles might take Baynes to visit the zoo. He also rejected a number of her drawings outright.[34] As the series went on, he made his suggestions to Baynes through Bles rather than directly. He reminded Bles that the swords in *The Horse and His Boy* should be curved because the text says that they are curved, and that she should try very hard to make Bree look like a warhorse.[35] To his surprise and delight, Lewis found that the illustrations for *The Horse and His Boy* had succeeded. He wrote to her a letter effusive with praise, though he did not comment on whether Bree resembled a warhorse.[36] With *The Magician's Nephew*, however, she had finally learned to draw a horse to Lewis's satisfaction, and he wrote to her to tell her so. Strawberry was "the real thing."[37]

Once the ordeal of illustrating the books had come to an end, Lewis wrote to Dorothy L. Sayers that the main trouble with Pauline Baynes was that even though she could draw plants, she could not draw animals. He thought she had done a much better job for Tolkien, but those illustrations mimicked those in medieval illuminated manuscripts, while Lewis wanted realism.[38] Baynes would go on to illustrate *The Adventures of Tom Bombadil and Other Verses from the Red Book* (1962) and *Smith of Wootton Major* (1967) for Tolkien. Most maddening for Lewis was that when he tried to explain to Baynes "how boats are rowed, or bows are shot with, or feet planted, or fists clenched," she took it as a "put down."[39] Thus, Lewis the tutor, who had confronted his students for five hours a day, five days a week, eight weeks a term, three terms a year for twenty-five years, found that he could only hint at criticism lest Baynes give up the job out of "sheer, downright, unresenting, pusillanimous dejection."[40]

For her part, Baynes had an entirely different recollection of the experience of working with Lewis. She said that he made no recommendations or criticisms unless she specifically asked for directions. She could only recall his observation that she had someone rowing a boat facing the wrong way, and that he had some concern about the faces of the children. She recalled that Lewis commented when she began work on *Prince Caspian*, "I know you made the children rather plain—in the interests of realism—but do you think you could possibly pretty them up a little now?"[41] Baynes had the idea that Lewis had no strong feelings about the illustrations at all since he criticized "so charmingly." When she wrote to congratulate Lewis on winning the Carnegie Medal in 1957 for *The Last Battle*, he wrote back to assure her that it was "'our' Medal" since the illustrations must have figured into the consideration of the judges.[42] When a German edition of the stories was illustrated by Richard Seewald in 1957, Lewis had a basis for comparison and found that he preferred the illustrations by Baynes.[43]

The World of Narnia

All seven of the Narnia stories follow the "there and back again" plot that Lewis had come to love as a teenager living with W. T. Kirkpatrick, with the exception of the final story, in which the children go farther in and farther up.[44] They stand in the tradition of the medieval allegorical tales that he expounded in *The Allegory of Love*. They are the same kind of tales as George MacDonald's *Phantastes*. They all involve the journey during which the travelers face great dangers and challenges in order to complete the object of their quest. It was the kind of story that had gripped Lewis and pierced his heart from the first time he read William Morris's *The Well at the World's End*. In writing *The Pilgrim's Regress*, Lewis demonstrated that he saw the journey story as his story and the story of every person on the spiritual journey to and with Jesus Christ. It was a plotline that would not let him go. So, the journey story is one of the unifying themes of the Narnia chronicles.

We have seen that the genesis of *The Lion, the Witch and the Wardrobe* was the visual image in Lewis's mind of a faun in a snowy wood carrying packages and an umbrella. He once explained to Kingsley Amis and Brian Aldiss how stories grew in his mind from an initial picture. With *Perelandra*, he began with a mental picture of floating islands—perhaps the sort that Odysseus encountered on his long trip home from Troy. Since floating islands do not actually exist in our world, he had to imagine the kind of world where they did exist. He did not yet have a story, just a world. Once he had a world, however, something had to happen.[45] With the Narnia stories, Lewis had the idea of four children before he had the idea of Aslan. He did not know about Aslan any sooner than the Pevensie children did, and the lion came as just as big a surprise to him as to them. He did not contrive to write an evangelistic story that explained the Christian faith with symbolic imagery. Instead, he started writing a story and discovered what it was about as he wrote.

Tolkien wrote in much the same way. He had no idea what Hobbits were when he wrote the famous first sentence to *The Hobbit* on a blank sheet in an examination book. He discovered all about Hobbits as he wrote. Likewise, he had no idea what would happen in his new Hobbit book *The Lord of the Rings*. Other writers, like Dorothy L. Sayers and William Faulkner, sketch out a full outline to their stories. Still others, like J. K. Rowling, suddenly have the complete plot of a multivolume novel in their minds. They know all the parts and how the story will end.[46] For Lewis, writing a story was almost like reading a story. He did not know what would happen next, and he had to keep writing to find out. Thus he called it "bubbling."

A fairy story must cross the boundary from this world to another. In *The Allegory of Love*, Lewis describes "the other world" as the world of imagination, "the land of longing, the Earthly Paradise, the garden east of the sun and west of the moon."[47] Except for *Smith of Wooton Major*, Tolkien's stories did not normally involve the intersection between our world and the other world. Except for *The Horse and His Boy*, all of Lewis's Narnia stories involve that intersection, and even this exception has the Pevensie children in the background. The first thing Lewis had to do with his children was to find a way for them to journey from our world to the other world. Lewis Carroll's Alice made the journey by following the white rabbit down a rabbit hole in Christ Church Meadow, where Lewis and his friends used to stroll. She also managed a return trip by going through a looking glass. In *The Wonderful Wizard of Oz*, Dorothy found that silver shoes (ruby slippers in the movie) worked just as well. Harry Potter used platform 9 3/4 at King's Cross Station. The richness of the story tradition taught Lewis that the other world had many entry points. Rings worked (*The Magician's Nephew*). A picture on the wall would do as well (*The Voyage of the Dawn Treader*). A disastrous train wreck could open the way (*The Last Battle*). He also found doors particularly useful: the door of a wardrobe (*The Lion, the Witch and the Wardrobe*), the door in a high stone wall (*The Silver Chair*), or the door to a stable (*The Last Battle*). One might even be summoned by a blast on a horn (*Prince Caspian*).

Once they crossed the bridge into the other world, the children found a world of talking animals where something would have to happen. The fun of source criticism involves imagining the influences on Lewis that allowed him to construct Narnia and the adventures that happen there. An obvious source for the world of talking animals would be Lewis's own childhood world of Animal Land, complete with illustrations.[48] Another might be the stories of Beatrix Potter, especially *The Tale of Squirrel Nutkin* (1903) with its lifelike illustrations, which first gave Lewis the taste of Joy as a young child.[49] Add to these the pleasure of reading about Mole, Ratty, and Toad in *The Wind in the Willows* as an adult, and Lewis had plenty of straw for making bricks. The idea, however, came from none of these previous experiences. It came from a picture in his mind of a faun. The faun is a figure from Roman mythology, half man and half goat, known for charm, hospitality, and skill at playing the flute or panpipe. Yet, sixteen-year-old Lewis imagined one carrying packages and an umbrella like an English gentleman of the Edwardian age. Lewis's initial vision contradicted all that Tolkien knew about mythology from the past. The vision not only bridged our world and the other world; it also bridged ancient classical culture with the British Empire. In his vision of the faun, a world of talking animals was presented to Lewis. The faun is the embodiment of the bridge between animals and humans.

As noted earlier, Lewis did not set out to present Christian doctrine in *The Lion, the Witch and the Wardrobe*. Revelation tells us about God. Theology ponders God by inquiring what revelation means. Apologetics removes obstacles to faith. Lewis does not present Christianity in *The Lion, the Witch and the Wardrobe*, nor does he explain how it works. Instead, he tells a story that demonstrates the reasonableness, rationality, and logical consistency of Christianity. He does not present a theological system or an explanation for the affirmations of Christianity. He simply tells a story with his Christianity latent, an approach he thought constituted the best apologetics.[50] He does not present the Christian teaching about the incarnation of God as Jesus, but he does tell a story that makes the idea of the incarnation reasonable. He does not explain how the substitutionary atonement of Jesus works, but he does tell a story in which the idea of substitutionary death makes sense. He does not describe how the resurrection of Jesus took place, but he does tell a story in which the idea of resurrection is logical. Apologetics does not aim at convincing anyone of the truth of the gospel story. The Holy Spirit reserves the exclusive prerogative to do that. Apologetics simply removes the intellectual barriers that prevent an honest hearing of the gospel story.

The incarnation, the substitutionary death, and the resurrection of Jesus represent the crisis moments in the gospel story, but twenty-first-century Christians in the West tend to forget that the apostles taught that the gospel includes more than these aspects of who Jesus is. The fulfillment of prophecy is a key element of the gospel that the apostles reiterated over and over again. Anyone could claim to be the Messiah, but God spoke by the prophets to give clear signs by which the promised one might be known. In *The Lion, the Witch and the Wardrobe*, the story requires that the reader accept the idea of prophecy. The White Witch certainly believes the prophecy and does all in her power to prevent it from coming true.

Another essential element of the gospel that the apostles insisted upon is the exaltation of Jesus as both Lord and Christ, ruler of the universe, who is given a name "above every name, so that at the name of Jesus every knee should bow, in heaven and on earth and under the earth, and every tongue confess that Jesus Christ is Lord, to the glory of God the Father" (Phil. 2:9–11). At the breaking of the stone table, Aslan is alive again, but not alive the way he once was alive. At his resurrection, he takes on an exalted glory and power. As exalted Lord, Aslan goes forth to conquer and exercise his power over evil. The fact of evil is not explained—it is merely shown—and its vanquishing is the mission of Aslan. Lewis shows through his storytelling how reasonable this idea is.

The apostles also insisted that the gift of the Holy Spirit is an essential aspect of the gospel story. Just as Jesus told Nicodemus that he must be born again, and just as the risen Christ breathed on the disciples on Easter evening that they should receive the Holy Spirit, so Aslan breathed on those who had turned to stone that they might have new life. Though they have not been regenerated or made holy as Christian doctrine would explain the gift of the Holy Spirit, the story makes clear the reasonableness of the divine power to transform lives in whatever state they might be found. Four of the subsequent Narnia stories explore more about the meaning of the exalted Christ and the presence of the Holy Spirit, but two of the stories consider the reasonableness of the last two essential elements of the gospel: the creation and the last judgment.

In *The Magician's Nephew*, Lewis explores both the end of a world and the beginning of a world. The story demonstrates the reasonableness of both ideas. The story does not prove that they are true of our world, but it does show that these ideas are both logical and rational. The story also explains how evil might come into a world from the outside, as Lewis showed in *Perelandra*. He makes no effort to explain evil; he only depicts its disruptive force. He had discussed the idea in a letter to Ruth Pitter in 1947 when he said that the prehuman earth already contained suffering because of the fall of the angels prior to the human fall. Adam and Eve did not create evil. Instead, they joined "the wrong side in a battle wh. had already begun."[51] Lewis, who had always been fascinated with science and its implications for faith, also does something fascinating with a scientific idea that has grown to prominence since his death. He shows the compatibility of the concept of multiple universes with Christian faith and the idea of divine creation. As Digory and Polly go into one pool after another, they journey not to different planets but to different worlds. Like *The Lion, the Witch and the Wardrobe*, this story did not begin with the intention of presenting a Christian doctrine. This was the story that Lewis began writing immediately upon finishing the first Narnia story, but it was the last one he finished writing. He found out that it was about the creation of Narnia only by writing the story.

In *The Last Battle*, Lewis pictures the reasonableness of the end of the world and a final judgment. In so doing, he also pictures the final journey from this world to Aslan's country, which is not Narnia any more than earth is heaven. Lewis never flinches from including suffering and death in his stories, but unlike James Fenimore Cooper, he does not dwell on gory details. Instead, he gives a picture of what it means to die for those who accept grace. He also shows what it means to refuse grace. The dwarfs in *The Last Battle* are like the big man in *The Great Divorce* who wants what is his, and no blooming charity. In all these ways, Lewis aims not at proving the truth of the gospel or winning a debate against an adversary, but at showing that the gospel story makes sense. Reasonable people, therefore, ought to consider the gospel on its own merits without prejudice. Lewis probably had an idea that the last Narnia story must be about the end of Narnia, but he probably had no idea how it would happen until he started writing.

Because the Christian doctrines of the exaltation and the gift of the Holy Spirit were largely neglected in the twentieth century and are now largely forgotten, the other four Narnia stories may not seem to have the same Christian background as *The Lion, the Witch and the Wardrobe*, *The Magician's Nephew*, and *The Last Battle*. For Lewis, however, most of his fiction writing focused on these two present realities of faith. Lewis is often characterized as a man of pure intellect who had no place in his life for religious experience or emotion in general. It is an odd characterization, given his lifelong experience of Joy, which continued after his conversion, and his perpetual experience of pictures in his mind, something the Bible calls visions. Lewis had a profound awareness of the journey, what the apostle Paul called the race, that is the Christian life. He knew that it involves conflict, temptation, pain, and loss, as well as joy, friendship, comfort, and fulfillment. He also knew that when he prayed every day, he was talking to someone who heard him and helped him.

In terms of its form, the story of *Prince Caspian* is like Shakespeare's *Hamlet*. An uncle has usurped the throne. It is the same story as *Richard III*, that wicked uncle who murdered the little prince who should have been king. Of course, Lewis developed the details in a way entirely different from either of Shakespeare's wicked uncle plays. As far as the Christian life is concerned, *Prince Caspian* is a story about calling and equipping for service. It is about divine help in the midst of earthly struggle. It shows that life often is not easy, even if we love God.

In *The Voyage of the Dawn Treader*, Lewis not only uses the journey plot, but he makes use of one of his favorite versions of the journey plot from antiquity: the *Odyssey*. Prince Caspian journeys from land to land and has a complete adventure in each place. The overarching plot, however, is the journey to the end of the world, a journey that only Reepicheep completes. In this sense, Reepicheep is the ideal knight of the chivalric tradition Lewis describes in *The Allegory of Love*. His devotion to Queen Lucy comes straight from the pages of the medieval literature Lewis loved.

With *The Silver Chair*, Lewis tells a story in which none of the original four children appear. In terms of the plot, this journey is like the story of Orpheus, who went down to Hades to retrieve his wife. Like the Christian journey, the children receive guidance and a fellow traveler in the form of a Marsh-wiggle to help them on their way, but they must make the journey and face the dangers themselves. With the classical background of Orpheus, it is not surprising that Lewis also incorporated a story that Plato told about people who have been chained to a wall in a cave for their entire lives and who know of other things only from the shadows cast on the opposite cave wall by people passing by. The inmates' perception of reality is a mere shadow of what is real. Lewis took this idea and turned it around for the debate between the Marsh-wiggle and the Green Lady. Reflecting Freud's view that the idea of God is merely a projection of the idea of a father on the universe, she says that the Sun is just a projection of the idea of a lamp. The lamp is the real thing; there is no Sun. And Aslan, the great lion, is only a projection of a cat. The Overworld is only a projection of the Underworld. Puddleglum, the Marsh-wiggle, resists the seductive influence of the witch by stomping his foot in the fire and getting a jolt of pain. In this way, Lewis reminds us that pain actually gives us information about reality. Puddleglum then says that he is on Aslan's side, even if there is no Aslan. This is Pascal's wager that it is better to bet there is a God. If there is no God, you have lost nothing. If there is a God, you have gained everything.[52] Finally, Puddleglum declares that he will spend the rest of his life looking for the world of Overland, thus renewing the story of the journey.

The exchange between the witch and Puddleglum also contains one fascinating feature in light of Lewis's earlier exchange with Elizabeth Anscombe over *Miracles*. Anscombe did not challenge Lewis's views on naturalism, but she challenged his language along the lines of linguistic analysis: What did he mean by *cause* and *because*? Wittgenstein's conception of linguistic analysis involved identifying how people use words that are meaningful to them but may lack real cognitive meaning. The witch uses the method of linguistic analysis when she asks Puddleglum what he means by the word *sun*. The whole debate is treated by the witch as an exercise in linguistic analytical critique.

Puddleglum is not the only one engaged in linguistic analysis. During the same period in which Lewis was writing *The Silver Chair*, he was editing and revising his four BBC broadcast series from three little books into a single volume called *Mere Christianity*. It was published by Geoffrey Bles on July 7, 1952.[53] After explaining why he avoided matters of controversy between denominations, Lewis turned to what he meant by "mere" Christianity and more particularly what he meant by the word *Christian*. In linguistic analytical fashion, he then acknowledged that different people mean different things by the word. Without naming him, Lewis's discussion reflects his disagreement with Owen Barfield over the very nature of Christianity and who is a Christian. He points out that the word *gentleman* originally meant something quite different from what it means to the modern world. In like fashion, he acknowledges that many people use the word *Christian* in a variety of ways, but he means to use it as it was originally understood in the first century. He insists that he is not making a moral or theological judgment in this case. Rather, he is only clarifying the meaning for better understanding.[54] Elizabeth Anscombe would be proud.

The Horse and His Boy is the only Narnia story in which no one travels from our world to Narnia. The action, however, takes place during the period when the Pevensie children reign as kings and queens of Narnia. The journey this time is from slavery to freedom, from Calormen to Archenland, and the boy is returning home at last. The greatest obstacle in his journey involves not all the hosts of Calormen but the spiritual flaws of those leaving their former lives behind. Aslan is just as present in this story as he is in *The Lion, the Witch and the Wardrobe*, but usually out of sight. His help sometimes involves pain, which is the only way some people ever learn, as Lewis argued in *The Problem of Pain*. Aslan claws Aravis in her flight from Calormen, just as he tore the dragon hide from Eustace in *The Voyage of the Dawn Treader*. Aslan explains to Aravis that when she drugged her stepmother's slave as part of her escape plan, the slave was severely beaten. Aravis needs to know what her actions have cost an innocent person and how it felt.

The point of the journey story, as Lewis explained in *The Allegory of Love*, is that it expresses internal conflicts of a person that reach resolution in the course of the journey. Throughout the journey, the traveler undergoes a change and ends the journey as a different person. In the first Narnia book, the story is about how four children who journey to Narnia change as a result of events along the way, especially the children's encounter with Aslan. Change comes not only to the Pevensie children but also to anyone in stories of travel with Aslan: Prince Caspian, Reepicheep, Shasta, Bree, Aravis, Whin, and even the witless donkey, Puzzle.

Both within and without The Chronicles of Narnia, Lewis makes clear that Aslan is meant to present a picture of Jesus Christ. At the end of *The Voyage of the Dawn Treader* when Aslan tells Lucy and Edmund that they will not return to Narnia, he explains that he is in their world and in all worlds, but he has another name in their world. They must learn to know him by that name. Yet Lewis did not mean for his Narnia stories to be a symbolic telling of the gospel. Instead, he said it was a supposal: "Suppose there were a world like Narnia and it needed rescuing and the Son of God (or the 'Great Emperor oversea') went to redeem *it*, as He came to redeem ours, what might it, in that world, all have been like?"[55]

In 1960 and 1961, Lewis wrote letters to children to explain how The Chronicles of Narnia relate to the gospel. Patricia Mackey had written with her understanding of how the stories represented Christianity. In response, Lewis distinguished stories as symbols from stories as supposals, and then he explained:

1. The creation of Narnia is the Son of God creating *a* world (not specifically *our* world).
2. Jadis plucking the apple is, like Adam's sin, an act of disobedience, but it doesn't fill the same place in her life as his plucking did in his. She was *already* fallen (very much so) before she ate it.
3. The stone table *is* meant to remind one of Moses' table.
4. The Passion and Resurrection of Aslan are the Passion and Resurrection Christ might be supposed to have had in *that* world—like those in our world but not exactly like.
5. Edmund is like Judas a sneak and traitor. But unlike Judas he repents and is forgiven (as Judas no doubt wd. have been if he'd repented.)
6. Yes. At the v. *edge* of the Narnian world Aslan begins to appear more like Christ as He is known in *this* world. Hence, the Lamb. Hence, the breakfast—like at the end of St. John's Gospel. Does not He say 'You have been allowed to know me in *this* world (Narnia) so that you may know me better when you get back to your own'?
7. And of course the Ape and Puzzle, just before the last Judgement (in the *Last Battle*) are like the coming of Antichrist before the end of the world.[56]

It is clear that Lewis saw The Chronicles of Narnia as a supposal series about Jesus Christ. He conceived of the series in the same order as the gospel story, as reflected in the Apostles' Creed. Another way to say it is that the essential unity of The Chronicles of Narnia is provided by the Apostles' Creed, including not only creation, incarnation, atonement, resurrection, and last judgment, but also exaltation and the gift of the Holy Spirit. To Anne Jenkins he wrote an explanation of the doctrinal flow of the stories:

> *The Magician's Nephew* tells the creation and how evil entered Narnia.
>
> *The Lion etc*—the Crucifixion and Resurrection
>
> *Prince Caspian*—restoration of the true religion after a corruption
>
> *The Horse and His Boy*—the calling and conversion of a heathen
>
> *The Voyage of the Dawn Treader*—the spiritual life (specially in Reepicheep)
>
> *The Silver Chair*—the continued war against the powers of darkness
>
> *The Last Battle*—the coming of Antichrist (the Ape). The end of the world, and the Last Judgement[57]

It is interesting to note that though *The Horse and His Boy* takes place before *Prince Caspian* chronologically, Lewis placed it after *Prince Caspian* in this explanation, just as the first twelve chapters of the Acts of the Apostles come before Paul's missionary journeys. In similar fashion, he placed *The Magician's Nephew* first, in order of Narnian chronology and theology, though it was the sixth book published; and *The Horse and His Boy* before *The Voyage of the Dawn Treader* in theological order, though not in Narnian chronology.

Lewis emphasized on several occasions that the stories were not allegories.[58] He had gone to a great deal of trouble to define and explain allegories in *The Allegory of Love*, and The Chron-

icles of Narnia do not work at all like *The Pilgrim's Progress* or
The Faerie Queene.[59] Furthermore, the stories do not symbolize
Christianity, even though they parallel the same plot as the gospel. The Harry Potter stories are not symbols for Edgar Allan
Poe's "The Gold-Bug," even though they all follow the same basic
plot: the detective must first realize that a mystery exists before
the mystery can be decoded and solved. Jules Verne's first science-
fiction story, *Five Weeks in a Balloon*, is not a symbol for Poe's
"The Balloon Hoax," even though it is based on Poe's plot of air
travel. Though Lewis shows the reasonableness and logic of the
gospel plot, he uses other details to do it. His apologetic concern
is for someone who has read The Chronicles of Narnia to realize
that the story actually came true once, just as he came to realize
that all those myths about the dying and rising God also came
true once. The point is that a person does not need to know anything about Jesus or the Bible to enjoy the stories. Someone who
knows the gospel will find familiar passages that remind him or
her of Jesus, but the suggestion is more like poetry than philosophy. Fong Choon Sam, dean of the Baptist Theological Seminary
in Singapore, once explained to me that as a young Buddhist boy
growing up in Malaysia, he read *The Lion, the Witch and the
Wardrobe*. It left him with a deep longing that was satisfied only
when he came to hear the gospel and realized that there was a
real Aslan in our world named Jesus.

Because The Chronicles of Narnia is a series of fairy stories
instead of theological treatises, the plot differs in details from the
gospel. For instance, Aslan does not die to take away the sins of
that world. He dies only as a substitute for Edmund. Lewis does
not attempt to explain the nature of sin; he only shows the fact of
sin. He makes no attempt to explain a theory of the atonement;
he simply shows the reasonableness of the concept of substitution.
He makes no attempt to explain the doctrines of inspiration and
revelation; he simply shows that prophecies come true. He leaves
to the reader to wonder about the source and nature of prophecy.

Planet Narnia

One of the most fascinating and imaginative theories for reading
The Chronicles of Narnia was proposed by Michael Ward, who
sees the medieval cosmology as "the secret imaginative key to the
series."[60] In brief, Ward believes that Lewis intended that each of
the seven books represents one of the seven heavenly bodies of the
medieval cosmos: the Sun, the Moon, Mercury, Venus, Mars, Jupiter, and Saturn. I first heard Ward present his ideas at a conference
led by Alister McGrath at Wycliffe College in the summer of 2007.
The audience was agog, because until then everyone believed that
Aslan was the key to the series. Ward published his ideas in *Planet
Narnia* (2008), which has enjoyed wide success and gone on to
become the basis for a BBC documentary featuring him.

The proposal has a number of problems, and the person who
has given the proposal its fiercest critique is Ward himself. Lewis
never suggested to anyone that the series has such a plan. Furthermore, such a plan would need to be envisioned from the first
book.[61] He could not have decided upon it when he started the
fourth book. It would have been too late. When he began writing,
Lewis never intended more than one book about Narnia. It was
in a letter to Laurence Krieg in 1957 that Lewis explained that
when he wrote *Prince Caspian*, he thought that was it, but then
he wrote *The Voyage of the Dawn Treader*, which he "felt quite
sure . . . would be the last."[62]

Lewis insisted that "the background has no hidden meaning."[63] Instead, Aslan provides the "underlying significance of the
Narnian series," a point that children often saw but adults often
missed.[64] In a letter to Sophia Storr, Lewis explained how Aslan
integrates the Narnia stories. The stories all focus on Aslan, beginning with the incarnation, passion, and resurrection in *The Lion,
the Witch and the Wardrobe*. The plot of *Prince Caspian* revolves
around the problems that arise from disbelief in Aslan. *The Voyage of the Dawn Treader* culminates with Aslan as the lamb. Old
Prince Caspian is raised from the dead by Aslan's blood in *The*

Silver Chair. *The Last Battle* culminates the series with the reign of the ape as antichrist falling under the judgment of Aslan with the end of the world. Lewis neglected to mention *The Horse and His Boy*, where Aslan is present and providentially guiding events throughout all the struggles, unbeknownst to the children.[65]

Ward accepts the idea that Aslan and a Christological idea may be found in *The Magician's Nephew* with creation; in *The Lion, the Witch and the Wardrobe* with redemption; and in *The Last Battle* with the last judgment; but he can see no Christocentric meaning in the other four books.[66] The difference between Lewis's claims about his books and Ward's reading of them is not so much literary as biblical. As with *The Pilgrim's Regress* and *The Screwtape Letters*, Lewis is concerned with how we live in this world and how Christ is present in our individual lives as well as the great events of this world. Between Pentecost and the last judgment, Christ is King of kings and Lord of lords. Aslan is present in every book of The Chronicles of Narnia, and he is the key actor in every book.

Much of Ward's grounds for supposing that the Narnia books have a secret meaning is that he regards Lewis as a secretive person. Lewis certainly had his secrets, and this is one of Ward's most persuasive arguments. The difficulty arises in moving from the secrets Lewis kept from his father to inserting secrets into his fiction. Ward's thesis is certainly possible, but it does not logically follow as an argument. We also do well to distinguish Lewis's secretive or, more accurately stated, his deceitful nature before his conversion and his manner after his conversion. He was always a private person in that he thought it impolite to talk about one's personal affairs unless asked. Yet he told all manner of personal details to his American correspondents who did not hesitate to ask.

Ward observed that Lewis wrote about the planets in *The Allegory of Love*. He lectured on the medieval understanding of the planets in his "Prolegomena to Medieval Literature," which eventually formed part of *The Discarded Image*. He also wrote a poem titled "The Planets." Most readers of Lewis also know that he incorporated the planets into his science-fiction trilogy.[67] It does not necessarily follow, however, that The Chronicles of Narnia also deal with the planets when they are so obvious in the other writings and so missing in The Chronicles. In the absence of the planets in the Narnia books, Ward argues that the planets are "evoked," rather than presented or symbolized, to form the atmosphere for each book. Thus, *The Lion, the Witch and the Wardrobe* represents the *joviality* of Jove, the other name for Jupiter, because the turning point in the story comes with the appearance of Father Christmas, who, as everyone knows, is a "right jolly old elf."[68] Yet King Lune is just as jolly and more magisterial in *The Horse and His Boy* at the turning point.

With this understanding of the role of the planets, Ward sees Mars as the governing planet for *Prince Caspian* because of its martial spirit. It does involve a war, but so do *The Lion, the Witch and the Wardrobe* and *The Horse and His Boy*. The Sun governs *The Voyage of the Dawn Treader* because the journey heads toward the sunrise, Ward believes, and the Moon governs *The Silver Chair* because the Moon represents wetness, and wetness happens throughout the story. Of course, wetness also happens throughout *The Voyage of the Dawn Treader*. Mercury is thought to govern *The Horse and His Boy* because Mercury's chief attribute is language, and the Calormenes liked to talk, and the horses are talking horses. This argument is one of the most difficult because talking beasts are throughout The Chronicles, as well as people and beasts who like to talk. Ward bolsters the argument by quoting a scene in which Lewis describes the desert under the Moon as gleaming like a silver tray. Mercury is also called quick silver, thus the association with the silver tray. Some of the arguments work more as free association.

Because Ward identifies Venus as the "laughter-loving goddess," he recognizes Venus as governing the story of *The Magician's Nephew* in that the people of London laugh at Jadis and this story is the lightest and most humorous of The Chronicles. In fact, Venus is the laughter-loving goddess, but not the laughter of ridicule or contempt, for Venus is the goddess of love, Lewis's *eros* love. In *Perelandra*, the first couple are bound by a love for one another that aids the mother of Perelandrians in her struggle with temptation. If Venus governs any book, it should be *The Horse and his Boy*, which ends, like all good Shakespearean love stories, with marriage. *The Magician's Nephew*, on the other hand, is one of the darkest of The Chronicles, for it begins with the gloom of anticipatory grief for the imminent death of Digory's mother and builds with the horror of the end of Charn and the invasion of evil with Jadis. It is not a laugh-filled story. Finally, Saturn is said to govern *The Last Battle* because Saturn is the god of time, and time comes to an end in this story. Saturn, depicted as Father Time, is actually presented in *The Last Battle*, though he also appears as the sleeping giant in *The Silver Chair*. Yet the point of the story is that Father Time does not pervade or govern the story, because the end of time comes like a thief in the night. Aslan governs the stories, always present though not always seen.

One of the biggest problems with Ward's reading is that he treats the stories as allegory, something Lewis always insisted they were not. The medieval cosmology was an allegorical view of the heavens. To say that Jupiter embodies and evokes joviality is to employ allegory. The notion of planets as representatives of the classical deities forms the very heart and essence of Lewis's explanation of allegory in *The Allegory of Love*. In classical mythology, the gods had the full range of interests, motives, and personality traits, but in allegory, the gods are finally embodied in their planetary hosts and have only one distinguishing trait. Of the shift from classical mythology to what became medieval allegory, Lewis said of Mars in Statius: "In other words, Mars is 'discovered raging' when the curtain rises and before he has reason to rage. Naturally; for when *War* is not raging he does not exist."[69] To see a planet of the medieval cosmology governing the action of a story based on the god's essential quality is to see the story as an allegory. Lewis learned his lesson about allegory with a modern audience when he wrote *The Pilgrim's Regress*. He was determined to communicate with his audience, unlike T. S. Eliot, and that meant no more veiled meanings hidden behind allegory that no one would recognize.

While Ward's theory of the planets may be true, it probably is not. The ethos of the planets could all fit several stories simply because the human qualities they represent appear in all stories regardless of the author's intent. That was the point of them for the medieval world. If the planets do not provide the unifying theme for The Chronicles of Narnia, however, that does not diminish in any way Michael Ward's achievement in his brilliant analysis of Lewis's use of medieval cosmology in his lectures, poetry, and science-fiction trilogy. Nor does it mean that Ward's planet theory has no value. His reading of The Chronicles belongs to that marvelous way that Lewis said, in *An Experiment in Criticism*, a story "works on" people. He explained it in a letter to Peter Milward:

> If you sometimes read into my books what I did not know I had put there, neither of us need be surprised, for greater readers have doubtless done the same to far greater authors. Shakespeare wd., I suspect, read with astonishment what Goethe, Coleridge, Bradley, and Wilson Knight have found in him! Perhaps a book *ought* to have more meanings than the writer intends?[70]

The Chronicles of Narnia worked on Ward, and he saw things that no one else has ever seen.

The "Final Agonies" of OHEL

Though Lewis had not particularly enjoyed writing the "infernal" *English Literature in the Sixteenth Century* for many years, he had come to hope that its publication would amount to dropping a bomb on the literary establishment.[71] He told Sister Penelope that he aimed to put an end to much of the popular "mythology about that fabulous monster called 'the Renaissance'."[72] Chancing to meet Lewis on Addison's Walk one day, Nevill Coghill was surprised to hear Lewis say: "'I *believe* I have proved that the Renaissance never happened in England. *Alternatively,*'—he held up his hand to prevent my astonished exclamation—'that if it did, *it had no importance!*'"[73]

With his sabbatical, however, the work on the book grew more "congenial" as he spent his days in the Duke Humphrey without the interruptions of pupils or Mrs. Moore. Yet Lewis feared making mistakes that would inevitably come to light when the reviewers had their turn. Perhaps betraying a hint of depression, Lewis confessed to Warfield Firor that he was a man who had been somewhat well known for his writings in his forties but who would die unknown and forgotten. On the whole, he thought it might do him good to experience true humiliation before death.[74] For fifteen years, the OHEL had been his most important academic work, even when he was not working on it, while "all the other books were only its little twiddly bits."[75] As it neared completion, he wondered if he would lose his moorings and drift away like a hot-air balloon without sandbags.

One gratifying and sad moment came in the midst of his sabbatical. After many years of Mr. Attlee's government, the voters returned Churchill to office. In his first New Year honors list, Churchill proposed recommending to the King that Lewis be made a Commander of the British Empire (CBE). Lewis received word on December 3, 1951, in a letter from Churchill. The next day, however, he wrote to decline the honor. He feared that his appearance on a Conservative Party honors list would give "knaves" the occasion to say that all of Lewis's religious writings were only "covert anti-leftist propaganda."[76]

Lewis managed to finish the massive OHEL volume by the time the new academic year began in October 1952.[77] He submitted his manuscript to the Oxford University Press and was responding to editing by Christmas.[78] He felt an enormous sense of freedom and found that he liked the idea of feeling like a balloon with all its sandbags cast out.[79] By the end of May 1953, he was correcting proofs and working on the bibliography, but he had managed to finish the last Narnia story, though he confessed to Roger Lancelyn Green that he had not been in good health.[80] Not quite fifty-five, Lewis would never again enjoy the robust health he had known in his younger days. Since turning fifty, he had felt like an old man. June found him still correcting proofs along with Warnie, who had finished his first book, *The Splendid Century*, about France during the reign of Louis XIV.[81] Warnie would write a total of seven books on the age of the Sun King. Jack was just happy to have his "big . . . dull, academic" book behind him.[82]

Between correcting the proofs and constructing the bibliography, the OHEL dragged on for more than a year after Lewis completed the text. In mid-July 1953 he wrote to Green that he feared it would not be finished before his vacation with Warnie in August.[83] He wrote to George Sayer that he felt "damned with doing Bibliographies."[84] In November, he wrote to Mary Neylan that he could not spare the time to visit with his goddaughter, Sarah Neylan, because all his time from eight thirty in the morning until quarter to ten in the evening was taken up with tutorials and his OHEL bibliography.[85] In December, he thought he had finally reached the "final agonies" of producing the book.[86] On December 7, 1953, he wrote to Edna Green Watson, one of his American food benefactresses, that the term had come to an end and he had finally finished his "troublesome academic book."[87] He told Dorothy L. Sayers that, having finished the OHEL, he planned "never to do any work again as long as I live."[88] Alas, he would do more work, because he still had to correct the proofs of the bibliography, which appear to have been completed by early January 1954, the year in which the book was finally published on September 16.[89] Like a bad infestation of kudzu, however, his work on OHEL never completely went away, for he continued to find mistakes that needed correcting for later printings.[90]

Helen Gardner observed that the first of many great merits of the book is that it is "a genuine literary history."[91] One might have expected a book in a series on literary history to actually be a literary history, but such is often not the case. Literary critics might often simply provide an introduction to important or favorite works within a period without giving a full history of the literature of the time. One reason why this book took so long was that Lewis thought a history of English literature in the sixteenth century ought to be a history of the literature of the sixteenth century. For him, it meant reading everything published in England in that century, whether good, bad, or indifferent. The second great merit of the book is its remarkable readability. Gardner, a fierce critic, called it "brilliantly written" so that "hardly a page . . . does not stimulate and provoke thought" while at the same time arousing "delighted laughter."[92] George Sayer found wit and humor on virtually every page.[93] Gardner said that she would have given much to have written the chapter on Shakespeare's sonnets. True to her calling, however, she found some problems. She thought that the book suffered from a polemic against humanism and the new learning, which Lewis suggested was the new ignorance—thus the title of his introduction, "New Learning and New Ignorance."[94] She also pointed out several places where Lewis was not aware of new developments in the scholarship of the period. This situation represents one of the side effects of Lewis's insistence on criticism based on the primary text without reference to what others have said about it.

Nevill Coghill thought that the prose of this critical volume had a "magisterial quality" that Lewis's conversational prose did not, though his conversational prose was impressive.[95] With his own prodigious critical skill, Coghill identified the essential elements of Lewis's critical writing that set it apart:

> The marks of this style are weight and clarity of argument, sudden terms of generalization and genial paradox, the telling short sentence to sum a complex paragraph, and unexpected

touches of personal approach to the reader, whom he always assumes to be as logical, as learned, as romantic, and as open to [argument] as himself.[96]

Based on Lewis's comment about the pleasure of having tea while reading a book in solitude, A. N. Wilson, whose controversial biography of Lewis did not shy from putting Lewis in an unfavorable light, remarked that it never failed as a book to read with tea, and "in so far as a book can increase the sum of human pleasure, there are not many higher terms of praise."[97] John Wain, who was assimilated into the Inklings for a few years after the war and made his mark as a poet and novelist, thought that Lewis's OHEL contribution was his best book.[98] Wain's good opinion of this book is significant, because he did not care for all that Lewis wrote and thought that the science-fiction stories were a "sign of imaginative bankruptcy."[99] Wain considered Lewis's OHEL volume a model for critical writing. Lewis managed to combine the wit and vitality that Gardner and Coghill experienced with a touch of the personal in order to help the reader feel interested in the most "deservedly forgotten book" or "crabbed" theological controversy.[100] And controversy it had aplenty. Lewis had hoped to drop a bomb on the literary establishment, and he succeeded.

Gardner had said that Lewis engaged in a polemic against the humanists, and George Sayer called it a crusade.[101] Most literary scholars specialize in their period, focusing their attention on what happens within the confines of a century or so. The humanists were the new avant-garde group of the sixteenth century and included people like Erasmus, Thomas More, John Calvin, and even Henry VIII. They were the exciting young Turks. Unlike modern literary critics, Lewis read the sixteenth century in light of his fifteen-hundred-year study in *The Allegory of Love* and his twenty-five-hundred-year study in *A Preface to Paradise Lost*. Latin was still a living, spoken, developing international language at the beginning of the sixteenth century, but Lewis blamed the humanists for killing it by their emphasis on the formal structure of Augustan Latin, in contrast to the developing structure of medieval Latin. Worst of all, he blamed the humanists for killing romance with their emphasis on the literal and the historical. This approach is most easily accessible to modern audiences through the humanist treatment of the Bible. While the medieval world saw all of the Bible as symbol and allegory, the humanists saw none of the Bible as symbol and allegory. The Bible was a collection of literal facts.

While the first half of the sixteenth century represents a rather drab period in English literature, the second half represents a golden age. Lewis denied that the humanists can take any credit for this "efflorescence" (he refused to call it a renaissance).[102] While acknowledging that humanism would play an important role in the development of ideas in later centuries, Lewis insisted that it was not yet determinative for literature in the sixteenth century. He explained that while historians of science or philosophy might focus on the ideas of the humanists, "The literary historian . . . is concerned not with those ideas in his period which have since proved fruitful, but with those which seemed important at the time."[103] While Lewis credited the humanists for editing many Greek, Latin, and Hebrew texts, he also reminded his readers that many ancient texts had not been lost, and that the work of recovery had been going on for three centuries before the humanists.[104]

Then Lewis came to the argument about which he told Coghill on Addison's Walk one day. He did not believe that the Renaissance ever occurred in England, because he thought that the Renaissance was a mental construct rather than a historical reality. The humanists invented the concept of the medieval and classical periods as ways of identifying themselves.[105] Lewis argued that once the educational establishment accepted the humanist view of the past, a view took hold that regarded good writing as that which "aped as closely as possible that of the chosen period in the past."[106] This was what they meant by a renaissance or rebirth of classical learning. Lewis charged, however, that "before they had ceased talking of a rebirth it became evident that they had really built a tomb."[107] It is important to recall that the humanists did not embrace the beginnings of the scientific revolution reflected in the work of Copernicus and Kepler. The humanists looked to the classical world of antiquity for knowledge, and from Aristotle and Ptolemy the humanists received confirmation that the earth lies at the center of the heavens. Thus, the reliance on ancient authority inhibited new knowledge.

Lewis also devoted a significant portion of his introduction to discussing the English Puritans, who arose within the Elizabethan Church of England after the ascension of Elizabeth I in 1558. Thus, the Puritans appeared and became a major force within Elizabethan society even as the golden age of English literature dawned with Shakespeare, Spenser, Marlow, and Jonson. Just as a heavy layer of myth has obscured the humanists, Lewis argued that the modern understanding of the Puritans has been obscured by nineteenth-century fictional accounts of the Puritans. He did not attempt so much to defend the Puritans as to describe them accurately. In contrast with the Protestants in general, who focused on religious belief and right doctrine, the Puritans focused on religious *experience* in addition to right doctrine.[108] The Puritans experienced the doctrine of salvation as a gift of God to all who have faith as a joy and hope.[109] It is possible that Lewis's exposition of the Puritans played a part in the growing distance between him and Tolkien, who became increasingly suspicious of a latent anti-Catholic bias in his friend. If true, it would be ironic, since Lewis did not accept the Puritan theology, especially as practiced in Ulster. After Lewis died, however, Tolkien wrote an article entitled "The Ulsterior Motive," which criticized *Letters to Malcolm* and accused Lewis of a prolonged prejudice against Catholicism, though he never published the article.[110]

Tolkien seems to have been distressed, if not offended, that Lewis did not become a Catholic when he became a Christian. As Tolkien grew older, he appears to have grown in his view that

Lewis harbored a deep-seated prejudice against Catholics related to his roots in Northern Ireland Protestantism, which would not be an illogical assessment. Warnie certainly had an anti-Catholic bias until he came under the care of the Irish nuns who nursed him during his worst alcohol binges. Tolkien probably did not realize that Lewis made a habit of recognizing his prejudices and facing them. Nor did Tolkien seem to know that Lewis had been engaged in correspondence with Giovanni Calabria—an Italian priest and founder of the Congregation of the Poor Servants of Divine Providence—between 1947 and 1954, the year Don Giovanni died.[111] The subject of the correspondence focused on the possibility of healing the rift between the branches of Christianity.

Tolkien never seems to have taken Lewis's theological objections to Catholicism seriously, tending to regard them as holdovers from Lewis's childhood teaching. Lewis rejected what he called "modernism," regardless of the century in which it became modern. For him, true Christianity involves those doctrines about which the Bible, the early church fathers, Eastern Orthodoxy, the medieval church, modern Roman Catholics, and modern Protestants agree.[112] He was also concerned about the schism between the ancient Eastern Orthodox Church and the Roman Catholic Church. He rejected any Catholic doctrine that deviated from the universal tradition, among which he counted the Catholic views of the Blessed Virgin Mary, the supremacy of the pope, and transubstantiation. From the point of view of Lewis, the reliance on tradition amounted to reliance on innovation, for every tradition begins by a deviation from the original. Thus, Catholicism, though older than Protestantism, was still a provincial, local departure from the original, just like Protestantism.[113] When Don Giovanni suggested that the pope was "the point of meeting," Lewis replied that Protestants disagreed with Catholics on nothing more than the authority of the pope, which is the grounds for almost all other disagreements.[114] Of course, in his introduction to the OHEL volume, Lewis had called Calvin's extrapolation of church government from the Scriptures one of the "strangest mirages which have ever deceived the human mind."[115] It is not difficult to see, however, that after enduring a lifetime of anti-Catholic prejudice in England, Tolkien might have sensed in the OHEL volume the same from Lewis, who grew up in Belfast, the front line of violence between Protestants and Catholics.

Perhaps Lewis's greatest satisfaction in writing the book was revealed to Ruth Pitter when he told her how "glorious" it was "*not to be doing it* any longer."[116] Within a few years, Alastair Fowler told Lewis that *English Literature in the Sixteenth Century* had become a popular volume from which undergraduates plagiarized their papers.[117] Both of the two great controversial declarations that Lewis had made about the Renaissance and the Puritans became the standard view in the decades after his death, though few scholars gave him credit for them. Historians in particular now recognize the gradual growth of learning and the arts, beginning with the blossoming of courtly love poetry in the eleventh century and the many advances in the thirteenth century—the century of Dante, Thomas Aquinas, Giotto, Marco Polo, Roger Bacon, Cimabue, and Magna Carta. Lewis's recognition that the Puritans were more than their nineteenth-century caricature would find resonance in the sudden surge in Puritan studies in the twenty years after his death.[118] Yet, perhaps to his relief, this major academic book did not produce the fan mail that required an answer, which his science fiction, "devil" stories, and Narnia tales had done.

5

The New Freedom

1951–1954

After the death of Janie Moore in January 1951, Lewis experienced a freedom he had not known for years. When she had gone into the nursing home, he had written to Warfield Firor that he had not enjoyed the freedom to plan his own days or to experience any domestic leisure for fifteen years.[1] He told Firor things he never mentioned to the Inklings—that she had a worrying, jealous, exacting, and angry disposition.[2] He wrote to Mary Van Deusen, another of his American correspondents, that he had rarely known twenty-four hours of peace at the Kilns, "amidst senseless wranglings, lyings, backbitings, follies, and *scares*," and that he "never went home without a feeling of terror as to what appalling situation might have developed in [his] absence."[3] Not until Mrs. Moore died did Lewis realized how bad his life had been.[4] Just before she went into the nursing home, Lewis had calculated that he had not had any freedom since 1929, which would add six years to his reckoning of fifteen. Whether fifteen or twenty-one years, it must have seemed like an eternity. When she died and he no longer attended her daily at her bedside in the nursing home, he wrote to Arthur Greeves, "I know now how a bottle of champagne feels while the wire is being taken off the cork."[5]

Though Lewis did not have complete freedom when Mrs. Moore went into the nursing home, because he visited her every day, he did at last have the freedom of his own house and his daily schedule. On the very day she entered Restholme, Lewis wrote to Roger Lancelyn Green to invite him for dinner and conversation.[6] A few days later, he wrote to give Greeves the news, but it meant that he would have to delay the long-anticipated vacation to Ireland. He also worried about the expense of keeping Mrs. Moore in a nursing home. The bill came to over five hundred pounds a year.[7] He was not sure how he could manage on his limited means. He rarely remembered that he had access to royalties and speaking fees that could help if he did not send them all to Owen Barfield for his philanthropies. Instead of thinking about how he might use the money for himself, he continued to think of how he could use it for others. His old friend Cecil Harwood, who had introduced Barfield to Rudolf Steiner and anthroposophy, had married a lady almost a generation older than he, and her health had declined dramatically, like Mrs. Moore's. Lewis wrote to Harwood to encourage him to take advantage of whatever money he might need from the trust, and Harwood did.[8] She died a few months later on July 14, 1950.[9]

As Lewis settled into the new routine with an hour every afternoon at Restholme, he issued more invitations. He asked Arthur to come for a visit, promising that the Kilns was no longer the "horrible" house it had been.[10] When Warnie was away in August, Jack invited George Sayer to come for any or all of the time, insisting that he could cut his visit to Mrs. Moore for a day or two if they wanted to take an all-day walk.[11] He invited Dom Bede Griffiths, whose regimen as a monk had its own restrictions, to lunch.[12] After Daphne Harwood's death, Lewis invited Cecil to visit him anytime he had a weekend free.[13] By September, he felt free enough to take the day off from visiting Minto to go on a sixteen-mile walk with Warnie along the old Roman road from Dorchester Abbey to Oxford.[14] It had become easier to skip a day from time to time because Mrs. Moore's mind had "almost completely gone."[15]

Two weeks after Mrs. Moore died, Lewis wrote to Arthur with the news and asked if he could come to Ireland for a two-week visit during the Easter break from March 31 until April 16, 1951.[16] This visit would not be to the old neighborhood where the two friends had grown up and spent so much time together in each other's homes. Arthur's mother had died in 1949, and Arthur moved to a small cottage twelve miles away in the village of Crawfordsburn. Lewis would stay at the Old Inn in Crawfordsburn from then on when he visited Arthur.[17] The same day, he wrote to Roger Green to invite him for a visit at the end of February for two nights during the week.[18] He next invited Sayer to visit after Jack returned from Ireland.[19] Lewis was in a sociable mood, and he appears to have missed the company of his friends—a situation he acted to rectify.

The visit with Arthur must have gone better than even Lewis had hoped, for upon his return to Oxford, he wrote to Arthur with plans for a few days' return trip to Crawfordsburn in early August, then a week with Warnie in Southern Ireland, followed by two more weeks with Arthur. By June, Jack had decided to add an extra week at the front of his vacation to visit Cornwall, the extreme southwest corner of England, where he had never been.[20] It is possible that this extension involved a visit to his old friend A. K. Hamilton Jenkin from his college days. While in Cornwall, he went sailing for the first time, which would have informed his treatment of the *Dawn Treader*.[21] Of course, he had crossed the Irish Sea dozens of time, but never under sail. Meanwhile, Green would visit at the end of May, when they could talk all about Narnia.[22]

Experiencing Forgiveness

Life was so good that Lewis asked Sister Penelope to pray for him. He thought he was in danger of being too comfortable, like Bunyan's pilgrim, who traveled across the Plain of Ease.[23] Though

Lewis recognized the danger of physical comfort, he also realized that spiritual comfort is far superior. In the context of his new freedom, he had also experienced the kind of freedom about which the apostle Paul spoke in Galatians. On Saint Mark's Day, which falls on April 25, Lewis had a profound spiritual experience of dramatic consequences. He wrote of it first to Sister Penelope and then to Father Don Giovanni Calabria.[24] Unfortunately, he did not provide any details of what happened and how. He simply wrote to Sister Penelope in early June 1951:

> I realise that until about a month ago I never really believed (tho' I thought I did) in God's forgiveness. What an ass I have been both for not knowing and for thinking I knew. I now feel that one must never say one believes or understands anything: any morning a doctrine I thought I already possessed may blossom into this new reality.[25]

On the day after Christmas of 1951, he wrote to Calabria:

> As for myself, during the past year a great joy has befallen me. Difficult though it is, I shall try to explain this in words. It is astonishing that sometimes we believe that we believe what, really, in our heart, we do not believe.
>
> For a long time I believed that I believed in the forgiveness of sins. But Suddenly (on St. Mark's Day) this truth appeared in my mind in so clear a light that I perceived that never before (and that after many confessions and absolutions) had I believed it with my whole heart.
>
> So great is the difference between mere affirmation by the intellect and that faith, fixed in the marrow and as it were palpable, which the Apostle wrote was *substance* ["Now faith is the *substance* of things hoped for, the evidence of things not seen" (Heb. 11:1 KJV)].[26]

Lewis gave this word of testimony in the context of responding to some struggle Calabria had confided to Lewis. Lewis then added,

"Jesus has cancelled the handwriting which was against us."[27] This statement is striking for several reasons, but most of all for his use of the personal name of Jesus. Normally in his letters, Lewis spoke of Jesus as our Lord or Christ or the Lord. The personal experience of the profundity of the forgiveness that came to him through Jesus made Jesus near, personal, and intimate to Lewis.

By March 1952, Lewis was already planning his August visit to Greeves in Crawfordsburn.[28] After spending two weeks with Arthur, he planned to meet Roger Green on the return trip and to visit several of the ruined castles of Wales, beginning with Beaumaris Castle.[29] As was often the case with Lewis, the actual dates for the vacation were subject to change. Apparently, Green offered to make the reservations at the hotel where they would stay, but Lewis replied with the wisdom of the world. If Green made a reservation for two, the hotel keeper would put them in the same room, likely with one bed. Instead, Lewis explained that he would make a reservation from Oxford and Green would make a reservation from Bebington, leaving the hotel keeper with no idea of a connection and no temptation to save a room for another guest.[30]

The Un-Wife

The most surprising event of 1952 probably involved the marriage of C. S. Lewis to Nella Victoria Hooker. At least, it certainly came as a surprise to Lewis. Ms. Hooker had checked into the Court Stairs Hotel in the seaside town of Thanet, on the eastern tip of Kent, where she registered as Mrs. C. S. Lewis. She told Alan and Nell Berners-Price that Lewis would pay the bill when he arrived later. After a year had passed, Lewis had not yet appeared to pay his bill, so Mrs. Berners-Price went up to Oxford to confront him and demand payment. In times like this, it was helpful that one of Lewis's best friends was a lawyer. Barfield advised Lewis to take out an injunction. Ms. Hooker was arrested in April and her trial was scheduled for May 8.[31] Between the news of the fraud and the trial, Lewis spoke at the Library Association conference in

Bournemouth, on April 29, where he read his paper "On Three Ways of Writing for Children."[32] He wrote to Roger Green that the paper was a success, judging from the report of one librarian, who said that Lewis had almost converted him to fairy tales from "the 'real life' stuff."[33]

Lewis had to appear in court in Canterbury to testify, and Nell Berners-Price invited him to stay at the Court Stairs, which was not far from there.[34] When he returned to Oxford the next day, he wrote a note of thanks to Mrs. Berners-Price, in which he gave his reaction to the first phase of the trial. He thought the whole scene had been "horrid" and that justice at work was "not a pretty sight."[35] In fact, he had witnessed for the first time what his father had done as a police court prosecutor. It is interesting to note that Lewis apparently had never seen his father in court. He wrote, "Any creature, even an animal, at bay, surrounded by its enemies, is a dreadful thing to see: one felt one was committing a sort of indecency by being present."[36] The case did not end on May 8. It was adjourned until May 19, so Lewis booked another night at the Court Stairs. A few days before the resumption of the trial, however, Lewis learned of a postponement.[37] Eventually, Ms. Hooker was convicted and sent to Holloway Prison in London.[38]

A by-product of Lewis's experience with the justice system was his new acquaintance with the Berners-Price family. He enjoyed himself at their little hotel. When he sent his thank-you note, he included a copy of *Prince Caspian* for their daughter, Penelope.[39] A correspondence continued for several years, but the entreaties to return to Thanet would have to wait for a return trip to the Court Stairs. As for Ms. Hooker, she corresponded with Lewis prior to the trial, and Lewis visited her in Holloway Prison.[40]

Growing Friendship with Ruth Pitter

In stark contrast with Ms. Hooker, visits with Ruth Pitter continued to give Lewis great pleasure. He had grown concerned about the movement to ordain women to the Episcopal priesthood, and he held a small, informal colloquium on the topic in his rooms at Magdalen, which Pitter attended on the Friday and Saturday after Christmas 1949.[41] She found it strenuous, but she thoroughly enjoyed the luncheon afterward, at which Lewis praised the poetry of Roy Campbell.[42] When she visited Lewis in Oxford, she stayed with Lord David and Rachel Cecil. By 1949, she was closer friends with the Cecils than with Lewis. She spent a weekend every year with them at Rockbourne, their country house in Hampshire.[43] While she addressed her letters to Mr. Lewis, she had progressed to addressing Cecil as David.

We do not have all the correspondence between Lewis and Pitter. Some of the letters allude to other letters now lost. For instance, in a letter to Pitter on November 28, 1950, in which he responded to one from her about *The Lion, the Witch and the Wardrobe*, Lewis commented on her lion image in a previous letter.[44] They continued to correspond about poetry—their own and poetry in general—and to exchange manuscripts for review, for they valued each other's critical opinion.[45] He continued to invite her to Oxford for lunch. We do not know how often she came, but we do know that some visits went unrecorded. For instance, on March 17, 1951, which would have been toward the end of Hilary term just before the Easter break, he wrote to invite her to lunch during the next term with the added incentive that she could reclaim her glasses case, which she left behind on her last visit.[46] She accepted this invitation and returned to Oxford on May 10, 1951.

Pitter was back in Oxford for the diocesan conference of the Worship and the Arts Association during the first week of July, but appears to have missed Lewis, who was on his excursion to Cornwall. This time she stayed at St Hugh's College, but she spent two afternoons with the Cecils.[47] In exchanging manuscripts, however, Lewis told her about going sailing for the first time.[48] She mentioned receiving a card from Lewis in September 1951, but the card is lost.[49] Lewis invited Pitter to attend his lecture on *Hero and Leander*, which he delivered before the British Academy on

February 20, 1952.[50] The lecture fostered another letter from Pitter, to which Lewis responded with elaborations on Greek poetry on April 16, 1952.[51] In May, she was back in Oxford visiting the Cecils, who invited Lewis to join them. In thanking Rachel Cecil for including Lewis, Pitter wrote "I do delight in him."[52]

Visit from an American Lady

Lewis learned in May 1952 that Vera Mathews, who had sent him numerous care packages during the rationing time in England, had married K. H. Gebbert. When she announced her plans to visit England in October, Lewis invited her to stay with him and Warnie at the Kilns.[53] When the time came, however, she came down with the flu while in London and had to cancel her stay in Oxford.[54] Vera Mathews Gebbert was not Lewis's only married female correspondent whom he invited to visit the Kilns. Mrs. Joy Davidman Gresham came for Christmas.

Lewis did not realize that Joy Gresham would be with him for Christmas. He told his godson Laurence Harwood that he had invited her for a week but that she had decided to stay for three weeks![55] In fact, it was barely more than two weeks, but it may have felt like three to Lewis, who has never been known for his grasp of time. She took up all his time so that he could not do any writing, and she talked "from morning till night."[56] He could not believe that it was happening, and he only hoped that Laurence would have a better Christmas than he had. To another correspondent, he wrote that he had to entertain a visitor and that his domestic help was sick, but he had "mountains of mail" to handle.[57] Her visit came during an unusually bad spell of winter weather, with gales, snow, and frigid temperatures. She did not complain about the weather, but she did complain about the heating at the Kilns.[58] She stayed from December 15 until January 3, 1953, which wrecked Lewis's plans to spend New Year's Day with George and Moira Sayer in Malvern. In sending them a note of regret and apology for breaking their plans, he told the Sayers

Joy Davidman, ca. 1940. Used by permission of the Marion E. Wade Center, Wheaton College, Wheaton, IL.

that his vacation had turned into a shambles in which "perpetual conversation [was] a most exhausting thing."[59]

Joy Davidman Gresham

Lewis first received a letter from Joy Gresham on January 10, 1950, when she was thirty-five years old.[60] To Charles Williams's widow, Lewis described her as "an old & valued pen-friend" in September 1952.[61] She was an unlikely person with whom Lewis might form a friendship, for she embodied many of the things he most disliked. She was an American who wrote modern poetry. Though Lewis referred to her as Joy Gresham, she maintained her maiden name and wrote as Joy Davidman. She was a modern woman. She was a woman with a shady past, having belonged to the Communist Party and worked as a writer for its magazine,

New Masses. By the time she began writing to Lewis, she had published a volume of poetry, *Letter to a Comrade* (1938), and two novels: *Anya* (1940) and *Weeping Bay* (1950). She also edited *War Poems of the United Nations* (1943) and *They Looked Like Men* (1944), a posthumous collection of communist poems by Alexander Bergman. Davidman was born into a family of secular Jews in 1915 and decided for atheism when she was eight years old as a consequence of reading H. G. Wells's *Outline of History*.[62]

Davidman met William Gresham at a Communist Party meeting. They fell in love and Gresham divorced his wife so that they could marry in August 1942. Their first son, David, was born in 1944, and their second son, Douglas, in 1945. In 1946, while Bill Gresham felt he was in the midst of a nervous breakdown, Joy had a profound spiritual experience, sensing that "God came in" and provided her with a spirit of peace and security during a period of chaos in which she recognized she was powerless.[63] Joy and Bill turned to the Christian faith and joined the Pleasant Plains Presbyterian Church. By 1949, she was a deaconess in her church.[64] Bill, who was also a writer, had a major success with his new novel, *Nightmare Alley* (1946), which was adapted as a movie in 1947 starring Tyrone Power and Joan Blondell. (Guillermo del Toro has produced and directed a new film version starring Bradley Cooper and Cate Blanchett with a release date of 2021.) With the sixty thousand dollars from the film contract, Gresham bought a fourteen-room house on twenty-two acres in Pleasant Plains, but he proved incapable of repeating his initial success.[65] Under the resulting financial strain, Gresham turned to alcohol for support.

As a new Christian, Davidman discovered the works of C. S. Lewis and found him a great encouragement to her faith. She told William Rose Benét, founding editor of *The Saturday Review of Literature* and older brother of Stephen Vincent Benét, that Lewis's writing had cleared her head of determinism.[66] She informed Kenneth Porter, prominent poet and historian, that though she was a Presbyterian, she really belonged with the Anglicans and

Joy Davidman Gresham, David (looking at his mother), William, and Douglas, ca. 1949–1950. Used by permission of the Marion E. Wade Center, Wheaton College, Wheaton, IL.

regarded Lewis and Charles Williams her teachers.[67] Though she said she was a convert of Lewis, she told Porter that she was less traditional than he.[68] In 1949, she read Chad Walsh's new book *C. S. Lewis: Apostle to the Skeptics* and began a correspondence with Walsh. She wrote to Walsh that she first read *The Great Divorce* because of her early love of fantasy, which she had suppressed as a Communist.[69] Because Walsh told Joy that "Lewis answered even asinine letters," she wrote her January 1950 letter to him—five single-spaced pages in which she told her own story.[70]

The Gresham marriage began to deteriorate as Bill struggled with his writing. In addition to alcohol, he sought solace in the arms of a series of willing women. In early 1952, Joy's cousin Renée came to stay with the Greshams, along with her young son and daughter. Renée had left her husband, Claude Pierce, who was once known as a violent drunk but is now remembered as an abusive husband. She escaped north from Alabama under the subterfuge that her mother was seriously ill and needed Renée.[71] Renée, who was more a homemaker than an intellectual, took over the household duties of cooking and cleaning, which left Joy free to write. Joy retained from her communist days a preference to dress in a plain, practical way, whereas Renée cultivated a more glamorous style. She had also abandoned her Catholic upbringing and enjoyed a secular approach to life.[72]

An American in London

With Renée to look after the house and children, Joy decided to take a sabbatical and finish her book on the Ten Commandments, which would be published as *Smoke on the Mountain*. No letters or other primary materials have survived that relate to her decision to take a lengthy vacation in England, but speculation has filled the gap. Lyle Dorsett suggested that Joy was already falling in love with Lewis when she made that first trip to England.[73] By this view, Joy's attachment to England came as an aspect of her romantic view of Lewis. Another view, however, seems more consistent with Joy's temperament and no-nonsense approach to life. While she was a person of deep passion in whatever mattered to her, she was also a woman of deep commitment and practicality. As a literary person, however, she had developed a lifelong infatuation with England that had stood at odds with her earlier communist period. Free from communism, she once again indulged her romantic imagination with a land that she loved through the books she read.

Her romantic view of England became a context for developing a romantic interest in England. In all likelihood, the progress went from regarding Lewis from *storgē*, to *philia*, to *eros* as her life situation changed. While Douglas Gresham cannot tell us how his mother felt about Lewis in 1952, he can tell us about how she felt about England. He recalled, "She wanted to see that land from which stemmed the literature she admired so much and she

ﻻ

also wished very much to meet and talk to the British Christian writer with whom she had exchanged letters for two years—C. S. Lewis."[74]

With Renée installed at home, Joy sailed for England in August 1952. She stayed with a new literary friend in London, where she finished writing *Smoke on the Mountain*. Through her own writing, Joy had developed a network of literary correspondents, and Phyllis Haring (who went by Phyl) was one of these. A South African, Haring lived in London for a few years with her lesbian lover, Selma (who went by Sel), in the 1950s before returning to Johannesburg.[75] Haring was a minor poet who published only a few dozen poems and whose most important work was the slim volume *A Taste of Salt*.[76] During more than four months in England, Joy went to Oxford several times to see Lewis. Sel, as it turned out, was a cousin of Joy's "loony cousin Neil Bernstein" on the other side of his family.[77]

Joy quickly settled into the London literary scene, discovering the White Horse in Fetter Lane, a pub near her where the London science-fiction writers gathered every Thursday night. She became a regular at their gatherings and soon got to know Arthur C. Clarke.[78] Phyllis Haring lived only five blocks from Mrs. Charles Williams, and Joy quickly made her acquaintance and regularly had tea or a meal with her and her son Michael. Early in her Christian life, Joy had been as interested in Williams as she had been in Lewis.[79] Florence Williams suggested that Joy wear something pretty when she went to Oxford to meet Jack. She said that the dons might lead a cloistered life, but they took notice and felt flattered by female attention.[80] In late October 1952, Florence explained that she was not anxious to find any manuscripts or letters that her husband had sent to admirers that might turn up anything indiscreet. Joy reported to Bill that Florence said Williams had an extended love affair over many years that continued to cause her pain. Joy then added that Michael Williams was very immature and seemed to have no close male or female friends, and commented, "Sons of wronged wives do seem to have a bad time; you should know."[81]

Meeting Joy

Joy went to Oxford to meet Lewis on September 14, 1952. She took Phyl Haring with her, and they stayed in Oxford with another friend of Joy, Veronica Ruffer.[82] Joy and Phyl met Lewis at the Eastgate Hotel for lunch.[83] The Eastgate had been a favorite restaurant and pub for Jack, Warnie, Tolkien, and Williams for thirty years. It has never enjoyed the popularity that the Eagle and Child has had for Lewis fans, but it was probably the more important place for Lewis. The luncheon went so well that Lewis invited them to join him a few days later for lunch in his rooms at Magdalen, prepared in the excellent kitchen of the college. He asked Warnie to come as well, but when he declined, Jack invited George Sayer to make up the fourth at the table.[84] Lewis and Sayer had spent much time together since Mrs. Moore entered the nursing home, and Lewis had come to rely upon him in many ways. Sayer recalled of his first meeting that Joy "was of medium height, with a good figure, dark hair, and rather sharp features. She was an amusingly abrasive New Yorker, and Jack was delighted by her bluntness and her anti-American views."[85] She was a rabid Anglophile who regarded everything in England better than in the United States. Sayer added that "Jack liked this."[86] These were not the only meals that Jack and Joy shared during her first trip to Oxford. Lewis introduced her to one of his favorite pub meals, pork pie with cider, at the Eagle and Child. They were also together one night when they had enough to drink for Joy to feel "a little sozzled" and began debating "reason vs. the Inner Light."[87]

Walter Hooper gave the date for the first meeting as September 24, but he also gave Phyllis's last name as Williams.[88] It is unlikely that they did not meet until ten days after Joy's arrival in Oxford. It would also have been difficult for them to fit in two other lunch meetings after September 24 since Joy went on an extended tour of England, visiting her friends the Matley Moores in Worcester, and traveling on to sightsee in Edinburgh before September 30.[89] She also appears to have spent at least one day on a ten-mile walk with Jack that took her over Shotover Hill and back to the Kilns. She included this expedition in "Bread-and-Butter Sestina," a poem she addressed to Jack, with a copy sent to Bill, in which she included the stanza:

And there was once a voice within a cloud
I would not hear, although it called aloud
In Love's own words; since I was bred too proud
For all gods but my bitter self, until
You taught me wisdom. Gratitude might fill
With hymns of joy, for that, your house and hill.[90]

She was flirting with Jack and telling Bill all about it.

After Joy and Phyllis left for London, Jack told Sayer that he had invited Joy to visit the Kilns at Christmas. It was the kind of courtesy he had extended to Vera Mathews Gebbert during the same period. With the holidays, however, he needed Sayer's advice about how to behave. Should he and Warnie behave as they always would at Christmas, or should they be "more conventional hosts"?[91] Sayer advised them to act the way they always did during their Christmas holiday.

In the meantime, Joy left Phyl and Sel on October 19. Phyl had serious psychological problems, for which she was well known, and Sel kept children for a friend, all of which made the small flat a difficult place to live and write. Joy had earned her keep by doing the cooking and cleaning, but never to the satisfaction of Phyl. Now she moved to the home of Clare Gay in Barnet, Hertfordshire, at the end of a London tube line. Gay was a woman Joy had met through dianetics circles in London. Dianetics was a form of mental therapy developed by L. Ron Hubbard before he moved on to Scientology, and Joy and Bill Gresham had gotten heavily involved in it by the time she went to England. Gay provided Joy with free lodgings in exchange for "dianetic runs," which involved such things as her "engrams, an "ESPER," "lock chains," "visio shut-offs," "grief charges," a "memory audit," and many more incomprehensible terms of questionable value.[92] While working with Clare on her dianetics and attending a dianetics group in London, Joy realized that Hubbard had gone far off on a tangent. He claimed he could take the spirits out of his followers' bodies to allow them to experience telekinesis, communicate with Mars, and similarly outrageous things. Joy told Jack that she had been doing dianetics to earn cash in London, and she wrote to her husband that Lewis responded by drawing a cartoon of her "opening my pack and walking down Cheapside crying, 'Dianetics! Fresh dianetics! All a-growing and a-blowing!' or 'Any old complexes to mend!'"[93] More interestingly, Lewis told her that if she ran out of money, she could come and stay at the Kilns.

On November 5, 1952, Joy left Clare Gay and moved to the Stanton House, a small hotel at 17 Nottingham Place in London. The combination of the flu, Clare's vegetarianism, the lack of heating, Clare's daily "dianetic runs," the distance from central London, and Clare's multiple neuroses finally overwhelmed Joy, who took to her bed and decided she had to leave. She managed to spend only fifty dollars in October by saving on housing and taking advantage of the hospitality of her friends for as many meals as possible. When she wrote to Bill on November 3, she still had a little over two hundred dollars left. A state of general depression comes through this letter.[94] In her many letters to Bill during her stay in England, she addressed him in the most affectionate terms: "Poogle" (the favored term), "Poogabill," "Turtle Hatcher," "Unconquerabill," "Unsinkabill," "Unforgettabill," "Sage of Staatsburg," "Ole Reliabill," Poogleface," "Ole never-let-a-girl-down Billy," and "Master Mind of Modern Mentalism." At the same time, she also sounds conflicted.

In the midst of her collapse and depression, Joy told Bill that she had "another sort of spiritual experience" in which she sorted out her emotions. She was attracted to Lewis, but part of her reason for going to England was to punish Bill and teach him a lesson for his philandering. She seems to have wanted him to be jealous of the other writer in Oxford. She confessed:

> I am sick to death of love-languishing; no man in the world, not even the greatest, is worth dying for, and I am BORED with the whole fruitless business. I really was clinging to suffering and self-pity, wasn't I? What a dreary time I must have given you, and no wonder you were so glad to pack me off! Well, I realized (like the dames in the magazine stories) that I was doing it to myself and didn't *have* to; so I stopped. As for That Man, he is certainly fond of me and rather attracted to me, but not enough to disturb his peace of mind (thank goodness); and if it were ten times as strong a feeling, his belief would be stronger. Funny; I've never before been with a man who looked at me and talked to me like that and then did *not* make a pass—and, do you know, I half like it! I'll be a Christian yet.
>
> So now I am feeling homesick for my poogle and my boys, and I shall get the most out of the rest of my stay and then come home, do my job, and be happy. And *you* will be happy too, if I can do anything about it![95]

Simple explanations of all that filled Joy Gresham's heart when she went to England will not do. It was complicated.

On November 10, Lewis spoke to a group of school children in London, and Joy went to hear him. It was not the sort of event that would have been advertised in the newspapers, so Lewis no doubt invited her.[96] On November 17, she returned to visit Veronica Ruffer in Oxford for three days so that she could hear Jack speak on Richard Hooker, a prominent Elizabethan theologian.[97] The lecture was sponsored by the new group Lewis was engaged with, the Fellowship of Saint Alban and Saint Sergius. The lecture was planned for the Senior Common Room of Christ Church, but so many people came that they had to move to a larger lecture hall. Joy wrote to Bill that before Lewis spoke, he looked about the room anxiously until he saw Joy, then he gave her "a delightful sunburst of a smile, and sat down content."[98]

After writing about Lewis's lecture, Joy turned to why she thought she had struggled so in her relationship with Bill. She said that her father had never been satisfied with her, regardless of how well she did in school. Her failure to satisfy her father transferred to her sense of failure at being a good wife for Bill. This sense of failure only turned on her sense of rage against the one who asked more than she could deliver. A vicious circle of expectation, failure, resentment, blame, and more failed expectations ensued. It was a sad letter.[99] Bill continued to write regularly, but Joy felt that something was missing. Though he was friendly, his letters were not affectionate.[100]

Joy made a fourth trip to Oxford for lunch in early December 1952. On December 9, Lewis wrote to Belle Allen:

> Talking of Americans, we have just had a 'pen friend' of long standing, from New York (state not city) stopping with us; she belongs to the small income group, and is delightful— a rolling stone, authoress, journalist, housewife and mother, and has been 'doing' England in a way which few Americans have done before. Last time I heard from her, she had been to a Cockney wedding in the East End of London, where the guests slept on the kitchen floor after the festivities! She comes back to us next week before sailing for America, and we look forward to hearing her experiences. She ran out of money a little while ago, but has apparently supported herself quite comfortably by giving treatment in 'dianetics' (whatever that may be).[101]

This brief paragraph tells a great deal. First, Joy spent her four months in England soaking up the local flavor of ordinary English life rather than on Lewis's doorstep. Second, her money ran out midway through her trip. Instead of the expected check from Bill to cover her continuing expenses, she received a letter from Renée saying there was no money left.[102] The financial situation explains in part why Joy overstayed her visit to the Kilns in December. She could not afford a hotel at the end of her time in England. Third, she took the initiative to earn some money through dianetics. Bill Gresham took up a variety of features of Zen, yoga, tarot cards, and dianetics as part of his general spiritual quest, of which Christianity was only a stop along the way. Joy credited the dianetics with helping to stabilize Bill for a while.[103]

Warnie did not meet Joy until she returned to Oxford in early December. He wrote in his diary about their first meeting in the winter of 1952. It was at another luncheon at Magdalen College. Lewis's letter to Belle Allen suggests that the occasion came at the end of term. It may have been another private luncheon arranged by Lewis, or perhaps a larger end-of-term luncheon to which guests were invited. In the midst of the party, Joy turned to Warnie in a company of several men and said, without any self-consciousness, "Is there anywhere in this monastic establishment where a lady can relieve herself?"[104] Warnie did not immediately warm to Joy, but initial reticence quickly turned to affection when he found that she liked walking with the Lewis brothers, drinking beer with the Lewis brothers, and laughing with the Lewis brothers.

On December 15, Joy went to Oxford for the fifth time, this time to spend Christmas at the Kilns.[105] She gave a full account of her visit to Chad Walsh when she returned to New York. Whereas Lewis thought he had not accomplished any writing during the Christmas break, Joy reported that he worked on his book on prayer (which he never completed), corrected the proofs for his OHEL volume, worked on an edition of Spenser for an American publisher, and finished *The Last Battle*. They went walking a great deal, including one long walk over Shotover Hill to the village of Horspath, on the other side, and across country to Garsington before coming back by way of Wheatley, which probably involved a little over ten miles, depending on the route. The walk gave her blistered feet, and the return trip up and over Shotover Hill was almost too much for her. They attended a Christmas pantomime, complete with audience participation in the songs, to which Lewis gave himself wholeheartedly. They also visited all their favorite pubs: the Eastgate and the Eagle and Child in Oxford, and the Ampleforth in Headington, among many others. She acknowledged that she was an "Anglomaniac."[106]

The Affair

By the time she wrote to Walsh on January 25, 1953, Joy had decided that she would "transplant" to London, where she felt more at home than anywhere she had ever lived. The decision to relocate came as the result of something else that happened when she was at the Kilns. She received a letter from Bill Gresham explaining that he and Renée had been in love since August and that he had done all he could to expedite Joy's trip to England, which suggests that it suited him to have her out of the house. He did not see any point in her determination to make their marriage work. Whereas Joy wanted to be a writer, Renée only wanted to make her husband happy. Bill explained to Joy that she could never make a real housewife. He thought the best solution would be for her to find someone she loved to marry and for Renée and him to marry, so that they could all live near each other. He thought this would be best for the boys.[107] He gave an overview of his finances to explain why he had not sent her any money, and finished with a dianetic explanation of how bright her future looked: "If you feel lost, forsaken and unloved, Poogle, just try to remember that there are a vast horde of lock chains that remain to be scanned off your case, including your year-long engram of your illness with Jenine [Davidman's mother] lying always underfoot like a krait in the dust."[108] Lock chains and engrams were all part of Ron Hubbard's dianetics scheme.

The letter arrived at the Kilns in time for Joy to discuss the situation with Lewis. Joy told Walsh that Lewis had advised divorce and had reinforced this view in correspondence after she returned to New York.[109] She shifted her allegiance from Geneva to Canterbury in February, when she was confirmed in the Episcopal Church at the Cathedral of Saint John the Divine in New York City, leaving Bill to the Presbyterians.[110]

The Business of Moving

By November 1952, Ruth Pitter had decided to leave London and move to a cottage near Oxford.[111] It would be a complicated move, because it also involved her business partner, Kathleen O'Hara, with whom she had lived since the early 1920s. The day before Joy Gresham left the Kilns to return to the United States, Lewis wrote a letter to Pitter to thank her for her Christmas present and to say that it was "thrilling to hear" that she was "'closing in on' Oxford."[112] In her letter, she had made reference to the night skies at Christmas, and Lewis responded with an uncharacteristically almost romantic word: "It was beautiful, on two or three successive nights about the Holy Time, to see Venus and Jove blazing at one another, once with the Moon right between them: Majesty and Love linked by Virginity—what could be more appropriate?"[113]

Pitter loved the country and gardening, and she had tired of the hectic life of London. She had grown up in Essex and regularly returned to visit her mother at Oak Cottage. When her mother died in October 1941, she and her sister inherited the cottage.[114] It was a place of retreat and restoration for her during the war years and through the bleak years of austerity afterward, but it was a bit Spartan and isolated for Kathleen O'Hara's tastes. It would not do as a permanent home outside London.[115] A move would mean selling her childhood home, but in truth, it was not a comfortable house. O'Hara was not as much interested in location, location, location as in comfort, comfort, comfort.[116] Their lease on the London flat in Chelsea ran until 1954, so they had the leisure to find the ideal country cottage near Oxford, the Cecils, and Lewis.[117] She told Rachel Cecil that after the sale of Oak Cottage, she hoped to find something within ten or twelve miles of Oxford.[118]

The house hunting was well along by June 1953 when Pitter returned to Oxford for another weekend with the Cecils and Lewis. In May, Lewis had been effusive and exuberant in his praise for her latest volume of poems, *The Ermine: Poems 1942–1952*, a copy of which she had sent to him. He told her the collection was "an absolute corker," which was "as sweet as sin and as innocent as milk," and that he was "drunk" on her poetry.[119] Dissatisfied with the measure of his praise, Lewis wrote two days later to say that "the brightness does not fade" from her "exquisite collection."[120] She called her time in June with Lewis "spirit renewing," but the weekend brought other pleasures as well within the Cecils' bounty of literary friends, from Joyce Cary to John Betjeman (one of Lewis's earliest students, who annoyed him).[121]

Pitter finally found the appropriate house in late September. The Hawthorns at Long Crendon stood at the border between Oxfordshire and Buckinghamshire on two and a half acres with its own garden and orchard. Built in 1905, it was not the older house that Pitter had wanted, but it was well priced and in good condition. Aesthetically, she could only say, "It's not exactly ugly, only very plain, with a tiny classical feeling."[122] Along with the new house, Pitter also had a change in her relationship with Lewis. After seven years, he began to address her as Ruth instead of as Miss Pitter. When she wrote to give him the news that she had found a house, she also asked if they might finally go by Christian names, alluding to the seven years that Jacob worked for Laban before he finally gained Rachel. Lewis responded with a letter addressed to her as Ruth, explaining that he had been ready for a long time, but he was raised to believe that familiarity with a lady must come at the invitation of the lady. Clearly, any woman who expected to get close to Lewis would have to take deliberate action without flinching—he began addressing the unreserved Joy Gresham by her first name much sooner.[123] Pitter told David Cecil that she was finally on a first name basis with Lewis after seven years of acquaintance.[124]

Lest anyone think that Lewis's formality about the use of Pitter's first name was mere shyness or disinterest, he had a similar experience with Dorothy L. Sayers, whom he always addressed as Miss Sayers and who addressed him as Mr. Lewis. This situation had gone on for over a decade when Lewis's changing status caused Sayers to ask if she should then call him Professor Lewis. Lewis finally asked her to call him Jack, and added, parenthetically, "I believe such suggestions ought to come from the lady, but years and the lady doesn't move!"[125]

By January 1954, Pitter had moved into the Hawthorns and greeted the Cecils as early guests. Lewis wrote on January 4 to say that he would like to come for a visit, but he had a case of gout and hoped she could come to Oxford for lunch.[126] In fact, he may not have had gout at all. He explained to George and Moira Sayer four days later that he had minor surgery to remove a sebaceous cyst, so he could not visit them.[127] Lewis may have thought that gout sounded less indelicate a thing to say to a lady than sebaceous cyst. On February 1, Pitter journeyed the thirteen miles to Oxford to have lunch at the Eastgate Hotel with Lewis.[128] To get to Oxford, however, she had to change buses, which she said made the trip "a great undertaking."[129] Lewis knew her new home well and the journey there. The village of Long Crendon had fond associations for Lewis, because Barfield had lived there before abandoning his literary career to enter his father's law practice.[130]

Shortly after Pitter found her new house, Joy Gresham moved to London with her two sons. They had sailed the first week of November 1953 on the *Britannia* from New York to Liverpool. Douglas turned eight years old aboard ship on November 10.[131] David was nine and would turn ten on March 27, 1954.[132] Ten months had passed since Joy left England to return home to New

York and the ruins of her family. She told Chad Walsh that Bill greeted her "by knocking [her] about a bit."[133] During the ensuing months, she wrote a series of letters to console and to counsel her cousin Renée, who went to Florida after a few months to file for divorce.[134] Joy kept Renée abreast of Bill's vacillations between wanting a divorce and wanting to stay with Joy. Lewis advised Joy to seek a divorce, and she had decided that the time had come, but she confided to Walsh that they could not afford the expense of a divorce with their precarious finances.[135] Even at his young age, David told his mother that it was time for a divorce, for "there is a point at which patience stops being a virtue."[136]

By July, Joy had signed the divorce papers with her lawyer.[137] Bill had moved out of their house, but then he broke up with Renée, who was distraught. Joy had refused his offer of reconciliation, saying that he was six months too late.[138] Joy told Renée that the divorce would proceed more easily if she would write a letter "specifically admitting adultery," but she need only sign her first name. Meanwhile, Bill took a job with a traveling carnival and was able to send Joy a check for fifty dollars at the end of July, but this was a hundred dollars behind what he had agreed to pay for the family's support.[139] At the beginning of August, Joy told Walsh that Lewis had written to her and advised her to disregard her own feelings and do what was best for her sons.[140] She was determined to put an ocean between Bill and her and the boys. She delayed her plans to sail, however, until November to allow Bill a chance to see the boys again before they left for England. During his time away with the Hamid Circus, he had written *Monster Midway*, based on his experiences of circus life, but he had not seen the boys in months.[141]

Joy wrote to Bill from their temporary lodgings at Avoca House Private Hotel, near Phyllis Haring at Belsize Park in London.[142] Joy found two furnished rooms with a grand piano for thirty-six dollars a week, but she needed something cheaper for the long term. She could not depend upon a steady allowance from Bill.[143] The biggest expense facing her involved the schooling for the boys. She estimated that a good school would cost thirty-five guineas, or four hundred dollars, a year. In her next letter to Bill, she said that she was inclined to put the boys in Dane Court at sixty-one guineas, almost twice what she had earlier estimated.[144] This school had the advantage of the enthusiastic approval of her new friend P. L. Travers, who wrote *Mary Poppins*. Her concerns in choosing a school reflected an idea already suggested, that her love of all things English preceded her love of Lewis. She wrote to Bill:

> What I want most for the boys is the coherent view of life which makes England tick—the tradition we recognized, for instance, in Burke's conservatism. I believe a great deal of the mental disturbance in America, and certainly much of the aimlessness and restlessness, comes from a lack of it. You and I had no stability to give the boys and they were beginning to suffer from its absence; but Dane Court people have it, all right.[145]

Lewis invited Joy and her boys to stay with him and Warnie at the Kilns for the weekend of December 17–20, 1953. He mentioned the visit of the boys in five letters to various correspondents in the following days. He said that the boys were very nice, but their table manners were not as good as those of English boys their age, which he estimated first at eight and six and a half, then nine and a half and eight, and finally nine and seven.[146] Lewis had been around young girls during World War II, when refugee children stayed with him, but he did not realize how much more strenuous young boys can be, especially American boys. He said the experience was like surf bathing, which may be pleasant but also leaves a person breathless and aching.[147] He found them completely exhausting, and he planned to escape to Malvern for a rest with the Sayers to get over the "domestic upsidedownedness."[148] To Ruth Pitter he mentioned that the mother of the boys was Mrs. Gresham, who wrote poetry as Joy Davidman. He asked Pitter if she knew Davidman's poetry. If either lady had romantic designs on Lewis at this point, it is evident that he was oblivious.[149]

By 1953, Lewis saw himself as an old man. He frequently described himself that way to his correspondents.[150] He no longer had the energy he once enjoyed. In the year since he had taken Joy on a ten-mile walk at Christmas, he found that a four-mile walk with the boys tested his limits.[151] He had a number of health complaints that slowed him down and taxed his energy, such as his rheumatism, which he regularly mentioned by way of apology more than complaint.[152] He said it was not bad, but it always made him feel as though he had just walked twenty miles on a hard road.[153] By the end of 1954, he amended his statement to say that after only fifty yards, he felt like he had walked twenty-five miles.[154] In general, Lewis did not feel good during 1953. He had his usual bouts with the flu, but he also had a severe case of sinusitis for over a month that was so painful, it affected his ability to concentrate.[155] It hampered his ability to do anything, and he found himself sleeping late and going to bed early. It even affected his sense of smell, which would have lessened his enjoyment of food.

Though sixteen years older than Joy Gresham, Lewis probably did not seem an old man to her. Her account of the Christmas weekend at the Kilns that she sent to Bill Gresham had an entirely different flavor. While the walks seemed strenuous to her, she saw Lewis as energetic as a schoolboy, "charging ahead with the boys through all the thorniest, muddiest, steepest places."[156] By comparison, Joy felt old. Nonetheless, she told Bill, "I shouldn't dream of visiting Jack often—we're much too exhausting an experience for that quiet bachelor household; but a little of it's probably good for them, judging by their reactions."[157]

Adjusting to Life in England

Joy and her boys were in a state of perpetual financial crisis in London. Breakfast and dinner were included in the cost of their rooms at the hotel, but for lunch, they ate peanut butter sand-

184

wiches. Dane Court School required the boys to wear a prescribed set of clothes, but Joy saved on clothes by not buying overcoats for the boys in hopes that the winter would not be too severe.[158] Joy found companionship with a literary set in London, and she made the effort to expand her literary circle. She hoped to earn money as a freelance writer, and she had always associated with writers in the United States. She saw Arthur Clarke regularly at a pub that catered to writers.[159] Aware of Jack's love of science fiction, she asked Clarke to send Lewis a copy of *Childhood's End*, which Jack greatly enjoyed. She wrote about this exchange to Bill, but she appeared to be unaware that Clarke and Lewis had already corresponded and that Clarke had earlier invited Lewis to speak to his science-fiction group in London.[160] Clarke asked Lewis if his publisher could quote from Lewis's letter to Joy in its publicity about *Childhood's End*, to which Jack agreed.[161]

Meanwhile, Joy could not manage to bring a story together. She struggled with a "Britannia story," which grew from a short story to a novella, but could never quite come to a satisfactory conclusion. *Collier's* magazine turned it down as a serial, and it disappeared as a part of Joy's active work.[162] Warnie suggested that she collaborate with him on a book about Françoise d'Aubigné, Marquise de Maintenon (aka Madame de Maintenon), the secret wife of King Louis XIV. Joy began work on it, but it also failed to come together.[163] By the beginning of April 1954, she had written a twenty-five-thousand-word novelette and three short stories, none of which sold to magazines or publishers.[164] She pinned her financial hopes on Bill's success with the book he was writing about Houdini, but he had only sent three hundred dollars for the support of his children during the first three months of 1954.[165]

Joy and the boys did not return to Oxford until Easter break in April 1954. She told Bill that the vacation in Oxford helped them get through the month financially by saving a week of expenses.[166] Jack and Warnie took them all to their beloved Whipsnade Zoo to see the lions, bears, wolves, and a rhinoceros. Along with Humphrey Havard, they also went to Studley Priory, a hotel in the remains of a medieval monastery near Oxford, which would become the new favored dining spot over the next few years.[167] From Joy's perspective, it had been an idyllic week. In writing to George and Moira Sayer, however, Lewis said that the visit was "bad luck," since it would mean canceling his planned trip to Malvern.[168] Still, Lewis asked if they might want to drive to Oxford and meet for lunch while Mrs. Gresham was in town. He said, "She's a queer fish and I'm not at all sure that she is either yours or Moira's cup of tea (she is, at any rate, *not* a Bore)."[169] It appears that Lewis had forgotten that George Sayer had met Joy and had lunch with her a year earlier.

Immediately after the week in Oxford, Joy had two teeth extracted—the first two of six that would have to come out. It had not gone well. The dentist had trouble pulling the teeth. Though she was numb to the pain in the dentist's office, the injections wore off as she was having tea with the novelist Angela Thirkell following a meeting of the Royal Literary Society to which Jack had arranged an invitation.[170] Joy had wanted to meet Thirkell, who presided at the meeting, but quickly left when the pain began. She needed codeine to survive the night. The extractions came with dry sockets and infections, low blood pressure followed by high blood pressure, and sinus pain. To make matters worse, she was having thyroid trouble.[171]

Probably during Joy's week with Lewis in April, he became aware of her strained financial circumstances and offered her the largesse of his Agapony Fund, as he had done with so many others. She did not accept at first, but used the offer as leverage with Bill to shame him into meeting his familial obligations rather than leaving it to "another man's charity."[172] She gladly accepted Jack's offer to write a preface for the London edition of *Smoke on the Mountain*, which would be published in the fall of 1954.[173] Meanwhile, Bill and Joy came to an agreement about a divorce. She acceded to a divorce as long as he agreed in writing to pay sixty

Studley Priory, 1950s

dollars a week for the support of the boys and to grant her sole custody, while Bill could have unlimited visitation privileges.[174] Bill may have once seemed a romantic figure as a writer, but that had all grown cold, and Joy pointed out to him that all the science-fiction writers she knew had jobs to support their families while they wrote on weekends.[175] She was as intellectual and literary as ever, but she also had her feet on the ground, and the boys came first. The divorce was finalized on August 5, 1954, in Florida, where Bill married Renée the same day.[176]

And Ruth Pitter

The friendship between Lewis and Ruth Pitter had by no means diminished. They continued to write and visit. Lewis mentioned to her his visit to Whipsnade Zoo with some children.[177] Between 1953 and 1955, George Sayer regularly drove Lewis to Long Crendon to see Pitter.[178] Sayer was not the only person who drove Jack to Long Crendon. On June 12, 1954, Lewis and Warnie went with David and Rachel Cecil to lunch at the Hawthorns with Ruth and Kathleen. Pitter bested Lewis in a discussion of *The Lion, the Witch and the Wardrobe*. After confirming that it was always winter and that the witch allowed no commerce beyond Narnia, Pitter asked where Mrs. Beaver got the oranges for marmalade, the potatoes, the suet and flour to make the rolls, and the hops for Mr. Beaver's beer. After Lewis suggested a more thorough literary critical study of the text, Warnie remarked, "Nonsense, Jack; you're stumped and you know it."[179] Beyond being a major poet, Pitter was witty, well informed, intelligent, and capable of keen critical insight. Lewis enjoyed her company.

August at the Kilns

Without any money, Joy lamented her inability to provide David and Douglas with a vacation trip during the long summer vacation of 1954. At this point, Lewis stepped forward and offered them the use of the Kilns for the month of August while he went to Ireland for his much-anticipated annual visit with Arthur Greeves. She gladly accepted and took up residence during August 4–31.[180] Lewis did not plan to leave for Ireland until the 6th.[181] He visited with Joy and her sons on the 5th as he made final preparations for his holiday. When the 6th came, however, Warnie was back in a nursing home owing to one of his bouts with alcohol, and Jack had to postpone his trip until later in the month.[182] Upon hearing the news of Bill's wedding, Joy wrote to him that she drank a pint of cider to their happiness at the Eagle and Child, and Jack "drank to the repentance and forgiveness of all sinners."[183]

During this month-long stay at the Kilns, Joy met Tolkien for the first time. It was not a planned meeting. Joy and Jack stopped by the Eastgate Hotel, where they came upon Tolkien and a former pupil whom Jack had examined. Tolkien had just come from the dentist and did not have his false teeth, and Joy thought this made him feel embarrassed in addition to what she took for a natural shyness. The next day, they chanced upon him again in the High Street. Joy wrote to Bill that Tolkien came running after them crying, "Now you can see what I look like with my teeth."[184]

In addition to the Eagle and Child and the Eastgate Hotel, Jack took Joy once again to Studley Priory, where they had tea with clotted cream and gooseberry jam. The boys got to play with the Studley dalmatian puppies, the hamsters, and a badger.[185] The entertainment continued as Lewis took them all punting on the Cherwell before heading off to Ireland with Warnie on August 16.[186] Behind in Oxford, Lewis allowed Joy the use of his rooms at Magdalen to work on her book about Madame de Maintenon, the same courtesy he had extended to Charles Williams fifteen years earlier.[187] Warnie kept all his books on the history of France during the reign of Louis XIV in the small study in Jack's rooms at Magdalen, where he did his own writing.[188]

Joy could not afford the tuition and board fees for David and Douglas at the beginning of the fall term. As usual, Bill was short on funds, and they had trouble sorting out the lawyers' fees following the divorce. By October, however, the money had arrived along with Joy's parents, who had come for a visit on their way to Israel.[189] During the Davidmans' stay in London, Lewis came to London on October 27 to take part in a debate, along with Dorothy L. Sayers. Before the meeting, Joy took Lewis to tea with her parents and with Phyllis Haring and Sel at the Piccadilly Hotel. Joy wrote to Bill that Jack had succeeded admirably at being charming to her parents in spite of her parents. Her father lectured Lewis on the "blessings of Prohibition," which led Joy to tell of how as a child she had poured her father's brandy down the drain after hearing him extol the virtues of Prohibition, for which he "walloped" her. When her father explained that his was a special case, Lewis had taken all he could without breaking silence. He remarked: "I think there was more than one prig in the family. Of course, our *own* case is always different, isn't it?"[190] Joy's mother, who had "a mania about her own beauty," was decked out in a "fancy black suit with rhinestone buttons, a pearl bracelet, a pearl choker, dingle-dangle pearl earrings, a pink lace blouse and a shocking pink hat." In a private moment, Joy complimented Lewis on how well he was doing with her parents, to which he replied, "I'm doing my best!"[191]

Having survived tea with her parents, Lewis invited Joy to bring them to Oxford for lunch at Magdalen College on November 3, 1954.[192] After they had a full tour of all the grand and historic sites of Oxford, Lewis asked Mrs. Davidman what had impressed her the most, to which she replied, "The Market!"[193] This small luncheon would be one of the last times Lewis would entertain guests at Magdalen College, for his life was changing.

6

Journey to Cambridge

1954–1955

While Lewis desperately worked at completing the editing and bibliography for his OHEL volume, in faraway Cambridge on January 18, 1954, the Council of the Senate of Cambridge University recommended the establishment of a "Professorship of Medieval and Renaissance English" to be held by someone who took a literary approach instead of a philological approach. The chair seemed designed for Lewis. It came with a salary of 1,950 pounds, which was more than triple the six hundred pounds Lewis received at Magdalen for his fellowship. The recommendation was approved on March 31, and applications were received until April 30.[1]

In establishing the professorship, the university also determined a process for its election. Sir Henry Willink, master of Magdalene College and vice-chancellor of Cambridge University, presided over the electoral committee, which had six other members—four from Cambridge and two from Oxford. Tolkien and F. P. Wilson, Lewis's former tutor, were the Oxford electors. One of the Cambridge electors was E. M. W. Tillyard, with whom Lewis had debated "the personal heresy."[2] Other electors included Basil Willey, who had offered a series of lectures at Cambridge titled "Christianity, Past and Present."[3] The other Cambridge members were Henry Stanley Bennett and David Knowles.[4] It was a committee friendly and sympathetic to Lewis. They would have been predisposed to view Lewis's application for the position favorably, but Lewis did not apply. This, however, did not deter the committee from doing what they wanted to do. They elected him unanimously without benefit of application.

Willink wrote to Lewis on May 11, 1954, to inform him of his election and to stress that the establishment of a new chair meant that the person to first hold the chair was of critical importance.[5] Lewis replied the next day, expressing his deep appreciation for the great honor and turned them down. He told Willink that his domestic situation was such that he could not leave Oxford. He had also encouraged someone else to apply for the position. Besides, he thought he was too old to accept a professorship.[6]

With a clear refusal from Lewis, the committee looked to a second choice. Before notifying the second choice, however, Willink wrote to Lewis again on May 14 to give him a second chance at acceptance. Lewis refused again, but this time he made his reasons more concrete. He had a brother who was not "always in perfect psychological health" and a handyman who had been with him for years.[7] He feared that his brother would not do well in moving to Cambridge, and the move would deprive his handyman of a living.

The situation must have been maddening to Tolkien. Though their friendship had ebbed in recent years, they still had a strong bond. Tolkien had done his best for Lewis to obtain a professorship at Oxford without success, but to have one in hand and throw it away was beyond belief. By 1954, the old regular Monday morning meetings must have lapsed, or Tolkien would have known Lewis's feelings about the Cambridge professorship. On May 17, Tolkien approached Lewis personally and convinced him that he could take the professorship at Cambridge, where he would have rooms in college, and continue to maintain his home at the Kilns, where handyman Fred Paxford could keep an eye on Warnie.[8] The next day, Tolkien wrote to Willink with the news that Lewis would accept the position if he could have suitable rooms in college where he could live during the week in term, allowing him to be at home with his brother on the weekends.[9]

Unfortunately, by the time Tolkien had closed negotiations with Lewis, Willink had already written to the second choice with the offer on May 16.[10] Rarely will anyone turn down a professorship at Oxford or Cambridge, but the thought that two people might turn down the same professorship is beyond reason. Without knowing what had transpired, Lewis wrote to Willink on May 19 to confirm his desire to accept the professorship if Tolkien's understanding of the situation was accurate. Rooms in college with an expectation of only four days a week residence during terms would make everything work. Besides, Lewis explained that he had been living and sleeping on trains for years, so the commute would not be a burden.[11] Willink must have read the letter with embarrassment, distress, and disbelief, for it had come too late for him to do anything about it.

Willink wrote to Lewis on May 24 to explain the situation. The offer had gone to "Choice No. 2," but a reply had not yet been received. As for residence, Willink explained that a professor could not be habitually absent from Cambridge for more than two nights a week during term, but outside of term, professors could go wherever they liked for as long as they liked.[12] Lewis must have felt terribly let down at this point. He wrote to Willink on May 26 that unless "No. 2" had as tricky a domestic situation as he had, *he* could not possibly turn down the offer.[13]

In her memoir of Lewis for the British Academy in 1966, Helen Gardner noted that when Lewis first declined the professorship

offered to him by Cambridge, the committee offered it to someone else. In elaborating, she explained, "Fortunately, the 'second
string' declined, partly on account of having heard that Lewis
was changing his mind, for it was obvious that this ought to be
Lewis's chair."[14] What she modestly neglected to mention was that
she was the "second string" who gave up the rare opportunity to
have a professorship in order that it might go to Lewis. The only
way Gardner could have known that Lewis had changed his mind
would have been for Tolkien to have told her. Ever the "Lord of
the Strings," Tolkien would not have hesitated to have such a conversation. It was a remarkably noble gesture on Gardner's part.
In due course, she obtained the Merton Chair at Oxford in 1966
and the next year was made a Dame Commander of the Order of
the British Empire.

On June 3, Willink wrote to Lewis to inform him that "No. 2"
had declined the chair and that it was his. He hoped Lewis would
accept it this time. When Lewis Carroll wrote *Alice in Wonder-
land*, he satirized English society in the nineteenth century, including Oxford, where he taught mathematics. Lewis's election
as Professor of Medieval and Renaissance Literature has echoes
of Alice. Until then, Willink corresponded with Lewis as chair of
the committee. He then told Lewis that he must now write to the
vice-chancellor of Cambridge University to indicate his acceptance
of the chair. He would also have to write to a head of college to
find a place of residence and membership. Willink advised Lewis
to write to the master of Magdalene College for a place. Faithful
to his instructions, Lewis wrote to Sir Henry Willink, the vice-
chancellor of Cambridge, to accept the chair, and he wrote another
letter to Sir Henry Willink, the master of Magdalene College, to
request rooms in his college. To the vice-chancellor, he begged
permission to delay his move from October 1954 to January 1955
in order to fulfill his responsibilities to Oxford and to allow his
college sufficient time to find his replacement.[15] To the master of
Magdalene College, he wrote with apologies for his impertinence

in requesting a place, but he would never have done it without the suggestion from the vice-chancellor, with whom the master was "intimately acquainted."[16]

The Inaugural Lecture

Warren Lewis did not always go to hear his brother's important lectures. He had spent his time strolling the streets and searching out the pubs of Newcastle during the war when Jack gave his "Abolition of Man" lectures. For the inaugural lecture at Cambridge, however, Warnie was present and proud. When someone commences a major professorship, that person traditionally delivers a lecture to set the tone for his or her tenure. Lewis delivered his inaugural lecture in the Mill Lane Lecture Hall on the evening of Monday, November 29, 1954.[17] It was his fifty-sixth birthday. According to Warnie, he spoke to a crowded house. G. M. Trevelyan, noted medieval and Renaissance historian and master of Trinity College, presided at the lecture. Trevelyan had issued the invitation for Lewis to deliver the Clark Lectures at Cambridge during the war, and Lewis had stayed with him in the master's lodge. In introducing Lewis, he remarked that Lewis's election was the only one in his experience that had come by a unanimous vote.[18]

Dorothy L. Sayers could not attend the inaugural lecture, but she sent her young friend Barbara Reynolds to hear Lewis and report back to her.[19] Sayers was pleased to hear that Lewis had a "good house" for his introduction to Cambridge. From Sayers's response to Reynolds's letter, Lewis appeared not to have had a manuscript. His personality came through as he engaged with his audience. Lewis *did* have a manuscript, which he published and later recorded for the BBC.[20] Nonetheless, he had learned the art of delivery without, as Sayers noted, "mumbling secretively into a typescript."[21] She was glad that Lewis had not tried any of his "naughty and provocative . . . capers" of the sort she had witnessed at the Socratic Club or when she had shared the stage with him in a debate. He was on his best behavior, probably because he had something of grave importance to discuss.

Taking up a theme he had explored in *The Abolition of Man*, Lewis discussed the way in which Western culture had changed and what the impact of this change might mean. With *The Allegory of Love* and *A Preface to Paradise Lost*, Lewis had sketched how culture had changed from classical Greece to Hellenistic Rome to Christianized Rome to the early medieval period to the High Middle Ages to the modern world. He understood change and continuity. He grasped the forces at work in cultural change. As might be expected from Lewis, he gave his lecture a Latin title: "*De Descriptione Temporum*," which might be rendered into English as "A Description of Time." He had long argued that the rigid way of describing the Renaissance as a sudden break with the past was simply incorrect. In fact, all of the great divisions of time lacked clear landmarks to set them apart. Change takes place over a period of many centuries, with one exception. He argued that a change between the period of Jane Austen and when he was speaking in 1954 was unlike any other change in culture throughout world history. He noted a recent symposium on T. S. Eliot's poem "A Cooking Egg" in which seven leading scholars could not agree on what the poem means. He noted the un-Christianizing of the West, which had accelerated since Austen's time. He noted the way in which politics had become "the organization of mass excitement," or what *Punch* called "Govertisement." Finally, he noted that with the success of the machine, the culture had moved to viewing what is new as good and what is old as bad. The result was that education has shifted from the development of character to the acquisition of technical skill and the assimilation of data.[22]

In his inaugural lecture, Lewis painted a picture of a world in which people had lost the ability to make value judgments because of the disappearance of values. Since his days at Great Bookham, when his awareness of right and wrong had begun to make him suspect that W. T. Kirkpatrick might not have an accurate view of the universe, Lewis had grown convinced that the existence of right and wrong is a clue to the meaning of the universe. In a world in which literary scholars could not understand the meaning of a short poem, Lewis envisioned a world in which a great nation of over three hundred million people might not be able to discern news from fake news and in which truth would become a casualty of technological progress. In his conclusion, Lewis reverted to type, as Sayers feared he might, and made a clever remark that has become the one idea people tend to remember from this lecture. He suggested that he was a relic of old Western man and a dinosaur in an age of technology. He advised his audience to "use your specimens while you can. There are not going to be many more dinosaurs."[23]

Joy Gresham had taken the train from London to Cambridge to hear Lewis speak. She wrote to Bill that she had "lurked modestly in the crowd" and did not go near Lewis, who was surrounded by caps and gowns.[24] She said the university had made "as much fuss" as the coronation a few years before, and she mentioned the dinosaur remark by Lewis. After recounting the lecture to Chad Walsh, she added, "How that man loves being in a minority, even a lost-cause minority!"[25] After the lecture, she slipped away without speaking to Lewis. It was a rainy November night, and Mill Lane is a narrow byway or alley that runs between Granta Place along the River Cam and the point at which King's Parade becomes Triumphing Street. It is not a place where taxis cruise in search of a fare. When she left the lecture hall, however, Joy found a taxi waiting. She jumped in and told the driver to take her to the train station. When she got to the station, the driver said, "Glad I found you, didn't know who I was to meet!" She had stolen someone's cab on a bleak, cold, rainy night when another taxi would not likely venture down Mill Lane. Then it occurred to her that Lewis usually had a taxi waiting for him when he finished a lecture away from Oxford so that he could quickly make his getaway.[26]

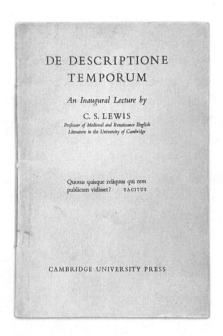

Cover of *De Descriptione Temporum*. Cambridge
University Press, 1955.

When Cambridge University Press printed Lewis's inaugural
lecture, he asked that copies be sent to several people in addition to the libraries of Magdalen and Magdalene. He sent copies to only three of the Inklings: Hugo Dyson, whom he listed
first; Ronald Tolkien; and John Wain. He also asked for copies
for two other friends: Owen Barfield and George Sayer. Then
he requested one for perhaps the most unlikely of people, T. D.
Weldon—the philosopher at Magdalen who had caused Lewis so
much distress—perhaps to say, "Top that." Finally, he asked that
a copy be sent to Mrs. Gresham at 14 Belsize Park in London.[27]
Over the next few months, he would ask that more copies be sent
to friends, including Sister Penelope, but they were not among his
first thoughts.[28] On the other hand, Lewis also requested three
copies for himself, and then an additional three copies.[29] We do
not know to whom he gave these three copies personally. We may

J. R. R. Tolkien and Hugo Dyson, 1954

speculate that Ruth Pitter, Dorothy L. Sayers, and Arthur Greeves received copies from Lewis with a note, but it is only speculation. Whether he gave Sayers her copy or not, she was "delighted" with it when she read the address.[30] What we do know is that he had six copies, which he probably gave to six people.

Not all of the thousands of letters Lewis wrote to strangers deserve mention, but the day after he delivered his inaugural lecture, he wrote to a young American serviceman from North Carolina who had read Lewis's works and taken great spiritual help from them.[31] Lewis would continue to correspond with the young man after he completed his military service, studied at the Virginia Theological Seminary, taught English at a private school, and pursued graduate study in English literature at the University of North Carolina in Chapel Hill. Ten years later, the young man called on Lewis in Oxford and became his secretary for the summer. His name was Walter Hooper, and he would spend the rest of his life editing Lewis's works, diary, and letters, and doing all he could to keep Lewis's works in print. He died in Oxford as this chapter was being written. Without him, this chapter and the three volumes of this biography would not exist. He was a dear and generous man who made himself available to one and all who were interested in Lewis. He was a mentor to scores and a blessing to millions.

The Move to Cambridge

At the end of Michaelmas term, on December 9, 1954, members of the English faculty of Oxford University gave an informal dinner in Lewis's honor to say goodbye to a colleague and friend of many years. Warnie noted in his diary who attended: Ronald and Chris Tolkien, Hugo Dyson, Lord David Cecil, Nevill Coghill, Jaw Bennett, and Humphrey Havard, all of whom had been part of the Inklings. Four others attended: John Bryson of Balliol College; Irvine Browning, who was one of Lewis's students; Frank Percy Wilson, who was Lewis's old tutor; and one young man whom Warnie did not know. The dinner won accolades of praise from Warnie, who enjoyed in particular the turtle soup, which he had never tasted before, and the wine, which he had. Coghill, who was Lewis's oldest friend in the English faculty, regaled the group with anecdotes, which also earned Warnie's commendation. It was a good send-off for a man who hated formal dinners and sentimentality but loved being with his friends.[32]

Lewis wrote to Edward Allen that he would "take up" his new chair at Cambridge on January 12, 1955, by which he meant that the term would begin and he would have work to do.[33] He took up residence in his new rooms at Magdalene College on January 7.[34] Before doing so, however, he had the arduous task of moving out of the rooms he had occupied at Magdalen College, Oxford, for thirty years. Joy Gresham volunteered to help with the move and brought the boys to the Kilns with her to spend the week beginning on December 30.[35] Lewis hired Pickford's moving firm to pack and transport his books, beginning on January 1, 1955.[36] Joy did not actually do any of the packing and moving, but Lewis needed someone to oversee the Oxford end of the move while he met the movers in Cambridge, where he spent much of the holiday involved in a fellowship examination.[37] When Jack was at the Kilns, Joy said he "went around muttering, 'Oh, what a fool I am! I had a good home and I left!'"[38] The lament appears to be a quotation from Mole in *The Wind in the Willows*, set on the River Cherwell upstream from Magdalen College, where Lewis had long loved to swim and punt.

Despite the trauma of moving for a man who did not like change, Lewis liked Cambridge. He wrote to Jill Freud that it was "fun" because it had such a "country-town feeling."[39] He had three large rooms and a private bath in the fifteenth-century first court above the parlor and old library on staircase three.[40] By the beginning of February, Joy had already been to Cambridge to help Jack buy a hearthrug, but mainly to walk, talk, eat, and drink. Her financial situation looked as bleak as ever, so Lewis hired her to type the manuscript for his spiritual autobiography, which he had finally finished at the end of 1954 after eight or so years of thought.[41] It would be published as *Surprised by Joy* in 1956. By this time, Jack had found that Warnie could no longer be relied upon for consistent service as a typist, and Warnie was also working on his own books about the age of Louis XIV.[42] Joy had finished the typing of the manuscript by April, when Lewis mailed it to Mr. Jocelyn Gibb, his new editor at Geoffrey Bles.[43]

One of Lewis's biggest concerns about the move to Cambridge had been Warnie. Though Jack would teach in Cambridge, he would spend the rest of his life, until his last illness, shuttling back and forth between Oxford and Cambridge on trains, taxis, and the automobiles of friends. The move meant a reorganization of the schedule of the Inklings, who had been meeting on Tuesday mornings for drinks and conversation at the Eagle and Child since the early days of World War II. Monday mornings had long been reserved for Tolkien, though those meetings had grown less frequent. With the move to Cambridge, the meetings with Tolkien came to an end, and the Inklings mornings moved to Mondays. On Monday afternoons, Lewis left Oxford by train at 2:34. He arrived back in Oxford on Saturdays at quarter past one.[44] The train with direct service to Cambridge from Oxford was known as the Cantab Crawler, because it took three hours to make the trip, stopping at every crossroad. Lewis explained to Edward Allen that he loved it because it was so slow that few people took it, and he could usually have the whole compartment to himself. He would read and even say his prayers.[45]

For Lewis's first and last journeys at the beginning and ending of term, however, Clifford Morris drove him between Oxford and Cambridge. Morris had a car-hire business in Oxford and had driven Lewis locally for several years before the move to Cambridge. At the start and end of term, Lewis had too much baggage, books, and papers to carry on the train. Normally, unless driven by Roger Lancelyn Green, George Sayer, or Humphrey Havard directly from their noon gatherings, Lewis rode with Morris to the train station on Mondays, and he met him again on Saturdays for the return. Morris continued to be Lewis's driver around Oxford until Jack's death in 1963.[46]

Lewis gave lectures on Tuesdays and Fridays at noon.[47] The rest of his week in Cambridge was relatively free except for the odd meeting from time to time. He had no undergraduate tutorials for five hours every day, as he had had in Oxford. He had free time to read and write. He told Derek Brewer that for the first time in his life he could ask himself when he woke in the morning what he would like to do.[48]

One of the shortcomings of this biography is its failure to convey the extent of the continuous expressions of Lewis's remarkable sense of humor, which reflected his sheer joy of life, even in difficult circumstances. An example occurred with the move from Magdalen College to Magdalene College. One cannot help but notice the irony—same name, different spelling, same pronunciation. Lewis enjoyed saying that he had left the Impenitent for the Penitent.[49] In the Gospels, Mary Magdalen was among those who went to the tomb on Easter morning. Jesus had freed her from demon possession, and tradition identified her with the woman who had a shady past who anointed Jesus with costly perfume (Luke 7:36–38; 8:1–2; John 20:1–2, 11–18). Lewis had not been happy at the Impenitent, which he referred to as the "leftist, atheist, cynical, hard-boiled, huge Magdalen."[50] Unlike the Impenitent, where he experienced much "opposition," Lewis found the Penitent Magdalene "much more congenial socially & spiritually."[51] Emrys Jones, a former pupil of Lewis, succeeded him at Impenitent Magdalen in 1955. Jones told me that upon his election, Lewis sent him a note with the warning, "Magdalen S[enior] C[ommon] R[oom] is a dangerous place."[52] Jones said that for Lewis, it was a place of spiritual warfare.

Richard Ladborough, university lecturer in French, became one of Lewis's closest friends at Magdalene. Ladborough wrote that when Lewis first arrived there, the fellows were a bit apprehensive of this person they suspected of being "very Oxford."[53] The rivalry between the two universities goes back centuries and continues to be reinforced. Lewis told Ladborough the old story that an Oxford don on a Cambridge street feels as though he were wearing patent leather shoes, but a Cambridge don on an Oxford street feels he is wearing big boots. Lewis explained that a Cambridge man is regarded in Oxford as rude and unsophisticated, but an Oxford man is always elegant, witty, clever, and sleek. As a result, Cambridge fears Oxford, and Oxford despises Cambridge. The punch line, of course, is that Lewis would have been wearing his trademark big, clodhopper shoes and shapeless tweed jacket at the time.[54] The members of the Combination Room of Magdalene College had no idea what to do with a professor who ate at high table in a tweed jacket!

With the move from Magdalen to Magdalene, Lewis also needed to learn a new vocabulary. What was the Senior Common Room in Oxford was the Combination Room in Cambridge. What was a quad in Oxford was a court in Cambridge. It has often been said the Americans and the English are divided by a common language. The same could be said of Oxford and Cambridge.

Soon, however, Lewis's warmth and good humor put everyone at their ease with him. He continued to dominate the conversation, but Ladborough and the rest began to realize that Lewis was a shy man who happened to know a great deal. Ladborough came around to accepting Jack when he received a note from him saying: "Dear Dick, May I call you that? Yours, Jack."[55] Though he held a prestigious university professorship, which placed him at an exalted rank in the academic world, as the most recent arrival at Magdalene, Lewis was the most junior fellow in seniority. The Magdalene Combination Room had a tradition that the most junior fellow would serve the port after dinner to all the other fellows. The other fellows tried to relieve Lewis of the ancient task, no doubt originally intended to teach young fellows their place, but he insisted upon pouring the drinks for all until he was replaced by a new man.[56] R. M. Dias, another colleague, reported that once the task was passed to a new junior fellow, Lewis always insisted that his glass be filled to the absolute brim. He then took delight in bringing it to his lips without spilling a drop.[57]

John Walsh, a historian at Magdalene, said that conversation with Lewis was part ordeal, part delight, and always education. He seemed unconsciously to pay his friends the compliment of assuming they had all read what he had read. Walsh said that he always felt that he was on the wrong side in a Socratic dialogue whenever he debated Lewis.[58] Simon Barrington-Ward, the young chaplain of Magdalene, concurred with Walsh and observed that conversation with Lewis was part ordeal and part formative education.[59] Before long, the other fellows realized that Lewis was not playing a game of one-upmanship or showing off. He simply knew a lot without being a know-it-all. In fact, he soon came to be regarded as an asset. One night, Ronald Hyam came into the Combination Room in a state of distress, for he had to deliver a lecture the next day for which he was not yet prepared. He hopelessly asked Lewis if he knew anything about race relations in the eighteenth century. Lewis reflected and then asked if Hyam had read Captain Cook's *Journals*. Of course, he had not. Lewis then proceeded to explain to Hyam all about race relations in the eighteenth century.[60]

The kindness and generosity of Lewis became widely known among the fellows when he helped John Stevens, another young fellow, in his efforts to learn Anglo-Saxon. Stevens would eventually hold Lewis's chair, but that was in the distant future. It may or may not have been generally known that Lewis was jealous of his time and disliked interruptions in his routine. Yet Lewis devoted two hours in the evenings each week for two years to teaching Stevens the delights of Anglo-Saxon. Of course, Lewis had his reward—friendly conversation with someone who loved the literature he loved, and someone with whom to share a bottle of wine.[61]

Magdalene the Penitent had a small number of fellows compared with Magdalen the Impenitent. After dinner in the hall, the fellows gathered in the Combination Room for their port and to talk, presumably in that order. In the winter, they formed their chairs in a semicircle around the great fireplace, and in the warm weather months, they shaped their chairs in a semicircle around the large window that overlooked the court. Though Lewis easily dominated the conversation with his vast knowledge and encyclopedic memory, the tone and topic of conversation was set by Francis Turner, the small but formidable senior fellow. Turner held the chair at the center of the semicircle. Lewis once remarked to a junior fellow, "Every common room needs a bully, but an amiable bully, such as Francis, who will do us good and keep us all in order."[62]

The fellows of the Combination Room at Magdalene provided Lewis with the kind of college experience he had never really known at the Impenitent Magdalen. He enjoyed friendship in their company. When he left Oxford, he wrote to Mary Van Deusen that he had loved his "own little circle" but that he also had "many other intersecting and adjacent circles."[63] The Combination Room at Magdalene would become a new circle, or semicircle, for Lewis, but it would never be a writing group like the Inklings had been until the late 1940s. Richard Ladborough remarked that Lewis never talked about what he was writing. His colleagues never knew what he had been working on until a new book came out.[64] For some years, he had to look for writing support beyond his academic circles from such people as Roger Lancelyn Green, Ruth Pitter, and Joy Davidman.

Lewis began his day early. He attended morning prayer in chapel every weekday at eight o'clock.[65] When Simon Barrington-Ward gave me a tour of Magdalene College in 2004, he showed me where Lewis sat every morning. Facing the altar, Lewis always occupied one of the massive, carved oak chairs to the left against the back wall. Following chapel, he ate a solitary breakfast in his rooms, which was a departure from eating breakfast in hall at Magdalen, Oxford.[66] Someone he described as a "little old man . . . who is exactly like Mime" from Wagner's *Siegfried* brought him his breakfast each morning.[67] Lewis also knew Milne, the aged butler who attended the fellows in the Combination Room.[68] Ladborough discovered that Lewis got on well with the college servants, who respected and admired him as a person without realizing that he was, in Ladborough's words, "a great man."[69] They called him a *real* gentleman, for he seemed to care about them. This manner of his reflects his greatness. He was not great because of the books he wrote; he wrote the kind of books he wrote because he was great.

In the afternoons, Lewis liked to take walks through the countryside around Cambridge. England is crisscrossed with public access walks that have cut across the fields, woods, and farms since medieval times. Those who take advantage of them are known as "ramblers," and maps have long been published that identify the location of the public paths for ramblers. Lewis bought a map and soon found the footpaths of Cambridgeshire. According to Richard Ladborough, he preferred to walk alone, which was a departure from his lifelong practice of finding friends who enjoyed walking, like Arthur Greeves, Leo Baker, Owen Barfield, and Warnie. From time to time, however, he invited others to walk with him. Ladborough walked with Lewis occasionally and noted how much Lewis preferred the beauty of nature to any human artifacts. Sometimes, Ladborough drove Lewis to a remote location to start a walk.[70]

It is possible that Lewis's lifelong habit of walking with friends had not changed, but his shyness and reluctance to put himself forward may have prevented him from asking more people to accompany him. He does not appear to have found the same kind of walking friends he had known. He told George Watson—one of his former pupils, who took up a post at St John's College, Cambridge, a few years after Lewis—where he could find the best country walks, but Watson never went with him.[71] Simon Barrington-Ward, however, told a different story from that of Ladborough or Watson. Barrington-Ward frequently walked with Lewis. Perhaps they had more in common as pedestrians. Not all walking companions are created equal, for Lewis enjoyed walks with Barfield but not with Tolkien. They had different rhythms.

On one of the rare occasions when Lewis went walking in the morning, Barrington-Ward recalled that Lewis quickened his pace as they drew near to the college at lunchtime. When Barrington-Ward asked why he had suddenly begun to hurry, Lewis replied, "Francis doesn't like us being late." "You don't mean to say *you're* a bit afraid of Francis too?" Barrington-Ward exclaimed. "Of course I am," he said. "Francis is one of the grown-ups."[72] Lewis then explained his view that some people have a grown-up status that others never acquire. Lewis did not consider himself one of the grown-ups.

On another walk, Barrington-Ward came to grasp the nature of Lewis's awareness of the "moral and spiritual framework . . . [that] held all his teaching and his critical writing together." Barrington-Ward had complained of the dullness of the Cambridge countryside, that vast, flat tableland punctuated by the occasional bog. He related how Lewis gravely contradicted him:

> "You should never condemn any genuine countryside in that way," he said almost severely to me. "In every landscape you should try to feel for its real nature and quality and let it grasp hold of you. The day is coming when, beyond this life, we shall recognize that quality in the eternal fulfillment in which it will have its true place."[73]

On another walk along the river when a flight of swans landed on the water, Barrington-Ward quoted Walter de la Mare's lines, "Look thy last on all things lovely, every hour." Lewis quickly disagreed with the sentiments of the poem and insisted, "No. No. It should certainly *not* be, 'Look thy last . . . ,' but 'Look thy *first* on all things lovely.' Every sight and sound that is good, every touch of beauty or rightness, is pointing ahead to its ultimate fulfillment in the world to come."[74]

Barrington-Ward had not yet read "The Weight of Glory" or the final chapter of *The Last Battle* when he had these walks with Lewis. On reflection almost fifty years later, however, then bishop Barrington-Ward understood that Lewis was expressing the sense of anticipation that Lewis called "eschatological Platonism," whereby all of creation is connected to that new creation to which it points.[75] Lewis ended *Surprised by Joy*, which was published shortly after his move to Cambridge, with this same observation. God has placed signposts all along the way, even in the deep woods where someone might be lost. The signposts set us on the right path: "But we shall not stop and stare, or not much;

not on this road, though their pillars are of silver and their lettering of gold. 'We would be at Jerusalem.'"[76]

Lewis quickly made the Pickerel, just opposite Magdalene College, his favorite pub in Cambridge. He regularly invited George Watson to join him there for a pint of draught Guinness. Watson later regretted that he had never gone, simply because he did not care for stout. Lewis had always assured Watson that Guinness was "a very good drink," but Watson was never won over. He said that Lewis stopped by the Pickerel to fortify himself because the dinners were so late at Magdalene College.[77] John Lawlor, on the other hand, did meet Lewis for drinks at the Pickerel. On one occasion, Lawlor was shocked to see Lewis impeccably dressed in a suit, and Lewis ordered a dry Martini instead of his usual (one might say "monotonous," since Lewis was fond of monotony) Guinness. Lawlor could only conclude on reflection sometime later that Joy Gresham probably had some momentary influence on him.[78]

Everyone agreed with Watson's assessment that Lewis's rooms, which should have been among the most charming in Cambridge, were "spartan and uninteresting."[79] Ladborough said that his rooms were only a "laboratory for his work and his writings."[80] The rooms with their windows overlooking the court were paneled and had the expected antique appearance of five-hundred-year-old rooms. The exquisite architectural beauty, mingled with the rich history of the buildings of Oxford and Cambridge, seemed to have no effect on Lewis, who appeared to Ladborough "to be oblivious of his immediate surroundings."[81] George Sayer described the Cambridge rooms as "depressingly bare and uncomfortable."[82] The room had book cases, two tables, and three or four hard chairs, but it had no armchair or sofa. Moira Sayer offered to lend Lewis a comfortable chair, but he declined the offer. While his friends who described his rooms in their memoirs tended to emphasize the stoicism and Lewis's disregard of creature comforts, another dynamic may have been involved. Lewis hated interruptions when he was writing. He mentioned this peeve a number of times. A comfortable armchair and sofa would only have invited people to drop by and chat. A hard, straight chair would not.

While Lewis must have been delighted to find that his Cambridge rooms included a private bath, Watson took note that the "ancient battered bathtub" stood in the middle of a small hallway."[83] In *Surprised by Joy*, Lewis remarked that his boyhood home contained nothing of beauty. The same could be said of Lewis's rooms in Oxford and Cambridge. Watson noted that the Cambridge sitting room had a cheap print of Michelangelo's creation of Adam from the Sistine Chapel. The cheap print would have stood out for Watson, who had sophisticated tastes in art. When I visited George Watson's rooms in St John's College forty-five years later, I found the walls covered with his collection of fine Dutch and Flemish paintings of the sixteenth and seventeenth century. In Lewis's rooms in Oxford, along with the "huge floral-patterned Chesterfield" and the "cliffs" of books was a reproduction of Botticelli's *Mars and Venus*, which he had seen at the National Gallery in 1922.[84]

Lewis had begun the practice of giving luncheons in college when he first grew acquainted with Ruth Pitter, and he found that such parties were a good way to maintain and grow friendships. Once settled in Cambridge, he began the practice of inviting friends, both old and new, to Magdalene for large luncheons and dinner parties.[85] On June 8, 1955, he gave a dinner party to which he invited Valerie Pitt, who had served as secretary of the Socratic Club a few years earlier, where the men would be wearing dinner jackets, ruling out his usual tweed.[86]

Though he spent the greater part of each week in Cambridge, he still tried to maintain his friendships in Oxford and his other special relationships. As a parting gesture, Magdalen College conferred upon Lewis the dignity of honorary fellow and the privilege of dining in hall with access to the Senior Common Room. Lewis regularly invited George Sayer to drive over to Oxford from Malvern and meet him in the smoking room at Magdalen before joining the Inklings at the Eagle and Child, known to all as the "Bird and Baby," and then driving him to Cambridge.[87] Sometimes, he invited Roger Lancelyn Green.[88] John Lawlor drove him once. When Lawlor stopped for lunch, an outrageously comic episode ensued in which Lewis, who always struggled with money and numbers, attempted to calculate who owed whom what for their share of the meal after deducting what Lewis thought must be the cost for the gasoline. Lawlor was surprised that Lewis, known for his generosity and munificent philanthropy, should struggle so over the bill for the meal at a wayside pub.[89]

An Adversary

Not everyone greeted Lewis warmly in Cambridge. Some were not happy about his arrival. The very idea of creating the chair for Lewis arose because of the belief that someone needed to offer an alternative to the direction that literary criticism had taken at Cambridge. I. A. Richards had dominated the School of English at Cambridge until 1939, when he left for Harvard. Lewis had taken strong exception to him. By the time Lewis arrived in Cambridge, no single figure dominated, but George Watson, who came to teach in Cambridge shortly after Lewis, maintained that F. R. Leavis held the preeminent place among all the "heresies" to literature in Cambridge at the time.[90] Lewis and Leavis had a history that went back to an article Lewis wrote in 1940, "Christianity and Culture." In that article, he criticized *Scrutiny*, a literary journal edited by Leavis from 1932 until its demise in 1953. Through *Scrutiny*, Leavis advocated, as an extension of the thought of Richards, the view of "a necessary relationship between the quality of the individual's response to art and his general fitness for humane living."[91] Leavis and this school of thought, which continued to develop after Richards left Cambridge, found in culture an alternative to God and salvation, from Lewis's point of view.

Though Lewis had believed that culture was good for its own sake and for the good of humans before his conversion, he objected to the glorification of culture soon after his conversion. He began to belittle culture until he realized that he spent most of his life involved in culture. This realization had prompted the writing of *The Pilgrim's Regress*. He recognized that culture, "though not in itself meritorious, was innocent and pleasant, might be a vocation for some, was helpful in bringing certain souls to Christ, and could be pursued to the glory of God."[92] Lewis could not accept a new morality and a new virtue based on cultural taste and artistic sensitivity cut loose from the divine source of right and wrong that he expounded in his broadcast talks. Leavis advocated a new moral order based on the writers whom the great critics like Leavis judged to be great.[93] In the concluding chapter of *A Preface to Paradise Lost* in 1942, Lewis had addressed Leavis by name and declared that while he and Leavis could see the same things in *Paradise Lost*, "he sees and hates the very same that I see and love." Lewis continued, "Hence the disagreement between us tends to escape from the realm of literary criticism. We differ not about the nature of Milton's poetry, but about the nature of man, or even the nature of joy itself."[94] Now Lewis found himself within the same English faculty as Leavis, at a university where Leavis had his own cult following.

In a letter to Christopher Derrick, who became a prominent author and journalist in later years, Lewis wrote in 1956 that he should read *The Lord of the Rings* instead of Lewis's OHEL volume, because it was "the book we have all been waiting for."[95] Lewis said that it shows "that there are thousands left in Israel who have not bowed the knee to Leavis."[96] When Basil Willey asked Lewis if he might consider becoming chairman of the Faculty Board of English, he answered with a definite no, but he suggested that if Leavis were chosen, he would finally become the object of criticism instead of the critic, and it might cure him.[97] When *Delta*, the Cambridge University literary magazine, published the unflattering article "Professor C. S. Lewis and the English Faculty," Lewis was invited to respond in a subsequent issue. Among his observations about undergraduate efforts at criticism, Lewis said, "It is not difficult, least of all when you are angry, to write as harshly as Dr. Leavis."[98] In this vein, Lewis described Leavis's literary criticism to George Watson as "yahoo howls."[99]

Derek Brewer, who survived the Leavis era at Cambridge to become master of Emmanuel College, explained that Leavis did not have a theory of criticism so much as a pronounced prejudice. Leavis advocated a canon of the acceptable authors, those to be admired and read. He also had his list of the vile and despicable writers to be repudiated and avoided. The first list of admired authors began with D. H. Lawrence. The despised authors included Spenser, Milton, Swift, and even T. S. Eliot after he became a Christian! Good writers were those who reflected the values of Leavis and bad writers were those who did not.[100] To say "reflected" does not quite capture the passion of Leavis. He wanted propaganda for his values.

When Charles Percy Snow delivered the Rede Lecture in Cambridge in 1959, "The Two Cultures and the Scientific Revolution," he argued that ignorance of science by those in the humanities was as barbaric as ignorance of the humanities by those in the sciences. Leavis exploded at this contradiction of his view and issued a rebuttal in *Two Cultures? The Significance of C. P. Snow* (1962), in which he defended his view that culture is what the great artists say about life.[101] Lewis was delighted. He told Nathan Starr that Leavis had built a pillory for Snow but put himself in it. Tongue in cheek, Lewis attributed Leavis's criticism to bad digestion.[102] In contrast to Leavis and his huge following at the universities and the major publishing houses, Lewis presented to J. B. Priestly in succinct form his vision for literary criticism: "My hope was that it would be primarily a historical study that wd. lift people out of (so to speak) their chronological provincialism by plunging them into the thought and feeling of ages other than their own: for the arts are the best

Time Machine we have."[103] The year before Lewis died, when John Lawlor told Lewis that he and others were planning a *Festschrift* in honor of his coming retirement in 1966, Lewis discouraged Lawlor from planning a dinner, because by then he could eat very little. Instead, he suggested "the head of F. R. Leavis in a charger."[104] A month before his death, however, Lewis sensed that the tide was beginning to turn as a younger generation grew tired of Leavis.[105]

John Wain, who had little in common with Lewis's literary preferences, regarded Leavis as a great man, but one, he said, who "is not for me."[106] His greatness involved his power within the literary world, but it was not a greatness of which Wain approved. He called Leavis "an absolutist, an all-or-nothing man."[107] Leavis decreed which books were great and which were bad, and Wain did not consider the whole approach as education. Wain thought that the Leavis approach, which dominated British education for a while, had undermined education. In describing the results of a Leavis education, Wain remarked, "I have met bigots enough in my lifetime, but never, not even in political or religious circles, have I met any so rigid, hidebound, blinkered and thoroughly shut-in as the typical Leavisite, the man on whom the master's teaching has thoroughly 'taken'."[108]

Despite the scathing bite of Lewis's comments in private correspondence, which he never expected the world to read, George Watson emphasized in his memoir of Lewis that he and Leavis "were always courteous to each other, and in a manner so elaborate that when they sat on committees one was reminded of the formality of a tea party before the First World War."[109] Watson added that this kind of formal courtesy in those days was a mark of distance. While Leavis viewed himself as the future and Lewis as the past, sixty years later, Leavis is all but forgotten and Lewis is not.[110]

The Lectures

Though Lewis had been the grand lecturer in Oxford who attracted hundreds of undergraduates to his lectures in the vast expanses of the upper rooms in the Examination Schools building, Brewer recalled that he attracted only a comparative handful to his lectures in Cambridge.[111] Lewis wrote to Nan Dunbar that it had been thirty years since he had lectured to such a small audience.[112] He confided to John Lawlor, another former pupil, that his Cambridge lectures were a flop, but that it was probably good for him.[113] Lewis regularly gave his two most famous sets of lectures: "Prolegomena to Medieval Literature" and "Prolegomena to Renaissance Literature." He eventually prepared these for publication as *The Discarded Image*, which did not appear until the year after his death. In Michaelmas term of 1955, he delivered "Some Major Texts: Latin and Continental Vernacular."[114] These were not, however, the only lectures he gave; or perhaps it would be better to say that *The Discarded Image* is not the only book that came from lectures he gave. In 1959 he sent to the Cambridge University Press his manuscript for *Studies in Words*, published the next year, based on his Cambridge lectures of Easter term 1956, titled "Some Difficult Words."[115]

Studies in Words

With *Studies in Words*, Lewis made an important contribution to his discipline, but he also demonstrated how his critical mind worked in a consistent universe in which all the parts interconnect. In the 1990s, his approach would be termed "the integration of faith and learning." He did not invoke God or insert devotional illustrations from the Bible, which tended to be as far as the integration of faith and learning went at Christian colleges when it was still in vogue. Instead, he showed how to think as a Christian in a universe made coherent by its Creator. With *Studies in Words*, Lewis answered the claims and method of linguistic analysis that had taken him off guard in his famous encounter with Elizabeth Anscombe. Anscombe was a disciple of Ludwig Wittgenstein, who had taught at Cambridge. In *Studies in Words*, Lewis provided a contrasting vision of how language works without actually debating the metaphysical assumptions that some people attach to linguistic analysis.

At first glance, the book may have the appearance of something thrown together without any connection between chapters. A lack of structure had been his criticism of *The Great Divorce*, in which the chapters might have come in any order once the day trippers arrived in heaven. *Studies in Words* devotes a chapter to each of seven words, together with an introductory chapter and a concluding chapter. From an apologetic point of view, the genius lies in the subtext. At the end of World War II, Lewis had expressed the view to a group of youth ministers that the best apologetics is not little Christian books, but little books on a variety of subjects by Christians with their Christianity latent in the text.[116] In that talk, later published as "Christian Apologetics," Lewis also devoted attention to the importance of understanding that people use words in ways that may be quite different from how they are used within the Christian faith. This idea represented the point Anscombe had made in her critique of *Miracles*.

For his seven words, Lewis chose *nature*, *sad*, *wit*, *free*, *sense*, *simple*, and *conscience/conscious*. By beginning with nature, he turned to his decades-long battle over the confusion of science with a particular philosophy of science that excluded the possibility of anything beyond the physical world of sensory experience. With the words he chose, he could examine the presuppositions built up within his culture over centuries through the changing meaning of words. The words he examined had particular significance in his apologetics during the 1940s, especially *The Abolition of Man*, *Miracles*, and *Mere Christianity*. J. A. W. Bennett, while praising this book for how Lewis brought a "logical and philosophical" dimension to the study of language and literature, pointed out that he had explored the terms *physis*, *natura*, and *kind* not only here, but "throughout his works."[117] *Studies in Words* is not, however, a popular book. Lewis intended it for college students interested in language. Since his encounter with the English textbook that led to his thoughts in *The Abolition of Man*, he came to see that English students who were untutored in philosophy were susceptible to philosophical ideas being slipped past them when they thought they were studying English. He worked on the book for several years, often slowed by his own health issues, and finally published it in 1960.

Tolkien did not care for *Studies in Words*. In a letter to his son Christopher, Tolkien excoriated Lewis and the book: "Alas! His ponderous silliness is becoming a fixed manner. I am deeply relieved to find I am not mentioned."[118] Tolkien had taken offense that Lewis had used only nine lines of "a long analysis of the semantics and formal history of *BHŪ with special reference to φυσις."[119] The offense came because Lewis felt that Tolkien did not have evidence to support his assertions about *physis* (which came into Latin as *natura*, the two words that provide the basis for *physics* and *nature*). Tolkien condescendingly remarked of Lewis, "He remains at best and worst an Oxford 'classical' don—when dealing with words."[120] Tolkien did not have a high opinion of the classical education Lewis had pursued in his undergraduate days.

For his part, Lewis had his own reservations about Tolkien's method and what he lost of literature with his emphasis on the morphology of language. In *The Discarded Image* Lewis remarked, "Those who ignore the relation of English to Anglo-Saxon as a 'merely philological fact' irrelevant to the literature betray a shocking insensibility to the very mode in which literature exists."[121] Tolkien was interested in how the spelling and pronunciation of words changed over time, but Lewis was interested in the stories and the worlds in which the stories arose.

The Faerie Queene

Lewis also gave lectures on Edmund Spenser. When Lewis arrived in Cambridge, he had been reading *The Faerie Queene* for forty years. He fell in love with it while reading it for pleasure in his bedroom at the end of the day in W. T. Kirkpatrick's house. His treatment of it formed the culmination of *The Allegory of Love*, the book that established his reputation as a major literary scholar. Lewis called *The Faerie Queene* the most difficult poem in English, yet he could summarize the plot of its narrative in one simple sentence: "St George defeats error, falls into pride, is dominated by despair, purged by penance, and raised by contemplation, and finally defeats the devil."[122] It was the great story that he loved, the story of the journey there and back again in which the knight is forever changed.

With the plot of the narrative, the simplicity ends. The modern reader will miss most of the poem for ignorance of how people in Spenser's world thought and expressed ideas. Lewis argued that the poem involved a "pageant," by which he meant a progression of allegorical figures in allegorical dress. The modern reader may know that during the Middle Ages, Christendom developed a sophisticated iconography or way of representing important people and ideas.[123] For instance, the apostle Peter was always shown with keys, which represented the keys to heaven. John the Baptist was always presented in animal skin. In *The Faerie Queene*, Spenser presented a succession of characters in his poem as the story unfolds, but each character in its setting also tells a symbolic story that would still have been common knowledge to the Protestant Elizabethan audience of the 1590s, even as the allegory of Spenser was quickly dying in the face of the realism of William Shakespeare.

In his series of lectures on Spenser, Lewis took up the discussion of *The Faerie Queene* from *The Allegory of Love* and carried it much further. Part of his discussion explains the cheap print of Botticelli's painting of Mars and Venus that hung in his rooms in Oxford. By the time of Spenser, Homer's view of Mars and Venus, the god of war and the goddess of love, had changed into allegories of immaterial qualities: "the victory of beauty over strength and peace over war, perhaps; or concord's resolution of discord."[124] Lewis continued, "And this is what it meant also to Botticelli, in whose picture of *Mars and Venus* the profound sleep of Mars and the waking tranquility of Venus powerfully present 'the lineaments of gratified desire': not their desire only but desire itself, the desire of all creation."[125] Thus, we have a clue as to why Lewis would hang this picture in his room. It connected him to the great story he loved. He mentioned the painting not only this once in his lectures. In a later lecture he said of Botticelli's scene: "It is by no means that of a sensual love-scene. The impression imparted is rather of a profoundly felt statement that the spirit of love can and should pacify strife."[126] Again, he returned to it in yet a later lecture: "Think, for example, of all the Renaissance pictures of Mars conquered by Venus, disarmed by Venus, bound by Venus."[127] Perhaps not surprisingly, the only way we know that Lewis had the picture on his wall in Magdalen is that Alastair Fowler, who edited Lewis's Spenser lectures, took note of it. Fowler published Lewis's edited lectures as *Spenser's Images of Life* in 1967.

In his lectures, we find another clue to what captivated Lewis. The first of the lectures dealt with the figure of Cupid, the son of Venus in the Roman version of Greek mythology. Lewis thought that Cupid and his mother were of central interest to Spenser in *The Faerie Queene*.[128] He had thought so for years, and this thought had fixed in him the desire to retell the myth of Cupid and Psyche. He had tried. In January 1917, he had mentioned Psyche to Arthur Greeves in a way that suggested he wanted to write his own version.[129] By May 1922, Lewis was attempting a poetic version of the Psyche myth, but it was proving too difficult in the meter he had chosen.[130] By November 1922, he was thinking about how to turn the story into a masque or play.[131] Through the 1930s and 1940s, he mentioned the Cupid and Psyche story from time to time in his letters, and always with a rich enthusiasm, as though he had just discovered it for the first time. Then, in 1955, he wrote to Katharine Farrer, a detective novelist and the wife of his friend Austin Farrer, that he had just returned to an idea he had worked on for twenty-five years—his own version of the story of

Cupid and Psyche. He declared to her that Apuleius, who had first written the story in antiquity, had "got it all wrong."[132]

Till We Have Faces

Joy Gresham finished typing the manuscript of *Surprised by Joy* in early March 1955. Rather than entrust the document to the Royal Mail, she decided to deliver it to Lewis in person in Cambridge. She had also finished the index for Warnie's book, and the publisher was so pleased with it that she said she would send Joy more indexing work at the rate of fifteen to twenty-five pounds per book. She had little money, and when Bill failed to provide the school fees for David and Douglas for the new term, the Agapony Fund stepped in. In Cambridge, she found Lewis in a state of distress over his writing, now that The Chronicles of Narnia and the OHEL volume were behind him. He had no ideas. Joy told Bill, "He's dried up."[133] Lewis had never suffered from writer's block before. His previous experience had been too many ideas. For some time, he feared that he had lost his edge, which contributed to his feelings of old age. He had written to Robert Walton at the BBC in 1951 that he had lost his "dialectic power."[134] At the same time that Joy was writing to Bill about Lewis, Jack was writing to Ruth Pitter from the Kilns that it had been a long time since he was able to write poetry. He ached a little over it and wanted so much to be "with poem" again.[135] He wrote to Carl F. H. Henry that he had decided not to write any more books that were "*directly* theological." Instead, following his idea of apologetics based on latent Christianity within books on any subject, he wanted to catch "the reader unawares—thro' fiction and symbol."[136] But what would he write?

In preparation for Easter 1955, Lewis reread Dorothy L. Sayers's *The Man Born to Be King* during Holy Week. Meanwhile, he encouraged Sayers to read Joy's new book, *Smoke on the Mountain*.[137] Also during the Easter vacation of 1955, Joy took Lewis in hand and recharged his imagination. The last week of March found Joy and the boys back at the Kilns, where they ate "at Jack's expense." Her account to Bill of the coming of the muse captures the way in which writer's block often breaks:

> One night he was lamenting that he couldn't get a good idea for a book. We kicked a few ideas around till one came to life. Then we had another whiskey each and bounced it back and forth between us. The next day, without further planning, he wrote the first chapter! I read it and made some criticisms (feels like old times); he did it over and went on with the next. What I'd give to have his energy![138]

Once back in Cambridge after his short vacation at the Kilns, Lewis wrote to Katharine Farrer to tell her the good news that he had found a story. Apparently, he had tried to work up a tale about a Phoenix, but it came to nothing. Without reference to Joy and the way inspiration finally came with talk over glasses of whiskey, Lewis described the new story to Farrer:

> I've given up the Phoenix story for the present, an old, 25 year old, idea having just started into imperative life. My version of Cupid & Psyche. Apuleius got it all wrong. The elder sister (I reduce her to one) couldn't *see* Psyche's palace when she visited her. She saw only rock & heather. When P. said she was giving her noble wine, the poor sister saw & tasted only spring water. Hence her dreadful problem: 'is P. mad or am I blind?' As you see, tho' I didn't start from that, it is the story of a very nice, affectionate agnostic whose dearest one suddenly 'gets religion', or even luke warm Christian whose dearest gets a Vocation. Never, I think, treated sympathetically by a Christian writer before. I do it all thro' the mouth of the elder sister.[139]

Lewis had set about to retell an ancient myth from a Christian point of view, the same way Tolkien had done with *The Lord of the Rings*. He finally had the right form. It would be not a poem but a novel. Lewis frequently remarked that his stories usually began with a picture in his mind, like the floating islands of *Perelandra* or the faun with an umbrella and packages in the snow of *The Lion, the Witch and the Wardrobe*.[140] *Till We Have Faces*, on the other hand, is one of his stories that began with an idea, like *The Screwtape Letters* and *The Great Divorce*. By the time Lewis wrote to Katharine Farrer, the story had developed a clear Christian theme, but it is important to note that Lewis had the idea of a retelling of the Cupid and Psyche myth from long before he became a Christian.

Lewis was particularly proud of what he had done with *Till We Have Faces*, because he thought he had accomplished something quite original. He explained to Mary Willis Shelburne:

> It is the story of Cupid & Psyche told by one of her sisters— so that I believe I've done what no mere male author has done before, talked thro' the mouth of, & lived in the mind of, an *ugly* woman for a whole book. All female readers so far have approved the feminine psychology of it: i.e. no masculine note intrudes.[141]

Whether he succeeded is not the main point. That he even tried to write from a female perspective represents a significant movement in Lewis's entire frame of reference. He had actually begun to think about women in a different way.

Once the words began to flow for Lewis, Joy decided to take him to her pub in London a few days later to meet with the circle of science-fiction writers who gathered there. He wrote to Alastair Fowler, with whom Lewis shared a love of science fiction and who had also tried his hand at it, that he had been taken to a London pub where science-fiction writers gathered every Thursday night. He said they were all very young and that it was "a merry party."[142] Perhaps Joy understood that Lewis missed the company of active writers talking about their work and the energy that such talk can provide to a writer. Since the Inklings had ceased to be a writing club, Lewis had not had that kind of company. On May 19, 1955, he wrote to Fowler again to thank him for the loan of a science-fiction book and to say that he was not reading anything unrelated to his lectures because he was so "occupied with my Cupid & Psyche story."[143] Lewis probably had finished his first draft by June 20, when he invited Katharine and Austin Farrer to join him for tea the following week. Lewis asked Katharine to give a critical reading of the new novel, which she completed and dropped off at the Kilns on July 8.[144] The Farrers would occupy an increasingly important place in Lewis's life until his death.

As spring passed to summer, Joy was desperately trying to make her own way writing. Hodder and Stoughton gave her a hundred pounds' advance on *The Seven Deadly Virtues*, a book she pitched to the publishers only thirty minutes after having the idea.[145] Macmillan and also Hodder and Stoughton rejected her manuscript about Madame de Maintenon, which she called *Queen Cinderella*.[146] She hoped to do some writing for the *Church Times*, probably through the efforts of Lewis, but she had to borrow money from her agent to survive.[147] She continued to beg Bill to get a job and send some money, but he never proved very reliable. Though she was only forty in 1955, she increasingly referred to herself as "an old woman."[148] She had one health complaint after another. None were serious, but they were enough to make her feel old.[149]

Joy visited Lewis at the Kilns during the first week of July. They went to the Trout at Godstow and then went swimming in the Thames amid a flock of geese and a swan. Joy wrote to Bill that it was the first time she ever tried swimming with a quart of beer "sloshing about in my inside."[150] She and Jack also went to the Eastgate Hotel bar to meet the poet Herbert Palmer, who had first encouraged the friendship between Lewis and Pitter. This time, Palmer wanted Lewis to meet Phoebe Hesketh, another poet, who would become a friend.[151] Such a literary gathering would have been a particular pleasure for Joy, who had once identified herself as a poet. The Eastgate continued to be Lewis's pub of first choice, where he would take people who were important to him. For a person who did not like change, Lewis found the Eastgate comfortable and full of good memories of early days in Oxford with his brother and Ronald Tolkien. In 1940, in a long letter to Warnie, who was in France awaiting the German invasion, Jack commented on "the charm of a *secret* restaurant—the charm which kept you and me and others faithful to the Eastgate long after its prices had become exorbitant and its food bad."[152]

A Summer Vacation

With the end of his first year at Cambridge, Lewis looked forward to his annual return to Ireland and a long visit with Arthur Greeves. It had not been a bad half-year for someone in fear of writer's block. He had finished *Surprised by Joy* and wrote *Till We Have Faces*. He planned to go to Ireland at the beginning of August and stay until the 20th, when he planned to sail for Liverpool.[153] Events at the beginning of August, however, forced him to change his plans. Writing to Dorothy L. Sayers on August 9, he stated in a postscript that he had loaned his house to Joy Gresham, who then found herself "in the unhappy position" of having him as her guest. The letter was typed. Lewis did not type. A postpostscript by Joy who had typed the letter added "I wouldn't precisely call it an unhappy position, would you?"[154]

Just before Joy's arrival with the boys at the Kilns in August, George Sayer had come to Oxford to overnight with Lewis. Lewis invited him to the "Bird and Baby" at noon, where he would find Lewis and a few others. That evening, they would dine at Magdalen. Lewis, who rarely did anything on the spur of the moment or without written notice, suggested that they drive out to Long Crendon to visit Ruth Pitter. She was not there that day, but Kathleen O'Hara, who met them in trousers, gave them the hospitality of the house. In reply to a letter from Pitter in which she apologized for missing him, Lewis assured her that he would try

Ruth Pitter, 1955. Photograph by Jane Bown, Camera Press London.

the experiment again. He and George Sayer would return, but it would be many years in the future. As they drove back to Oxford, Lewis confided to Sayer that if he were not a confirmed bachelor, he would like to marry Ruth Pitter. Sayer said, "It's not too late," but Lewis replied, "Oh yes it is. . . . I've burnt my bridges."[155]

The same day that Lewis wrote to Sayers, he also wrote to Vera Gebbert to mention that Warnie was away in Scotland.[156] He did not explain to Sayers why his trip to Ireland had been delayed, but it probably had to do with Warnie's sudden visit to Scotland. The brothers always planned the August excursions to Ireland together. They normally spent a week traveling together and then separated with Jack spending an extra fortnight with Arthur Greeves. Warnie's alcoholism had grown much worse over the previous two years. His binges regularly ended with a stay for a few days or more in Restholme or some other nursing home near Oxford that would still take him. In June 1955, Lewis told Cecil Harwood that "after a half year of debauches," Warnie had "agreed to go into a hygienic bastille at Dumfries."[157] The cure took six months, but Jack said that Warnie might be out in three months with good behavior. As soon as the clinic had a place for Warnie, Jack planned to take him immediately to Scotland. The chance probably came suddenly at the end of July, for Lewis wrote to Christian Hardie on July 31 that he had "been away for a few days."[158] Furthermore, when Lewis wrote to Arthur to explain the change of plans and the revised schedule, he added that Warnie would not be coming to Ireland at all that year.[159]

Warnie's sudden departure from the scene left Jack alone at the Kilns with Joy for a prolonged stay with her sons. It was a time of intense happenings. While she was at the Kilns on August 19, Joy wrote to Bill Gresham to say that she had decided to leave London and take a house in Headington, where she hoped to live more cheaply. Her stay at the Kilns ended on September 2, when she returned to London to pack up her things.[160] The same day, Lewis landed in Larne, Northern Ireland, on his way to visit Arthur Greeves.[161]

7

Jack and Joy

1955-1957

While she was staying with Lewis at the Kilns in August 1955, Joy found a two-story, semidetached brick house, what Americans would call a duplex, in Headington, not far from the Kilns. Located at 10 Old High Street, the house stood only a block from the main shopping district on the London Road.[1] The rent was fifteen dollars a week.[2] The small flat in London had cost thirty-six dollars a week. Lewis's plans had called for him to remain with Arthur Greeves from September 2 until the 20th, but he changed his plans and was back at the Kilns by the 14th, when Warnie was typing his correspondence.[3] Jack probably returned early to help Joy move into her new house. She and the boys had moved by September 17 when she wrote to Bill with all the details and to thank him for sending a check. They had ridden in the cab of the moving van to save money on train fare from London. It was a crowded cab with the three Greshams, their cat Sambo, two moving men, and one Australian customer.[4]

Lewis's relationship with Joy had rapidly developed during the month of August 1955 with Warnie away in Scotland. As soon as Warnie returned from drying out in Scotland after only a month, he immediately went on a two-week bender before landing in his usual nursing home. Lewis probably did not tell Warnie the extent of his thinking at this point. At least, Warnie's diary gives no indication of what was in the air. To Arthur Greeves, however, Lewis had floated an idea while they were together in Ireland. Lewis told Arthur that the Home Office was not prepared to renew Joy's permit to live in the United Kingdom. If she married a citizen, however, that citizenship would be extended to Joy.[5] Lewis suggested that it could all be done in a civil ceremony instead of a Christian wedding, and it would only be a formality. No one need know, and they would continue to live separately and have their own lives. It would only mean that Joy could enjoy citizenship and also work. Later, Lewis would give the same explanation to George Sayer.[6] As soon as Lewis returned from his vacation with Arthur, Geoffrey Bles released *Surprised by Joy* on September 19.[7]

Lewis had strong opinions about remarriage after divorce. Joy would have known how he felt from discussions arising from the news that Bill and Renée were having an affair. It would not have been necessary, however, for them to discuss other options, because Lewis had explained his view on civil marriage in his broadcast talks, which had just been republished in a combined edition as *Mere Christianity* in 1952. After expressing his dogmatic view that Christian marriage is for life and has no place for divorce, he acknowledged that the majority of the British people were not Christians. He did not think that Christians should impose their practices on people who did not share their faith, any more than he would want Muslims to impose their prohibition of alcohol on him. Under these circumstances, Lewis argued:

> There ought to be two distinct kinds of marriage: one governed by the State with rules enforced on all citizens, the other governed by the Church with rules enforced by her own members. The distinction ought to be quite sharp, so that a man

knows which couples are married in a Christian sense and which are not.[8]

This view horrified Tolkien when Lewis first expressed it during the war. Though he believed that God intended marriage universally as a permanent state between a man and a woman, Lewis allowed the state permission to establish marriage on other grounds.[9] The odder point, however, is not that Lewis would not impose his faith on unbelievers but that in 1955 he thought the Christian view need not apply to Christians who did not want to follow the Christian view of marriage.

Joy Gresham, who is often referred to by her maiden name, Davidman, remains a highly controversial figure among people who study and write about C. S. Lewis. Some regard her as an angel, and some as a devil. Some call her a "gold digger" who was only after Lewis's money, while others call her Lewis's savior.[10] We have the record of how Lewis felt about her, how she felt about him, and how others felt about her. We have anecdotes about her flashes of temper. We have anecdotes of her consideration. Speculating about motivations, however, is a tricky endeavor.

Lyle Dorsett appears to have endorsed the view that Joy "forced herself on Lewis, hounded him continually, and in essence became a nuisance."[11] To support this view, he pointed to the way she "pursued a relationship" with Lewis in the early months of her move to England in 1953. The problem with this view is that she had very little contact with Lewis when she first moved to London. They only gradually came to have more interaction over a three-year period, as we have seen. On the other hand, as her letters suggest, she had a strong attraction to Lewis. The intensity of this attraction is evident in the love sonnets she wrote to Lewis.[12] It is difficult to say, however, whether Lewis actually saw these sonnets when Joy first wrote them, if ever.

Following Alan Jacobs, Alister McGrath concluded that Lewis had become Joy's "sugar daddy," and that her interest in him was purely mercenary.[13] One of the problems with this view is that Joy did not approach Lewis about money at first, but appears only reluctantly to have accepted financial assistance from him at last. Throughout her years in England, she maintained a long, detailed, and regular correspondence with Bill Gresham, through which we know most of the information about her and the boys and their relationship with Lewis. Money was always a matter of discussion, and she elaborated financial issues in detail. Through these letters we know that Lewis eventually helped with school tuition for the boys through his Agapony Fund. According to Douglas Gresham, who was nine years old at the time, Lewis also paid the rent for number 10.[14] What comes through clearly is that she was a proud woman and a modern woman who believed in hard work.

We know that Lewis helped with the school fees because Joy mentioned this help in an effort to shame Bill into getting a job and supporting his sons.[15] After moving to Headington, she wrote to Bill expressing, on the one hand, that she appreciated his own financial difficulties but emphasizing, on the other: "I will *not* go to Jack with my hand outstretched! Once was enough. So come across, please!"[16] On December 13, 1955, she wrote to Bill that she had no idea where she would get the school fees for the next term, and then added, "Or rather I fear I know only too well; and I don't like it."[17] Rather than the schemes of a gold digger, Joy's discussions of help from Jack have the tone of embarrassed mortification. She frequently told Bill that she did not want to retain another lawyer to force Bill to support his children, but that the children came first.[18] The threat of legal action for child support always remained.

It is not odd, under the circumstances, that Joy made no mention of the plan to marry Jack in a civil service. Perhaps she thought that Bill would feel relieved of financial responsibility for his sons if he knew that Joy had married Lewis, regardless of Lewis's view that it would not be a real marriage. What is odd, however, is that Joy mentioned nothing to Bill about the Home Office refusing to renew her visa. McGrath has pointed out that it already had been renewed once before, through May 31, 1956.[19] It is odd that she never mentioned it to Bill when she told him about all her other personal matters. On December 3, 1956, she wrote to him from Wingfield Hospital to tell him that she and Jack had been married for several months and that it would soon be announced in the papers. She told him that they had a civil wedding and hoped to have a church wedding, but she mentioned nothing of the visa problems.[20]

The only reason we know the story of the visa problems with the Home Office is that Jack told Arthur Greeves, George Sayer, and a few others. Joy appears never to have mentioned it to anyone. Here we have the problem of the absence of primary sources. The absence of evidence leaves one to wonder if there ever was a visa problem at the Home Office. Might Joy have concocted the story to play on Jack's sympathies? Might Jack have concocted the story to provide a rationale for a marriage to Joy Gresham? By a strange coincidence, Bill Gresham's new wife, Renée, had a similar problem in the United States. She was born in Cuba and came to the United States as a child with her parents, but she had never become an American citizen. After her father's death in the spring of 1955, Renée had to fly to Cuba to begin the naturalization process.[21]

A few months later, Jack reported to Arthur that Joy would be deported when her visa expired. Yet C. S. Lewis was not without connections. He had friends in the highest places. Lord David Cecil's brother, the fifth Marquess of Salisbury, held the prestigious post of lord president of the council. Lewis himself was known to members of the conservative government, which had offered him a CBE only a few years earlier. No effort seems to have been made, however, to influence the decision of the Home Office. On the other hand, if Lewis had not been trying to use his influence to help Joy, then why would he have waited until the last minute before her visa was due to expire before taking the extreme measure of marriage?

Whether the Home Office actually put Joy on notice or Renée's situation suggested to Joy the precariousness of her own situation remains a matter of speculation. What the incident did bring to Joy's mind was that she could never become a permanent resident, much less a citizen, of the United Kingdom because, as she wrote to Renée, "You can't do that over here—they accept nobody except refugees for permanent residence."[22] Whatever the circumstances may have been, Jack and Joy married on April 23, 1956, a week before her visa would have expired, at the registry office in St Giles in Oxford.[23] Dr. Robert Havard and Rev. Dr. Austin Farrer stood with them as witnesses.[24]

Havard, now widowed by cancer, continued to be a close friend to Lewis whatever the fortunes of the Inklings. Austin Farrer, who served as chaplain of Trinity College and would soon become warden of Keble College, had become a better and better friend since the war years. Lewis asked him to speak several times at the Socratic Club. Farrer was a theological polymath who came to be recognized as one of the great English theologians of the twentieth century. He excelled not only at theology but also at New Testament interpretation, philosophy, and preaching. He also appears to have been good company. His wife, Katharine, known as Kay to her friends, had befriended Joy upon her arrival in Headington, presumably through introductions from Lewis. She was one of the women whom Jack asked to read the manuscript of *Till We Have Faces* for her opinion on how well he succeeded at writing from a female point of view.[25] She had literary interests that coincided with those of Lewis and Tolkien, for she was one of the few people whom Tolkien allowed to read the manuscripts of *The Silmarillion* and *The Lord of the Rings*.[26]

Friends and Relations

Kay Farrer asked Joy to type the manuscript of her detective novel *Gownsman's Gallows* for ten pounds, which Joy desperately needed.[27] Joy was not very flattering about Kay's skill as a detective novelist in a letter to Bill. Joy said that Kay wrote like an angel but that her plots reminded her of Bill's "contempt for the artificial whodunit with no knowledge of real crime and real police."[28] Kay's detective was an inspector from Scotland Yard, and Joy thought Scotland Yard should sue.

Some biographers have suggested that Lewis secretly supported Joy because, under the terms of her visa, she could not work. As we have seen, the law never stopped Joy from earning money. Lewis's fund helped supplement her income, but his support of her was no more "covert" than his support of dozens of other people.[29] Joy constantly sought ways to earn a few pounds doing typing, editorial work, and writing. If Joy were merely a gold digger, a smart lady like her would have stayed in New York, where she could have made some real money.

Warnie appears to have been skeptical of Jack's relationship with Joy when she first moved to Headington. Some years later he wrote in his diary that Jack was at Joy's house every day when she first moved to that suburb of Oxford.[30] This claim would have been one of Warnie's exaggerations, probably based on his sense of neglect when Jack spent time with Joy, combined with the merging of memories over the lapsed time. Jack could not have spent every day with Joy, because when she moved to Headington, Jack no longer lived in Headington. Though the Kilns remained his official address, Lewis spent only two nights a week at the Kilns. If Joy had wanted to "hound him continually," she would have done better to move to Cambridge. Of course, it probably felt to Warnie as though his brother spent every day with Joy. A key point about the move to Cambridge had been that Jack would be home with Warnie every weekend. Warnie found that he had to share those weekends with the American, about whom he had not yet made up his mind. Long after he made up his mind about Joy, however, he noted in his diary that the evening of March 16, 1960, had been the first time in three years, except for the fifteen-minute walks back from St Mary's twice a month, that Warnie had alone with Jack.[31]

Money was always an issue for Joy because her two sons were her greatest concern and preoccupation. While her sonnets to Lewis show that Joy had fallen in love with him and that she wanted him to be in love with her, her biggest concern to which she devoted her time and energy was her sons. She may have been determined to win Lewis's love, but she appears to have taken her time about it so as not to frighten him away. She went about setting up housekeeping at 10 Old High Street with its garden, which was producing cabbages, tomatoes, and runner beans from the labors of the previous tenants. She had plans to expand the garden as a major food source. It also had a plum tree and apple trees. No sooner had she moved in than she began canning her own plum jam.[32] A month after moving, she had added blackberry, apple, and mint to the jellies she had canned.[33] She may not have realized that Jack hated the making of jams. In her spare time, she learned how to play the recorder.[34] She also made the White Hart her pub of choice in Headington.[35] For church, she appears to have chosen St Andrew's, near her, rather than Holy Trinity Church in Headington Quarry, where the Lewis brothers attended.[36]

Joy did all she could to make ends meet with her meager, sporadic allowance from Bill and her small earnings. She burned old wood paving blocks (wood blocks impregnated with tar) instead of coal for a while.[37] She often ate a sparse diet, such as sprats, which she described as "little silver fish, sardine size, that you fry."[38] By February 1956, she wrote to Bill that she had learned to live on crumpets, tea, and fish paste, except when Jack took her out to eat.[39] In early December 1955, he took her to a luncheon at a country club where she dined on venison and burgundy and met Sir John Rothenstein, director of the Tate Gallery in London. Later that month, he gave another dinner party at Magdalen in her honor so that she could meet some people. She was grateful that she still had her "nine-year-old Hollywood evening dress."[40] Less formally, Joy and the boys had Christmas dinner at the Kilns. Jack provided the raw materials and Joy cooked the meal: turkey, plum pudding, mince pies, and all that would make a proper English Christmas dinner.[41] After Christmas, Jack, no lover of the movies, took them all to see the new rerelease of *The Wizard of Oz*.[42]

Colin and Christian Hardie attended a luncheon Jack gave to meet Joy, but it did not go well. Walter Hooper confided to Ruth Pitter what Christian Hardie had told him about the meeting. Christian was one of the women Jack asked to read the manuscript of *Till We Have Faces* for their critique of his attempt to write the story from the female perspective.[43] She thought that Jack hoped she would befriend Joy and help her find her way in Oxford. Instead, Christian disliked Joy so much that she could not bring herself to be kind to her at all. At this point in the conversation, Colin interrupted his wife and blurted out, "Jack should have married Ruth Pitter."[44] David and Rachel Cecil socialized with Jack in the 1940s and 1950s, but their closer friend was Ruth, who remained close to them until they died. It would have been difficult for them to accept Joy over Ruth, though Cecil spoke graciously of their love and marriage in his review of Humphrey Carpenter's *The Inklings*.[45] Cecil described Joy as intelligent and lively.

Lewis went with Joy when she lectured on Charles Williams at Pusey House in Oxford on February 26, 1956. Gervase Mathew may have had a hand in arranging the lecture. Joy went with Jack to Cambridge for a performance of *The Bacchae* in Greek about the same time.[46] Richard Ladborough recalled that Lewis enjoyed going to the college plays in Cambridge.[47]

Meanwhile, Lewis plodded on with his own affairs. During February, he traveled to Edinburgh, where he delivered an after-dinner talk for the annual dinner of the Walter Scott Club. He sat next to Sir John Garnett Banks, Lord Provost of Edinburgh, who reminded Lewis of Bailie Nicol Jarvie, a figure in Scott's *Rob Roy*.[48] Lewis included this address simply as "Sir Walter Scott" in *They Asked for a Paper* (1962). In this lecture, he explored (borrowing from Jane Austen) Scott's "Sense and Sensibility."[49] Perhaps not surprisingly, Lewis examined these two related words in *Studies in Words* (1960).⁵⁰ Perhaps even less surprisingly, he used the lecture as an opportunity to expose the failings of the modern literary criticism of Leavis and his ilk in their treatment of Scott. Lewis also paid tribute to G. M. Trevelyan, the master of Trinity who had introduced him at his inaugural lecture, who first brought to his attention the importance of Scott in creating what we now call historical fiction. The historian pointed out that Edward Gibbon's *History of the Decline and Fall of the Roman Empire* reads as though all the emperors were contemporaries of Gibbon. In Thomas Macauley's *History of England*, however, the figures are distinctly different from Macauley's time. Trevelyan attributed this difference in historiography to the fact that Scott had written between the other two.⁵¹ The reference demonstrates Lewis's memory for conversation, as well as his generosity in giving credit for ideas.

As for his sideline, Lewis had more books coming into print. *Till We Have Faces* went to the press at the end of February 1956, and The Bodley Head released *The Last Battle* on March 19, 1956.⁵² Originally, Geoffrey Bles planned to release the Narnia books at Christmas each year. When Bles retired from his firm at the end of 1954, Lewis contracted with Spencer Curtis Brown to represent him as his literary agent. Curtis Brown did well for Lewis financially, but this new approach to publishing resulted in Lewis signing with John Lane, The Bodley Head to publish his last two Narnia books. Jocelyn Gibb, who replaced Geoffrey Bles as head of the firm, was disappointed, to say the least, at losing the last two volumes of a popular series. Thus, The Bodley Head did not wait until Christmas to publish the last of the series, which had a ready market.⁵³ It has been suggested that Joy Gresham persuaded Lewis to sign with an agent with an eye toward eventually enriching herself.⁵⁴ The influence might have come from Joy, Ruth Pitter, or both. Though Joy had published only two novels and a volume of poetry, she was aware of the advantage of having a literary agent and was represented in New York by Brandt and

Brandt.[55] Ruth, on the other hand, was a client of Curtis Brown and seems the more likely source of Lewis's thinking about an agent.[56]

Joy began her life in Headington with minor health problems. Her first week at 10 Old High Street, she broke a tooth.[57] This mishap came on top of her teeth extractions earlier in London. By January 1956, she had an exposed nerve in one tooth, a case of intestinal flu, and what she called "a peculiar hop-skip-and-jump rhythm" in her heart.[58] Then, while out for a walk with Jack in late winter, Joy "did something" to her leg, and several weeks later it still bothered her. At first, she was lame, but by April 13, when she wrote to Bill, the leg had become "weak and wobbly and painful."[59] She hoped it would not be rheumatism. By June, she had a diagnosis of fibrositis in her leg, back, and chest. She had trouble walking, and she was in a great deal of pain.[60]

The third week of April 1956 proved particularly busy for Lewis. He began by inviting himself to lunch with Ruth Pitter and Kathleen O'Hara at Long Crendon. Pitter was quite surprised, because Lewis never did that sort of thing. This time, he did not have one of his friends drive him. He went by himself on the bus. Pitter took pity on him for the cheap and laborious way he went about traveling, so she hired the local driver to take him back to the Kilns after lunch. Pitter's niece Mary was with her, and both ladies decided to ride along with Lewis to see where he lived. She had never been to the Kilns. All their meetings for lunch and dinner had taken place at Magdalen College. She remarked to Arthur Russell that Lewis's house "looked pretty forlorn."[61]

Later that week, Jack took Joy and the boys to Cambridge. They had never been there before, and Jack gave them the tour. They returned to Oxford on the Saturday morning train, which took four hours. When they finally arrived in Oxford, the boys caught the bus for Headington while Joy and Jack ran some errands in Oxford. When the couple caught *their* bus, it stood still on High Street near the Carfax, a central intersection, for half an hour because of a reception for Nikita Khrushchev, the premier of the Soviet Union. Between the heat, the confined quarters, the smell, and the thought that his life had been disrupted by the international communist conspiracy, Jack insisted that they get off the bus and make their way to Magdalen College, where they could refresh themselves with beer from the buttery and wait out the Soviet threat. No sooner had they gotten their beer, than Khrushchev turned up at Magdalen, the site of the reception! Jack immediately sprang for the Fellow's Building, because protocol dictated that, as an honorary fellow, he could not appear without his gown at an official function. Joy, on the other hand, enjoyed the parade of the vice chancellor of the university with Khrushchev and his foreign minister in tow.[62] Two days later, on Monday, April 23, Jack and Joy married in a civil service at the registry office in St Giles near the Eagle and Child. Perhaps they stopped at the "Bird and Baby" for a private reception.

That Lewis invited himself to lunch with Pitter the week before he married Joy suggests some degree of conflict within—the old *bellum intestinum* of *The Allegory of Love*. What to do, what to do?

Poor Health

In his memoir of his brother in *Letters of C. S. Lewis*, Warnie Lewis mentioned that Jack already had been in poor health by the time he married Joy.[63] The combination of several conditions that would eventually claim his life were already taking their toll on him. In the end, Lewis had a heart condition, kidney failure, and a severely enlarged prostate.[64] The symptoms were in place before he met Joy Gresham.[65]

George Sayer recalled that Lewis urinated much more frequently than most other men when he was in his thirties.[66] Alastair Fowler noted that Lewis regularly had to interrupt a tutorial as early as 1952 to make use of a chamber pot in his room because of his acknowledged "weak bladder."[67] Most men begin to experience prostate problems in old age, but Lewis's troubles came in his early fifties. Several things contribute to and aggravate an enlarged prostate. A major culprit is caffeine. Sayer observed that Lewis was as addicted to tea as he was to tobacco.[68] Walter Hooper reported Lewis's now famous remark, "You can't get a cup of tea large enough or a book long enough to suit me."[69] Hooper told me that Lewis favored Typhoo tea, a particularly strong, dark tea favored by the working class for its inexpensive price. Usually when he had a cup of tea, he actually had two cups. Lewis drank tea all day long, beginning with an early morning cup when he first woke up. Then he had tea at breakfast. He always had tea in the afternoon after his walk, and then again after dinner, and once again before bed.[70] He consumed enormous amounts of caffeine. Though caffeine does not cause prostate enlargement, it aggravates an enlarged prostate.

A second factor contributing to Lewis's enlarged prostate was overeating. He not only ate too much; he also ate the wrong things. He did not care for many vegetables but preferred meat and starches. He gobbled his food and then had second helpings.[71] When eating at a pub, he would consume a pork pie chased by a second. Obesity exacerbates the problems of an enlarged prostate.

Another factor that aggravates an enlarged prostate is alcohol. C. S. Lewis did not have the drinking problem his brother had, but he drank a great deal of alcohol in a day. Anecdotal evidence from memoirs creates a certain picture of Lewis. He often visited the pub in the morning for beer, not just on Tuesdays with the Inklings.[72] He ended his day with several glasses of port in the Magdalen Senior Common Room or the Magdalene Combination Room.[73] He often had two pints of beer with lunch when not eating at the Kilns or in college.[74] He normally had sherry before supper and several glasses of wine with supper.[75] He drank alcohol all day long according to the anecdotal evidence. Except, the anecdotal evidence does not provide a comprehensive picture. He may have had two pints for lunch while walking twenty miles across the moors, but he did not have alcohol for lunch when dining in college. He may have had two pints in the morning with the Inklings, but not when he was going to have two pints for lunch when out walking. Lewis believed that beer and wine helped with digestion and overall good health. He also knew where to draw the line. At the end-of-term feast at Magdalene in December 1956, Lewis informed Vera Gebbert that there had been plenty of good food and good wine but no hangover the next day. He explained that you need never worry about a hangover if you "stick to what you drink at table." The trouble comes for those who begin drinking "spirits" after the meal.[76] Nonetheless, alcohol consumption may account for the broken blood vessels on Lewis's face in the 1950s.[77]

In addition to the behaviors that made his enlarged prostate an increasingly dangerous problem, he also had issues that contributed to his heart condition. Lewis began smoking as a little boy, probably before his mother's death. He smoked all his life, and he had what Americans once called a two-pack-a-day habit. John Lawlor claimed that Lewis smoked sixty cigarettes a day.[78] He occasionally smoked a pipe, but he preferred cigarettes. Walter Hooper once told me that his preferred brand was Golden Flakes. Smoking puts a terrible strain on the heart, especially when combined with obesity and excessive alcohol consumption. With his susceptibility to colds and flu, however, Lewis believed that smoking helped build up his resistance to disease by drying out his lungs. For centuries before the twentieth century, tobacco was promoted for its health benefits.

Finally, Lewis probably suffered from sleep apnea before it was well known as a medical problem. With sleep apnea, the patient stops breathing throughout the night, which results in strain on the heart and a variety of other problems. Warnie Lewis complained of Jack's snoring. Not all who snore have sleep apnea, but people who have sleep apnea tend to snore. Lewis could sleep through a violent storm that woke everyone else.[79] He quickly fell asleep despite his enormous caffeine consumption, but he had trouble waking.[80] He fell asleep in college meetings.[81] Lewis's "heavily pouched eyes" are another symptom of sleep apnea's constant interruption of the flow of oxygen to the brain.[82] One of his students observed that Lewis's breathing was "symptomatic of heart disease."[83] Obesity exacerbates sleep apnea. Lewis may not have had sleep apnea, but if he did have it, it would help explain the severity of his heart condition—though the alcohol and tobacco would have been enough to shorten his life.

Add to all of these issues the chronic pain Lewis had experienced from arthritis since the trenches of World War I, and it is not hard to see why he had begun to see himself as an old man by the age of fifty. He could no longer take the long walks he had once enjoyed without pain. It even hurt to write. Lewis always wrote with a steel-nib pen, which he dipped into a bottle of ink. As his correspondence increased to thirty or forty letters a day after World War II, he had increasing pain in his hand, which he attributed to arthritis. He told Lawrence Krieg in 1955 that his handwriting had gotten bad because of the pain in his wrist.[84] It is possible, however, that he actually had carpal tunnel syndrome from repetitive motion.

In his biography, A. N. Wilson laid great blame on Dr. Robert Havard for Lewis's early death. This charge may not be fair or represent Havard's efforts for the health of his friend. As early as 1948, when Lewis collapsed and had to spend a week in the hospital, Havard had put Lewis and Warnie on notice that Lewis was not in good health. He had placed Lewis on diets several times in the 1950s, which Lewis abandoned in short order. In November 1954, Lewis wrote to Mary Willis Shelburne that he had to give up potatoes, milk, and bread for medical reasons.[85] When he invited Kay and Austin Farrer to tea in June 1955, he could not eat any crumpets, scones, or cakes.[86] In December 1956, he wrote to Vera Gebbert that he was trying to lose weight.[87] A drug to deal with an enlarged prostate was not developed until long after Lewis's death.

The health warnings related to tobacco use did not appear until after he died. The correlation between caffeine and high blood pressure was not known until much later. Apart from diet, there was little that Havard could do for Lewis at the time. With all of these health complications, however, Lewis may not have felt in the mood for love.

John Lawlor, who knew Lewis from his undergraduate days in the 1930s and was one of the few who attended Lewis's funeral, thought he saw something else in Lewis's attitude toward his health, which he called "a stoical contempt for illness."[88] Lawlor had been one of those many students filled with "frustration that easily shaded into annoyance" by Lewis's annual two weeks in bed at the beginning of Hilary term to convalesce from flu while catching up on his reading and drinking tea.[89] Lawlor thought Lewis made for a docile patient if the doctor prescribed bedrest, but that he would pay no attention if the doctor warned of "a prospect of dying." Flu was serious, but dying was not. Flu interrupted his life, but death opened the way to life. Lewis's attitude toward health is reflected in a letter he wrote to Shelburne in 1955:

> I get the impression, not only from you but from many other correspondents, that in your country people are far too medically minded: they read and think too much about health and go to doctors too often! It seems to me crazy ever to have an operation unless it is either a quite trivial one or quite clearly necessary. My own doctor, who happens to be also one of my most intimate friends (he's a R.C.) says that the vast majority of illnesses are either incurable or (which is fortunately the larger class) cure themselves in due course. I said 'But my cough *does* get better after I've been taking cough mixture for a day or two.' He replied 'Yes, because you didn't start the mixture until the cough has become a real nuisance, which means until it was reaching its peak after which it wd. have gone away in about the same time whether you had taken the mixture or not.'[90]

Lewis was accustomed to flu running its course three times a year for decades. His mistake was comparing flu to heart disease and enlarged prostate, which do not get better when left alone.

Life Goes On

Lewis showed no signs that he thought his civil marriage made any difference to his well-established routine of life. Yet he seems to have shown signs that his old views on women were beginning to shift. He mentioned to Dorothy L. Sayers, when Joy was staying at the Kilns in August 1955, that he did not like either the "ultra feminine or the ultra masculine."[91] In January 1956, he asked to be remembered to Chad Walsh's wife and then added parenthetically: "One usually says after a visit 'I was glad to see X again. It was a pity his wife had to come along.' With you it is 'I hope he'll come again *and bring* his wife.'"[92] The comment reflects how his attitude had changed since his twenties when he thought nothing ruined a friendship like a friend getting married.

He continued to invite George Sayer and Roger Lancelyn Green to dine with him and visit with him during the summer vacation. He made his usual plans to visit Arthur Greeves in Ireland during September 1956.[93] He planned to stay with George and Moira Sayer in Malvern for four days in August.[94] He tried to arrange a visit with Roger Green on his way back from Ireland, but it could not be worked out with all parties.[95] Most interestingly, he hoped Ruth Pitter had been invited to a garden party at Buckingham Palace on July 12, 1956, to which he had been invited, and hoped she might return to Oxford for dinner, almost three months after his civil marriage.[96] Perhaps Pitter seemed a more appropriate companion than Joy because she had only recently had a private audience with the queen, who presented to her the Gold Medal for Poetry.[97] In any event, Pitter had not been invited to the garden party.[98] Lewis wrote her a jocular letter after the event to inform her that she was "well out of it."[99] He was one of eight thousand guests, a likely exaggeration, and he could only accept the report in the newspapers that the queen had been present, for he never saw her, nor could he get any tea. No one seemed to know anyone else, and he would have felt completely alone if he had not run into Gervase Mathew's brother, Archbishop David Mathew of Apamea. In short, he thought the party "simply ghastly."[100] After assuring Pitter that she did not miss anything, he invited her to come to Oxford to have lunch with him later in July.

Jack and Warnie went off to the Republic of Ireland for two weeks on August 14. They rambled about, as the return addresses on his few letters from this period demonstrate. To Mary Van Deusen he wrote from Annagassan, in County Louth. To Mary Willis Shelburne he wrote from "Somewhere in Eire." To Stephen Schofield he wrote from "On Tour in Eire." To I. O. Evans he wrote "From a momentary address in Eire."[101] In Annagassan, they rented a bungalow by the sea where Jack could hear the waves sounding all through the night. From the little house, they had a view across the bay to the mountains in the distance.[102]

When the brothers parted, Warnie returned to Oxford and Jack went on to visit Arthur for an additional two weeks, returning to England on September 17. In Northern Ireland, Jack and Arthur stayed in their beloved County Donegal with its "fine, wild country with green mountains, rich secretive valleys, and Atlantic breakers on innumerable desolate sands."[103] While Lewis was in Ireland with Arthur, Geoffrey Bles released *Till We Have Faces* on September 10, 1956.[104] Jack told Jocelyn Gibb that his time in Ireland had been a "glorious holiday" and that his leisure proved to be "an addiction drug which one's system aches at discontinuing."[105] While Lewis must certainly have spent some time, if not much time, visiting Joy at her house in Headington after their civil marriage, he also certainly did not spend every day with her, as Warnie had felt, more than remembered, several years later.

The Dark Specter of Cancer

In his biography of Lewis, Alister McGrath noted that Lewis had agreed to Joy moving into the Kilns in October 1955. The date is one of those unfortunate but inevitable typographical errors by which book collectors identify first printings of books. In his diary, Warnie recalled years later that Jack had agreed to the new living arrangement in October 1956.[106] Warnie's diary entry, however, fails to capture the drama that surrounded the decision. While it is possible that Joy pressured Lewis until he agreed to her moving to the Kilns, the decision appears to have been in response to other circumstances.

Lewis did not settle into his rooms in Cambridge until the end of the second week of October. The term began on October 9, so he had three weeks at the Kilns with Warnie before beginning his duties at Magdalene. Jack and Joy must have seen a lot of each other during those three weeks, but not necessarily to the satisfaction of his friends. After declaring Joy to be a possessive, jealous woman lacking in emotional self-control, George Sayer related an experience between Moira Sayer and Joy that probably took place at the beginning of Michaelmas term in the first week of October. This would have been after Joy's move to Headington but before she moved to the Kilns. Sayer had come to Oxford for the confirmation of a former Malvern pupil upon his going up to Oxford. Moira came with her husband, and after lunching at the Eastgate Hotel with Lewis, she asked if she might go to the Kilns to read instead of attending the ceremony. Lewis agreed, though the Sayers thought he seemed embarrassed by the request. Jack and Moira went back to the Kilns, where he offered her a George MacDonald story to read in the common room while he went upstairs for a nap. Soon, Joy came in whistling and carrying a load of laundry. Upon seeing Moira, she blurted out, "Who the hell are you and what the hell are you doing in this house?" Though Joy had eaten with Moira and George Sayer the year before, she did not recognize her at first. Not to be outdone, Moira rose to the occasion and replied: "We've met before: I'm Mr. Lewis's guest. I have as much right to be here as you." Joy swore in reply, slammed the door behind her, and stormed off. Moira reported to George that Jack seemed miserable when she told him the story.[107]

No sooner had Lewis resumed his professorial life in Cambridge than Joy had a calamitous fall at her house on the evening of Thursday, October 18, 1956. Kay Farrer had the sudden feeling that something was wrong with Joy, and she immediately called her. At that moment, Joy tripped over the telephone cord and crashed to the floor. Her left femur had broken, resulting in enormous pain. The Farrers came to her house and helped her get to the Wingfield Hospital, where she had X-rays. She wrote to Bill Gresham that the bone looked "moth eaten," that she had cancer, and that she would probably die. Her letter to Bill is as matter of fact as usual, without any histrionics for herself, but with deep concern for her boys. She had a will drawn up to appoint Jack and Owen Barfield as their guardians and had Jack's promise that he would see to their education. All her emotion went into her plea that Bill not try to gain custody of the boys.[108]

Her painful fibrositis was actually cancer. In a letter to Bill just a month earlier, she had commented on how she once had radiation doses on her face to treat her sinuses. Later, she had radiation doses to treat her thyroid condition. Her London doctors were horrified when they learned of the cavalier way in which she had been subjected to radiation therapy, and she gathered that radiation treatments may not be a very good idea.[109] It is possible that the radiation contributed to the cancer, which was not isolated to her hip. Joy thought so.[110] She had malignant tumors in her left breast, her right leg, and her right shoulder, in addition to her left femur.[111]

Lewis was back in Headington on Saturday, and plans were made. Joy would spend many months in the hospital and would undergo three operations.[112] In the meantime, the boys would move to the Kilns along with all their belongings. Warnie rose to the occasion, and Kay and Austin Farrer oversaw the move. The Farrers were two of the few people who knew about the civil marriage, and Lewis asked Kay to tell Colin and Christian Hardie about their "innocent little secret."[113] The move probably represented Lewis's acceptance of his guardian responsibilities for the boys rather than a plan for Joy to move to the Kilns as Mrs. Lewis. Though the boys would move to the Kilns, everyone expected Joy to move to the cemetery. Neither she nor Jack expected her to live. He asked Mary Neylan for her prayers and confided that he soon expected to be "both a bridegroom and a widower."[114]

In the midst of the crisis on October 26, Lewis suffered a further distressing and morbidly comical intrusion on his privacy when the Keystone Press photo service issued a photo of Lewis with the following caption:

PROFESSOR C.S. Lewis (68) world famous author and poet—yesterday denied that he was to marry 46 year old MISS LOUISE KITTY MARTIN, tomorrow. Miss Martin is alleged to have "arranged" the wedding for Marleybone Register Office tomorrow[.] Professor Lewis said "I have never met the woman". Miss Martin hopes that the Professor will change his mind—and the licence for marriage lasts a month.[115]

The brief teletype story must have been amusing to those in the news service who sent it out globally, but it must have dismayed Lewis at such a time. It gave his age as sixty-eight when he was actually fifty eight, and it also identified Martin as an antiques dealer, perhaps suggesting that Lewis was the antique. Yet the age difference in this outrageous story fit Lewis's actual situation with Joy.

Lewis explained to Greeves in a letter on November 25 that Joy had "a tiny 100th chance of ultimate cure," that she might live for a few years, or that she might die soon.[116] If she lived, she would have to come to the Kilns, where she could be taken care of, because she would be too frail to live alone. Coming to the

C. S. Lewis, ca. 1956. Used with the Keystone Press story of the alleged forthcoming marriage to Louise Kitty Martin.

Kilns meant that their civil marriage would have to be publicly acknowledged to avoid a scandal. Warnie wrote to their family in Belfast to tell them that Jack was getting married. He also wrote to Mary Willis Shelburne that he was marrying a woman who was very sick and probably dying, and that he would soon be "both a husband and a widower."[117]

Just as they had told the Farrers about their civil marriage, Joy wrote to Chad and Eva Walsh at the beginning of December to tell them that she and Jack had been married for months and would soon publish an announcement. She declared proudly that when she finally got to leave the hospital, she would go to the Kilns as Mrs. Lewis.[118] With Jack in Cambridge during the week, Warnie stood in for Jack with daily visits to Joy's bedside throughout

October and November. As December approached, however, he fell off the wagon. Though Bill Gresham had returned to Alcoholics Anonymous, Joy explained that Warnie refused to consider AA. He wanted to overcome his alcoholism by will power. His will power appears to have worked, except when he wanted a drink. Joy said that when his binge began, Warnie would drink two quarts of gin by himself, day and night, until he got terribly sick, then quietly go to a nursing home. He could continue to talk lucidly and politely in a drunken state, but he could not walk![119] Thus, the little family approached Christmas with Warnie a bit the worse for wear.

The public announcement came on Christmas Eve 1956 and appeared in the *Times*: "A marriage has taken place between Professor C. S. Lewis, of Magdalene College, Cambridge, and Mrs. Joy Gresham, now a patient in the Churchill Hospital, Oxford. It is requested that no letters be sent."[120] The notice gave the impression that they had a Christmas wedding. Lewis neglected to mention to most that he and Joy had been married for eight months. The day the notice appeared, Lewis wrote to Dorothy L. Sayers to explain:

Thanks for your kind card. You may see in the *Times* a notice of my marriage to Joy Gresham. She is in hospital (cancer) and not likely to live; but if she gets over this go she must be given a home here. You will not think that anything wrong is going to happen. Certain problems do not arise between a dying woman and an elderly man. What I am mainly acquiring is two (nice) stepsons. Pray for us all, and God bless you.[121]

After Christmas, Jack wrote to Mary Neylan, Bill Gresham, and Vera Gebbert to apprise them of the situation. In addition to Joy, whom he visited every day in the hospital, he had Warnie sick in bed from his binge, two stepsons to feed, one dog, one cat, four geese, umpteen hens, two stoves, three pipes in danger of freezing, "eternal, merciless letter-writing," and no domestic help over the holiday.[122]

Christian Marriage

By December, Jack had already explored the possibility of Christian marriage with the bishop of Oxford. The Church of England did not allow for remarriage of divorcees at that time. The country had fallen into a constitutional crisis when King Edward VIII had announced his intention to marry the American divorcee Wallis Simpson less than twenty years earlier. Joy told the Walshes that they had asked the bishop to rule her former marriage invalid, but he refused.[123] Jack's argument to the bishop was based on the fact that Bill Gresham had been married before he married Joy; therefore, their marriage was not valid. While the Catholic Church accepts this understanding of the validity of marriage, the Church of England does not, Henry VIII notwithstanding.[124] In the emotion attendant with her illness, she and Jack probably did not realize what the invalidation of her marriage to Bill would mean for the legal and social status of David and Douglas. They would appear illegitimate.

The sudden realization of Joy's imminent death had a powerful effect on Lewis. Both of his parents had died of cancer, and it loomed as a dreadful specter before him. When he told Greeves of Joy's condition, Lewis had declared that it would be "a great tragedy" for him if Joy died. The eternal pessimist, he did not expect her to leave Wingfield alive, but Joy nurtured the hope that her radiation treatment might be effective against the tumors for a while, and Jack allowed the hope.[125] By February, however, hope had flown away. The cancer resisted the treatment on which Joy had pinned her hopes. She wrote a discouraging letter to the Walshes in which she said that the most that could be done for her at that point was to make her last time as comfortable as possible. Joy struggled to hold to her faith while feeling the cruelty of such an end at the moment when she and Jack had finally moved from friendship to love. While she experienced the grace to endure her death, she grieved for Jack, who was "terribly broken-up" by her coming death. She lamented that she had only wanted to make him happy, but now she was only bringing him pain.[126] She appears to have succeeded in masking her feelings to Jack, for just as she wrote to the Walshes out of her despair, Jack wrote to them to say that Joy had a "wonderful peace" about her situation.[127]

After her discouraging—or, more properly, despairing—letter to the Walshes, Joy's letters reflected a peace that had come over her. Her usual sense of humor returned even in the midst of a dreadful condition. She had not walked in months. Confined to a wheelchair, she now aspired to walk again before she died. She found hope where she could, such as the ability to sit in a chair again. Jack said that it had been wrong of them to surrender to "utter hopelessness," and her faith revived. On the other hand, every visit from Humphrey Havard left her feeling like she should order her coffin.[128]

For months, Joy had a half-body cast for her leg. By the end of February 1957, a full four months after her fall, she was still in the Wingfield Hospital. Her left leg was more than three inches shorter after surgery than her right leg. On the hopeful side, she was beginning to learn to walk again, which must have been an arduous task. What buoyed her spirits most was Jack's attention to her. She wrote to Bill that Jack was "more madly in love" with her than she was with him, "which is saying plenty."[129] She explained that Jack's outward reserve resembled an H-bomb that needed an atomic bomb to set it off, but once ignited "—Whee! See the pretty fireworks! He is mucho hombre, my Jack!"[130] In her body cast, the fireworks to which she referred would have been emotional rather than physical.

David and Douglas

With all of Joy's tragedy playing out at the Wingfield Hospital, Jack had the responsibility of caring for David and Douglas. Maureen Blake volunteered to take the boys to Malvern after Christmas, but David had resented this abrupt decision without being consulted.[131] Lewis wrote to Bill Gresham that they were both intelligent boys, but they did not like to work hard at school. In an afterthought, Lewis added that nobody does. He also added that the boys got along well with him, but they did not get along well with each other.[132] Their relationship had been a problem for many years. Douglas was a cheerful child with a sweet nature who loved the outdoors and animals. Once in Headington, Doug developed an interest in gardening.[133] David tended to be sedentary and bookish. Douglas had many friends, while David did not. They often fought.[134] When they first went to Dane Court, Doug was out on the playing field with the other boys while David was in the library.[135] In some ways, he was like Lewis at the same age, but there were differences.

While Douglas had a steady disposition and tended to live out his life like the other boys his age, David tended to become obsessed with particular interests that set him apart from his peers. Joy told Bill that Davy got "enthusiasms" and then quickly discarded them, just like Bill.[136] In November 1954, David decided to become a Muslim.[137] Rather than oppose him, Joy bought him a Qur'an and urged him to learn about the different Islamic sects, memorize passages from the Qur'an, and pray toward Mecca. She wrote to Bill, "That sort of cat is best killed by choking it with cream."[138] By March 1956, the interest had shifted from Islam to Judaism, and Davy was learning the Hebrew alphabet.[139] Perhaps to head off a growing enthusiasm for Judaism, Lewis bought David a Greek New Testament combined with the English text.[140] By March 1959, David had turned to materialism and was in what Joy called his "science-is-all phase."[141] With September 1959, David entered his "Jewish-nationalistic phase," his final phase, which he would continue for the rest of his life.[142]

Lewis gave his own assessment of the boys to Mrs. Johnson, one of his many regular correspondents, whom he did not actually know:

> The younger stepson is an outdoor, cheerful boy, everyone's friend, just the right amount of mischief, and certain to fall

on his feet anywhere. The elder is our problem child. V. like what I was at his age. V. studious, a bit of a pedant, perhaps a bit of a prig, lots of brains, but inclined to use them in every subject except his school work (tries to teach himself Hebrew and neglects his Latin!), a bad mixer, can be spiteful and feels his mother's situation (poor little devil—I was thro' all that at about his age) dreadfully. He'll either be a great scholar or a total waster. No one can tell.[143]

The boys appear to have concealed from their mother just how much they hated Dane Court. Douglas recalled being beaten relentlessly for his crime of having an American accent and of being hung upside down from a tree limb by his ankles to the amusement of the other boys. He enjoyed school as much as Jack had.[144] David's sharp tongue kept getting him into fights with schoolmates.[145] He was a violent child who bullied his younger brother. Douglas Gresham has related how David tried to kill him several times when they were children. On one occasion, before they left New York for England when Douglas was only five or six, David tried to drown his younger brother in a swimming hole. After they moved to the Kilns, David dropped a bucket of gasoline on Douglas from the top of the iron staircase outside the house and tried to strike a match to his brother. These were only two of many episodes. Douglas recalled that he had to be ever careful as a child because his brother's "main object in life seemed to be to kill me."[146] Throughout their childhood, however, the boys concealed the worst of David's behavior from their mother. According to Douglas, his brother was diagnosed as a paranoid schizophrenic in New York City, but he refused treatment. After meeting him, Richard Attenborough decided to write him out of the script of his film *Shadowlands* for fear that his instability would only create trouble. After being estranged from his brother for many years, David Gresham died on Christmas Day 2016 at a secure psychiatric hospital in Zurich. It was a family of great tragedy, but Jack accepted the responsibility of loving the boys.

The Faith Healer

Lewis believed in miraculous healing by faith, as he mentioned to a Mrs. Johnson, a lady who peppered him with questions over many years.[147] As Joy's case seemed hopeless, Jack turned to one of his former pupils for help. He asked Rev. Peter Bide to lay hands on Joy for healing. During the polio epidemic of 1954, Bide had prayed for healing at the bedside of a boy who was expected to die. He then went to conduct his evening Lenten service, where he asked those gathered to have faith that the little boy would live. The boy immediately began to recover, though it troubled Bide's theology that he had prayed for many dying people before, and they had all died. He had visited Lewis from time to time after going down from Oxford, so he went to talk with Jack about what happened. Now, when approached about Joy's impending death, Bide could not recall what Lewis had said about the earlier incident or about faith healing, but Lewis wanted him to come and lay hands on Joy for healing.

When Bide arrived at the Kilns to meet Jack and go with him to the hospital, Lewis also asked him to marry them. Jack explained that the bishop would not allow it, because Joy was divorced, and none of his clergy friends could do it against the bishop's ruling. Bide came from another diocese under a different bishop, and he had long disagreed with the position of the Church of England on marrying divorced people. Still, Bide had great respect and a sense of obligation to those in authority. Furthermore, he was intruding into another parish and diocese, where he did not belong. In the end, however, he simply asked himself what Christ would do. That settled the matter for him, and he performed the ceremony at Joy's bedside with Warnie and the ward nurse as witnesses. Then he laid hands on Joy for healing.

The next day, Bide went to see Bishop Harry Carpenter, the bishop of Oxford, to explain and confess what he had done. Rather than deal with Bide himself, Carpenter sent him to his own bishop, George Bell. Upon calling Bell's secretary for an appointment, he was told that the bishop had been trying to locate him for the past day. Bell listened patiently to Bide's explanation of what had happened and then told him not to do it anymore. The Lewis wedding was not why the bishop wanted to see Bide. He offered Bide the parish of Goring-by-Sea, one of the choicest parishes in the diocese of Chichester.[148]

The wedding took place on the morning of Thursday, March 21, 1957. Warnie entered the event in his diary, but he began by saying, "Sentence of death has been passed on Joy, and the end is only a matter of time."[149] Warnie put away his diary after that entry, busy with writing another book of French history and having another binge. On November 13, 1958, he returned to his diary and wrote: "The last entry makes curious reading now when Joy is busy in the kitchen cooking our dinner. A recovery which was in the truest sense a miracle—admitted to be such by the doctors."[150] In a scientific world that can be shut down with a tiny virus, such experiences seem far-fetched. I saw it happen three times in three years as a pastor.

8

Married Life

1957–1960

A week after her wedding to Jack, Joy moved from the Wingfield Hospital to the Kilns.[1] A nurse came with her, because she still required continuing care. Joy could do nothing for herself and had to be lifted by the nurse onto the bed pan. Jack wrote to Arthur Greeves that she was no better but the hospital could do nothing more for her. Though Lewis could not visit Arthur in Ireland that summer, he expected to be "free" once again the next year.[2] He told Chad Walsh that he expected every day to be worse than the day before.[3]

In this context, the greatest crisis came with Bill Gresham's announcement that he intended to take custody of the boys.[4] On April 6, 1957, Jack wrote a carefully phrased, diplomatic letter to Bill in which he said that he could not judge between Bill's and Joy's accounts of their marriage, but he thought the important thing was the happiness of David and Douglas. Bill did not have the power to help the boys, but Lewis did. Whatever his intentions had been regarding child support, he had not fulfilled his responsibilities. Lewis told Bill that it would be good for him and the boys to have a genuine reconciliation, but at the moment, their view of him was of the man "who fired rifles thro' ceilings to relieve his temper, broke up chairs, wept in public, and broke a bottle over Douglas's head."[5] He urged Bill to wait until the boys had time to experience some healing. To force the boys to go back to America with Bill would only create a further barrier between them. Furthermore, he had to think of Renée and the burden that would be created by two more mouths to feed.[6]

Having written his own diplomatic letter, he then on the same day wrote a letter on behalf of Joy, who was too sick to write herself. In a very polite way, Lewis charged Bill with torturing Joy at a time when she was in a state of both physical and mental anguish. Furthermore, he would also torture the boys by proposing to take them when they regarded him as a "figure of terror."[7] Then he delivered the warning:

> If you do not relent, I shall of course be obliged to place every legal obstacle in your way. Joy has, legally, a case. Her (documented) desire for naturalization (which there may still be time to carry out), and the boys' horror of going back, will be strong points. What is certain is that a good deal of your money and mine will go into the lawyers' hands. You have a choice to soothe, instead of aggravating, the miseries of a woman you once loved. You have a chance of recovering at some future date, instead of alienating for ever, the love and respect of your children. For God's sake take it and yield to the deep wishes of everyone concerned except yourself.[8]

Though Jack may not have believed that he had the funds to engage in a protracted legal battle, Bill would have thought that Jack did, given the popularity of his books. At the same time, Bill knew that he had no money for legal fees.

The next day, Joy must have struggled to write a letter to Bill on her own. While she called Bill's "alcoholism, neuroses, sexual and financial irresponsibility," and "destruction of the boys' education" minor matters, she said that the main reason Bill should not have custody of their sons was that they both loathed, disliked, and despised him.[9] After mentioning a few concrete examples of why they hated their father, Joy concluded by pointing out that they were old enough to tell their story in court. Then Joy wrote a second letter to Bill on the same day, after Lewis showed her a letter from Bill to him accusing her of a variety of things, from running up a nine-hundred-dollar bill in a shopping spree to going to England the first time because she had fallen in love with Lewis.[10] Some might cite this letter as evidence that Joy had fallen in love with Lewis before she ever left the United States, but Bill is not a reliable witness, especially in the context of a bitter custody battle. Such things must be weighed. In response to Bill's charges, Joy wrote a short but emphatic letter in which she called his statements all lies "in some degree."[11]

Bill backed down but did not entirely give up for the time. In response to a support check at the end of April, Joy wrote a long chatty letter as though nothing had happened. In a sense, nothing had happened that was not routine for Bill Gresham. Joy had handled him again, and then she resumed her usual way of relating to him as the father of her children with a convenient ocean between them. She told him that her cancer had been arrested, "at least for the time being."[12] Surprisingly, or perhaps not, she also coached Bill on how to get along better with his sons through the way he wrote his letters. Then she concluded by saying, "I'm sorry to have written as sharply as I did in my last letters; for I believe your love for the boys is a genuine one in spite of its lack of understanding." Still, she added, not able to leave it alone, "But you certainly brought it on yourself."[13]

In contrast to Bill's behavior at the time, Ruth Pitter showed remarkable grace. In early May, she wrote to Jack to offer him financial assistance if he needed it with all the expenses he would face. She had seen the way he lived, and she knew the way he dressed. To all appearances, he was a desperately impoverished man. She was a lady of limited means who continued to support herself by painting trays and other decorative items. He declined the offer and told her he had "a good deal in the kitty."[14] Exactly how large a kitty, we shall see.

Joy continued to improve. She could sit comfortably in a wheel chair after spending three months in a plaster body cast. She could not yet walk, but she had hope that her broken leg would heal enough for her to hobble about. She had the use of her right arm again and no longer relied on pain medicine. By the end of May, she no longer needed a night nurse to care for her, but Jack hurt his back trying to lift Joy. The injury meant he would undergo physical therapy while experiencing severe pain himself.[15] The injury turned out to be what doctors then called a slipped disk or what is now usually called a ruptured disk.[16] He confided to Dorothy L. Sayers that it was "among the severest" pain he had ever known.[17] By July, however, the diagnosis had changed again. Lewis had osteoporosis.[18] He often screamed in pain, which was unusual for a man who had learned to mask his own suffering, and he could neither sit nor stand comfortably[19] By August, Lewis wore a surgical belt that he described as "your grandmother's corset," which brought him some relief.[20] He also began sleeping with a board under his mattress.[21] By September, his pain was greatly reduced, and he had adjusted to his new physical restrictions. Though much improved by November, he realized that he would never again be able to go on the kinds of walks he had always loved.[22] As much as he had loved the walks, he thought it was wonderful "how mercifully the desire goes when the power goes."[23] He assured Dom Bede Griffiths and Arthur Greeves that his disease was neither curable nor fatal, but it accompanied the fatal disease of senility. His was a disease that normally came twenty years later in life.[24]

He told Sheldon Vanauken, "The intriguing thing is that while I (for no discoverable reason) was losing chalcium [*sic*] from my bones, Joy, who needed it much more, was gaining it in hers. One dreams of Charles Williams [*sic*] substitution! Well, never was a gift more gladly given: but one must not be fanciful."[25] Vanauken, a young man whose wife had only recently died, had received great support through his own experience of grief from Lewis. Williams had developed a speculative theological theory that he called co-inherence, whereby a person might take the sufferings of another person. The theory is rooted in the same feudal concept of the king's champion fighting on another's behalf that Anselm used as the basis for his satisfaction theory of the atonement. Lewis thought it a fanciful notion, but an intriguing coincidence nonetheless.

By the end of October 1957, Joy was able to walk with the aid of a stick and an elevated shoe to compensate for the loss of three inches to her leg.[26] The Kilns had become a different place since Joy's arrival. For years it had been an unhappy house full of bickering, jealousy, rage, and malice. Joy seemed to change all that. Lewis told Dorothy L. Sayers that the servants all loved Joy, him, and each other. The house was full of "laugher and esoteric jokes," all from Joy's influence.[27] Joy had gradually become more active. She could stand for a few moments at a time by June, when she could also turn on her side after nine months on her back. With the use of her arm again, she began to crochet.[28] A year after her fall, however, she still had a day nurse but lived with the hope that she might one day be able to bathe and dress herself without help.[29] By the end of November, she could climb two or three stairs, walk fifty feet, and use the toilet by herself. Her next goal was to ride in a car, which she was able to do by March 1958.[30]

In January 1958, Joy felt well enough and strong enough to undertake the restoration of the Kilns. She attacked the house one room at a time, beginning with her bedroom and moving to the common room. She had walls painted and furniture stripped of its old finish. With the completion of each project, she found more repairs that needed doing. Perhaps most telling, she no longer needed a nurse.[31] She wrote to Bill that the house had not had any maintenance in thirty years. The walls and floors had holes, and

Jack and Joy in the garden at the Kilns, 1958. © University of
Dundee, The Peto Collection.

the carpets were worn to rags.[32] Outside, she had a barbed-wire
fence put up around the woods on Shotover Hill to keep trespass-
ers away. She patrolled the property with either a starting pistol
or a shotgun and her dogs, regularly firing into the trees to scare
intruders.[33] Douglas Gresham tells the story of his mother and
Jack going out for a walk in the woods when they came upon a
belligerent trespasser. Jack immediately sprang forward to place
himself between the miscreant and Joy, when he heard an irritated
voice behind him yell something to the effect: "Dammit, Jack. Get
out of my line of fire!" Though thoroughly converted and devout,
Joy still recalled her Brooklyn vocabulary on occasion.[34]

Throughout the long ordeal of Joy's precarious health, Warnie
had been a pillar of strength, an unshakeable rock, a sure and

certain anchor. During term, Jack still had to be in Cambridge during the week, so Warnie rose to the occasion and abstained from his beloved gin. Once it became clear that Joy was improving, however, Warnie indulged in a long-contemplated celebration. He began 1958 in Restholme.[35] This time, Joy was feeling well enough to take up Warnie's secretarial duties as she began typing Jack's correspondence.[36] Instead of planning her funeral, Joy made application for naturalization as a subject of the queen.

As Joy continued to feel better, she had a new set of friends and some old ones for company. Her cousin Eddy Rosenthal and his wife, Bess, came to see Joy and Jack while on a European tour of seven countries. Chad and Eva Walsh came for a visit with three daughters after a year in Finland. The poet W. H. Auden, a former student of Coghill and a devotee of Tolkien's stories of Middle-earth, came to tea. Joy also had her new local literary friends. Gladys Stern, a writer of short stories and novels, came to dinner.[37] Jean Wakeman, another writer who lived near Oxford, became Joy's closest friend.[38] Thus, she had a new circle of friends to keep her company when Jack had to be away, such as at the beginning of June when not even a Professor of Medieval and Renaissance Literature could escape the duty of grading the Cambridge tripos. Lewis explained to Mary Willis Shelburne that the Cambridge tripos are the examinations before one takes a degree. The word refers to the tripod, or three-legged stool, on which the candidate once sat in olden times, when the exam involved a disputation.[39] Lewis was away from the Kilns with examinations for two weeks.[40] In spite of all the pain and drama, Lewis was happy as he had never been happy before.

On one occasion, when Joy was finally able to be up and about, Jack gave a luncheon in her honor at Magdalen College in a room in the Chaplain's Quad.[41] It was a large mixed party that included Peter Bayley and his wife, as well as Nevill Coghill. After dessert, the men left the ladies and went out onto the quad. Lewis confided to Coghill and Bayley, "I never expected to have, in my sixties, the happiness that passed me by in my twenties."[42] Lewis also told Coghill that he had the experience of co-inherence that Williams had talked about at their Inklings meetings, with which Coghill was aware. Lewis believed that through his osteoporosis, the pain left Joy and entered his body, which gave him a sense of delight in the endurance of the pain he suffered, as though it were a gift to her.[43]

Reflections on the Psalms

In the midst of all the travail, Lewis got an idea for a new book. He would write a little volume about the more difficult psalms.[44] He began writing it at the beginning of June 1957, and by October 22, when he sent a note to Kay Farrer, his handwritten manuscript was with the typist.[45] He told Arthur Greeves that it was a "very unambitious little work."[46] It is not a work of biblical scholarship in a technical sense, for it was aimed not at scholars but at ordinary people with honest questions about the Bible. It grapples with profound issues that many people have with the Old Testament. In this way, it is a major work of apologetics. Apologetics is not necessarily the construction of philosophical arguments for the existence of God; it is the effort to answer questions by people who struggle with faith. For many people, the Bible itself is the stumbling block, as it was for Saint Augustine and Lewis.

The little book was *Reflections on the Psalms*. In his introduction, Lewis acknowledged all his limitations, but he also admitted that the problems he discussed were problems he had met when reading the Psalms. Lewis wrote "as one amateur to another," and he was not being modest.[47] The one thing he insisted upon, however, was reading the Psalms as poetry meant to be sung and not as doctrinal treatises or sermons. They must be read "as lyrics, with all the licenses and all the formalities, the hyperboles, the emotional rather than logical connections, which are proper to lyric poetry."[48] He then laid out some of the more important features of Hebrew poetry, just as he had done for allegory in *The*

Allegory of Love and for epics in *A Preface to Paradise Lost*. Foremost of these is the pattern found in parallelism, or "the practice of saying the same thing twice in different words."[49] Our eighth-grade English teachers taught us not to be redundant by saying the same thing more than once. An eighth-grade Hebrew teacher would have taught the students to be redundant and say the same thing more than once. Lewis provided several examples of what he meant, but one, familiar to listeners of Handel's *Messiah*, will suffice:

> He that dwelleth in heaven shall laugh them to scorn;
> the Lord shall have them in derision. (Ps. 2:4)

The one who dwells in heaven, from line 1, is the Lord, in line 2. Laughing them to scorn, in line 1, is the same as derision, in line 2.

This parallelism continues throughout Hebrew poetry in several basic forms. People who do not recognize the pattern of Hebrew poetry may assume several different points are being made instead of one. The parallelism can then be expressed in a variety of combinations. For instance, in the example given, the order of ideas is the same in both lines: ab/ab. But consider this example from the children's "Cherry Tree Carol":

> Joseph was an old man
> And an old man was he.

In this example of parallelism, the order of the ideas reverses: ab/ba. Lewis commented that it is either just good luck or the provision of God that Hebrew poetry works regardless of the translation, because it does not depend upon the sound of words rhyming, which is lost when we go from one language to another.[50]

Moreover, Hebrew parallelism appears as a feature of Hebrew thought in general, apart from poetry. Prophecies and teachings regularly make use of parallelism. Jesus illustrates this aspect of the Hebrew world in the Sermon on the Mount when he says, "Ask, and it will be given to you; seek, and you will find;

knock, and it will be opened to you" (Matt. 7:7). The importance of the saying is heightened by saying it not once, not twice, but three times.

At this point in his introduction to Hebrew poetry, Lewis did a most interesting thing. He began to discuss the incarnation of God in Christ and the idea that Jesus, in taking on humanity, also took on a particular culture with its own practices and learned his style from "His Mother." Here Lewis explored the extent to which Jesus "was His Mother's own son."[51] Observing a mother's ways with her sons, Lewis noted that when Jesus speaks, "There is a fierceness, even a touch of Deborah, mixed with the sweetness in the *Magnificat* to which most painted Madonnas do little justice."[52] Lewis had begun to see something in women that he had not noticed before.

Interestingly, Lewis did not use the King James Version of the Psalms, which had been the standard translation for 350 years. Instead, he used Coverdale's translation—one of several that the King James translators consulted—the translation found in the Psalter of the Book of Common Prayer. It was the translation he used every day when he said his prayers. He then explored the ideas in the psalms that he had difficulty understanding or reconciling with his view of God seen through Jesus Christ. The problems he met included the idea of judgment, the curses bred in hatred, the understanding of death before the resurrection of Jesus, the exuberance of temple worship, the veneration of the law, how to behave in the presence of very bad people, the manifestation of God in nature without the deification of nature, God's expectation of praise, a reader's injection of hidden meanings, the nature of Scripture as revelation from God, and "spiritual" meanings in the Psalms. Lewis said that this book did not fall under the category of "what is called" apologetics. He said he was not trying to convince anyone that Christianity is true but was writing for people who already believed. Then he added, "or those who are ready, while reading, to 'suspend their disbelief.'"[53] It is real apologetics after all. It is to help people resolve questions they have about biblical faith.

The Four Loves

In May 1958, Bishop Henry Louttit of the Episcopal Diocese of South Florida wrote to Lewis to ask if he would tape a series of programs for *The Episcopal Radio Hour* in the United States.[54] Lewis agreed at once and proposed a series of talks on the four loves—*storgē, philia, eros,* and *agapē*. He had referenced the first three of these in connection with Spenser in *The Allegory of Love* more than twenty years earlier, and he had regularly mentioned them in his letters over the years. On a September night in 1931 when he took his late-night stroll along Addison's Walk with Tolkien and Dyson, they ended their discussion of myth and Christ with reflection on the relationship between love and friendship.[55] Lewis dealt with the subject in a variety of ways in his fiction and nonfiction in the 1940s and 1950s, but the subject continued to be on his mind for several years.

In 1957, at the peak of his experience of pain related to his osteoporosis, Lewis had written to Dorothy L. Sayers, "I have bad spasms both of body and soul, but they all go on amidst a sort of ballet of agape, storge, and eros."[56] Earlier, when he first told Sayers about his marriage, he acknowledged that his feelings toward Joy had changed since the last time he had written to Sayers. He explained, "They say a rival often turns a friend into a lover."[57] In Joy's case, the rival who wanted her was death. In September 1957 as Joy grew stronger, he wrote to Dom Bede Griffiths about his relationship to her, "which began in Agape, proceeded to Philia, then became Pity, and only after that, Eros. As if the highest of these, Agape, had successfully undergone the sweet humiliation of an incarnation."[58] He had discussed *agapē* and *eros* in a letter to Mary Van Deusen in December 1954.[59] In February 1954, he had discussed all four of the loves in a letter to Mrs. Johnson.[60] With Dom Bede Griffiths, he had discussed *storgē* and *agapē* in

January 1954, referencing a comment made by Lord David Cecil that Walter Scott may not have had a civilized mind, but he did have a civilized heart.[61]

Lewis wrote ten talks on the four loves for *The Episcopal Radio Hour*. Caroline Rakestraw came from America to oversee the tape recording of the talks by Lewis in London. She had asked Lewis for advance copies of the talks, but he declined to provide them since he only had his handwritten copies and was still working on those on August 8. He spent the night of August 18 at the Athenaeum Club, his private club in London, and met Rakestraw to record the talks on the 19th.[62]

The recording session and the entire relationship with *The Episcopal Radio Hour* was not a happy one for Lewis. Joy described the session in pithy terms to Chad and Eva Walsh. Rakestraw began by suggesting that Lewis change his opening statement from "Today I want to discuss . . ." to "*Let us think together, you and I.*"[63] Lewis declined. Rakestraw said her proposed introduction would give the audience the sense of feeling embraced. Lewis said that if she wanted an embracer, she had come to the wrong man. When she made no headway with his words, Rakestraw asked him to sit quietly before the microphone for a minute and a half in complete silence so the audience "could feel his living presence."[64] Joy thought the idea of a silent C. S. Lewis would make for a unique listening experience.[65]

By December 1958, Lewis was thinking of turning the talks into a book, the way he had done with *Mere Christianity*. By the end of March 1959, the book was well underway.[66] He told John McCallum of Harcourt Brace in New York that he had hopes it would be a substantive book. At the time, McCallum was collecting Lewis's essays for an edited book, *The World's Last Night and Other Essays*.[67] By the end of June, the four-loves book was finished.[68] The typed manuscript went to his agent at the end of August when he wrote to Chad Walsh to ask permission to dedicate it to him.[69] Lewis had to provide the publisher with the inside front-flap description of the book, which he wrote as though an astute observer of "Dr Lewis." He concluded his praise of himself, which must have been difficult or tongue-in-cheek, by writing, "Dr Lewis' power of expressing easily thoughts not very easy in themselves has never been more fully exhibited."[70] The statement is not one of conceit but of detached self-awareness. He finished the corrected proofs by the end of December.[71] The book was published in time for Lewis to receive his author's copies on March 31, 1960, just before he and Joy flew to Greece.[72]

As for the radio broadcast that had created the occasion for finally writing the book on the various aspects of love, *The Episcopal Radio Hour* decided, in the end, that Lewis's section on *eros*, with its "'startling frankness' on sexual matters," was entirely too racy for them.[73] Caroline Rakestraw and a friend flew back to England to discuss the problem with Lewis. George Sayer recalled that Lewis was both astonished and indignant that he was regarded as too shocking for the American Christian radio audience, but he enjoyed telling the story of his encounter with Rakestraw. Sayer's *Jack* includes how Lewis told the story to him:

> Mrs. Rakestraw said, "The trouble, Professor Lewis, is that you have several times brought sex into your talk on *Eros*."
>
> He replied, "My dear Mrs. Cartwheel, how can I talk about *Eros* without bringing it in?" Of course I burst out laughing.
>
> "Was her name really Mrs. Cartwheel?" [asked Sayer.]
>
> "I can't remember. But whatever it was, I don't think I got it right. The woman she was with had a name like Clara Bootlace. They were very nice. But isn't it incredible that the inhabitants of a country so used to every sort of pornography should object to my most circumspect discussion of married love? The wonder is that many admirable Christian people manage to live there."[74]

The recordings were never broadcast widely but were aired locally in several areas. A series of ten pamphlets was printed, which

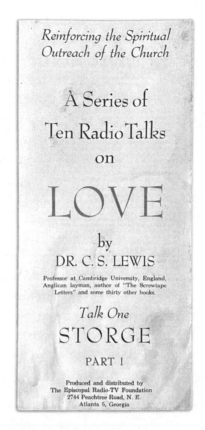

*Reinforcing the Spiritual
Outreach of the Church*

A Series of
Ten Radio Talks
on

LOVE

by
DR. C. S. LEWIS

Professor at Cambridge University, England,
Anglican layman, author of "The Screwtape
Letters" and some thirty other books.

Talk One
STORGE

PART I

Produced and distributed by
The Episcopal Radio-TV Foundation
2744 Peachtree Road, N. E.
Atlanta 5, Georgia

The first of ten pamphlets on the "four loves": *Storge*, 1959

contained the text of the recordings and was available upon request.[75] The recordings were later produced and sold as a record album, and still later as cassette tapes.

The book *The Four Loves* was well received by critics and the public alike. It continues to be one of Lewis's most accessible and appreciated works. In the book, Lewis distinguishes between the various natural loves and divine love. He finds some aspects of natural love among higher animals, and he acknowledges the extent to which these aspects of love relate to survival, but he is no Darwinian in the sense that biology explains everything. He starts by distinguishing gift-love from need-love. By gift-love, parents will sacrifice for the future well-being of the family—an outcome they may not themselves share. Even as he wrote this section, Lewis would have been aware of Joy's sacrifices for her sons, whose future she would not live to see. Need-love compels a frightened child into the mother's arms. Divine love is gift-love, most clearly seen in the incarnation and sacrifice of Jesus Christ. The natural loves are all need-love, but Lewis is careful to clarify that they are not necessarily selfish. Even the human love for God is a need-love, because of the insufficiency of humans. We need God. We were made to need God. The natural loves that originate in God can become a pathway to God. The Bible teaches that "God is love" (1 John 4:8, 16), but the inverse is not true, for love is not God. Lewis warned: "We may give our human loves the unconditional allegiance which we owe only to God. Then they become gods: then they become demons. Then they will destroy us, and also destroy themselves. For natural loves that are allowed to become gods do not remain loves."[76]

Lewis explored how natural love can become twisted in *The Screwtape Letters*, *The Great Divorce*, and *That Hideous Strength*. He had seen it happen. He had experienced it himself. It happens in subtle ways. With *storgē*, Lewis explores the experience of human affection. Affection is best seen in a parent's feelings for a child. Almost anyone can become the object of affection, including "the ugly, the stupid, and even the exasperating."[77] Parental affection, however, can become corrupted and twisted by a possessive jealousy. The second kind of natural love is *philia* or friendship. Neither mere companionship nor alliance, friendship involves a common interest rather than a self-interest. Friends enjoy something together, and the enjoyment increases by the togetherness. Whereas the section of *The Four Loves* on *storgē* reflects the jealousy and control that Lewis saw in Mrs. Moore, the section on friendship contains echoes of his own friendships.[78] Without naming names, he repeats the story of becoming friends with Arthur Greeves that he wrote in *Surprised by Joy*, and he describes Barfield's walking-tour parties.[79] Then he mentions Charles Williams and Ronald Tolkien by name.[80] Though friendship can be a school of virtue that brings out the best in people, it can also be corrupted into a school of vice that brings out the worst.[81] In his discussion of friendship, Lewis devotes an unusual amount of space to what happens if a man and a woman begin as friends and *eros* arises. With *eros*, Lewis explores "being in love" in a passionate, sexually attractive way. It is quite different from mere lust, in which anyone will do, for with *eros*, the heart is set on one particular person and no one else will do. This section reflects Lewis's new experience of being in love with Joy. He had done his research. Even *eros* can have a dark side when it descends to the demanding and giving of worship or falling in love with falling in love.[82]

The only thing that can save the natural loves from corruption is the fourth love, divine love, *agapē*. Lewis follows the King James translation in calling this "charity." The modern translations lump it together with the other loves the Greeks enumerated, but the age of Shakespeare still recognized the difference. Perhaps the greatest gift of divine gift-love is the gift of divine love. The love of God received into a person gives that person the capacity for *agapē* and transforms what has been corrupted of the natural loves.[83] This exploration of how the love of God in Christ indwelling believers by the Holy Spirit bestows the capacity for selfless love may be one of Lewis's most helpful apologetic works.

Summer in Ireland

Since Minto's death, Jack had tried to spend several weeks in Ireland with Arthur Greeves at the end of his summer vacation every year. When Arthur wrote to ask if Jack could come in 1958, Jack replied that he was afraid to make plans due to Joy's precarious health, which could turn at any moment. He added that, unlike Minto, Joy would "not breathe a word against" his going.[84] Arthur countered that Jack should bring Joy with him. Jack responded enthusiastically to the proposal and agreed to make plans. Greeves must have said something in his letter about who might do all the talking, for Jack said that Joy had "the extraordinary delusion" that he did most of it. He insisted that between Arthur and Joy, he would have no chance to say anything.[85]

Jack and Joy spent a fortnight in Ireland beginning July 4, 1958.[86] Neither had ever flown before, and Jack always loved crossing the Irish Sea on the ferry, but they decided to fly to avoid the kind of lurches that happen with a ship at sea. Though terrified of the idea of flying, once aloft, Jack found it "enchanting." They flew above scattered clouds in England and then had clear skies over the Irish Sea when he first spied the bright green of Ireland against the dark sea.[87] They drove through the Carlingford Mountains, through the Mourne Mountains, and to Donegal, presumably with Arthur Greeves as chauffeur.[88] It was their first vacation together. It was their honeymoon—with Arthur along, of course.

The boys were still away at school while Jack and Joy were in Ireland, but Joy always wanted them to have some kind of vacation trip every year. The first few years in England, the vacation meant a trip to the Kilns. This year, Jean Wakeman volunteered to drive Joy and the boys to Wales.[89] They went to the fishing village of Solva, in Pembrokeshire. Joy took the boys out in a fishing boat to visit a bird sanctuary on the island of Skomer where they climbed the cliffs and saw puffins and a variety of other birds. Doug helped with the lobster pots, and between them, the boys caught a dozen mackerel.[90]

Joy continued to improve and grow stronger through the fall. She undertook more of the work of keeping house and cooking. Jack mentioned to many of his correspondents how she limped through the woods "shooting—or anyway shooting *at*—pigeons" and how they walked together to the Ampleforth Arms, a pub about a quarter mile from the Kilns.[91]

Maintaining Friendships

While Joy and the boys were in Wales, Warnie went to Ireland for a holiday. Jack took the opportunity to invite George Sayer for a visit. Sayer countered with an invitation to Malvern, where Jack had always enjoyed walking the hills. His walking days behind him, Jack suggested that George drive to the Kilns on September 1, 1958, and spend the night. The next day they would drive to Malvern. On September 4, they would drive back to the Kilns, and George would spend another night. Then he would drive back to Malvern on the 5th. He suggested that they invite Tolkien and Humphrey Havard to join them for lunch on one of the days in Headington.

When Sayer arrived at the Kilns, Joy had not yet left for Wales. This was the first time he had seen her since her hospitalization almost two years earlier. She had gained weight and her face was puffy. In addition to everything else, Joy's thyroid condition was aggravated. The combination of the thyroid imbalance, her forced inactivity, and the cancer treatment had aged her considerably. She was only forty-three, but there is a dramatic difference between her photo in 1950 at age thirty-five and the photos of her at the Kilns in 1958. Her direct conversational style appears to have always made Sayer feel uncomfortable. She discussed how much more money Jack could make if he only knew how to sell his work. Then she took Sayer on her rounds through the woods, firing her shotgun into the trees. Sayer thought that Jack must not have liked her behavior; at least he hoped he did not.[92]

That evening, Humphrey Havard brought Tolkien in his car and drove all the men out to Studley Priory, the medieval monastery that had become a manor house after the dissolution of the monasteries by Henry VIII and eventually became a hotel and restaurant, Jack's favorite by the time Joy arrived on the scene. Sayer described it as a hilarious evening. While Jack went to pay the bill, however, Tolkien lamented all the cares Jack had to endure: Warnie's alcoholism, the two stepsons, and his "strange marriage" to Joy, whom he described as "a sick and domineering woman."[93] What concerned him most was that Joy was a divorcée. Havard, who served as best man at the civil service, and Sayer, who were both Catholic, accepted the view that since Bill Gresham had a previous wife, Joy's marriage to him was not valid. Never mind what this view meant for the boys. Tolkien, on the other hand, would have none of it, even though it was the position of the Catholic Church. Before they could discuss the matter in scholastic fashion, Jack returned to the table and the subject was dropped.

Lewis tried as best he could, given his declining health and domestic responsibilities, to stay in touch with his friends. He invited Roger Lancelyn Green, and possibly his wife, June, to dinner at the Kilns on Monday, September 29, 1958.[94] Dinner at the Kilns would have been out of the question in the dilapidated days of the Kilns, with quarrelsome house servants and a tyrannical mistress of the house. It would have been equally unlikely in the days after Mrs. Moore, when Jack and Warnie allowed the house to sink into shabbiness. But the Kilns under Joy's supervision was a house of hospitality and brightness. Lewis's socializing was not restricted to entertainments with Joy. At the end of the summer, he attended a get-together of old pupils hosted by J. A. W. Bennett at Magdalen College, which included Derek Brewer.[95] By the end of 1958, he was making plans for Roger Green to spend the night with him at Magdalene in Cambridge.[96] By January 1959, he had arranged a grand reunion at Magdalene with Owen Barfield and Cecil Harwood. Harwood would stay for three days, but Barfield could only get away for one day.[97]

In classic Lewis fashion, Jack managed to confuse dates in February, other obligations, and guests such that he had Barfield, Harwood, Green, and Joy all booked for the same mid-week in Cambridge, along with the annual Pepys dinner at the college, in honor of Samuel Pepys, who had given his famous library to Magdalene. Not only did Lewis have to attend the dinner; he learned that he had to give the address on Pepys! Despite the confusion, Richard Ladborough thought that the speech on Pepys was the best he had ever heard.[98] Joy was coming to see the Greek play *Antigone* by Sophocles. In trying to work it all out, Lewis managed to place Monday of the appointed week in February on both the 22nd and the 23rd.[99] By the time it was all sorted, Joy's overnight stay on Monday had extended though the rest of the private boys' week.[100]

Lewis continued to spend his Monday mornings with the remnants of the Inklings and those who replaced earlier members. Christopher Tolkien began attending again in the fall of 1958, after a period of absence. Ronald Tolkien had dropped out of the group some time earlier. When Tolkien announced his retirement as Merton Professor to take effect in 1959, Lewis had the opportunity to write him a note that would be appropriate and timely without seeming awkward. Just as Tolkien had been an elector for Lewis's chair in Cambridge, Lewis was an elector for Tolkien's chair in Oxford. He wrote for any recommendation Tolkien might have and then added that it was nice to see Christopher again on Monday mornings, but it would "be nicer still if he were accompanied by his Aged P."[101]

In his biography of Lewis, A. N. Wilson reported an interview with Christopher Tolkien that hit on this period. Several times in conversation with Christopher over drinks, probably on one of the Monday mornings, Lewis asked why his father had grown so distant from their old friendship. Though Lewis seemed genuinely pained by the loss of friendship, the younger Tolkien felt too embarrassed to venture an explanation.[102] In later years, J. R. R. Tolkien claimed that Joy was the issue, though it may be fairer to say that she was the occasion.[103] With apparent pain, Tolkien confided to his son Michael after Lewis's funeral, that Lewis had never even told him about his marriage to Joy.[104] This reluctance on Lewis's part is not surprising, since Tolkien and Lewis apparently had not seen each other in some time when Lewis married Joy. In a note to Kay Farrer on the day of the bedside wedding, Tolkien made mention of her involvement with "the troubles of poor Jack Lewis" and remarked that he knew little about Lewis's troubles except for "the cautious hints of the extremely discreet Havard."[105] From the remark and the chronology of Lewis's troubles with Joy's health, it is probable that Tolkien had dropped out of the Monday mornings at the Eagle and Child by late 1956, and probably much earlier.

At times, Wilson's biography seems to be arguing a point rather than pursuing answers to questions, and the way he presents material from his private interviews sometimes contrasts with the interviewees' accounts of the same interviews. George Sayer was most disturbed by Wilson's account of what Sayer said.[106] Lest judgments fall too hastily on Tolkien, it is important to remember that the Tolkiens also had their share of health difficulties at the same time Joy and Jack had theirs. Both Edith and Ronald Tolkien had bouts of illness that would reasonably have limited Tolkien's ability to continue the Monday morning meetings.

Publishing and Controversy

At the end of the summer, *Reflections on the Psalms* was published by Geoffrey Bles, on September 8, 1958.[107] Harcourt Brace would publish the book in the United States the following November 5.[108] In October, Jocelyn Gibb of the Geoffrey Bles publishing house wrote Lewis to say that William B. Eerdmans wanted to publish *The Pilgrim's Regress* in the United States. Gibb was under the impression that it had never been published in America, but it had actually been published there by Sheed and Ward of New York in 1935. Eerdmans wanted Lewis to write a new introduction, which he declined to do.[109] The new edition was published in time for the Christmas trade in December 1958. In 1981 Eerdmans issued a deluxe edition with full color illustrations by Michael Hague, printed on slick paper.

Though Lewis continued to have a following in the United States with his popular books maintaining robust sales and the Narnia books going into second printings, he also had fierce critics. In the October 1, 1958, issue of *The Christian Century*, Norman Pittinger of the General Theological Seminary in New York wrote a scathing critique of Lewis and his apologetics. Pittinger was an early proponent of process theology, and as a professor of apologetics, he took the throw-in-the-towel approach by insisting that traditional Christian doctrine was incompatible with the modern world. Lewis replied to Pittinger in the November 26 issue of the journal. After making clear that he and Pittinger had radically different conceptions of the incarnation of God in Christ, he pointed out how Pittinger had distorted what Lewis wrote in *Miracles*. Pittinger wrote that Lewis defined a miracle as a "violation" of the laws of nature, the old eighteenth-century straw man that materialists had used against Christianity for over two centuries. What Lewis had actually said is that a miracle is the "interference" with nature by a supernatural power. On this statement, and its difference from what Pittinger and the Enlightenment materialists had alleged, rests the whole point of *Miracles*.

From that beginning, Lewis proceeded methodically to take Pittinger apart piece by piece. In so doing, he made an admission that many have not noticed. He declared, "Most of my books are evangelistic" and were addressed to the average person and not to theologians.[110] He saw it as his task to translate the faith of Christ into the vernacular. Lewis concluded, nearly white-hot with fury though expressing himself with cold precision: "One thing at least is sure. If the real theologians had tackled this laborious work of translation about a hundred years ago, when they began to lose touch with the people (for whom Christ died), there would have been no place for me."[111] Lewis had not really lost his touch or his dialectic ability. Of historical note, Clyde Kilby, who would later develop and become the first director of the Marion Wade Center at Wheaton College, which is the primary repository of Lewis letters and manuscripts, also wrote an article in response to Pittinger in defense of Lewis, which appeared in the December 8 issue of *Christianity Today*.[112]

The Revision of the Psalter

In the wake of the publication of *Reflections on the Psalms*, Lewis received an invitation from Geoffrey Fisher, archbishop of Canterbury, to serve on the Commission to Revise the Psalter of the Book of Common Prayer. The commission was charged with removing "obscurities and serious errors of translation" while retaining as far as possible the general character, style, and rhythm of Coverdale's original translation from the sixteenth century.[113] On November 14, 1958, Lewis wrote a brief letter to the archbishop to agree to serve. The commission convened for the first time on January 22, 1959, at Lambeth Palace, the official London residence of the archbishop of Canterbury.[114]

Upon acceptance, Lewis discovered that he would serve on the commission with his arch enemy, T. S. Eliot! Worse than that, he began to like Eliot. Immediately after the first meeting of the commission in January, Eliot had flown off to the Bahamas, which led Joy to call him a brute for "leaving Jack holding the bag."[115] Charles Williams, who had known and liked Eliot, had introduced the two men at the Mitre Hotel in Oxford, where he had invited them to tea during the war. Gervase Mathew was among those present, and he told the story of the meeting and how Eliot began by saying, "Mr Lewis, you are a much *older* man than you appear in your photographs." Lewis received the remark with a blank poker face, so Eliot started again, "I must tell you, Mr Lewis, that I consider your *Preface to 'Paradise Lost'* your best book." Lewis had lampooned Eliot in that book, so he had trouble believing Eliot. Mathew said that the tea degraded from that point, and "a bad time was had by all" except for Williams, who thought it was all rather funny.[116]

By July 1959, all had changed. Eliot and his wife invited Jack and Joy to dinner. Eliot extended the hospitality to Joy that Tolkien, Dyson, Hardie, and Cecil had failed to give. Joy's attitude changed as she told Bill that she was looking forward to the dinner with the Eliots because she "always wanted to meet him."[117]

The two couples may have gotten together more than once. Two months later, Joy told Bill that a meeting with the Eliots "was great fun all around." The "brute" turned out "to be a sweet, genial, but rather vague old boy (he's almost seventy!)—quite unlike the rather bleak and unhappy tone of his work."[118] She also noted that Eliot had a beautiful, young, blonde wife who adored him. Eliot had borne with dignity his own share of troubles. He had first married Vivienne Haigh-Wood in 1915, but she had a number of medical complaints, accompanied by mental instability that resulted in her spending long periods of time away from her husband at clinics. They separated in 1933, and her brother had her committed to a mental institution in 1938, where she remained until her death in 1947. In 1957, Eliot married Valerie Fletcher, who had been his secretary at Faber and Faber since 1949. She was thirty and he was sixty-eight. Eliot, an American from Missouri, would have had complete sympathy with Lewis's "strange marriage."

Though the commission had its organizational meeting at Lambeth Palace, it met at different locations. Lewis had offered to arrange a meeting place at Magdalene College for the July meeting. Unfortunately, he lost the name and address of the commission's secretary and could not make the necessary arrangements and communicate the plans. He wrote to Eliot to ask if Eliot might let the secretary know that he had secured the use of the inner library at Magdalene and if the secretary might send him the schedule for the benefit of the college staff.[119]

The commission had seven members. Lewis and Eliot were the "literary men," with Lewis also serving as a scholar of the sixteenth century who had written about Coverdale, whose translation of the Psalter was incorporated into the Book of Common Prayer. The other scholar was Winton Thomas, Regius Professor of Hebrew at Cambridge. The commission had two bishops: F. D. Coggan, bishop of Bradford, who would successively become archbishop of York and archbishop of Canterbury, and G. A. Chase, bishop of Ripon, who also had an academic career as master of Selwyn College. Finally, the commission included two musicians: Gerald H. Knight, director of the Royal School of Church Music, who rarely turned up for meetings, and J. Dykes Bower, organist at St Paul's Cathedral.[120]

As might be suspected, Lewis and Eliot often took opposite positions. One would expect Eliot, the ultramodernist, and Lewis, the ultraconservative, to clash. The one would defend the old order and the beauty of the traditional forms while the other would insist on a modern rendering for the modern world. What one would not expect is that Eliot defended the past and Lewis pushed for the modern.[121] Lewis, the conservative, came dressed in his usual scruffy tweed jacket while Eliot, the avant-garde poet, came dressed in an immaculate suit. Lewis told Francis Warner that whenever he proposed a change, Eliot wanted to retain the Prayer Book language. Mrs. Eliot later told Warner that it was all too true: "I remember him coming in late one night from a meeting of the Commission, and when I asked him how it had gone he said with a tired grin, 'Well, I think I have saved the twenty-third psalm.'"[122]

Doctor of Letters

On May 13, 1959, Manchester University conferred on Lewis the honorary doctor of letters degree.[123] Jocelyn Gibb had asked to meet with Lewis on May 12, but Lewis said only that he could not meet then because he had to go to Manchester.[124] Typical of Lewis, he made no mention of receiving an honorary doctoral degree. In the face of his larger-than-life personality and reputation, it is easy to forget just how shy and humble he was for a man whose self-confessed besetting sin was pride. While in Manchester, he stayed with Professor Eugène Vinaver and his wife. The next week, Lewis wrote thank-you notes to both Professor and Mrs. Vinaver. Vinaver had given Lewis a copy of an article he had written on medieval poetry, which prompted a surprising walk down memory lane of Lewis's earliest experiences with medieval authors.[125] To complete the medieval motif, he told Mrs. Vinaver that the visit had been like a night in Joyous Gard, the castle of Sir Lancelot.[126]

Money Woes

Jack and Arthur's old friend Janie McNeil, to whom Jack dedicated *That Hideous Strength*, died on March 24, 1959. Lewis wrote to Arthur the next day to acknowledge her death and observe that he did not *feel* anything yet, and to let Arthur know that he and Joy could not return to Ireland that summer. He had problems with his taxes. Two years earlier, he had a particularly profitable year from royalties, but the bill from the government had come due, and they were strapped for the next eighteen months.[127] On April 3, he wrote to Arthur again to say that instead of paying more tax, they would get a refund, since Jack had erroneously paid more tax than was due earlier. He happily told Arthur that they could come to Ireland in the summer after all.[128]

The confusion over finances had plagued Lewis for years. Once he set up the Agapony Fund, his royalties from specific books went directly to Owen Barfield to administer. The royalties were tied to the fund. Once Lewis married, Joy advocated for holding something back to support the family. Joy complained to Bill in a letter on July 14, 1959, that she had failed so far to untangle Lewis's royalties from the lifetime charitable trust he had established. It meant that brisk sales of *The Screwtape Letters* or the Narnia books did not affect their income at all. Only the Agapony and its beneficiaries stood to gain.

In September 1954, however, Lewis began to take direct royalties from Geoffrey Bles, and probably John Lane, The Bodley Head, and Harcourt Brace as well. Jocelyn Gibb maintained Bles's correspondence file with Lewis, and in his letters to Gibb, Lewis (and Warnie) acknowledged fourteen royalty checks between 1954 and 1963:

September 28, 1954	£1156–12–10
March 19, 1955	£704–14–5
April 11, 1956	£378–11–6
April 28, 1956	£656–15–10
May 2, 1956	£821–13–7
October 20, 1956	[amount not stated]
May 7, 1957	£1340–0–0
October 15, 1957	[amount not stated]
May 5, 1958	£1499–0–4
October 22, 1958	£1820–7–2
April 24, 1959	£1350–0–1
April 4, 1960	£1714–3–9
April 8, 1961	£1981–5–3
March 7, 1963	£1625–2–0[129]

These were significant sums, considering that Lewis's annual salary at Magdalene College was 1950 pounds and that his salary in Oxford had been only six hundred pounds per year. Why did Lewis suddenly feel that he needed so much extra money when he lived so frugally?

One of the problems for biographers, as evidenced in several biographies of Lewis, is that in the absence of evidence, a biographer's fancy takes wings. We may speculate, but we must realize that speculation is not the same as fact or reason based on evidence. Speculation attempts to fill in the blanks between the facts. Any number of things suggest themselves. Joy Gresham had trouble finding the money to send her sons to Dane Court School in the fall of 1954. Did Lewis need the extra money to pay the fees? There was plenty of money in the Agapony to pay the fees without taking the royalties and incurring the taxes when he was only going to give the money away. But maybe he did not want Owen Barfield to know. This should not matter, because there wasn't anything for Barfield to know in 1954 except that Lewis was helping yet another woman he hardly knew, of which there were many. Closer to home, he had the problem of his brother, who had the very expensive habit of spending weeks at a time in private nursing homes not covered by the National Health. Only a few months after receiving his first check, Jack had mentioned to George Sayer that Warnie had never had so many and such long "debauches" as in the previous year.[130] No doubt, Warnie's binges had cost Jack more than he could afford before his new salary began in Cambridge. On the extravagant side, having a bit of ready cash allowed Lewis to join the Athenaeum Club, where he could stay overnight when in London or take friends to lunch.[131]

After he went to Cambridge, however, he did have the regular significant expense of David's and Douglas's school fees. Then came marriage and further expenses unknown to a bachelor, while Warnie's binges only increased. Lewis needed money, especially once Joy came home to the Kilns and required nursing care. Even when the nurse was no longer needed, Joy undertook the refurbishment and redecorating of the Kilns. More money was needed. Though Joy loved Jack's mind and had always loved the romance of writing, she had a strong practical side that faced the fact that the bills had to be paid. She had recognized that Lewis knew nothing of the business side of writing. His articles in journals and church newspapers were important, but he would make a lot more money if he wrote for the *Saturday Evening Post*, which he finally did. For the December 19, 1959, issue he wrote a new Screwtape story in which "Screwtape Proposes a Toast" at the banquet where the infernal companions feast on Wormwood. The *Saturday Evening Post* paid very well for stories in its heyday, and Lewis probably received a fee of several thousand dollars.

While he was editing and proofreading *The Four Loves* and preparing a revised chapter 3 for a paperback edition of *Miracles*, which took into account Elizabeth Anscombe's critique from the Socratic Club meeting in 1948, Lewis and Jocelyn Gibb began work on a new edition of *The Screwtape Letters*, which included "Screwtape Proposes a Toast." Writing a book is the fun part for authors. Correcting the proofs is the miserable drudgery, and Lewis mentioned a number of times in his letters that he was very poor at it. He was hardly better at spelling than he was at math. So with Herculean effort, he managed to bring out four books in 1960: *Studies in Words*, *The World's Last Night*, *The Screwtape Letters and Screwtape Proposes a Toast*, and *The Four Loves*, which he regarded as the most important of the four.

Despite her practical bent, Joy misjudged The Chronicles of Narnia. She dismissed them to Bill as "Jack's juveniles."[132] Though she spoke well of them on other occasions, when she spoke in terms of cold, hard cash, she concluded that Jack would "never get rich from *those*."[133] Jack calculated that they would produce between three hundred and five hundred pounds a year. He, however, was never the most astute person at understanding business, publishing, market forces, and money. While acknowledging that the Narnia stories produced a steady income year after year, Joy lamented that "only the most successful juveniles go on forever."[134] While it is true that the Narnia books will not go on forever, sales are stronger than ever after seventy years in print. Joy never seems to have been concerned about money for herself, but she wanted her sons to have a good education, which she regarded as the key to a successful start in life, and security when she was gone. As it turned out, Aslan provided that security in more than one way.

One of Joy's first shocks about the way Jack handled his business affairs came shortly after her arrival at the Kilns as Mrs. Lewis. Maureen Moore Blake had taken David and Douglas to stay with her in Malvern after the Christmas following Joy's diagnosis of cancer. A. N. Wilson included in his biography of Lewis an exchange between Joy and Maureen that Maureen had told to him. In substance, Joy remarked that after she and Jack were dead, her sons would inherit the Kilns. Maureen, never one to let a false premise go unchallenged, attempted to correct her by explaining the terms of her mother's will. Joy interrupted her explanation and declared emphatically that the house would go to her sons. Maureen suggested that she ask Jack how matters stood. Joy then said that she had already told Jack where matters stood. Wilson stated that Mrs. Moore had been a joint owner of the Kilns with Jack and Warnie, but actually she was the sole owner.[135] Though the Lewis brothers put up the lion's share of the money, they put the house in Mrs. Moore's name and retained the right to reside there as long as they lived. By the terms of her mother's will, Maureen already owned the Kilns after 1951. This reality would have made Joy all the more anxious over her sons' security after she died.

Narnia on the BBC

One reason for the increased royalty income was the popularity of the Narnia stories in the United Kingdom and the United States, where The Chronicles of Narnia remain in print. In May 1956, the BBC had approached Jocelyn Gibb about producing a radio dramatization of Lewis's first Narnia book. Lewis readily agreed, provided he had veto power over the script. From his own perspective, a dramatic reading would be more effective than a dramatization.[136] Walter Hooper, who taught a sixth-grade elementary class in Chapel Hill, North Carolina, wrote to Lewis in November 1956 to say that he had written a dramatization of the book, which his class had performed. Lewis was happy to hear it but said that he would never allow a commercial production of the book as a play, because of "what theatrical managers are like."[137]

By March 1958, a BBC script was underway. Lance Sieveking, a veteran BBC producer and writer, wrote the initial treatment, which Lewis approved and allowed to proceed, with the understanding that he would see each new episode when completed so that he could make any necessary recommendations for revisions.[138] The script was finished by May 1959, and Lewis gave it his full approval. He had asked for only a few minor changes, which Sieveking had accepted without argument. Sieveking had only insisted on keeping one section to which Lewis had objected, but he convinced Lewis that his words were right for the dramatization.[139] The BBC broadcast the radio drama in six forty-minute episodes on successive Friday evenings at quarter past five as part of *The Children's Hour* between September 18 and October 23, 1959.[140]

As it turned out, Lewis heard only the first installment of the radio production. He would still have been in Oxford on the first Friday evening, but once the preliminaries of the new term at Cambridge began, he would be occupied on Friday evenings with formal hall. He assured Sieveking that he approved of what he had heard and would be glad to have the series broadcast abroad. What he would never approve was a television production with humans dressed as animals. An actor dressed as Aslan would be blasphemy to Lewis. He would accept a cartoon production for television so long as it did not have the vulgarity that Lewis associated with Walt Disney's cartoons. Lewis had been horrified by Disney's comic depiction of dwarfs in *Snow White*.[141]

Four years after the death of C. S. Lewis, the BBC produced a nine-episode adaptation of *The Lion, the Witch and the Wardrobe* for television. It would have required the approval of Owen Barfield and Cecil Harwood, who were Lewis's literary executors. It involved Lewis's fear—people dressed as animals. Perhaps Lewis would not have been as horrified as he thought. Warnie watched the full series and recorded his first and last impressions in his diary. On Sunday, July 9, 1967, he wrote:

> On television last night I saw the opening installment of J's *Lion, Witch and Wardrobe* by which I was agreeably surprised. Lucy is good, and looks the part, and Tumnus comes off. We got only so far as Lucy's return from her first visit to Narnia so one cannot yet form an opinion of the whole thing, but so far it's very promising and I think J would have been pleased with it—no hint so far of what he feared, a touch of Disneyland. . . . The scenery was first rate, and there really was

something of magic about the transition from the wardrobe to the dim lit snow covered Narnia. How I wish J was here to talk it over with me![142]

On Sunday night, September 10, Warnie gave his final verdict after apparently viewing the full series. He thought the adaptation had been "admirable both as regards acting and production, not a jarring note in either from start to finish. How I wish J could have seen it!"[143]

In later years, the Episcopal Radio-TV Foundation and the Children's Television Workshop would produce a cartoon version of *The Lion, the Witch and the Wardrobe*, which was broadcast in two parts on April 1 and 2, 1979.[144] The showing was so successful that an encore broadcast was made later that year, sponsored by Kraft foods. The BBC-TV produced a series of the Narnia stories between 1988 and 1990 that included *The Lion, the Witch and the Wardrobe*, *Prince Caspian*, *The Voyage of the Dawn Treader*, and *The Silver Chair*. In the early 2000s, three feature length films were made of *The Lion, the Witch and the Wardrobe*, *Prince Caspian*, and *The Voyage of the Dawn Treader*, with Douglas Gresham serving as advisor to the productions. Since then, the rights to produce the entire series have been granted to Netflix by the C. S. Lewis Company, which owns the rights to Lewis's literary estate.

The Long Vacation Ends

Jack and Joy spent three weeks in Ireland in the summer of 1959 from June 21 until July 10. They spent several days at the Old Inn in Crawfordsburn, County Down, where Arthur lived, then a week or so at the Port Royal Hotel in Rathmullan, County Donegal, then back to Crawfordsburn.[145] By the time they left for Ireland, Lewis had completed the manuscript for *The Four Loves* and was ready to send it to the typist.[146] While they were in Ireland, they received the invitation from the Eliots to dine.[147]

It was a wonderful summer. The long vacation almost always was, but the long vacation eventually came to an end with October. In October 1959, Joy's long vacation ended with the discovery that her cancer had returned with a vengeance. It was as bad as could be. It came back in many parts of her body.[148] Lewis spoke of it to his friends in military terms: the doctors could only perform "rearguard actions"; the tide had turned, and they were in retreat.[149] She had come through it once before, but Lewis held out no real "hope for a second resurrection."[150]

By the end of November, Jack had slumped into something I have seen many times as a pastor—anticipatory grief. Harking back to *The Pilgrim's Progress*, which he had loved to read before his conversion and which inspired his own conversion story as *The Pilgrim's Regress*, Lewis told Roger Green that he felt "like being recaptured by the giant when you have passed every gate and are almost out of sight of his castle."[151] In Bunyan's allegory, the giant was Giant Despair, and the castle was Doubting Castle. He told Mary Van Deusen that "one of the drawbacks to living in a tragedy is that one can't very well see out of the windows."[152] To Jessie Watt he wrote on Christmas Day, "The cat had let the mouse run so far away that it thought it had escaped."[153] In anticipation of the inevitable, he was experiencing the loss, the denial, the confusion, and much more that comes after someone greatly loved has died. By June 1960, he was blaming Humphrey Havard for failing to diagnose the cancer in time.[154] Though not a fair charge, blame is a normal feature of grief. Some biographers have taken the charge against Havard as a fact, because spoken by C. S. Lewis, instead of the expression of misery from a man who could do nothing to prevent his wife's death.

In the face of the unacceptable, Lewis and Joy stayed busy. It was in the context of Joy's looming death that Jack frantically worked to bring out four books if possible before Joy died. It was in this context that he gave a luncheon party for Joy at Magdalene College so that his Cambridge friends could meet her. He invited Joan and Stanley Bennett. Stanley had been one of the electors who chose Lewis for his professorship. He also invited George Watson, his former pupil who was by then a fellow at St John's College, one of the grandest of the grand Oxbridge colleges. Watson had his own set of stereotypical expectations of what Joy would be like, having lived in New York and known a number of Jewish intellectuals. Instead, Watson recalled many years later, he met

> a frail, distinguished, soft-spoken being, supporting herself on two sticks—above all a woman of letters. There was nothing brash about her. In fact, Lewis was noisier than she, by far. Perhaps I too was surprised by Joy, on the only occasion I met her. I am certainly surprised by what filmmakers have made of her.[155]

In defiance of death's grim shadow, Jack and Joy moved forward with a trip to Greece that they had planned with Roger and June Green.[156] When Lewis gave Arthur Greeves an update on Joy's condition, he told him that they planned to make the trip to Greece by air during the Easter vacation because they dared not put it off until summer. She was declining rapidly.[157] To top off matters, he told Arthur that he had developed high blood pressure. In addition to the stress under which Lewis had lived the past few years, he had an increase in symptoms suggesting sleep apnea, which often results in high blood pressure. He mentioned to Mary Willis Shelburne that he fell asleep immediately, but he often woke several times during the night. While he had trouble sleeping all night, he had trouble staying awake during the day.[158]

Jack and Joy flew to Greece with the Greens on Sunday, April 3, 1960. Walter Hooper retells Jack's description of their departure from the Kilns:

> "There I was, with a wife who was dying, and we were flying in an airplane, which was very new to both of us, going to a

foreign country where we didn't know, really, what was going to happen." [Just as the taxi arrived and Jack and Joy had settled in, Paxford the gardener, the model for Puddleglum the glum Marsh-wiggle in *The Silver Chair*, stuck his head in the window to bid them a fond farewell.] "Well, Mr. Jack, there was a bulletin just going on on the wireless about a plane just went down. Everyone killed, burnt beyond recognition. Did you hear that, Mr. Jack? Burnt beyond recognition." As Lewis said, "on that happy note, we flew to Greece."[159]

They toured Greece and several Aegean islands until April 14 on a package Wings Tour of about thirty people. In those pre-jet days, the plane from London made stops in Lyon, Naples, and Brindisi to refuel before flying on to Athens late the same night. These were also before the days of covered ramps that meet planes at terminals. The party had to hike across the tarmac to reach each terminal, which added an extra strain for Joy. They stayed at the Hotel Cosmopolis in Athens, but Joy did not feel like going to Marathon the next morning. Roger and June met them for lunch and the afternoon tour of Athens, when they climbed the Acropolis.[160] After making her way to the top, Joy sat with Jack on the steps of the Propylaea, where they gazed at the Parthenon and the Erechtheum. Instead of going on to the Agora and Plaka with the rest of the party, Joy went back to the hotel to rest.[161]

The next day, the tour group left by coach early in the morning to travel to Mycenae, fabled city of Agamemnon, the king who led the Greeks against the city of Troy. There they saw the Lion Gate and the Treasury of Atreus, which Green called the most impressive of the Mycenaean buildings, but Joy could go no further. They then ate lunch and drank the local Nemean wine, which legend says was the wine that Hercules drank after defeating the lion of Nemea. On the way back to Athens, the coach went by ancient Corinth.[162]

On Wednesday, April 6, the Greens and Lewises took a day away from the group, rented a car with driver, and drove down to the Gulf of Corinth. They visited the ruined temple of Apollo at Delphi. When he returned to England, Lewis wrote to Chad Walsh that "at Delphi it was hard not to pray to Apollo the Healer. But somehow one didn't feel it wd. have been very wrong—wd. have only been addressing Christ *sub specie Apollonis.*"[163] They stopped along the way several times for Roger and June to climb rocky cliffs to explore ruined castles, but Jack and Joy simply enjoyed being in the midst of vineyards, pine woods, olive groves, and tiny villages beside the "misty blue" sea. They dined on octopus, squid, and mullet for lunch with ewe's milk cheese and fresh oranges. To drink, they had ouzo and retsina. They sat at their table for several hours with the sound of waves, bees, and cicadas filling the air. Green recalled that Lewis said it had been "among the supreme days of his life."[164]

They flew to the Island of Rhodes on Thursday, where they stayed until Sunday. Lewis adored Rhodes and described it as "an earthly paradise—all orange and lemon orchards and wild flowers and vines and olives, and the mountains of Asia on the horizon."[165] After the Easter service at the Orthodox Cathedral, they flew to Crete, where the Wings Tour failed them in the way of food, and they made their own way to a little restaurant to dine on dolmades, squid, globe artichokes, and Minos wine. The step to the coach on Crete was so high that Joy hurt herself getting on and off, so they rented a car and driver for the rest of their time on Crete. Roger Green realized that Joy was in pain for much of the time and also that the only thing that helped her was alcohol. While June helped Joy and Jack to the nearest taverna, where they would eat, Roger arrived ahead of them to be sure they would have drinks on the table when they arrived. On Wednesday, April 13, they flew from Crete to Pisa and then, the next day, back to London.[166] It was an arduous trip, but also the trip of a lifetime for someone whose life was rapidly coming to an end. Lewis observed that Joy "performed prodigies of strength, limping to the top of the Acropolis and up through the Lion Gate of Mycenae and all about the medieval city of Rhodes. . . . It was as if she was divinely supported."[167]

In the midst of his own despair, Lewis wrote to two other men who faced the same ordeal he faced. Rev. Peter Bide's wife had contracted cancer, and Sir Henry Willink's wife died. The letters are touching in the depth of their empathy and consolation, coming as they did out of Lewis's own poverty of spirit at the time. To Willink he said, "People talk as if grief were a feeling—as if it weren't the continuous renewed shock of setting out again and again on familiar roads and being brought up short by the grim frontier post that now blocks them." And then he added, "It is quite useless knocking at the door of Heaven for earthly comfort: it's not the sort of comfort they supply there."[168] Belief in the life everlasting in heaven does not take away the sense of loss on earth.

With Bide, he was able to go deeper, for Bide was a clergyman who knew God well. He remarked that Joy had said they did not need to be afraid of questioning why it was all happening, because "it was the impatience of Job not the theodicies of Elihu that were pleasing to God."[169] Lewis thought that God might actually like people to stand up to him and speak their mind instead of masking resentment as submission. Surely God would not care for "mere flattery" like that. Joy's looming death impressed upon him the significance of the incarnation and how God shared "the horrors of the world He made!"[170] Until the death of their wives came, Lewis urged Bide to join him in keeping up their spirits as best they could, because "the less miserable we succeed in being, the more we can do for *them*."[171]

Joy's health deteriorated quickly upon the return from Greece. She had a right mastectomy on May 20 and promptly declared that she had been "made an Amazon."[172] Her sense of humor never diminished. After two weeks in the hospital, she returned to the Kilns. Warnie, who could be on his best behavior for Joy, pushed her in her wheelchair all about the grounds of the little estate to inspect the flower beds and the greenhouse and up to the pond. This was two days before his sixty-fifth birthday. The next few days were bad for her with terrible sickness all through the nights. On Monday, June 20, Joy felt that the end had come and told the nurse to send a telegraph to Doug to come home from his school in Wales. David was nearby at Magdalen School, across the bridge from Magdalen College. She was administered a powerful pain drug, which put her into a coma, but before going under she remarked in typical form, "I've got enough cancers now to form a Trades Union of the darned things."[173]

She was taken to the Acland Hospital to die on Tuesday afternoon, June 21. She did not. Warnie thought he had said his goodbyes, but wrote in his diary that "Joy has made fools of the doctors and nurses" and returned to the Kilns on June 27. By Sunday, July 3, she was able to go to Studley Priory for dinner, which had become a weekly custom for them. On Monday, she went for a drive into the Cotswolds. She then had a bad week but seemed to get better. Then on Tuesday night, July 12, Warnie took tea to her and Jack, who were playing Scrabble. She seemed fine. As Warnie dropped off to sleep, he heard Jack and Joy reading a play together. On Wednesday morning, July 13, 1960, Warnie was wakened at quarter past six by the sound of Joy screaming. Warnie rushed downstairs and called for Jack, who telephoned the doctor, presumably Humphrey Havard, who arrived before seven and gave her a shot of painkiller which did little to relieve her pain, so a subsequent shot was given. Warnie described a rather chaotic effort to find a hospital that could take her immediately, but finally Jack persuaded her surgeon to make way for her at the Radcliffe Infirmary, where she went by ambulance that afternoon at one thirty with Jack at her side. Austin Farrer arrived in time to give her Absolution. Jack returned to the Kilns that evening at 11:40, and Warnie went to meet him as soon as he heard him arrive. Jack gave him the news that Joy had died about twenty minutes earlier.[174]

9

Life without Joy

1960–1963

As she lay dying, Joy asked that Jack arrange for her cremation. She declared that "posh coffins are all rot."[1] The funeral took place on Monday, July 18, 1960, a sunny but blustery day. The family left the Kilns in one taxi, with the household servants and the nurse in another. Just as they reached the roundabout at the London Road, they met the hearse by chance and fell in behind it along the road that would have taken them to Studley Priory, where Jack and Joy had gone so often to eat on Sundays. Kay and Austin Farrer were the only friends of Jack who attended the service. Austin read the service, but he was too overcome by emotion to manage it well, which was unusual for such a seasoned minister as he. Jack did not have any music at the service.[2] In defense of Tolkien, Havard, Dundas-Grant, Mathew, and Sayer for not attending the funeral, it is important to note that a raucous discussion of cremation at an Inklings meeting in 1940 had made it surprisingly clear to Lewis that Catholics had a passionate objection to it.[3]

Lewis had known the death of people he loved before, but no one's death had ever affected him the way Joy's death did. He felt very little with his father's death, though in the long aftermath, he gradually felt a sense of guilt. As close as he was to Charles Williams, he felt a deep peace and confidence in the resurrection after his death. With Joy's death, he felt the most absolute desolation. In writing to Mary Willis Shelburne, he said, "I'm like a sleepwalker at the moment."[4] Three days after the funeral, he wrote to Kay and Austin that he never dreamed that "between the moments of acute suffering," grief would be "so like somnambulism or like being slightly drunk. Nor, physically, often so like fear."[5] Joy had left Kay her fur coat, and Jack wanted her to know, and he wanted to tell the Farrers how much they had meant to Joy. He told them that Douglas and Warnie had been "absolute Bricks" through Joy's death and funeral, but Douglas went back to school and Warnie fled to Ireland to console himself.

A few days later, Jack wrote another letter to Kay Farrer in which he made clear how he was feeling. She had let him know that they would not bother him so that he could get some rest. He replied:

> Come up any day that suits. Not seeing you two wd. never be a 'rest.' Nor am I sure that rest is what I need. I'm learning a good many things about grief wh. the novelists and poets never told me. It has as many different facets as love or anger or any other passion. In the lulls—between the peaks—there is something in it v. like fidgety boredom: like just 'hanging about waiting'—tho' what the deuce one thinks he is waiting for I don't know.[6]

Vera Gebbert had written to offer the comfort of the resurrection, but Lewis already believed in the resurrection. He did not question everlasting life, "but the state of the dead *till* the resurrection is unimaginable. Are they in the same *time* that we live in at all[?] And if not, is there any sense in asking what they are 'now'?"[7]

When I first became a pastor years ago, our small church had a funeral every week for eight weeks, and then it slacked off to one every other week. The questions Lewis asked are among the standard questions that people of faith who have loved dearly tend to ask. They are questions that occur to few people—even, or especially, pious people—before death intrudes and the great separation comes. Lewis handled himself in a very healthy way. He did not cut himself off from others but sought company. He did not withdraw from his work but threw himself into it and stayed busy. He let his emotions flow and did not try to be "appropriate."

Once school was out, Douglas returned to the Kilns to be for Lewis "an absolute brick, and a very bright spot" in his life.[8] The Greens invited Lewis to visit them in September, a visit he would have enjoyed but had to decline because he did not know when and in what state Warnie would return from Ireland, and he needed to be on hand, just in case.[9] Instead, he invited Peter Bide to come for a visit a few days after Bide's wife died. By September, Lewis was ready to offer comfort and support to Bide. Lewis now knew what it was like and could now help the man who had helped him. In writing to Bide, he said that he hoped their wives would be "allowed to meet and help one another. You and I at any rate." He also mentioned something he had learned by then about grief that Bide may not yet have known: "At first one is sort of concussed and 'life has no taste and no direction'. One soon discovers, however, that grief is not a state but a process—like a walk in a winding valley with a new prospect at every bend."[10]

A Grief Observed

While Warnie was away in August, Lewis invited Roger Lancelyn Green to visit at the Kilns.[11] Green arrived on Wednesday, August 31, and stayed for several days.[12] During the visit, Jack showed Roger what he had written since Joy died.[13] He began keeping a diary in which he poured out his anguish, all his "blackest doubts," all his anger with God, all his confusion, all his fear.

In addition to writing the book, by the end of August his weight had dropped from 182 pounds to just under 154.[14] Because we are often told that the grief process takes a year (a remarkably arbitrary figure), the impression might arise that this book, published in 1961 as *A Grief Observed*, covers a long period of time. In fact, it represents little more than a month. Lewis told Sister Madeleva a little over a month before he died that, though the book "raises all the blackest doubts," "it ends with faith."[15] Lewis and Green discussed whether Lewis should publish the remarkably candid book. Would a book so full of doubts and anger be a help or a hindrance, coming from such a well-known apologist? Would he be a stumbling block or a source of comfort? In the end, he swore Green to secrecy and decided to publish the book under an assumed name. His pseudonym would be Dimidius, which means halved or divided in two.[16] As it happened, Dimidius did not appear on the title page.

Lewis turned the manuscript over to his agent, Spencer Curtis Brown, who submitted it to Faber and Faber instead of Lewis's usual UK publisher, Geoffrey Bles or John Lane, The Bodley Head. Brown submitted the manuscript with the explanation that the author preferred to remain anonymous. When the manuscript by an unknown author came to Faber and Faber, T. S. Eliot managed its consideration. Eliot assigned the manuscript to Charles Monteith, who had taken a double first at Magdalen College, where he had been a pupil of Lewis. Monteith recognized Lewis's handwritten corrections to the manuscript.[17] Eliot accepted the manuscript with a letter to Curtis Brown:

> I and two other Directors have read *A Grief Observed*. My wife has read it also, and we have all been deeply moved by it. We do in fact want to publish it. . . . We are of the opinion that we have guessed the name of the author. If, as you intimate and as I should expect from the man I think it is, he does sincerely want anonymity, we agree that a plausible English pseudonym would hold off enquirers better than Dimidius.

The latter is sure to arouse curiosity and there must be plenty of people amongst those who know him, and perhaps even among the readers of his work who do not know him, who may be able to penetrate the disguise once they set their minds working.[18]

Lewis agreed. He had for many years published poetry in *Punch* under the initials N. W., which stood for Nat Whilk, the Old English for "I know not whom." For this book, he kept the initials and added a last name, Clerk, which represented his medieval status as one who wrote. The book by N. W. Clerk was published a year later on September 29, 1961.[19]

Exactly twenty years had passed since Lewis published *The Problem of Pain*. In its preface, Lewis confessed that he found serious pain intolerable, but that he did not write to address the feelings associated with pain or suffering. Instead, Lewis said:

> The only purpose of the book is to solve the intellectual problem raised by suffering; for the far higher task of teaching fortitude and patience I was never fool enough to suppose myself qualified, nor have I anything to offer my readers except my conviction that when pain is to be borne, a little courage helps more than much knowledge, a little human sympathy more than much courage, and the least tincture of the love of God more than all.[20]

A Grief Observed provides the other bookend to *The Problem of Pain*, giving the expression of the feelings associated with suffering, without any intellectualizing. In *The Abolition of Man*, Lewis had explored what happens when the head and the belly roam free without the magnanimity of the chest to keep them in balance. With these two books, we see exactly what he meant, and we see how balance finally came at the end.

We can almost give a date to when Lewis began writing his thoughts and feelings that became *A Grief Observed*. The first sentence states, "No one ever told me that grief felt so like fear."[21]

He had written these sentiments to Kay and Austin Farrer on July 21, 1960.[22] Lewis had begun *The Problem of Pain* by asking, "If the universe is so bad, or even half so bad, how on earth did human beings ever come to attribute it to the activity of a wise and good Creator?"[23] It was a brilliant stroke. With *A Grief Observed*, however, he faced the counterpoint. What if God were a monster and we had been wrong all along to call God good?

Lewis gave his feelings full vent over how God had failed him. He wailed: "Go to Him when your need is desperate, when all other help is vain, and what do you find? A door slammed in your face, and a sound of bolting and double bolting on the inside."[24] Lewis never felt in danger of losing his belief in God. The real danger for him was "coming to believe such dreadful things about Him."[25] While he had felt a rush of assurance about the continued life of Charles Williams after he died, he begged for "even one hundredth part of the same assurance about" Joy, but nothing came.[26] He had a bundle of fears, most notably the fear of losing his memory of Joy.[27]

Small lines he had written to friends in letters appear in expanded form in *A Grief Observed* as major preoccupations of his mind during August, such as "Where is she now?' . . . [at] 'the present time,'" and, "If the dead are not in time, or not in our sort of time, is there any clear difference, when we speak of them, between *was* and *is* and *will be*?"[28] This question of the relationship between time and eternity was one he had explored in *Mere Christianity* and other places as an intellectual problem, but now it was a very personal problem. Then he began to worry that Joy's suffering had not ended with death. If God had allowed Joy to suffer in life, then it would be consistent for God to allow her suffering to continue beyond death.[29]

The thoughts and fears must have come fast and furious for Lewis, and he poured himself onto the pages of his little notebook. He probably wrote the first half of *A Grief Observed* between Thursday, July 21, when he wrote to the Farrers about his experience of grief as fear, and Monday, July 25, when he wrote to Kay that it felt like "hanging about waiting."[30] On page 29 of the 59 page book, Lewis wrote: "And grief still feels like fear. Perhaps, more strictly, like suspense. Or like waiting; just *hanging about waiting* for something to happen."[31]

Lewis's fears that God might actually be a Cosmic Sadist began to subside as the sun came out following a series of cloudy days, and as he finally was able to get a good night's sleep. He gradually came to feel "that the door is no longer shut and bolted," and he wondered if his own "frantic need" had slammed it in his face.[32] Early on, Lewis had feared he would lose his memory of Joy. He noticed, "For some reason—the merciful good sense of God is the only one I can think of—I have stopped bothering about that."[33] As soon as he stopped worrying about losing the memory of Joy, he met her everywhere.[34]

By the last third of his rambling thoughts—for this book, in contrast to all of his other books, is not a well-organized and logical progression from one point to the next—Lewis had reached a state of peace and confidence in God, who he realized had not abandoned him or treated him cruelly. He wrote: "God has not been trying an experiment on my faith or love in order to find out their quality. He knew it already. It was I who didn't."[35] Lewis realized that he had not "got over it" so much as he had learned to "get about on crutches" following an amputation, but he felt better.[36] A major crutch was young Douglas Gresham, who returned home from school while Jack was in the depths of his despair just before the tide turned. Lewis wrote to Mary Willis Shelburne, "My youngest stepson is the greatest comfort to me."[37] Douglas was continuously described by Joy and Jack as a sweet boy, but he also has much of his mother about him, and no doubt, his mere presence uniquely brought comfort to Lewis and refreshed the memory of Joy.

By the last section of the book, Lewis had recovered his ability to think reflectively about death as a true believer with confidence in God. He had come to know a great deal more about the *bellum intestinum* about which he wrote in *The Allegory of Love*. His chest finally had gained control over his belly, with its wild emotions, and his head, with its equally wild speculations. Equilibrium had returned. At the beginning of the last section, he wrote that he had learned that grief is "not a state but a process" and that this process was "like a long valley, a winding valley where any bend may reveal a totally new landscape."[38] He would continue to repeat these phrases in letters to others.[39] He would continue to hurt. A month or more later, on September 20, Lewis wrote to Peter Bide a letter of consolation in which he said with authority, "Grief is not a state but a process—like a walk in a winding valley with a new prospect at every bend."[40] He would never really "get over" Joy's death, because that is the price and the proof of love, but he would become active again. When his goddaughter, Sarah Neylan, married in November, he sent a present with a note apologizing that he could not attend "for the reasons you know, would turn me inside out now."[41] He was fragile and he recognized it, in spite of his brave public face.

It had been a dreadful summer, but with September it was time to prepare for a return to Cambridge and his work there. On September 9, 1960, the Cambridge University Press released *Studies in Words*, a book he had finished writing two years earlier.[42] Throughout the end of September and beginning of October, Lewis was embroiled in a continuous exchange of letters with Jocelyn Gibb at Bles about details related to the forthcoming new edition of *The Screwtape Letters* combined with "Screwtape Proposes a Toast."[43] It would be published by Bles on February 27, 1961.[44] By the first week of October 1960, he was back in Cambridge to resume his duties.[45] He continued to receive invitations. The BBC wanted him to do another talk, which he declined.[46] The Bodley Head wanted him to write a book on George MacDonald, which he was willing to consider but in the end declined.[47]

An Experiment in Criticism

On January 25, 1961, Lewis wrote to Arthur Greeves to thank him for proofreading the manuscript of his new book, *An Experiment in Criticism*. Greeves, whose grammar, spelling, and punctuation Lewis had mocked when they were teenagers, was a much better proofreader than Lewis, who was hopeless at spelling the first time around, let alone catching his mistakes the second time around. Arthur had helped him in this way before.[48] Cambridge University Press published the book on October 13, 1961, but when did Lewis write it?[49]

In one sense, Jack began writing this book on February 1, 1916, when he wrote to Arthur, "You really lose a lot by never reading books again."[50] As a teenager, Lewis had developed the lifelong habit of reading the books he liked over and over again. This habit became the basis for *An Experiment in Criticism*. He laid out many of its basic ideas in his letters to Greeves from Great Bookham. When Arthur asked Lewis not to tell anyone that he thought *Frankenstein* badly written, Lewis replied forcefully, "And you ought to rely more on yourself than on anyone else in matters of books—that is if you're out for enjoyment and not for improvement or any nonsense of that sort."[51]

Through his pleasure reading at Great Bookham, Lewis had formed his basic ideas about literary judgment that he finally organized and expressed in *An Experiment in Criticism*. On November 1, 1916, he wrote to Greeves:

> If a person was really a book-lover, however ignorant, he wouldn't go and look up a text book to see what to buy, as if literature was a subject to be learned like algebra: one thing would lead him to another & he would go through the usual mistakes & gain experience. I hate this idea of 'forming a taste'. If anyone like the feuilletons in the 'Sketch' better than Spenser, for Heaven's sake let him read them: anything is better than to read things he doesn't really like because they are thought classical.[52]

Jack had recognized early on the flaws in relying on the professional arbiters of taste to establish which books a person ought to read. Echoes of these early ideas appear in *A Preface to Paradise Lost*, where Lewis challenged the opinion of T. S. Eliot that only the best practicing poets could legitimately judge an epic like *Paradise Lost*.[53] Lewis pointed out the fallacy of Eliot's view in a few biting paragraphs.

Eliot was one thing, but with F. R. Leavis and his devoted followers at Cambridge, Lewis found a more pervasive and pernicious approach to literary criticism that had come to dominate literary thought. Leavis set himself up as the judge of what was good and bad in literature. Usually, old books were bad books. In a letter to J. B. Priestly on September 18, 1962, Lewis expressed his concern for the state of English Literature as a subject. His concern centered on Leavis and his approach to literature:

> My hope was that it would be primarily a historical study that wd. lift people out of (so to speak) their chronological provincialism by plunging them into the thought and feeling of ages other than their own: for the arts are the best Time Machine we have.
>
> But all that side of it has been destroyed at Cambridge and is now being destroyed at Oxford too. This is done by a compact, well-organized group of whom Leavis is the head. It now has a stranglehold on the schools as well as the universities (and the High Brow press). It is too open and avowed to be called a plot. It is much more like a political party—or Inquisition.
>
> Leavis himself is something (in the long run) more fatal than a villain. He is a perfectly sincere, disinterested, fearless, ruthless fanatic. I am sure he would, if necessary, die for his critical principles: I am afraid he might also kill for them. Ultimately, a pathological type—unhappy, intense, mirthless. Incapable of conversation: dead silence or prolonged, passionate, and often irrelevant, monologue are his only two lines. And while he is in fact the head of the most powerful literary

Establishment we have ever had since Boileau, he maddeningly regards himself as a solitary martyr with his back to the wall.[54]

In his approach to criticism, Leavis judged literature good or bad depending on its moral perspective, by which he meant *his* moral perspective. The quality of composition or form mattered little in comparison. In constructing his lists of good and bad books, Leavis easily dismissed poetry (Milton) and novels (Dickens) that Lewis valued.

Rather than approaching literary criticism by judging the books, Lewis proposed that an alternative approach might be to judge the readers of the books. He had a simple standard for judging who the real literary people were. He had demonstrated the folly of Eliot's appeal to the great poets as great critics in *A Preface to Paradise Lost*. Lewis said that most people never read a book twice. Literary people, "on the other hand, will read the same work ten, twenty or thirty times during the course of their life."[55] He concluded that a book is a great book if a literary person reads it multiple times. Most people read to fill the time when nothing else is happening. Today we might think of reading on an airplane, in a waiting room, or at the beach. In contrast to this view of reading, literary people look for opportunities to read. When they are kept from reading by the vicissitudes of life, they feel denied.[56]

When most people read a novel, they have the satisfaction of finding out what happened. When a literary person reads a novel, it has an effect on them. The better the work of literature, the more significant the effect. Lewis said that a first reading of a piece of literature can create "an experience so momentous that only experiences of love, religion, or bereavement can furnish a standard of comparison."[57] Lewis did not exaggerate at this point, for he probably wrote these words in the context of the dying of Joy Lewis. We have the documentary evidence of the impact of a number of novels and poems on him during his years in Great

Bookham. The stories of the journey to the end of the world and back again ultimately resulted in his conversion. Finally, most people attend to a book while they are reading it, but then it passes out of their life. Literary people cling to the books that they read over and over, talking about favorite passages or quoting favorite lines. The literary person may interpret the world through experience of the books he or she has reread.[58] During his last term in Cambridge, Lewis gave an interview to Kingsley Amis and Brian Aldiss on science fiction in which he remarked about a book he thought pretty good: "I only read it once. Mind you, a book's no good to me until I've read it two or three times—I'm going to read it again. It was a major work, certainly."[59]

The difference between literary people and nonliterary people is not that literary people like good books and nonliterary people like bad books. The difference does not involve good or bad taste. It involves the very way a literary person engages or reads a book.[60] Lewis observed that the same sort of distinction can be found in all the other arts. Lovers of music can listen to the same Bach piece many times and continue to experience the same pleasure they did the first time they heard it. Movie people can watch *Casablanca* over and over without ever growing tired of it, even though they know exactly what will happen in the end. They do not watch again to find out what happens; they already know what happens. Not everyone feels that way about movies.

Lewis argued that it is a mistake to confuse nonliterary people with people who like popular literature, such as science fiction, mysteries, and Westerns. He refused to classify a particular genre in the whole as good or bad literature. Credentialed professional critics who teach literature at great universities may belong to the many who are not literary people. For some of these, reading has become a mere tedium, a necessary evil to hold down a job. Others read for the status of having read the things that everyone who is anyone has read. Others may be devotees of culture to be recognized as cultured, but with no real love of literature. These approaches to reading can leave the young with the mistaken idea that there is something meritorious in reading. For these, reading fails to bring the pleasure that the author intended.

While *An Experiment in Criticism* launched a full-scale attack on the Leavis school of criticism, it may have included a gentle rebuke of Tolkien, who did not measure up to Lewis's definition of a literary person. First of all, Tolkien was a not a person who read a book twice, for Lewis the critical aspect of a literary person. Tolkien observed of himself, "I am a very 'unvoracious' reader, and since I can seldom bring myself to read a work twice I think of the many things that I read—too soon!"[61] He felt sad that so many young people read *The Lord of the Rings* before they could properly appreciate it, because he could not imagine that anyone would read it more than once. He regarded modern literature as "very remote" from his taste and seldom found any modern books that held his attention.[62] He read more widely from time to time as a matter of academic duty or expectation, but he preferred to read mostly fantasy and science fiction, while confessing that he was a man of "limited sympathies" in literature.[63]

Holly Ordway's recent research has forced a closer assessment of Tolkien's reading of modern literature. She has identified about two hundred books of modern literature that Tolkien read during his lifetime, which came as a surprise to many.[64] By modern literature, Ordway means books written after 1850. While Tolkien had a working awareness of his contemporary literary world, it is important to distinguish modern literature from "modern literature." For Tolkien and Lewis, modernity was not a chronological matter so much as a cultural matter. "Modern literature" referred to an attitude toward writing that abandoned the old norms, forms, and cultural commitments in favor of an avant-garde rebellion against tradition. A book might be written after 1850 while not being what Tolkien and Lewis would call "modern literature." For them, *modern* and *contemporary* were not equivalent terms. For instance, Tolkien himself wrote books after 1850, but he was not a modern writer. Ruth Pitter was a modern poet, but not a "modern" poet. T. S. Eliot, on the other hand, was a "modern" poet. C. S. Lewis was not a "modern" novelist, but Virginia Wolfe was.

These distinctions are important in understanding Tolkien's reading habits and the influence of "modern" writing on Tolkien. He could like a passage or a description in a "modern" book without liking the book. He could like a book written after 1850 without liking "modern" literature. As for the bulk of his reading, for an academic scholar to have read two hundred modern books in a lifetime is not a great achievement. C. S. Lewis read about the same number between the ages of sixteen and eighteen when he lived at Great Bookham. Lewis and Tolkien simply read in different ways.

In spite of other literary exposure, Tolkien believed in his head and felt in his heart that Chaucer stood at the autumn of English Literature.[65] Even though he had read Homer, Virgil, and Greek tragedy as a schoolboy, by the time he had entered Exeter College, he changed his allegiance to the Germanic ideal "in reaction to the 'Classics.'"[66] Again, Tolkien did not qualify for what Lewis regarded as a literary person. Perhaps ironically, Humphrey Havard, who always insisted that he was not a literary person, did qualify.[67] In fact, Lewis may have settled on this term of distinction in honor of Havard. Tolkien's real interest was words and not stories. This preference may have formed the greatest divide between him and Lewis. The preference certainly affected how Tolkien read a novel or a poem. Lewis probably referred to Tolkien's way of reading when he remarked in *The Discarded Image*, "Those who ignore the relation of English to Anglo-Saxon as a 'merely philological fact' irrelevant to the literature betray a shocking insensibility to the very mode in which literature exists."[68] I have a very dear friend of long standing with whom I share a love of movies. Whereas I love the stories and their plots and how the director uses all the tools available to create an effect on the audience, he is only interested in the photography.

Back to Work

What would Lewis write next? In response to the endless stream of questions he received from total strangers about this subject, which he felt obliged to answer, Lewis wrote, "I have, as usual, dozens of 'plans' for books, but I don't know which, if any, of these will come off. Very often a book of mine gets written when I am tidying up a drawer and come across notes for a plan rejected by me years ago, and now suddenly realize I can do it after all."[69] While we pause for a moment over what writing project Lewis would next undertake, dear reader, we should note that he wrote a special note to you and me on January 3, 1961, via Don Luigi Pedrollo concerning his letters with Don Giovanni Calabria. Lewis remarked that he always burned correspondence after two days of having received it to insure that nothing would be read by posterity: "For nowadays inquisitive researchers dig out all our affairs and besmirch them with the poison of 'publicity' (as a barbarous thing I am giving it a barbarous name)."[70] So much for those who write and those who read biographies of C. S. Lewis.

The work of the Commission to Revise the Psalter was not yet done by January of 1961, when they continued to meet. Even as Eliot fought to retain the beauty of the Coverdale translation, Lewis continued to fight against the impulse to retain inaccurate translations, what he called "mere howlers," simply because they were so beautiful.[71] Whereas Lewis aimed at truth, Eliot aimed at beauty. External forces were at work that wanted to retain the old translation because of its familiarity, and many wrote to Lewis. In response to one such letter, he explained that he did not think "a Commission appointed by the Archb. to *correct* Coverdale, and preserving what they *knew* to be a mistranslation, cd. claim" their work to be inspired or blessed by God.[72] Eliot and his wife invited Lewis to dine with them when the commission met again in London at Lambeth Palace in April, but Lewis pointed out that the meeting would probably go into the evening and include supper. He closed with a remark that illustrates the growing cordiality of their relationship, for Lewis said supper with the Eliots would have been "fun," especially since they had so much in common: they had both taught John Betjeman (Eliot was his teacher at Highgate School), and neither had been called to testify in the Crown case against the publication of *Lady Chatterley's Lover* in 1960.[73]

By virtue of his status as the Professor of Medieval and Renaissance Literature at Cambridge, the Nobel Committee invited Lewis to submit a nomination for the Nobel Prize for literature in 1961. Lewis had several possible candidates on his mind: E. M. Forster, T. S. Eliot, Robert Frost, and his old friend Tolkien. It probably did not take much reflection to settle on Tolkien. Lewis's letters of the previous ten years are strewn with references to Tolkien's *The Lord of the Rings* prior to and after its publication, and his commendation of it to anyone who could read. However Tolkien might have felt about Lewis after *The Lion, the Witch and the Wardrobe* and his marriage to Joy, Lewis continued to admire and miss his friend. The Nobel Committee did not agree with Lewis, preferring to present the prize in 1961 to Ivo Andrić of Yugoslavia.[74]

Harcourt Brace, Lewis's American publisher, had approached Lewis in April 1959 about bringing out a collection of his old essays and articles.[75] Apparently without consulting his agent or his English publishers, he agreed, with the understanding that some of the titles be changed. The final choice of essays remained substantially as Lewis agreed in the first correspondence. Jocelyn Gibb learned about the American edited volume somehow, and Lewis learned that Gibb knew somehow, which led Lewis to write to Gibb to explain himself while on his trip to Ireland with Joy. He said that his real book was *The Four Loves*, which he was about to send to Gibb, and he did not want a collection of essays standing in the way of its publication. Besides, it had all been initiated by Harcourt Brace and only included old articles that no one in England would be interested in, but Americans would not know any better.[76] Harcourt Brace published the American collection as *The World's Last Night* on February 10, 1960, in time for Joy to see it, but Gibb was not to be thwarted. He wanted a collection too.[77]

By March 1961, Gibb and Lewis began a tug-of-war over which of Lewis's essays to include in a collection from Geoffrey Bles for an English audience. Lewis sent Gibb a "pile" of his published articles with instructions for Gibb to propose the articles he wanted in the collection. Lewis would consider the proposal and send a counterproposal. Then they could meet in Cambridge and "hammer things out."[78] It was a much more complicated process than for *The World's Last Night*, but that proposal had come when Joy was dying and Lewis did not want to be bothered. After her death, he wanted to be bothered. He seems to have wanted the give-and-take of any kind of exchange, perhaps with a meal thrown in.

On April 12, Lewis had received Gibb's proposal, and he issued his counterproposal with an invitation to come to Cambridge on May 16, which would give Lewis plenty of time to consider Gibb's reply. In fact, he thought it would be a good idea for Gibb to make a "preliminary call" on May 3. On April 16, Lewis wrote again to Gibb explaining what he had found so far that might be included in a collection.[79] In the end, Bles published eleven of the thirteen original suggestions from Lewis. It is important to remember that editing a collection of Lewis's essays constituted a gargantuan task, because Lewis did not keep copies of his writing. He rarely had copies of books he had written. He had to remember what he had written and where he had published it and then secure copies of the journals or magazines. Only when we properly understand the enormity of the task can we begin to appreciate Walter Hooper's great work in bringing numerous volumes of Lewis's uncollected essays, articles, lectures, and sermons to print when Lewis himself did not have a list of what he had done or where it might be found.

Lewis and Gibb continued their exchanges into the summer, throwing out and adding back the essays to include. Lewis's next big problem involved a name for the volume. He suggested the pithy title of *Collected Papers* on June 3.[80] In response to Gibb's proposal of *Literary Criticism* through *Ethics and Culture to Theology*, Lewis categorically refused and said it would have to be after his death for the word "culture" to appear anywhere in a title of something he wrote. He could not abide the word. Instead, he gave Gibb a list of alternative titles: *Vacation Exercises, Shotover Essays, Holiday Tasks, They Asked for a Paper*, or *Essays in Truancy*.[81] Lewis always had a difficult time with titles for his books and essays. The publishers frequently changed them. They settled on *They Asked for a Paper*, which Bles published on February 26, 1962.[82]

On April 20, 1961, Lewis sent Gibb another package of "snippets" that might be considered for the collection.[83] These offerings were probably never real offerings. Lewis had decided what he wanted to include from his earlier list, but he drew out the discussion. Gibb declined the "preliminary call" on May 3 but came to lunch with Lewis on May 16 to discuss the project.[84]

Lewis began planning his summer vacation by late April when Owen Barfield came for a visit. He then wrote to Cecil Harwood to suggest that he and Barfield join Lewis in the summer "for a few days in some village," the way they had done before the war.[85] Harwood's wife had died several years earlier, and Lewis wrote to him as one who understood when he asked, "Isn't it rather like after an amputation?"[86] Arthur Greeves also announced that he planned to come in June for one of his rare visits to England. Lewis invited him to come for a visit at the Kilns from Thursday, June 22, until Saturday, June 24. He even offered to hire a car to meet him in London and drive him to Oxford. This time, he could offer Arthur a comfortable bed, thanks to Joy's renovation of the Kilns, in contrast to conditions under Mrs. Moore's regime.[87] Jack brought sandwiches to eat along the way because Clifford Morris, his usual driver, was not available, and his alternate was a man whom Jack did not feel comfortable taking into a hotel dining room, which is where they would usually have stopped for lunch. The primary problem appears to have been that he was "one of the most vociferous bores in England."[88]

Declining Health

Lewis had a growing collection of health issues over the years. There was one problem he appears not to have brought to the attention of Dr. Havard. He wrote to Arthur on June 27, 1961, following their time together at the Kilns to let him know that his trouble had been diagnosed as an enlarged prostate and that he would soon go to a nursing home for surgery to treat it.[89] Men do not suddenly need prostate surgery, which suggests that the urinary problem had been neglected for some time. Three days later, Lewis wrote to Greeves again to tell him that he would enter Acland Nursing Home on Sunday, July 2, for the operation.[90]

Failure to deal with an enlarged prostate results in the accumulation of urine in the bladder and the danger of kidney infection, which is exactly what happened to Lewis. To complicate matters further, the doctors believed Lewis's heart could not take the stress of surgery. They postponed the operation in an effort to deal with his heart issues and kidney infection. Three weeks later, he was still in the Acland when he sent Jocelyn Gibb a short note about some of the articles he had located for possible inclusion in *They Asked for a Paper*. On August 4, the doctors sent Lewis home after concluding that the operation entailed too much risk.[91]

In 1961, the doctors had few medical options for treating Lewis. No pharmaceutical solutions had yet been developed for an enlarged prostate. They had begun giving him regular blood transfusions in an effort to raise his hemoglobin to deal with his severe anemia. They also put him on a no-protein diet to treat his damaged kidneys.[92] A month later, Lewis wrote to Roger Lancelyn

Green that he still awaited his operation. His blood tests (and transfusions) continued at weekly intervals. In addition to the diet and the transfusions, the surgeon had inserted a catheter to drain his bladder. Lewis moved his bedroom to the ground floor because his heart could not take the strain of climbing the stairs. He now occupied what had been the music room. The doctor also insisted that he no longer sleep in his bed but sleep upright in a chair. Sleep apnea was not identified as a medical condition until 1965, but sleeping upright would have been an early treatment to reduce the obstruction of breathing. Lewis hoped Green could visit, with the understanding that he might have to go for his operation just when Green appeared. Fortunately, Lewis experienced no pain and had plenty of time to read.[93]

When Lewis went back to the Acland for another series of transfusions on September 20, 1961, he asked Warnie to bring him a "bottle of whiskey."[94] While the doctors detected some slight improvement, it was not substantial. They took him off his restrictive diet, and he began cooking his own breakfast once he returned to the Kilns after about ten days in the Acland. He was able to walk for about half an hour every day, and from Warnie's perspective, the best sign was that he had grown bored and wanted to get back to work. At his rate of recovery, however, the doctors did not think the surgery could be attempted any sooner than six or even twelve months.[95] He was still having blood transfusions at the Acland when Lewis wrote to Chad Walsh on October 16 to say that it would not be convenient for him to come for a visit.[96] He had another transfusion on October 21 and then again on October 24–25. He expected to be taken back for yet another at any moment, but it depended on how bad his condition became and on bed availability. The transfusions left him feeling in a "drowsy, muzzy state."[97]

At the end of October, after nursing Jack all summer, Warnie left for a holiday in Ireland.[98] Chad and Eva Walsh spent some time in Oxford in November and visited Lewis at the Kilns.

Though he was not in pain, it would be too much to say that he felt better. When he wrote to Greeves on November 12, he made no mention of his health but wrote of books and closed by saying, "This is curiously like the sort of letters we used to write 45 years ago."[99] A few days later, he heard from Harcourt Brace, who wanted to publish a volume of selections from his works. He turned them down flat with the reply that such books make living authors look ridiculous.[100] A few days after that, he received a request from Clyde Kilby, who developed the Lewis collection at Wheaton College, for materials, but Lewis said he did not have anything of the sort Kilby wanted. He did not save letters and manuscripts.[101]

At the end of November, Lewis still had to undergo transfusions on a regular basis, but he told Laurence Whistler that he was "*nearly always* well enough to be visited."[102] Lewis thanked Jocelyn Gibb for a "lovely lunch" and bottle of wine in early December, which suggests that Gibb brought a lunch to the Kilns, for Lewis was still too ill to go out to eat.[103] When Lewis thought of something clever to say with just the right turn of phrase, he would repeat it in his letters to many people. He now had just the right description of his situation, which he shared with one and all: "The position is that they can't operate on my prostate till they've got my heart and kidneys right, and it begins to look as if they can't get my heart and kidneys right till they operate on my prostate. So we're in what an examinee, by happy slip of the pen, called 'a viscous circle.'"[104] He joked freely about his situation, but to Dom Bede Griffiths he confided, "I am in some danger—not sentenced but on trial for my life."[105]

During Christmas week Lewis had to have more transfusions, and his blood count showed that he had made no real progress in six months.[106] By January 26, 1962, he reported that the doctor said he "had turned the corner," but three days later, his blood count had fallen again, and he had to have another round of transfusions.[107] In early February, he told Gibb that he was still on a low protein diet, but he could "drink all the generous liquors" he wanted.[108] Lewis looked forward to a visit from Cecil Harwood in late February and told him that his blood count had improved. He hoped that the ups and downs of his blood count were merely the "foot-hills that prelude a real ascent."[109] On February 26, Geoffrey Bles released *They Asked for a Paper*.[110]

Lewis had his usual bout of flu at the end of February, which must have been particularly difficult for him with his other issues. He did not feel like writing any letters, and he may not have felt like reading the way he normally did when he had the flu. During the long period of transfusions, rest, and a sparse diet, Warnie had handled much of Lewis's correspondence, because he tired so easily. Warnie intercepted all but business letters.[111] On the positive side, however, his doctors began to talk about the possibility of his returning to Cambridge for the spring term after Easter.[112] Jack told Mary Van Deusen in early March that he would likely "escape an operation" but would be "condemned to [his] low diet for the rest of [his] life."[113] It meant his doctors had given up on Lewis ever improving enough to endure an operation. He assured Mary Willis Shelburne that he had learned to tolerate his condition and believed he could "carry on indefinitely in a semi-invalid way without surgery."[114]

Throughout Lewis's invalid life for ten months, Douglas stayed at the Kilns while attending Magdalen College School in Oxford, just across Magdalen Bridge from Magdalen College. He continued to be a source of comfort and joy as well as company to Lewis during his confinement and relative isolation. David had continued with his interest in Judaism and his mother's family heritage. This phase turned out to be not just another of David's phases. On April 10, he met with Rabbi M. Y. Young to discuss how he should proceed. At Young's advice, David enrolled in the North West London Talmudical College on April 15 to complete his A-level studies, the equivalent to an American high school course of study.[115]

Return to Cambridge

Lewis managed to return to Cambridge on April 24 for the Easter term. Both Oxford and Cambridge have three eight-week terms a year with vacations between. Though both universities begin with Michaelmas term at the outset of October, the names for the terms differ after that. Oxford's term after Christmas is Hilary term, but Cambridge's is Lent term. Oxford's third term, after Easter, is Trinity term, but the third term at Cambridge is Easter term. For Easter term 1962, Lewis delivered his lectures on *The Faerie Queene*.[116]

Lewis's life had a different tone in Cambridge after his return to work from what everyone had known before. His osteoporosis had certainly restricted his activity somewhat when Joy was still alive, but his activity was much more restricted in 1962. He told Muriel Bradbrook that he could no longer enjoy protein or "*loco-motion*." He invited her to visit him at Magdalene to enjoy a glass of sherry at six o'clock or lunch at noon, but he warned her that it would be like "visiting the sick."[117] He told T. S. Eliot, who had almost become a friend, that he would be an invalid the rest of his life, "condemned to a catheter and a low protein diet."[118] He also explained that he could not attend the commission on May 29, when it met at Bishopthorpe Palace, the seat of the archbishop of York, because of the ordeal of the journey and the stairs. He told Mary Willis Shelburne that he had to "reduce stair-climbing to a minimum," which meant that he had to think about everything he might need before he descended the stairs, "as if one were planning an expedition to the North Pole or central Africa."[119] It was not a theoretical problem, for Lewis's rooms at Magdalene were up a long flight of stairs. Avoiding stairs was not merely a recommendation from the doctors. Climbing stairs had become a physical ordeal. On the positive side, Lewis was no longer having blood transfusions every week or two, and the color had returned to his hands.[120]

Part of his reluctance to travel arose from the state of catheters in the 1960s. The Foley catheter had been invented in the

1930s, and it was better than nothing, but just barely. It required a surgeon to insert it, and it had to be replaced from time to time. While it did not hurt once in place, having it installed was a painful experience. Plastics were not yet the solution to all problems, and the valve by which Lewis emptied the bag did not have a long life. The valves always developed eventual leaks, but Lewis never knew when a leak would come. This situation caused him constant anxiety, which is not good for the blood pressure of a man with a weak heart.[121] Another feature of the Foley catheter, discovered later, was that it could actually lead to kidney infection!

The story has often been repeated that the catheter was a makeshift contraption of Humphrey Havard's design, as though he put it together in his garage. But Havard was not Lewis's surgeon. The Acland staff attended him when he went in for his regular transfusions and for the replacement of his catheter. In the late 1980s when A. N. Wilson wrote his biography of Lewis, the Foley catheter was already regarded as a primitive instrument compared with the improvements that came in the 1970s, but Wilson wrote as though Lewis had been denied care that did not yet exist.[122] Wilson's writing is an excellent example of what Lewis called chronological snobbery. Wilson might just as easily have criticized Havard for not implanting a pacemaker or stents, since those medical procedures and technologies either were not in common use or did not yet exist.

The Discarded Image

In addition to delivering his lectures on *The Faerie Queene*, Lewis spent Easter term working on a project he would complete in July 1962. He turned his famous prolegomena lectures into a book that would be published by Cambridge University Press as *The Discarded Image*. Though more profound in its depth of insight and a more important monograph on the medieval world than *English Literature in the Sixteenth Century*, *The Discarded Image* would have been a much easier book to write and one that Lewis wrote quickly. He told George Watson that he managed to write only one chapter a year for *The Allegory of Love* as a young tutor struggling to keep up.[123] Not so *The Discarded Image*.

Lewis did not lecture from a full manuscript, but he did have heavily detailed notes that gave him a full outline for the book. Furthermore, he did not have to do any research for this monumental classic, because he had been doing the research and adding to his lectures for thirty years. I visited Barbara Reynolds shortly after the publication of her magnificent *Dante: The Poet, the Political Thinker, the Man* (2006). She was terribly thrilled with what she had accomplished in a relatively short period of time. She told me that each chapter contained one new major idea or understanding about Dante. She was able to do it because she had lived with Dante for the previous sixty years! She advised me that when we grow older, some of our faculties diminish—we forget where we put our glasses or a phone number or a name. With age, however, we acquire a much broader grasp of vast landscapes of data and can recognize patterns that were not evident when we were younger and less experienced. In *The Discarded Image*, Lewis presents his grasp of the medieval world's view of reality from the perspective of forty years of immersion in the literature, history, theology, and science of that world.

When Cambridge University Press asked Lewis for information about his new book for use in promotion, Lewis explained that he wrote the book primarily for university students, but that scholars might be interested in the first two chapters, which deal with the classical background influences on the medieval world and the transitional period from classical to medieval. He also envisioned a third, broader audience of general readers, because he wanted to give a picture of the medieval world's view of the universe and all reality beyond mere curiosity about a bygone day or a tool for understanding the literature of that age, but instead for its "emotional and aesthetic impact." In the end, the book provides an occasion not just for considering the medieval model of the universe but also for reflecting on all cosmic models, including our modern model, which Lewis thought people ought to think about.[124]

It has become fashionable in recent years among some Christians to think of the "medieval synthesis" as the high-water mark of Christianity. If we think of Christianity as a culture, then they are almost right, provided they disregard the eleven centuries of Constantinople before its conquest by the Ottoman Turks. If we think of Christianity as faith in Jesus Christ, however, the medieval West had its share of problems along with the Renaissance, the Enlightenment, the Industrial Revolution, and the Christian century. It was a hodgepodge of classical pagan, Celtic pagan, barbarian invader, and biblical influences that illustrate the West European genius for syncretism. Lewis referred to the integrated system of beliefs and values about the universe as the "Model." He explained that the "medieval synthesis" was "the whole organization of their theology, science, and history into a single, complex, harmonious mental Model of the universe."[125]

This model worked for both a Platonic view in its first six hundred years and an Aristotelian view for its last three hundred years. As it turns out, in what seems to all a discussion of the culture in which a certain kind of literature appeared, Lewis actually was discussing the nature of scientific theories and the danger of confusing a model with a fact. He was doing sophisticated apologetics of the sort he had advocated in "Christian Apologetics"—he was writing a book on the medieval worldview with the Christianity latent. He was critiquing modern materialism through a look at the past.

Lewis did not believe the medieval model to be true or preferable to modern cosmology. He did not think it a Christian model.[126] He did not defend it as a model preferable to any other age. Lewis understood that the kingdom of this world is always the kingdom of this world. He described the model's understanding of the heavens, an understanding he incorporated into his science-fiction trilogy, with the spheres of Pythagoras, Plato, and Aristotle, their mathematical description by Ptolemy, and their sentient dynamics. The model looked at reality in a different way. Modern people think of the universe as a dark place because of our experience of night, but medievals saw the universe as a bright and colorful place because of their experience of day. Night was just a shadow through which they looked at the universe.[127]

Lewis also explored the Longaevi, the long-lived ones, the fairies, as part of the medieval model. Even though he gave a thorough description of their place in the medieval world, Lewis declared, "How far, by how many, and how consistently they were believed in, I do not know."[128] He believed that education would accomplish more if more people learned to say, "We don't know."[129] In the end, what has he said in *The Discarded Image*, and what does it have to do with literature and other art? Eventually, the beliefs and values of a culture permeate the whole culture, and not just the elites. Even after Copernicus and Galileo had laid the foundations for a new world, the old model lingered, just as most people in the twenty-first century still live in the universe of Isaac Newton instead of that of Einstein, Hubble, Heisenberg, and Bohr. People assumed it.

Returning to the problem he identified in *The Abolition of Man* and *De Descriptione Temporum*, in the great change from one culture to another, Lewis suggested that something has been lost. Even as Plato and Aristotle once governed the direction of science, new philosophies of science govern the direction and application of science until "now, in some extreme forms of Behaviourism, the subject himself is discounted as merely subjective; we only think that we think. Having eaten up everything else, he eats himself up too. And where we 'go from that' is a dark question."[130]

Getting By

Once the term ended in June 1962, Clifford Morris drove Lewis back to the Kilns from Magdalene College. The car provided Lewis with a more peaceful and comfortable way to travel, and he could stop at any moment he needed to. Morris was in no hurry. Despite his restrictions, Lewis had the company of colleagues he enjoyed even if he could not eat everything from the larder of Magdalene. Back at the Kilns, he did not have as much company. He told Sheldon Vanauken that "loneliness increases as health returns."[131] To Mary Willis Shelburne he was more specific: "As I get better I feel the loss of Joy more."[132]

Summer had once meant a walking tour across England with Barfield and Harwood, a thirty-mile forced march every day for a week! It had meant diving deeply into cold water and swimming for hours. In August 1962, when he would have been on his way to Ireland for a jaunt with Arthur Greeves, he found himself bound to the Kilns, no longer able to swim or take the long jaunts. Yet he told Dom Bede Griffiths that he had some consolation in the discovery that "nature seems to remove the desire for exercise when the power declines."[133]

Regardless of what was lost, Lewis never appears to have descended into self-pity. His letters of comfort to distressed people reveal how he found strength, peace, comfort, and a complete sufficiency in Jesus Christ on a daily basis. He continued to correspond with needy people who wrote for spiritual help. His letters after Joy's death often involved his own testimony of how he dealt with his grief, loss of health, personal disappointments, and daily struggles with temptation. He continued to attend to the gift of friendship as he found it physically possible. That usually meant writing letters, but it also involved inviting old friends to visit. He often talked about what it means to be "in Christ" and how the process of becoming like Christ that begins in this world is not completed until we reach the next world.[134] He warned of the danger of becoming too introspective. He told Keith Manship the prayer he prayed in his own struggle with temptation as he sought to be more like Christ: "Lord, show me just so much (neither more nor less) about myself as I need for doing thy will *now*."[135] He also rooted his spiritual counsel in specific biblical teachings, so he discussed his declining health in relation to his belief in the resurrection.[136]

Owen Barfield drove Lewis to visit Ruth Pitter on July 12, 1962. Then, Lewis invited Ruth to visit him on August 15, 1962. He invited her for "elevenses," that Hobbit occasion for eating again between breakfast and lunch, which corresponded to afternoon tea, only in the morning. He felt embarrassed that he could not invite her for lunch, but he explained that his "domestic arrangements hardly [made] that possible."[137] It is not clear what he meant. At this point Mrs. Molly Miller, who served as his cook and housekeeper, should have been able to provide a noon meal for Lewis and one guest. It may have meant that he was embarrassed for Pitter to see what a meal was for him at that point with his restricted diet. She brought him a bottle of her homemade elderberry wine.[138] Pitter noted on the envelope in which the invitation to visit had come that this meeting was the last time she saw him.[139]

In addition to writing *A Grief Observed*, *An Experiment in Criticism*, and *The Discarded Image* since Joy's death two years earlier, Lewis also managed to write some popular and academic articles. John Bunyan's *Pilgrim's Progress* played a part in Lewis's conversion, for he read it a number of times in the years leading up to his conversion. It became the model for his own testimony in *The Pilgrim's Regress*. In August 1962, the BBC approached Lewis again to give a talk. They wanted him to speak about *The Pilgrim's Progress*. After turning them down time after time since the war, this time Lewis agreed. He had something to say on the subject. He wrote quickly and recorded the talk at the Kilns on September 11 for broadcast on October 16.[140] He published the text as "The Vision of John Bunyan" in *The Listener* in December 1962.[141] It remains one of the few recordings of Lewis, and copies are available still.

As Michaelmas term approached, Lewis began to arrange meetings and visits with his friends. He made a date to meet Roger

Lancelyn Green at the "Bird and Baby" on Monday, October 29, as they had done so many times before. The day and place demonstrate that Lewis still met with his old friends at the Eagle and Child when his health permitted.[142] He proposed that Kay and Austin Farrer come by the Kilns any afternoon before he left for Cambridge on October 8.[143] He invited his godson Laurence Harwood to visit him in Cambridge some weekday at Magdalene during term.[144] The younger Harwood then lived near Cambridge. All the effort to keep up Lewis's spirits met with a crushing blow in the middle of September, however, when Jack had to tell Douglas and David that their father had committed suicide by an overdose of sleeping pills. Renée Gresham had informed Lewis that Bill died on September 13. He had learned he had cancer.[145]

On a happier note, John Lawlor told Lewis that he and a number of his friends and former students had decided to produce a *Festschrift* in his honor upon his retirement, which Lewis calculated would come in 1966. Lewis was deeply touched and honored, but as usual, his humility in such matters caused him to worry that people might feel they had to work up something for the book. If people had something they wanted to write and the book gave them a place to publish it, that would make "a useful book."[146] Lewis thought the idea of a dinner on the occasion of its publication would suit the guests better than him with his diet, unless Lawlor could serve the head of F. R. Leavis on a charger![147]

Tolkien, who was several years older than Lewis, had a *Festschrift* presented to him at the end of term in December 1962. Tolkien must have been touched and honored that Lewis contributed an essay entitled "The Anthropological Approach." The book was *English and Medieval Studies Presented to J. R. R. Tolkien on the Occasion of His Seventieth Birthday*. Tolkien invited Lewis to the celebratory dinner at Merton College, but Lewis declined the invitation with regret, owing to his diet, his catheter, and his need to go to bed early. It was a short letter without going into a more expansive explanation of all that had befallen him since

Joy's death.[148] The episode, however, forms part of a series of events that constituted a bit of a rapprochement between Tolkien and Lewis.

Earlier in the year, the publishing firm of George Allen and Unwin had written to Lewis asking if he would write an endorsement for Tolkien's little book of verse *The Adventures of Tom Bombadil and Other Verses from the Red Book*, published later in 1962. Lewis was not paranoid but realistic about the reach of F. R. Leavis in the literary world and what an endorsement from him might mean in the hands of literary critics at large. He wrote to Tolkien directly to explain that he thought an endorsement might actually harm the book for an additional reason: "The public—little dreaming how much you dislike my work, bless you!—regard us as a sort of firm and wd. only laugh at what wd. seem to them mutual back-scratching."[149] After making a few suggestions for improvement of the verses, which Tolkien may not have appreciated, Lewis closed by saying, "I wish we cd. ever meet." When Lewis wrote this letter, he sent it to Merton College, which A. N. Wilson interpreted as the degree of the estrangement between the two, since Lewis did not even know where Tolkien then lived.[150] By then, Tolkien had moved near Lewis in Headington at 76 Sandfield Road. Hugo Dyson lived just down the street from Tolkien. Such a conclusion, however, does not logically follow. Lewis received most of his mail at college, and it would have been normal to send a colleague a letter at his college too. The fact that Lewis marked the envelope "Please Forward" is only a sign that he sent the letter at the end of term, after which Tolkien would not likely go by the college every day. Wilson is correct, however, in conveying the idea that Tolkien and Lewis had drifted far apart.

Having received Lewis's regrets about the *Festschrift* dinner, Tolkien wrote another note to Lewis after the dinner. We do not have the letter, which probably said something about the dinner and how sorry he was to learn of Lewis's health problems. Humphrey Carpenter's edition of Tolkien's letters gives the impression

J. R. R. Tolkien, 1960s. INTERFOTO / Alamy Stock Photo.

that he did not have the heavy correspondence that Lewis inflicted, to a certain degree, upon himself. Holly Ordway has argued that Tolkien engaged in a heavy correspondence, most of which has not been published or otherwise made available to scholars.[151] All we know of the letter is that Lewis called it "most kind" when he replied to Tolkien on Christmas Eve 1962 with hopes for him and Edith. Sometime later that winter, Christopher Tolkien drove his father to visit Lewis at the Kilns. We only have Wilson's interpretation of the visit as told to him by Christopher.[152] The significant matter is that Tolkien responded to his old friend's desire to meet again after so long.

Tolkien was not the only one who braved the weather to visit Lewis that harsh winter of 1963. When George Sayer planned a visit in early January, Lewis advised him to leave his car on the road and walk "(or wade)" up the muddy lane to the house.[153] It was a winter of rain and snow that reduced the long dirt lane leading from the road across most of the estate to a muddy slough. Snow covered England from just after Christmas 1962 until March 1963.[154] Cars could not navigate the lane at the Kilns without getting mired in mud or snow, so visits were few until the thaw. Lewis made arrangements to meet Roger Lancelyn Green in Oxford on Monday, March 11, 1963. Green had joined Lewis and his friends at the Eagle and Child many Mondays since the late 1940s, but Lewis told him that there would be a change now. He hated to break with tradition, but by the end of January 1963, the friends had changed their loyalty from the Eagle and Child to the Lamb and Flag, just across broad St Giles', because their old favorite pub "had become too intolerably cold, dark, noisy, and child-pestered."[155] Though the location changed, the gathering did not. Neither winter's fierce gale nor the body's afflictions nor the entreaties of a demanding public could infringe on Lewis's Monday morning appointment. As he wrote to Sherwood Wirt on April 13, 1963, "Monday mornings happen to be always occupied."[156]

The third week of January, Lewis's catheter came apart in the middle of the night. At one thirty in the morning, he hiked down to the road through the snow drifts that blocked his lane so that he could meet the ambulance that would take him to the hospital to have a new catheter fitted. The ambulance arrived about 2:20, and off Lewis rode to the Acland, where they cared for his needs. He was back home in bed by six that morning.[157] He described this adventure not to Sayer, Green, Greeves, or Barfield but to Mary Willis Shelburne! The story is important for two reasons. First, it demonstrates that Dr. Havard was not the person to blame for the performance of a state-of-the-art catheter in 1963. Second, Jack's telling this story at all illustrates that he was not as secretive as is often alleged. He had a private side, but the only reason we know of his private side is that he told people about it. Not everyone was entitled to know everything about him, but he told people about his private life all the time. Often, he told total strangers or American correspondents he had never met. The only reason Humphrey Havard could quip that *Surprised by Joy* should have been named *Suppressed by Jack* is that Lewis had told Havard so much about himself.

Letters to Malcolm

In 1949, Mary Van Deusen had suggested that Lewis write a book about prayer, to which he replied that he thought it would be "rather 'cheek'" of him to write such a book.[158] By 1954 he had changed his mind and thought he was ready to write a book on prayer. He started writing it but could not finish.[159] During the bleak winter of 1963, however, he returned to the book, but this time in the form of a series of letters to an imaginary person. It was *The Screwtape Letters* from the other way around. On April 22, 1963, he wrote to Shelburne that he had finished the book. He called it *Letters to Malcolm Chiefly on Prayer*.[160] On May 16, Lewis informed Jocelyn Gibb that the manuscript was with his typist, but that he needed to rewrite one of the letters, so Gibb would not have the text immediately.[161]

In many ways, he had written the book many times before, for it captures the kind of dialogue he had once had with Arthur Greeves in his teens and Owen Barfield in his twenties. Since then, this kind of extended discussion of a subject had occurred only with some of his female American correspondents like Shelburne, Mrs. Frank Jones, and Van Deusen. In his opening paragraph, Lewis reveals how the idea for this form finally came to him:

> I am all in favour of your idea that we should go back to our old plan of having a more or less set subject—an *agendum*—for our letters. When we were last separated the correspondence languished for lack of it. How much better we did in our undergraduate days with our interminable letters on the *Republic*, and classical metres, and what was then the "new" psychology! Nothing makes an absent friend so present as a disagreement.[162]

Possibly the heavy snow that winter, which kept England blanketed with white from Christmas to Easter, set his mind back to the winter in Great Bookham when he first had the image of a faun in such a snow. He may have missed writing to a friend. Over the previous twenty years, he had neglected writing to his friends the way he had once written to Greeves and Barfield, because he felt an obligation to answer the mountain of letters from strangers that buried his letter box every day. He often mentioned it in notes he wrote to his closest friends. Of course, he would not have felt in any way sentimental like his father, because he deplored sentimentality, but he might have felt nostalgic.

In *Letters to Malcolm* Lewis explored private prayer. He had told Don Giovanni Calabria, when he first attempted the book, that he wanted to help new converts begin a life of private prayer. Much had been written for the religious, but he saw a need for those unaccustomed to the life of faith.[163] He had no interest in treating public prayer, which he associated with liturgy, a subject that disinterested him almost as much as sports.[164] He endured the liturgy of the church as he endured the hymns, almost as an act of penance, but certainly as a duty and obligation.[165] He told Dom Bede Griffiths that he thought "liturgiology" was more a snare for the laity who spoke of it "as if it were itself the Christian faith."[166] In a letter to the editor of the *Church Times* in 1949, Lewis had expressed the view that he was much less interested in liturgy than in doctrine, except when a change in liturgy would result in a change of doctrine.[167] His position should not be seen in any way as opposition to liturgy so much as opposition to innovations in liturgy.[168] In a letter to Mary Van Deusen, he had explained the problem with public extemporaneous prayer: "We don't know whether we can mentally join in it until we've heard it—it might be phoney or heretical. We are therefore called upon to carry on a *critical* and a *devotional* activity at the same moment: two things hardly compatible."[169] For Lewis, the advantage of the liturgical prayers, fixed for centuries, was that they set "our devotions *free*."

Several people had urged Lewis to write a book in answer to Bishop John A. T. Robinson's *Honest to God*, which had caused a great stir by its effort to synthesize the views of German theologians Paul Tillich, Rudolf Bultmann, and Dietrich Bonhoeffer. Dale Moody, one of my theology professors, had been at Oxford at the time finishing his DPhil degree and wrote reviews for Blackwell's Book Shop. He used to tell us that Robinson had poured three German beers together and only gotten a lot of froth. Lewis resisted the urge to write a full-on rebuttal because he did not want to give Robinson any more publicity, but he thought he had answered many of Robinson's views implicitly in *Letters to Malcolm*.[170] Lewis had already been involved in revising the Psalter of the Prayer Book, but the bigger project involved revising the entire Book of Common Prayer, and Lewis feared what would result with bishops like Robinson at large.[171]

Lewis's first effort at *Letters to Malcolm* had stalled when he came up against questions he could not answer. For instance, he told Don Giovanni that he wondered how a person could believe that God would answer a prayer and at the same time submit to the will of God possibly not to answer the prayer.[172] He found that "the simplest questions about [prayer] seem to be the ones no one has ever dealt with."[173] He could not simply ply his trade and do more documentary research to find the answers. He had to discover the answers through prayer. In many ways, the experience he documented in *A Grief Observed* taught him all about private prayer.

Though *Letters to Malcolm* imagines a recipient of the letters, in fact, most of what Lewis says in the book he had already said in letters to real people. In 1967, Clyde Kilby edited the letters from Lewis to Mary Willis Shelburne, which he published as *Letters to an American Lady*, with her name withheld.[174] These letters, beginning in 1950, illustrate the kind of spiritual counsel Lewis gave to spiritually needy people, and they are echoed in *Letters to Malcolm*. His description of an Orthodox service in a letter written in 1956 is repeated in *Letters to Malcolm*.[175] Letter 3 begins with an echo of his exchanges with the Episcopal Radio Foundation about mentioning sex in his "Four Loves" recordings.[176] In letter 7, he addresses the problem he had raised with Don Giovanni about how we can ask for God to do something and still pray that God's will be done.[177] Then, in letter 8, he discusses prayer when someone we love deeply has died.[178]

Lewis learned about prayer in the midst of the trials he had faced, the greatest of which was the death of Joy. *Letters to Malcolm* bears witness to the confirmation of Lewis's faith. Those who believe that the first half of *A Grief Observed* demonstrates that Lewis lost his faith simply have not read the whole book, or the rest of the story told in *Letters to Malcolm*, his final testimony.

10

The Last Summer

1963

Even in the midst of the dismal winter, Lewis began making plans for the summer of 1963. He intended to go to Ireland at the end of July, this time with Douglas. He wanted Arthur to meet them on July 29 and travel about with them. Lewis would hire a car and driver. He wanted to see Castlerock again or the Glens of Antrim.[1] Arthur suggested the village of Portballintrae in Antrim. Lewis approved the choice and asked Arthur to book three rooms for them until August 12, when he and Douglas would sail back to England.[2] In the end, Arthur could not get reservations, because the summer trade had already taken all the rooms, so he found places for them in Portstewart, in Londonderry. Lewis said that it did not matter where they stayed since the main thing was to find a few days together—"We're both too old to let our remaining chances slip!"[3]

As summer drew closer, Lewis asked Roger Lancelyn Green to meet him at the Lamb and Flag and then stay the night at the Kilns once the term ended on June 7, or to come on some Monday sooner.[4] Nathan Starr wanted to meet Lewis in Ireland when he would also be touring there, but Lewis was not inclined to have any intrusions on his time with Arthur. He suggested that Starr visit him in August at the Kilns.[5]

On June 7, Clifford Morris drove Lewis home from Cambridge for the summer, and that afternoon Walter Hooper came to the Kilns to have tea with Lewis.[6] Hooper had corresponded with Jack for nine years. He had wanted to write a biography of Lewis, who discouraged him from proceeding.[7] In 1963, Hooper taught English literature at the University of Kentucky, where he learned that the greatest advantage to an academic career was June, July, and August. He was spending his summer in Oxford, where Lewis invited him to meet on Monday mornings at the Lamb and Flag. In those days, the Monday morning regulars were Colin Hardie, Gervase Mathew, R. B. McCallum, James Dundas-Grant, Humphrey Havard, and Warnie when he was not in Ireland.[8] Hooper and Lewis then began meeting each week on Monday at the Lamb and Flag, Wednesday at the Kilns before going to the nearby Six Bells pub, and Sunday at the Kilns before proceeding to church together.[9] After church, they returned to the Kilns, where Lewis cooked breakfast. If it was his idea of a low protein diet, that explains a lot. He always cooked eggs, bacon, and sausage with toast and scones![10] Hooper met an important need for Lewis, for Warnie was in Ireland recovering from a binge, and Lewis hated solitude.[11]

On July 9, Lewis told Mary Willis Shelburne that he feared that his doctor, presumably Humphrey Havard, would not allow him to go to Ireland the next Monday. He had swollen ankles again, which were a "Red Light" for Lewis that his heart was in trouble. He would see Havard on July 10.[12] On the 11th, he wrote to Arthur Greeves to say that his heart trouble had returned, and he had to cancel all their plans for Ireland.[13] On the 13th, he was waiting for admission to the hospital as soon as a bed came available. His anemia left him feeling "a most debilitating effect on the mind."[14] The most disturbing thing to Lewis was the loss of his ability to concentrate. He was terribly sleepy and fell asleep three times while trying to write a letter.[15] He could no longer handle his own correspondence, and Warnie was away in Ireland as drunk as a lord.

The Heart Attack

On Sunday, July 14, Lewis was not well enough to go to church when Walter Hooper arrived at the Kilns. Without Warnie any-more as a reliable helper with his correspondence, and feeling his own steady decline, Lewis asked Hooper if he would consider serving as his private secretary. After discussing it, Hooper agreed to resign his post at the University of Kentucky at the end of the fall semester and return to help Lewis. In the meantime, he would help Lewis through the summer.[16] The next day, on Monday, July 15, at five in the afternoon, Lewis arrived at the Acland Nursing Home, where he promptly had a heart attack and went into a coma.[17]

With Warnie away, Lewis must have given Kay and Austin Farrer as his emergency contacts, for the Acland notified them of Lewis's condition. They contacted Douglas Gresham and Walter Hooper. On Tuesday afternoon, July 16, Lewis received extreme unction from Rev. Michael Watts of the Church of St Mary Mag-dalen. Then he woke up and asked for a cup of tea.[18]

For two days, Lewis appeared to be doing better, but then he slipped into what he called his "black period." For a week he suffered from nightmares, hallucinations, and a general disori-entation interspersed with lucid moments.[19] Several of his oldest and dearest friends visited him in the Acland, including Tolkien, Alastair Fowler, Douglas and David Gresham, James Dundas-Grant, John Walsh, Maureen Moore Blake, and George Sayer. When Dundas-Grant visited Lewis, he suggested that Lewis write a book on prayer, to which Lewis replied with a twinkle in his eye, "I might."[20] Dundas-Grant did not know that Lewis had just finished writing *Letters to Malcolm*, which suggests how far the remaining Inklings had departed from being a writing club aware of what each other was writing.

When Douglas went to visit Jack, they chatted for a while as usual, but then Jack asked if Doug should not be going to the train station. Doug asked why. Jack said he needed to pick up the au pair girl who was coming to help Mrs. Miller with the housework. He was surprised that Mrs. Miller had not told Doug. Doug immediately went to the hospital office to call a taxi, then he went back to Jack to ask for money to pay for the taxi. Jack asked why Doug needed a taxi. Doug said he needed a taxi to meet the au pair girl. Jack wanted to know what au pair girl. Doug explained that Jack had told him to go to the train station to meet the au pair girl who would be helping Mrs. Miller. Jack smiled and began to laugh as he told Doug it must have been another hallucination. Jack said that all he had left was his mind, and that was going too. Then he began laughing again.[21]

As Doug left the hospital that day, he met one of Jack's old friends coming in. "I don't know if you remember me," the man said as he offered his hand. "I'm Ronald Tolkien." Of course, Doug knew him. They talked for a few moments, but as they parted, Tolkien said, "If I can ever be of help to you, if you ever need a place to stay, please don't hesitate to let me know."[22]

Maureen Moore Blake visited Lewis when he was in the midst of his incoherent state. Walter Hooper met her and explained his condition. Maureen's father had died shortly after her mother, and a distant relative of her father died a few months before Lewis's illness. By one of those fairy-tale quirks of British history, Maureen succeeded to the lands and title of her distant relative as Lady Dunbar of Hempriggs, the first woman in three hundred years to succeed to a baronetcy in the United Kingdom. Maureen had not seen Lewis since she inherited the title. Hooper recalled that Lewis opened his eyes when Maureen took his hand: "'Jack,' she whispered, 'it is Maureen.' 'No,' replied Lewis smiling, 'it is Lady Dunbar of Hempriggs.' 'Oh, Jack, how could you remember that?' she asked. 'On contrary,' he said. 'How could *I* forget a fairy tale?'"[23] When his disorientation occurred, however, it could be alarming.

When Sayer entered his room, he found Lewis out of bed in his dressing gown. He walked toward Sayer and clutching him said: "Thank God, a friend. You see a dying man. For God's sake, and as you value our friendship, go and get me some cigarettes and matches. And don't, on any account, let them see you bring them in."[24] While smoking the offered cigarette, Lewis explained to Sayer that he had been named Charles Williams's literary executor, but Mrs. Williams was giving him trouble. Williams had left a number of valuable manuscripts that he needed to publish, but Mrs. Williams refused to turn them over unless he paid her ten thousand pounds. She kept them under her mattress, and he feared he would have to sue to get them. While Sayer tried to take in all this information, Lewis went on to talk about Mrs. Moore, who Lewis apparently thought was still alive. Sayer realized that Lewis was in a delusional state. He then asked if Sayer had met Walter Hooper, whom Lewis had engaged as his secretary. Sayer assumed that this new friend whom Lewis wanted everyone to like was another delusion. On his next visit to see Lewis, Humphrey Havard explained that Hooper was real and would make it possible for Lewis to go home.[25]

Warnie Lewis did not yet know about Jack's condition, so Sayer volunteered to go to Ireland and find Warnie. When Sayer arrived at Our Lady of Lourdes Hospital, at Drogheda, where Warnie had been going since the late 1940s to get over his Irish binges, he found that Warnie was in Dublin for the day. The sister in charge and Warnie's doctor explained that Warnie was free to go where he wanted during the day, just so long as he returned for the evening meal. They decided to break the news to Warnie gradually so that he would not spiral into depression and resume his serious drinking. They would keep Warnie with them until they decided he was fit to travel again without danger of going on another binge.[26]

Home to the Kilns

When Lewis returned to the Kilns on August 6, he went with Alec Ross, a male nurse from Scotland, and Walter Hooper and Douglas Gresham. Hooper took Lewis's old bedroom and study upstairs. Douglas, whose bedroom had been the old music room, had moved to the bedroom next to the kitchen by the tradesmen's entrance when Jack needed a bedroom downstairs.[27] Mrs. Miller cooked the meals, but her idea of low protein was similar to Jack's, for her meals included a lot of chicken, cheese, and eggs. In fact, they may actually have believed that low protein simply meant no roast beef. The doctors' advice to give up tobacco fell on deaf ears. Sayer believed that the doctors would also have been alarmed if they knew how much tea Lewis drank every day, but that was Sayer's perspective in health conscious 1988 and not 1963.[28]

Beginning on July 17, Hooper undertook the handling of Lewis's correspondence. He picked up the mail every day at the Kilns and took it to the Acland, where Lewis, when his mind was clear, dictated his letters to Hooper. At Lewis's behest, Hooper wrote letters to Lewis's friends who had not yet learned of his hospitalization, including Roger Lancelyn Green. Lewis asked Hooper to write Green a letter and explain that Hooper was a collector of "Lewisiana" like Green and to work out with Green if they were "competitors or collaborators."[29] Time would prove that they were the best of collaborators as coauthors of the first true biography of Lewis, *C. S. Lewis: A Biography* (1974).

Lewis probably recognized his condition better than most. He knew he would die sooner or later. Not wishing to create a burden for Cambridge University and Magdalene College, his academic home for nine years, he sent a letter resigning his chair, probably as soon as he returned home.[30] On August 12 and 13, Lewis wrote to Jock Burnet, the bursar of Magdalene College, to make arrangements for Hooper to pack his things and remove them from the college. He apologized for the trouble he was causing, but he explained that his "situation [was] rather desperate."[31] The college needed to reclaim its furniture and sell Lewis's. He also asked that the painting of his grandfather Hamilton be sent to St Mark's Church, Dundela, Belfast, where he had served as rector. It still hangs in the Parish Hall today.

Douglas Gresham went with Walter Hooper to pack Lewis's belongings on August 14. When they arrived, they found that the floor had fallen in! It meant they had to walk on a plank that bridged one side of the room to the other as they cleared out all the books and papers. Lewis gave Hooper seven pages of instructions about what to do with all the books in his study. It took them three days to complete their work. Lewis offered the college a keepsake from his books, and the *Complete Works of Shakespeare* was chosen. As for his own works, Lewis told Hooper to throw them away unless he wanted them. When they finally finished on August 16, they loaded several thousand books onto a truck and hauled them to the Kilns.[32] These books now reside at the Marion E. Wade Center at Wheaton College.

When he returned to the Kilns, Hooper told Lewis about meeting Derek Pepys Whiteley, a librarian at Magdalene College. Hooper said that Whiteley managed to interest him because of "the very intensity of his boredom."[33] In 1959 a question had arisen within the college about dismissing Whiteley. Lewis wrote to Dick Ladborough to plead for his retention. Whiteley had undertaken the cataloging of the Pepys Library, and Lewis found him to be "a friendly, decent, straightforward" man, but also "a very great Bore."[34] Lewis acknowledged that Whiteley's conversation fatigued and dejected him more than that of anyone else he knew. Yet Lewis thought it "dishonourable" to turn him out because of his "boringness" when he provided good service. He disclosed to Ladborough, "I feel v. strongly that to suffer bores patiently— 'gladly' may be impossible—is a plain duty, and that it is even plainer when we owe them some gratitude."[35] To Hooper, Lewis added, "Let us not forget that Our Lord might well have said 'As ye have done it unto one of the least of these my bores, ye have done it unto me.'"[36] The Christian faith was not merely true for Lewis; it made a difference in how he treated people.

Toward the end of August, Tolkien wanted to see Lewis again. Tolkien's eldest son, Father John Tolkien, took Tolkien to see Lewis at the Kilns. Father John recalled: "We drove over to the Kilns for what turned out to be a very excellent time together for about an hour. I remember the conversation was very much about the *Morte d'Arthur* and whether trees died."[37]

Ready for Death

Walter Hooper was back in the United States when Lewis wrote to him on September 3 to let him know that all was well at the Kilns. Though Warnie was still in Ireland behaving badly, the gardener and handyman, Fred Paxford, slept in the house in case Lewis had trouble during the night.[38] After much wringing of hands and worry about his looming poverty, Lewis offered Hooper five pounds a week when he would return the first week of January 1964 to resume his work as Lewis's secretary, now that Warnie had proved such an unreliable disappointment.[39] To others, Jack regularly referred to himself as an "extinct volcano."[40] When asked how he managed his retirement, he came up with another line he rather liked. He said he would never have to read A. L. Rowse on Shakespeare's sonnets, but he could reread the *Iliad* instead.[41] On a deeper level, he had something to say to many about how close he came to death. The nurses all thought he had come to the Acland one last time to die. He said to many of his correspondents that it was a pity he had come to the very gates of Heaven so easily not to be allowed to enter. Now he would have to go through it all over again.[42]

Warnie finally returned home in early October.[43] His return meant some relief from what Lewis regarded as the worst part of his invalid existence. The newspapers had reported Lewis's illness and retirement, so he was flooded with letters of condolence, to which he felt obligated to reply.[44] In spite of everything, he remained cheerful and grateful. He especially valued his friends who came to see him.[45] The letters he did not mind were those from friends who might come for a visit. He asked several to come when they could: Cecil Harwood, Richard Ladborough, Nathan Starr, Nan Dunbar, Basil Willey, and Kathleen Raine.[46] He made plans with Muriel Bradbrook for a visit on December 8 and with Nan Dunbar for a visit on December 14.[47] He wrote to Mrs. Frank Jones, an American lady who had sent him food packages during the shortages, about his life as an invalid:

> I rarely venture further afield than a stroll in the garden. Once a week I attend a reunion of old friends at one of the Oxford taverns. (*Beer* thank goodness is not on the list of things denied me). Sometimes some kind person takes me out for a run in a car. Otherwise I write, read, and answer letters; one day is like another. But you are not to think of me as unhappy or bored.[48]

The reunion, of course, was with the Inklings. The friends who took him driving were Humphrey Havard, Roger Lancelyn Green, and George Sayer. The only real sadness he had about his deteriorating condition was that he and Arthur would "never meet again in this life."[49] He ended his last letter to Greeves, "But oh Arthur, never to see you again!"[50]

On one autumn afternoon, Sayer took Lewis for a drive along the London Road, up Beacon Hill to the crest of the Chilterns, and then along the crest past Christmas Common. The beech trees were in full fall color and the sun shone brightly, but the air had a crispness to it. They stopped so that Lewis could get out and enjoy the country. He said, "I think I might have my last soak of the year."[51] Having a soak was an expression Lewis adopted soon after he and Arthur Greeves became friends to refer to the idyllic experience of walking in the country and stopping to rest, smoke a cigarette, and soak it all in. They drove back to the Kilns on back roads by way of Garsington and Chiselhampton. It was not a very long drive. The Chiltern Hills cross the southeastern boundary of Oxfordshire. Evening falls early in England as the days draw closer to winter, and the stars had come out before they reached home. Lewis, gazing at the first bright star, quoted Plato in Greek when Sayer asked if it was Venus or Hesperus. When Sayer asked for a translation, Jack quoted Shelley's translation in *Epigram to Stella*.[52]

Of course, Lewis could no longer write. His body was spent and he worried that his mind had gone. Yet he wrote anyway. On October 17 he sent a note to Thomas Congdon, an editor at the *Saturday Evening Post*, accepting a request to write an article about "the right to happiness." Lewis accepted with the understanding that he would have to discuss the American ideal of the right to "life, liberty and the pursuit of happiness" with the restriction that "people have a right to do only whatever they have a right to do."[53] Lewis wrote the article, but it was not the article requested. It was "We Have No Right to Happiness," which the *Post* published in its Christmas issue a month after Lewis died.[54]

After reading *Les Liasons dangereuses*, a rather racy eighteenth-century French novel, Lewis asked Richard Ladborough, his friend from Magdalene who taught French, to visit him and tell him about it. Ladborough went to see Lewis in mid-November, but he reported, "Of course it was Jack who told *me* about it, and not the other way round."[55] Roger Green spent the night with Lewis on November 15, but he was disturbed when Lewis kept falling asleep as they talked after dinner. More alarmingly, he often stopped breathing—a symptom of sleep apnea. When the following Monday came, however, Lewis felt good enough to drive to the Lamb and Flag to meet his friends.[56]

Just as Jack had gone through anticipatory grief over Joy's coming death, Warnie had gone through the same thing in his own way over Jack's inevitable death. Yet he had pulled himself together and returned to the Kilns. His company would have meant so much to Jack. Of those last days together, Warnie wrote:

Joy had left us, and once again—as in the earliest days—we could turn for comfort only to each other. The wheel had come full circle: once again we were together in the little end room at home, shutting out from our talk the ever-present knowledge that the holidays were ending, that a new term fraught with unknown possibilities awaited us both.

Jack faced the prospect bravely and calmly. "I have done all I wanted to do, and I'm ready to go", he said to me one evening.[57]

Then, Oxford University invited Lewis to deliver the Romanes Lecture, its oldest and most distinguished endowed lectureship. It would have been a nice note to end on, but the invitation came too late. Jack asked Warnie to "send them a very polite refusal."[58]

The End

Warnie was always famous for preparing the tea on Thursday nights when the Inklings had gathered so long ago. He also brought the late-night tea to Jack and any guest he might have as they talked away. Even with Mrs. Miller in the house, Warnie brought Jack his tea in the afternoons that last autumn. He described the last time in the memoir he wrote that became a foundational piece of biography Roger Lancelyn Green and Walter Hooper would build upon, along with *Surprised by Joy*, when they wrote their biography of Lewis. Warnie said:

> Friday, the 22nd of November 1963, began much as other days: there was breakfast, then letters and the crossword puzzle. After lunch he fell asleep in his chair: I suggested that he would be more comfortable in bed, and he went there. At four I took in his tea and found him drowsy but comfortable. Our few words then were the last: at five-thirty I heard a crash and ran in, to find him lying unconscious at the foot of his bed. He ceased to breathe some three or four minutes later.[59]

He was a week shy of his sixty-fifth birthday.

Douglas had left Magdalen College School the previous school year to go to Applegarth, in Surrey, a school designed to help boys pass their O levels. In a short time, he had grown close to Mr. Stevens—one of the teachers, who was a partner in the school—and his family. It was Pam Stevens, the elder daughter, who came to get Douglas so that he could be told the news of Jack's death. Douglas guessed and Pam confirmed the worst before they reached her parents.[60] Jean Wakeman, Joy's great friend who lived near Studley Priory, drove down to Surrey to bring Doug home. She had told Doug when Jack became very sick that if anything happened to Jack, Doug would come and live with her, which he did.[61] Warnie rode with her, though he was in a sorry state that only got worse as he drowned his anguish.[62]

The death of C. S. Lewis came on the same day John F. Kennedy was shot in Dallas, and all the news media were focused on that event, which gripped not only the United States but people around the world. Word of Lewis's death had not gotten out. Douglas called Walter Hooper in the United States, and Hooper notified those he knew of who should be told.[63] David Gresham had gone to New York to study at Mesivta Rabbi Chaim Berlin Talmudical college when he finished his studies in London, so he could not attend the funeral.[64] Warnie was too intoxicated and overwhelmed by grief to attend. The funeral took place on November 26 at Holy Trinity Church, the parish church where Jack and Warnie had attended since moving to the Kilns. Only a small group attended. Ronald Head, the vicar of Holy Trinity, led the service, and Austin Farrer read the lesson, so we may assume that Kay was with him.[65] The small party of mourners included Owen Barfield, Cecil Harwood, Ronald Tolkien, Colin Hardie, Robert "Humphrey" Havard, James Dundas-Grant, John Lawlor, Peter Bayley, Peter Bide, Molly and Len Miller, Fred Paxford, Maureen (Lady Dunbar) and Leonard Blake, and Douglas Gresham.[66]

George Sayer remembered that David Gresham was present, which illustrates how the memories of different people can provide conflicting accounts of the same event. This feature of memory is why memoirs are not primary sources and must be weighed judiciously.[67] Of all those who gave accounts of the funeral, only Sayer recalled that David Gresham had followed Lewis's coffin out of the church with Douglas and Maureen.[68] He might have flown from New York to London in time to be there. On the other hand, Dundas-Grant specifically mentioned the sadness of seeing Lewis's "younger stepson" following the coffin without reference to the other stepson. Douglas Gresham mentioned nothing of his brother being present, but that would be an argument from silence. Perhaps he was there, and perhaps he was not. In fact, we do not really know how many people were present. Sayer mentioned fourteen people, but Dundas-Grant only mentioned the three Catholics (Tolkien, Havard, and Dundas-Grant), who had attended a Requiem Mass for Lewis earlier that morning before the funeral. Peter Bayley mentioned no one. As with the rest of Lewis's life, in all likelihood, not everyone at the funeral knew everyone else who attended.

A large gravestone covers the length and breadth of the grave of C. S. Lewis. When Flora Hamilton Lewis died in 1908, the quotation for the day on her Shakespearean calendar came from *King Lear*:

> Men must endure
> Their going hence, even as their coming hither;
> Ripeness is all.[69]

On Lewis's gravestone, Warnie had the epitaph engraved:

IN LOVING MEMORY OF

MY BROTHER

CLIVE STAPLES LEWIS

BORN BELFAST 29TH NOVEMBER 1898

DIED IN THIS PARISH

22ND NOVEMBER 1963

MEN MUST ENDURE THEIR GOING HENCE.

When Warnie died almost ten years later, he was buried with his brother, and his epitaph added below that of Jack:

WARREN HAMILTON LEWIS
MAJOR ROYAL ARMY SERVICE CORPS
BORN BELFAST 16TH JUNE 1895
DIED IN THIS PARISH
9TH APRIL 1973

II

The Completion of a Life

Between his late thirties and his mid-forties Lewis wrote his three science-fiction books, but during this period he also wrote his most popular apologetics, all while a world war raged. In the last period of his life, his productivity changed. He was just as prolific, but he self-consciously entered a new phase of life. As he approached his fiftieth birthday, after the war, he saw himself as entering old age. In *The Screwtape Letters* and *The Great Divorce*, Lewis meditated upon the enormity of temptations that come our way. With The Chronicles of Narnia and *Till We Have Faces*, Lewis meditated on the great victory over temptation that is available to those in Christ. Even as he was finishing The Chronicles of Narnia and writing *Surprised by Joy*, Lewis had an experience of God's forgiveness that in some ways was more profound than his unwilling conversion. He had learned to accept and enjoy grace.

Some commentators suggest that Lewis's most important work was behind him by the time he left Oxford for Cambridge. In terms of fame and popularity, that assessment has something to it. In terms of his own life, however, his most important work was in full mobilization. All of the pieces were coming together as he approached death. The New Testament makes much of the Christian life after a person first has faith in Christ, but the modern world pays little attention to it, as though coming to faith is the end of the process instead of the beginning. Because of the nature of his own conversion, Lewis understood at once that the journey lay ahead of him, and that much would need to happen before he died. He captured the idea in the title of his first apologetic book, *The Pilgrim's Regress*. He could not go off and become a hermit. He had to go back to his everyday life, where everyone knew him. He had to become like Christ. He never thought he had to do something or learn something in order to earn or confirm or deserve salvation. Instead, he understood that Christ was going to change him. Lewis could either cooperate or kick against the goads. Like Aslan clawing the hide from the dragon, Christ would change him into what he was supposed to be in the first place. In the last phase of his life, Lewis embraced the belief that his faith meant dying daily with Christ.

Owen Barfield often remarked that he believed in evolution but had never changed his mind about anything, while Lewis did not believe in evolution and was changing his mind all the time. A change of mind is the definition of the Greek word *metanoia*, which English translations of the New Testament render as "repentance." The heart of dying with Christ involves constantly changing one's mind about things: attitudes, habits, behaviors. In his last years, Lewis moved steadily toward being the whole person Christ intended. In our health-conscious world, some readers may fall into the trap of judging Lewis for not living according to our current attitudes about smoking and diet, or reduce the goal of life to avoiding death. The goal of life is to become human.

To Replace Prejudice with Affection

Like many natives of the British Isles, Lewis developed at an early age an abhorrence for Americans and all they stand for. He was aided in his prejudice by never having had any actual contact with an American. Part of growing up involved changing his mind about Americans. After World War II, when austerity and shortages of food and almost every consumer good made life bleak, Lewis learned to accept the "abominable Americans" as he became the recipient of a flood of packages, which he shared with his friends. Acceptance gradually gave way to affection, and affection led to friendship. In the early church, the original Jewish believers had trouble shaking their old prejudices against Gentiles. As persecution of Christians grew stronger in Jerusalem in the years leading up to the Jewish War of AD 66, the apostle Paul conceived of a way to help the Jewish believers change their minds about the Gentiles. He took up a collection among the Gentile churches of Asia Minor, Macedonia, and Greece to give to the church in Jerusalem for their relief. Lewis was a "mighty warrior" for the faith during World War II, but he had prejudices that had to die, and by the late 1940s, his prejudice had turned to *philia*, affection for Americans.

To Love and Be Loved

If Lewis knew anything by his late forties, it was that he was a confirmed old bachelor who would never marry. He was too set in his ways. Marriage would have cost him too dearly in terms of his freedom to come and go. Having Mrs. Moore in the house for three decades had taught him how easily his time could be stolen. One of his early objections to the existence of God had been that he did not want to be accountable to someone who might infringe on his time. As he entered what to him felt like old age after a lifetime as a bachelor, Lewis learned to love a woman and to receive love. He discovered what the troubadours of eleventh-century France had sung about, and he changed his mind about marriage. Once he changed his mind about marriage, driven largely by his long-felt desire to help a damsel in distress, he encountered *eros*, the passionate desire for the only one who can satisfy the desire. It was not the mere lust of adolescence in which any woman would do. Ruth Pitter might have made more sense from a practical point of view, but that would not have been marriage for love.

To Love the Unlovely

Lewis hated intrusions into his private writing time. They had caused great difficulty for him while Mrs. Moore still lived. Nothing intruded into his writing time more than the interminable stream of correspondence he felt obligated to carry on with largely unknown well-wishers. Yet, through his daily letter writing, often to needy people with great physical, financial, emotional, and spiritual burdens, Lewis learned to care for people who could give nothing in return and who cost him his precious time. Ladies like Mary Willis Shelburne and Mrs. Johnson taxed his patience, and through them he grew in his capacity to love the unlovely. He had struggled with loving the unlovely as Mrs. Moore grew older and more disagreeable. He may have felt bad that he felt so good when she finally died. This may have been the issue that occasioned his experience of forgiveness. We can only speculate about that, but what we do know is that Jack's love for Joy in her dying years involved the costly love of *agapē* as much as the passionate love of *eros*.

To Grieve

When his father died, Lewis did not grieve. He took note at the time that he felt nothing. It concerned him. When Mrs. Moore and Charles Williams died, he did not grieve. The death of Mrs. Moore resulted in feelings of relief. Williams's death brought a renewed confidence in the resurrection. With the death of Joy Lewis, however, the dam finally burst. The depth of feeling that had been stoppered since the death of his mother finally came uncorked, and he learned to grieve at last, which resulted in one of the most honest and penetrating expressions of grief ever penned when he wrote *A Grief Observed*.

To Let Resentment Go

After harboring bitter resentment and loathing of T. S. Eliot for forty years, in the twilight of his years Lewis learned to love his enemy. Perhaps they did not become friends, but Lewis came to appreciate Eliot all the more as they faced off in their committee meetings and had honest debates without malice or rancor. It was like an Inklings evening!

To Accept the Loss of Health

Unlike many people, Lewis learned to accept his declining health and meet death as a friend. This three-volume biography began as an exploration of how Lewis formed most of his basic likes and dislikes during his teenage years. His preferences for the foods he liked to eat and his love of long walks and swimming, as well as writing, developed in these years. At the end, he could not take walks or swim, and he could not eat what he most enjoyed, yet he found that he did not miss the things he had once loved. The desire left as the capacity left. His attitude was one of peace and contentment. In spite of his physical constraints, he could still enjoy his greatest pleasure, talking with his friends. Somehow, he continued to meet with them every week at the Lamb and Flag across broad St Giles' from the Eagle and Child. Friends came to see him at the Kilns. His brother came home from Ireland. He said that he had done all he wanted to do. He was finished. He was ready to die.

Conclusion

In *The Allegory of Love*, Lewis first discussed the importance of being a whole person. Allegory arises and is always at its best when it expresses the internal conflict of a person—the *bellum intestinum*. Lewis certainly understood the internal conflict that the Bible calls temptation. For him, pride always posed the greatest threat. It led to anger, resentment, selfishness, and so many more attitudes and behaviors that he found so unattractive for someone in whom Christ dwelt. The conflict between the flesh and the Spirit that Paul discussed in Galatians was one Lewis knew well. To be at peace is to be whole, undivided in mind, at one with Christ. Those who read only the first half of *A Grief Observed* miss what happened in the second half. That awful month in which Lewis's world collapsed was also the month in which he was finally pulled together. Joy had died, and he was going to die too. Then the journey would be over.

The biblical concept for the opposite of internal conflict is expressed by the Hebrew word *shalom*, usually translated as "peace." Peace does not mean the opposite of conflict or war. It means wholeness in the face of strife. Some will say that it was a tragedy for Lewis to have died so young. I think it remarkable that he became complete so young.

Notes

Chapter 1: The Dreary Aftermath of War

1. Walter Hooper, ed., *The Collected Letters of C. S. Lewis*, vol. 2 (New York: HarperSanFrancisco, 2004), 649–50.
2. Hooper, *Letters*, 2:650–51.
3. This essay would be reprinted in Tolkien's *Tree and Leaf* (London: Allen & Unwin, 1964).
4. This essay is included in Lewis's *Of This and Other Worlds*, ed. Walter Hooper (London: Collins, 1982).
5. Barbara Reynolds, ed., *The Letters of Dorothy L. Sayers*, vol. 3, *1944– 1950: A Noble Daring* (Cambridge: Dorothy L. Sayers Society/Carole Green, 1998), 148.
6. Reynolds, *Letters of Sayers*, 3:149.
7. Hooper, *Letters*, 2:654–55.
8. Hooper, *Letters*, 2:657.
9. Hooper, *Letters*, 2:655.
10. Hooper, *Letters*, 2:658.
11. Hooper, *Letters*, 2:661.
12. Hooper, *Letters*, 2:662.
13. Reynolds, *Letters of Sayers*, 3:154.
14. Hooper, *Letters*, 2:662.
15. Hooper, *Letters*, 2:663 and 663n63. M. Cato refers to Marcus Cato, who admitted penitent souls to purgatory in Dante's *Purgatorio*.
16. Reynolds, *Letters of Sayers*, 3:155.
17. Hooper, *Letters*, 2:663.
18. Reynolds, *Letters of Sayers*, 3:176.
19. Reynolds, *Letters of Sayers*, 3:177n3.
20. Reynolds, *Letters of Sayers*, 3:176.
21. Hooper, *Letters*, 2:681.
22. Hooper, *Letters*, 2:686.
23. Hooper, *Letters*, 2:697, 699.
24. Hooper, *Letters*, 2:703.
25. Hooper, *Letters*, 2:703.

26. Hooper, *Letters*, 2:704.
27. Hooper, *Letters*, 2:704.
28. Hooper, *Letters*, 2:704.
29. Hooper, *Letters*, 2:708–9.
30. Hooper, *Letters*, 2:816–17, 821.
31. Hooper, *Letters*, 2:865–67; Reynolds, *Letters of Sayers*, 3:378–79.
32. Hooper, *Letters*, 2:861.
33. Hooper, *Letters*, 2:655–56.
34. Hooper, *Letters*, 2:744–45.
35. Hooper, *Letters*, 2:767–68.
36. Hooper, *Letters*, 2:885.
37. Hooper, *Letters*, 2:891.
38. Hooper, *Letters*, 2:892–93. One of the few recordings of Lewis's voice is this treatment of Charles Williams.
39. Hooper, *Letters*, 2:645.
40. Hooper, *Letters*, 2:698.
41. Hooper, *Letters*, 2:698.
42. Hooper, *Letters*, 2:744.
43. Hooper, *Letters*, 2:796, 798, 803.
44. Hooper, *Letters*, 2:806.
45. Hooper, *Letters*, 2:832.
46. Hooper, *Letters*, 2:836.
47. Hooper, *Letters*, 2:838.
48. Clyde S. Kilby and Marjorie Lamp Mead, eds., *Brothers and Friends: The Diaries of Major Warren Hamilton Lewis* (New York: Harper & Row, 1982), 219.
49. This sheet is frequently reproduced in books about Lewis, including volume 2 of Walter Hooper's *The Collected Letters of C. S. Lewis* and his *Through Joy and Beyond: A Pictorial Biography of C. S. Lewis* (New York: Macmillan, 1982).
50. Hooper, *Letters*, 2:849–50.
51. Hooper, *Letters*, 2:850.
52. Hooper, *Letters*, 2:859.
53. Hooper, *Letters*, 2:878–79.
54. Hooper, *Letters*, 2:888–89.
55. Hooper, *Letters*, 2:896.
56. Hooper, *Letters*, 2:918.
57. Hooper, *Letters*, 2:931, 934.
58. Hooper, *Letters*, 2:922n38.
59. Hooper, *Letters*, 2:913.
60. These are only the letters that Walter Hooper had tracked down for the publication of the massive three-volume collection of Lewis's letters. Most of Lewis's letters were probably thrown away by the recipients, but others were tucked away and will continue to come to light in the decades to come. By the time Hooper finished editing volume 3, he had

to add over 150 pages of letters that had come to light since he published the first two volumes.

61. Hooper, *Letters*, 2:798, 840, 846, 852.
62. Hooper, *Letters*, 2:929.
63. Hooper, *Letters*, 2:812.
64. Kilby and Mead, *Brothers and Friends*, 213.
65. Hooper, *Letters*, 2:841.
66. Hooper, *Letters*, 2:851.
67. Hooper, *Letters*, 2:852.
68. Hooper, *Letters*, 2:858, 1004. Chad Walsh also sent Lewis some cooking fat, 2:890.
69. Hooper, *Letters*, 2:890. Walter Hooper told me about Lewis's Golden Flakes preference.
70. By Christmas of 1949, tea and sugar were still in short supply. See Hooper, *Letters*, 2:1012.
71. Hooper, *Letters*, 2:900.
72. Hooper, *Letters*, 2:904.
73. Kilby and Mead, *Brothers and Friends*, 212.
74. See also Hooper, *Letters*, 2:912.
75. Hooper, *Letters*, 2:984–85.
76. Kilby and Mead, *Brothers and Friends*, 219.
77. Hooper, *Letters*, 2:856.
78. Hooper, *Letters*, 2:925.
79. Hooper, *Letters*, 2:710.
80. Hooper, *Letters*, 2:803.
81. Hooper, *Letters*, 2:812.
82. Hooper, *Letters*, 2:827, 837.
83. Hooper, *Letters*, 2:833.
84. Hooper, *Letters*, 2:869.
85. Hooper, *Letters*, 2:833, 837, 918, 932, 965.
86. Hooper, *Letters*, 2:840.
87. Hooper, *Letters*, 2:846.
88. Hooper, *Letters*, 2:852.
89. Hooper, *Letters*, 2:853.
90. Hooper, *Letters*, 2:889.
91. Hooper, *Letters*, 2:892. Lewis normally read the papers only during a period of crisis in which real news happened. See also Hooper, *Letters*, 2:899, 910, 916, 920, 923, 931, 938.
92. Hooper, *Letters*, 2:897.
93. Hooper, *Letters*, 2:909.
94. Hooper, *Letters*, 2:917, 923.
95. Hooper, *Letters*, 2:928.
96. Hooper, *Letters*, 2:923, 931.
97. Hooper, *Letters*, 2:923, 931.
98. Hooper, *Letters*, 2:927, 930–31.

99. Hooper, *Letters*, 2:932, 938.
100. Hooper, *Letters*, 2:932.
101. Hooper, *Letters*, 2:992.
102. Hooper, *Letters*, 2:681, 701. By 1948, Lewis reported that the number of students at Oxford had increased from four thousand to seven thousand. See Hooper, *Letters*, 2:852.
103. Hooper, *Letters*, 2:694.
104. Hooper, *Letters*, 2:709.
105. Hooper, *Letters*, 2:702.
106. Hooper, *Letters*, 2:706.
107. Hooper, *Letters*, 2:698, 847, 908.
108. Hooper, *Letters*, 2:719.
109. Hooper, *Letters*, 2:757.
110. Hooper, *Letters*, 2:809.
111. Hooper, *Letters*, 2:767.
112. Hooper, *Letters*, 2:766.
113. Roger Lancelyn Green and Walter Hooper, *C. S. Lewis: A Biography* (New York: Harcourt Brace Jovanovich, 1974), 228.
114. Hooper, *Letters*, 2:767.
115. Hooper, *Letters*, 2:842.
116. Hooper, *Letters*, 2:755.
117. Kilby and Mead, *Brothers and Friends*, 198.
118. Kilby and Mead, *Brothers and Friends*, 198–99.
119. Kilby and Mead, *Brothers and Friends*, 199–200.
120. Kilby and Mead, *Brothers and Friends*, 207.
121. Kilby and Mead, *Brothers and Friends*, 207–8.
122. Hooper, *Letters*, 2:806.
123. Hooper, *Letters*, 2:812.
124. Hooper, *Letters*, 2:817.
125. Hooper, *Letters*, 2:817–18.
126. Hooper, *Letters*, 2:818.
127. Kilby and Mead, *Brothers and Friends*, 216–17.
128. Hooper, *Letters*, 2:844.
129. Hooper, *Letters*, 2:887.
130. Hooper, *Letters*, 2:904.
131. Robert E. Havard, "Philia: Jack at Ease," in *Remembering C. S. Lewis: Recollections of Those Who Knew Him*, ed. James T. Como, 3rd ed. (San Francisco: Ignatius, 2005), 366.
132. Hooper, *Letters*, 2:706.
133. Kilby and Mead, *Brothers and Friends*, 201–3.
134. Kilby and Mead, *Brothers and Friends*, 210, 220.
135. Kilby and Mead, *Brothers and Friends*, 209.
136. Kilby and Mead, *Brothers and Friends*, 216.
137. Kilby and Mead, *Brothers and Friends*, 217.
138. Kilby and Mead, *Brothers and Friends*, 217.

139. Kilby and Mead, *Brothers and Friends*, 225–26.
140. Hooper, *Letters*, 2:934.
141. Hooper, *Letters*, 2:939.
142. W. H. Lewis, ed., *Letters of C. S. Lewis* (London: Bles, 1966), 17. See also Hooper, *Letters*, 2:927, 931, 935, 944, 973, 983, 1005.
143. Green and Hooper, *C. S. Lewis*, 303.
144. Hooper, *Letters*, 2:920, 921, 939, 957.
145. Kilby and Mead, *Brothers and Friends*, 226.
146. Kilby and Mead, *Brothers and Friends*, 226; Hooper, *Letters*, 2:944.
147. Hooper, *Letters*, 2:946, 960, 973.
148. Kilby and Mead, *Brothers and Friends*, 226.
149. Hooper, *Letters*, 2:946.
150. Hooper, *Letters*, 2:952–53.
151. Hooper, *Letters*, 2:952–53, 957.
152. Kilby and Mead, *Brothers and Friends*, 227. See also Hooper, *Letters*, 2:973, 983, 984.
153. Kilby and Mead, *Brothers and Friends*, 232–33.
154. Walter Hooper, ed., *The Collected Letters of C. S. Lewis*, vol. 3 (New York: HarperSanFrancisco, 2007), 28.
155. Kilby and Mead, *Brothers and Friends*, 233.
156. Kilby and Mead, *Brothers and Friends*, 233.
157. Hooper, *Letters*, 3:37.
158. Hooper, *Letters*, 2:905.
159. Hooper, *Letters*, 2:906.

Chapter 2: Work, Work, Work
1. Humphrey Carpenter, ed., *The Letters of J. R. R. Tolkien* (London: Allen & Unwin, 1981), 116.
2. Joel D. Heck, "Chronologically Lewis," December 27, 2021, 858. Heck makes this important resource available as a Word document on his website: www.joelheck.com. The page numbers here reflect that document.
3. Heck, "Chronologically Lewis," 866.
4. Clyde S. Kilby and Marjorie Lamp Mead, eds., *Brothers and Friends: The Diaries of Major Warren Hamilton Lewis* (New York: Harper & Row, 1982), 186–88.
5. Kilby and Mead, *Brothers and Friends*, 189.
6. Heck, "Chronologically Lewis," 871.
7. Kilby and Mead, *Brothers and Friends*, 189.
8. Heck, "Chronologically Lewis," 873.
9. Derek Brewer, "The Tutor: A Portrait," in *Remembering C. S. Lewis: Recollections of Those Who Knew Him*, ed. James T. Como, 3rd ed. (San Francisco: Ignatius, 2005), 119.
10. W. Brown Patterson, "C. S. Lewis: Personal Reflections," in *C. S. Lewis Remembered: Collected Reflections of Students, Friends and*

Colleagues, ed. Harry Lee Poe and Rebecca Whitten Poe (Grand Rapids, MI: Zondervan, 2006), 95.

11. Paul Piehler, "Encounters with Lewis," in Poe and Poe, *C. S. Lewis Remembered*, 120.
12. Peter Bayley, "From Master to Colleague," in Como, *Remembering C. S. Lewis*, 165.
13. George Bailey, "In the University," in *C. S. Lewis: Speaker and Teacher*, ed. Carolyn Keefe (Grand Rapids, MI: Zondervan, 1971), 82.
14. John Lawlor, "The Tutor and the Scholar," in *Light on C. S. Lewis*, ed. Jocelyn Gibb (London: Bles, 1965), 71.
15. Brewer, "The Tutor," 118.
16. Alan Bede Griffiths, "The Adventure of Faith," in Como, *Remembering C. S. Lewis*, 76.
17. George Sayer, *Jack: C. S. Lewis and His Times* (New York: Harper & Row, 1988), 117–18.
18. Patterson, "C. S. Lewis," 91.
19. Sayer, *Jack*, 118.
20. Brewer, "The Tutor," 136.
21. Lawlor, "The Tutor and the Scholar," 72.
22. Lawlor, "The Tutor and the Scholar," 74–75.
23. George Watson, "The Art of Disagreement," in Poe and Poe, *C. S. Lewis Remembered*, 81.
24. Piehler, "Encounters with Lewis," 121.
25. Alastair Fowler, "C. S. Lewis: Supervisor," in Poe and Poe, *C. S. Lewis Remembered*, 108.
26. A. N. Wilson, *C. S. Lewis: A Biography* (New York: Norton, 1990), 99.
27. Piehler, "Encounters with Lewis," 124; George Sayer, "Recollections of C. S. Lewis," in *C. S. Lewis and His Circle: Essays and Memoirs from the Oxford C. S. Lewis Society*, ed. Roger White, Judith Wolfe, and Brendan N. Wolfe (New York: Oxford University Press, 2015), 175; Fowler, "C. S. Lewis," 102–3; Patterson, "C. S. Lewis," 91; Watson, "The Art of Disagreement," 81.
28. Bailey, "In the University," 81.
29. Brewer, "The Tutor," 116.
30. Brewer, "The Tutor," 124.
31. Brewer, "The Tutor," 123.
32. Patterson, "C. S. Lewis," 91.
33. Piehler, "Encounters with Lewis," 123.
34. Brewer, "The Tutor," 131.
35. Patterson, "C. S. Lewis," 91; Fowler, "C. S. Lewis," 100; Piehler, "Encounters with Lewis," 121, 123.
36. Piehler, "Encounters with Lewis," 121.
37. Patterson, "C. S. Lewis," 89. After completing his two years as a Rhodes scholar studying literature with Lewis, Patterson returned to the United States, where he earned the bachelor of divinity (precur-

sor to the renamed master of divinity), was ordained in the Episcopal Church, and completed a PhD in history at Harvard. He taught history at Davidson and Sewanee while serving several Episcopal parishes that were too small to support a full-time rector.

38. Patterson, "C. S. Lewis," 92.
39. Watson, "The Art of Disagreement," 80.
40. Heck, "Chronologically Lewis," 885.
41. Heck, "Chronologically Lewis," 911.
42. Watson, "The Art of Disagreement," 77.
43. He once offered them to me for ten thousand pounds, but I declined the offer.
44. Watson, "The Art of Disagreement," 77; Piehler, "Encounters with Lewis," 122.
45. Watson, "The Art of Disagreement," 78; Piehler, "Encounters with Lewis," 122.
46. Watson, "The Art of Disagreement," 78; Fowler, "C. S. Lewis," 107–8.
47. Fowler, "C. S. Lewis," 108.
48. Brewer, "The Tutor," 133.
49. Fowler, "C. S. Lewis," 108.
50. Fowler, "C. S. Lewis," 108.
51. Kilby and Mead, *Brothers and Friends*, 190; Heck, "Chronologically Lewis," 877.
52. Kilby and Mead, *Brothers and Friends*, 190.
53. Kilby and Mead, *Brothers and Friends*, 190.
54. Kilby and Mead, *Brothers and Friends*, 190.
55. D. M. Baillie, quoted in the *St Andrews Citizen*, June 29, 1946, cited by Walter Hooper, *C. S. Lewis: A Companion and Guide* (New York: HarperSanFrancisco, 1996), 43–44.
56. Kilby and Mead, *Brothers and Friends*, 191.
57. Kilby and Mead, *Brothers and Friends*, 191.
58. Brewer, "The Tutor," 138. See also Peter Bayley, "From Master to Colleague," in Como, *Remembering C. S. Lewis*, 79.
59. Kilby and Mead, *Brothers and Friends*, 192.
60. Walter Hooper, ed., *The Collected Letters of C. S. Lewis*, vol. 2 (New York: HarperSanFrancisco, 2004), 808.
61. James McNeish, *Dance of the Peacocks* (New Zealand: Random House, 2003), 29.
62. Hooper, *C. S. Lewis*, 627.
63. Sayer, *Jack*, 199.
64. Fowler, "C. S. Lewis," 98–100.
65. Bailey, "In the University," 91.
66. Sayer, *Jack*, 199.
67. Hooper, *Letters*, 2:849.
68. Alister McGrath, *C. S. Lewis: A Life* (Carol Stream, IL: Tyndale, 2013), 243.

69. Isaiah Berlin, "A Close Colleague's Assessment," in *David Cecil: A Portrait by His Friends*, ed. Hannah Cranborne (Stanbridge, Wimborne, Dorset: Dovecote, 1990), 102–3.

70. David Cecil, "Oxford's Magic Circle," *Books and Bookmen* 24, no. 4 (1979): 11–12.

71. Helen Gardner, "Clive Staples Lewis, 1898–1963," *The Proceedings of the British Academy* 51 (1966): 425.

72. Gardner, "Clive Staples Lewis, 1898–1963," 418.

73. Heck, "Chronologically Lewis," 920.

74. For a more detailed discussion of the points at issue, see Victor Reppert, *C. S. Lewis's Dangerous Idea* (Downer's Grove, IL: InterVarsity Press, 2003).

75. Oxford and Cambridge, where Anscombe had a distinguished career for many decades, abound with apocryphal stories of Anscombe's antics aimed at rattling those enclaves of male superiority. She usually succeeded. Nonetheless, her high drama would never have been tolerated had she lacked a prodigious intellect to go along with her escapades.

76. I had the pleasure of knowing Mitchell in the last years of his life. We met at the Austin Farrer Centenary Conference at Oriel College, which he planned and directed in September 2004. He contributed to *C. S. Lewis Remembered* (2006), which Rebecca Whitten Poe (Hays) and I edited, and I visited in his home at Woodstock on several occasions, when we talked about Lewis and Anscombe.

77. Antony Flew, "A Conversation with Antony Flew and Gary Habermas," July 29, 2005, C. S. Lewis Summer Institute, St. Aldate's Church (Redlands, CA: C. S. Lewis Foundation, 2005), DVD recording.

78. Brewer, "The Tutor," 139–40.

79. G. E. M. Anscombe, *Metaphysics and the Philosophy of Mind*, vol. 2 of *The Collected Philosophical Papers of G. E. M. Anscombe* (Oxford: Basil Blackwell, 1981), x.

80. Minutes of the Socratic Club, February 2, 1967.

81. I met Lucas, as well as Mitchell, at the Austin Farrer Centenary Conference at Oriel College in September 2004. When they learned of my interest in Lewis, they were both keen to discuss the re-enactment. Mitchell, who was at the original meeting in 1948, had been surprised to hear, from people who wrote about the event but were not present, that Lewis had lost a debate! Besides being a brilliant philosopher, Mitchell was a kind and generous man who invited me to tea in his home in Woodstock on several occasions before his death in 2011. He gave me a copy of the handwritten minutes of the Socratic Club during his presidency until the club disbanded in the late 1960s.

82. Email message from John Randolph Lucas to Jerry Walls, August 28, 2003. A few typographical errors have been corrected, and italics have been applied where Lucas used asterisks.

83. Sayer, *Jack*, 186.

84. Lucas to Walls; conversation with Mitchell, September 2004; conversation with Walter Hooper at his home, August 2007. Hooper told me that during the question period, he asked Anscombe whether, if the C. S. Lewis estate offered one million pounds to the charity of her choice, she could undertake to correct the third chapter so that it would meet the challenges of her critique. Silence fell over the audience as Anscombe considered the question for a full two minutes. She then replied that she did not believe she could do it.

85. Anscombe's original paper from 1948 was published in *The Socratic Digest*. Her paper given to the Oxford C. S. Lewis Society was published as "C. S. Lewis's Rewrite of Chapter III of *Miracles*," in White, Wolfe, and Wolfe, *C. S. Lewis and His Circle*, 15–23.

86. Wilson, *C. S. Lewis*, 211–18.

87. Wilson, *C. S. Lewis*, 218–20.

88. Wilson, *C. S. Lewis* 220.

89. McGrath, *C. S. Lewis*, 256.

90. Hooper, *Letters*, 2:747.

91. C. S. Lewis, *Mere Christianity* (New York: Macmillan, 1952), 23.

92. Lucas to Walls.

93. See Alexander Hutton, "An English School for the Welfare State: Literature, Politics, and the University, 1932–1965," *English: Journal of the English Association* 65, no. 248 (2016): 3–34.

94. Wilson attributes his information to Helen Gardner, who told Wilson about it. With Wilson, it is important for the reader to reserve judgment. His biography has been challenged by George Sayer and Alister McGrath, among many others, over both factual matters and issues of interpretation. Of course, he wrote his biography when creative nonfiction was the new thing and many people tried their hand at it. All biographers, however, will inevitably allow their biases to affect their telling of the story, and Sayer, McGrath, and I are no exceptions.

95. Wilson, *C. S. Lewis*, 209.

96. Gardner, "Clive Staples Lewis, 1898–1963," 418.

97. Holly Ordway has written an important new book that challenges this view of Tolkien. She argues that Tolkien actually liked modern literature and was influenced by it. See Ordway, *Tolkien's Modern Reading: Middle-earth beyond the Middle Ages* (Park Ridge, IL: Word on Fire Academic, 2021). Tolkien used the term "Frenchified" as early as 1908 in a letter to Father Francis Morgan.

Chapter 3: A New Agenda and New Friends

1. Walter Hooper, ed., *The Collected Letters of C. S. Lewis*, vol. 2 (New York: HarperSanFrancisco, 2004), 855.

2. Hooper, *Letters*, 2:887.

3. Hooper, *Letters*, 2:883.

4. For a complete list of what Lewis published during this period and throughout his entire life, see Walter Hooper, "A Bibliography of the

Writings of C. S. Lewis, Revised and Enlarged," in *Remembering C. S. Lewis: Recollections of Those Who Knew Him*, ed. James T. Como, 3rd ed. (San Francisco: Ignatius, 2005), 387–492.

5. C. S. Lewis, "Meditation in a Tool Shed," in *God in the Dock: Essays on Theology and Ethics*, ed. Walter Hooper (Grand Rapids, MI: Eerdmans, 1970), 212.

6. Robert E. Havard, "Philia: Jack at Ease," in Como, *Remembering C. S. Lewis*, 358.

7. Hooper, *Letters*, 2:167–68.

8. Hooper, *Letters*, 2:221, 877.

9. Hooper, *Letters*, 2:812.

10. A. R. Wooley, *The Clarendon Guide to Oxford* (Oxford: Oxford University Press, 1979), 86.

11. C. S. Lewis, "Christian Apologetics," in Hooper, *God in the Dock*, 99.

12. Audio interview with Bishop A. W. Goodwin-Hudson, Forest Falls, CA, Marion E. Wade Center, Wheaton College, Wheaton, IL, cited by Philip G. Ryken, "Winsome Evangelist: The Influence of C. S. Lewis," in *C. S. Lewis: Lightbearer in the Shadowlands*, ed. Angus. J. L. Menuge (Wheaton, IL: Crossway, 1997), 60.

13. The Methodist Central Hall in Westminster should not be confused with Westminster Chapel, where Martin Lloyd-Jones preached.

14. Interview with Heather Brown Olford at the Olford Center of Union University, Memphis, TN, 2007. I had the pleasure of knowing Mrs. Olford from the time the Stephen Olford Center became a part of Union University in 2007 until her death in 2013.

15. Hooper, *Letters*, 2:702–3.

16. Hooper, *Letters*, 2:755–56.

17. Hooper, *Letters*, 2:747.

18. Hooper, *Letters*, 2:830.

19. Clyde S. Kilby and Marjorie Lamp Mead, eds., *Brothers and Friends: The Diaries of Major Warren Hamilton Lewis* (New York: Harper & Row, 1982), 219–20.

20. Hooper, *Letters*, 2:877.

21. Hooper, *Letters*, 2:929.

22. Hooper, *Letters*, 2:1005–6.

23. Walter Hooper, *C. S. Lewis: Companion and Guide* (New York: HarperSanFrancisco, 1996), 181. See also Andrew Lazo's discussion of the early dating for this manuscript in Lazo, "'Early Prose Joy': A Brief Introduction," *SEVEN* 30 (2013): 5–12. The manuscript is printed in full as C. S. Lewis, "'Early Prose Joy': C. S. Lewis's Early Draft of an Autobiographical Manuscript," ed. Andrew Lazo, *SEVEN* 30 (2013): 13–49.

24. Lewis, "Early Prose Joy," 13.

25. Kilby and Mead, *Brothers and Friends*, 189.

26. Kilby and Mead, *Brothers and Friends*, 213.

27. Kilby and Mead, *Brothers and Friends*, 223–24.
28. See Hooper, "Bibliography," 447–52.
29. Hooper, *Letters*, 2:812.
30. Kilby and Mead, *Brothers and Friends*, 212.
31. Hooper, "Bibliography," 446.
32. Hooper, *Letters*, 2:756, 812.
33. Hooper, *Letters*, 2:712.
34. Hooper, *Letters*, 2:679.
35. Hooper, *Letters*, 2:684–85.
36. Hooper, *Letters*, 2:688, 691–92.
37. Hooper, *Letters*, 2:705.
38. Don W. King, *Hunting the Unicorn: A Critical Biography of Ruth Pitter* (Kent, OH: Kent State University Press, 2008), 143.
39. King, *Hunting the Unicorn*, 118.
40. King, *Hunting the Unicorn*, 82.
41. King, *Hunting the Unicorn*, 114.
42. King, *Hunting the Unicorn*, 144.
43. King, *Hunting the Unicorn*, 144. She sent him *The Bridge*; *The Spirit Watches*; and *A Mad Lady's Garland*.
44. Hooper, *Letters*, 2:720.
45. Hooper, *Letters*, 2:721.
46. Hooper, *Letters*, 2:724.
47. Hooper, *Letters*, 2:893.
48. I do not intend these remarks as criticism of the Inklings or Barfield. Having published some forty poems myself, I know what it means to write poetry but not to be a poet. These are the cold, hard facts of life.
49. Hooper, *Letters*, 2:738.
50. King, *Hunting the Unicorn*, 142.
51. Hooper, *Letters*, 2:742.
52. King, *Hunting the Unicorn*, 146.
53. This form was developed by Edmund Spenser for *The Faerie Queene* and employs eight lines of iambic pentameter followed by an alexandrine line in iambic hexameter with a rhyme scheme of ababbcbcc.
54. Hooper, *Letters*, 2:753.
55. Lewis, "Christian Apologetics," 93.
56. Hooper, *Letters*, 2:725–28, 758–61, 790–95.
57. Hooper, *Letters*, 2:777.
58. Hooper, *Letters*, 2:778.
59. Hooper, *Letters*, 2:780.
60. King, *Hunting the Unicorn*, 148.
61. King, *Hunting the Unicorn*, 148.
62. King, *Hunting the Unicorn*, 148.
63. Hooper, *Letters*, 2:874.
64. King, *Hunting the Unicorn*, 296n31.
65. Hooper, *Letters*, 2:881.

66. King, *Hunting the Unicorn*, 149.
67. Kilby and Mead, *Brothers and Friends*, 183–84.
68. Hooper, *Letters*, 2:687.
69. Coghill's story and his impact on the Oxford Dramatic Society is told in Christopher Carpenter, *OUDS: A Centenary History of the Oxford University Dramatic Society, 1885–1985* (London: Oxford University Press, 1985).
70. Nevill Coghill, "The Approach to English," in *Light on C. S. Lewis*, ed. Jocelyn Gibb (London: Bles, 1965), 63.
71. Hooper, *Letters*, 2:853.
72. James Dundas-Grant, "From an 'Outsider,'" in Como, *Remembering C. S. Lewis*, 368–70.
73. Kilby and Mead, *Brothers and Friends*, 218.
74. Kilby and Mead, *Brothers and Friends*, 239.
75. Kilby and Mead, *Brothers and Friends*, 212, 216.
76. John Wain, *Sprightly Running* (London: Macmillan, 1962), 143.
77. Wain, *Sprightly Running*, 180.
78. Wain, *Sprightly Running*, 184–85.
79. Kilby and Mead, *Brothers and Friends*, 195, 196, 198, 200, 211, 212.
80. Kilby and Mead, *Brothers and Friends*, 194, 212.
81. Kilby and Mead, *Brothers and Friends*, 211.
82. Kilby and Mead, *Brothers and Friends*, 198.
83. John Lawlor, *C. S. Lewis: Memories and Reflections* (Dallas: Spence, 1998), 32–33.
84. Lawlor, *C. S. Lewis*, 34–35.
85. Lawlor, *C. S. Lewis*, 33–34.
86. Kilby and Mead, *Brothers and Friends*, 235, 239, 242, 243.
87. Hooper, *Letters*, 2:828.
88. Hooper, *Letters*, 2:183, 219; Havard, "Philia," 365.
89. Hooper, *Letters*, 2:684.
90. Wain, *Sprightly Running*, 185.
91. Kilby and Mead, *Brothers and Friends*, 193.
92. James Houston, "Reminiscences of the Oxford Lewis," in *We Remember C. S. Lewis*, ed. David Graham (Nashville: B&H, 2001), 130–31.
93. Hooper, *Letters*, 3:9.
94. Hooper, *Letters*, 3:1199.
95. Walter Hooper, *Through Joy and Beyond: A Pictorial Biography of C. S. Lewis* (New York: Macmillan, 1982), 138–39.
96. Hooper, *Letters*, 3:720.
97. Hooper, *Letters*, 2:1039.
98. Hooper, *Letters*, 2:236–37.
99. Hooper, *Letters*, 2:1040.
100. Hooper, *Letters*, 2:670–72.
101. Hooper, *Letters*, 2:767.
102. Hooper, *Letters*, 2:896–97.

103. Roger Lancelyn Green and Walter Hooper, *C. S. Lewis: A Biography* (New York: Harcourt Brace Jovanovich, 1974), 241.

104. Hooper, *Letters*, 2:373.

105. Hooper, *Letters*, 2:802.

106. Green and Hooper, *C. S. Lewis*, 241.

107. Hooper, *Letters*, 2:883n74.

108. Hooper, *Letters*, 2:881.

109. C. S. Lewis, "It All Began with a Picture . . . ," in *Of This and Other Worlds*, ed. Walter Hooper (London: Collins, 1982), 79.

110. George Sayer, *Jack: C. S. Lewis and His Times* (New York: Harper & Row, 1988), 189.

111. Green and Hooper, *C. S. Lewis*, 241.

112. Roger Lancelyn Green, *C. S. Lewis* (London: The Bodley Head, 1963), 37.

113. Green, *C. S. Lewis*, 37.

114. Sayer, *Jack*, 189.

115. Alan Bede Griffiths, "The Adventure of Faith," in Como, *Remembering C. S. Lewis*, 77.

116. Hooper, *Letters*, 2:911.

117. Hooper, *Letters*, 2:942–43.

118. Hooper, *Letters*, 2:961.

119. Sayer, *Jack*, 189.

120. Walter Hooper, ed., *The Collected Letters of C. S. Lewis*, vol. 3 (New York: HarperSanFrancisco, 2007), 847–48.

121. Hooper has printed the Lefay manuscript in full in Walter Hooper, *Past Watchful Dragons: The Narnian Chronicles of C. S. Lewis* (New York: Collier Books, 1979), 48–65.

122. Green and Hooper, *C. S. Lewis*, 242–43.

123. Green and Hooper, *C. S. Lewis*, 242–43.

124. Walter Hooper suggested that the idea may have been for *Prince Caspian*, but since Lewis had already discussed elements of that story with Roger Lancelyn Green, a later story seems more likely. See Hooper, *Letters*, 2:952, 980n140.

125. Lewis mentioned in many places that his fiction usually began with a mental picture that then required the construction of a world and a plot within which that picture fit. See Lewis, "It All Began with a Picture . . . ," 79; Lewis, "Sometimes Fairy Stories May Say Best What's to Be Said," in Hooper, *Of This and Other Worlds*, 71–72; Lewis, "On Three Ways of Writing for Children," in Hooper, *Of This and Other Worlds*, 68; C. S. Lewis, Kingsley Amis, and Brian Aldiss, "The Establishment Must Die and Rot . . . ," in *C. S. Lewis Remembered: Collected Reflections of Students, Friends and Colleagues*, ed. Harry Lee Poe and Rebecca Whitten Poe (Grand Rapids, MI: Zondervan, 2006), 236.

Chapter 4: Narnia and Beyond

1. Roger Lancelyn Green and Walter Hooper, *C. S. Lewis: A Biography* (New York: Harcourt Brace Jovanovich, 1974), 239.

2. Roger Lancelyn Green, "C. S. Lewis," in *Puffin Annual*, no. 1 (Harmondsworth, UK: Puffin, 1974), 104.

3. Walter Hooper, ed., *The Collected Letters of C. S. Lewis*, vol. 2 (New York: HarperSanFrancisco, 2004), 670–72.

4. C. S. Lewis, "Sometimes Fairy Stories May Say Best What's to Be Said," in *Of This and Other Worlds*, ed. Walter Hooper (London: Collins, 1982), 71–73.

5. C. S. Lewis, "It All Began with a Picture . . . ," in Hooper, *Of This and Other Worlds*, 79.

6. Green and Hooper, *C. S. Lewis*, 245.

7. Hooper, *Letters*, 2:942.

8. Green and Hooper, *C. S. Lewis*, 243.

9. Walter Hooper, ed., *The Collected Letters of C. S. Lewis*, vol. 3 (New York: HarperSanFrancisco, 2007), 12.

10. Hooper, *Letters*, 3:90, 94; Green and Hooper, *C. S. Lewis*, 244.

11. Hooper, *Letters*, 3:300, 332; Green and Hooper, *C. S. Lewis*, 247.

12. Hooper, *Letters*, 3:307; Green and Hooper, *C. S. Lewis*, 245, 246.

13. Hooper, *Letters*, 3:431, 442; Green and Hooper, *C. S. Lewis*, 247–48.

14. Hooper, *Letters*, 3:563–64.

15. Hooper, *Letters*, 3:45.

16. Hooper, *Letters*, 3:44–45.

17. Helen Gardner, "Clive Staples Lewis, 1898–1963," *The Proceedings of the British Academy* 51 (1966): 419.

18. Hooper, *Letters*, 3:112, 141.

19. Clyde S. Kilby and Marjorie Lamp Mead, eds., *Brothers and Friends: The Diaries of Major Warren Hamilton Lewis* (New York: Harper & Row, 1982), 236. See also Hooper, *Letters*, 3:89; Green and Hooper, *C. S. Lewis*, 257. Green and Hooper dated Mrs. Moore's death as January 17, but in *The Collected Letters of C. S. Lewis*, Hooper corrected the date to January 12. Lewis mentioned her death in a letter to Arthur Greeves on January 31, saying that she had died a fortnight earlier (fourteen days). Two weeks earlier would have been January 17. As was often the case, Lewis was careless about dates. Warnie, who noted Minto's death in his diary, was more careful with dates. When Green and Hooper wrote their biography, they did not have access to Warnie's diaries, but they did have Lewis's letters to Arthur, which Hooper would later publish as *They Stand Together*.

20. Hooper, *Letters*, 2:1015; 3:181–82.

21. Kilby and Mead, *Brothers and Friends*, 239.

22. Gardner, "Clive Staples Lewis, 1898–1963," 425. Gardner, who by this time was a leading voice in the English faculty owing to her leadership in revising the syllabus over Lewis's objections, would have been in a position to know.

23. Kilby and Mead, *Brothers and Friends*, 239.

24. Kilby and Mead, *Brothers and Friends*, 239.
25. Humphrey Carpenter, ed., *The Letters of J. R. R. Tolkien* (London: Allen & Unwin, 1981), 351.
26. Hooper, *Letters*, 3:90n20.
27. Hooper, *Letters*, 2:1009.
28. Hooper, *Letters*, 2:1009; 3:83n6, 84.
29. Hooper, *Letters*, 2:1008.
30. Hooper, *Letters*, 2:818, 1053–54.
31. Hooper, *Letters*, 3:84.
32. Hooper, *Letters*, 3:264–65.
33. Hooper, *Letters*, 3:290, 412.
34. Hooper, *Letters*, 3:299.
35. Hooper, *Letters*, 3:322.
36. Hooper, *Letters*, 3:412–13.
37. Hooper, *Letters*, 3:511.
38. Hooper, *Letters*, 3:638–39; Carpenter, *Letters of Tolkien*, 280.
39. Hooper, *Letters*, 3:639.
40. Hooper, *Letters*, 3:639.
41. Hooper, *Letters*, 2:1020.
42. Hooper, *Letters*, 3:850.
43. Hooper, *Letters*, 3:888.
44. C. S. Lewis, *The Last Battle* (London: The Bodley Head, 1956), 160, 172, 173. While the London edition says "farther," the American edition says "further." See C. S. Lewis, *The Last Battle* (New York: Macmillan, 1956), 149, 162, 163.
45. C. S. Lewis, Kingsley Amis, and Brian Aldiss, "The Establishment Must Die and Rot . . . ," in *C. S. Lewis Remembered: Collected Reflections of Students, Friends and Colleagues*, ed. Harry Lee Poe and Rebecca Whitten Poe (Grand Rapids, MI: Zondervan, 2006), 236.
46. I had this experience in writing *The Romanov Files*. As I sat listening to Robert Massie deliver an excellent lecture on the forensic investigation of the bones of the Romanov family that were discovered in the woods near Yekaterinburg, he remarked that it would have been impossible for anyone to survive the execution in the Ipatiev House. In a moment, I knew the full story of how someone could have escaped several weeks earlier. It was a remarkable experience and a valuable insight into the working of the imagination.
47. C. S. Lewis, *The Allegory of Love: A Study of Medieval Tradition* (Oxford: Clarendon, 1936), 75–76.
48. C. S. Lewis, *Surprised by Joy* (London: Bles, 1955), 13, 19–20.
49. Lewis, *Surprised by Joy*, 21, 22–23.
50. C. S. Lewis, "Christian Apologetics," in *God in the Dock: Essays on Theology and Ethics*, ed. Walter Hooper (Grand Rapids, MI: Eerdmans, 1970), 93.
51. Hooper, *Letters*, 2:754.

52. Lewis acknowledged to Nancy Warner—the mother of Francis Warner, who had been Lewis's graduate assistant in Cambridge—that Puddleglum's answer to the witch involves Anselm's ontological argument and Pascal's wager. See Walter Hooper, "It All Began with a Story," in *C. S. Lewis and His Circle: Essays and Memoirs from the Oxford C. S. Lewis Society*, ed. Roger White, Judith Wolfe, and Brendan N. Wolfe (New York: Oxford University Press, 2015), 159.

53. Walter Hooper, "A Bibliography of the Writings of C. S. Lewis, Revised and Enlarged," in *Remembering C. S. Lewis: Recollections of Those Who Knew Him*, ed. James T. Como, 3rd ed. (San Francisco: Ignatius, 2005), 396.

54. C. S. Lewis, *Mere Christianity* (New York: Macmillan, 1952), viii–xi.

55. Hooper, *Letters*, 3:1158. See also 3:1244.

56. Hooper, *Letters*, 3:1158–59.

57. Hooper, *Letters*, 3:1245.

58. One of Lewis's clearest explanations of the distinction between allegory and a supposal was given to Mrs. Hook in a letter dated December 29, 1958. See Hooper, *Letters*, 3:1004–5.

59. For an excellent discussion of why The Chronicles of Narnia were not written by Lewis as allegories, see Peter J. Schakel, *Reading with the Heart: The Way into Narnia* (Grand Rapids, MI: Eerdmans, 1979), 1–18.

60. Michael Ward, *Planet Narnia: The Seven Heavens in the Imagination of C. S. Lewis* (New York: Oxford University Press, 2008), 5.

61. Ward, *Planet Narnia*, 5.

62. Hooper, *Letters*, 3:847–48.

63. Hooper, *Letters*, 3:1281.

64. Hooper, *Letters*, 3:1281.

65. Hooper, *Letters*, 3:1113–14.

66. Ward, *Planet Narnia*, 12.

67. Ward, *Planet Narnia*, 23–27.

68. Ward, *Planet Narnia*, 57.

69. Lewis, *The Allegory of Love*, 51.

70. Hooper, *Letters*, 3:1116.

71. Hooper, *Letters*, 3:86, 112.

72. Hooper, *Letters*, 3:158.

73. Nevill Coghill, "The Approach to English," in *Light on C. S. Lewis*, ed. Jocelyn Gibb (London: Bles, 1965), 61.

74. Hooper, *Letters*, 3:149–50.

75. Hooper, *Letters*, 3:194.

76. Hooper, *Letters*, 3:147.

77. Walter Hooper gives the period of completion as July 1952. See Hooper, *Letters*, 3:215n154.

78. Don W. King, ed., *Out of My Bone: The Letters of Joy Davidman* (Grand Rapids, MI: Eerdmans, 2009), 138.

79. Hooper, *Letters*, 3:270, 288.
80. Hooper, *Letters*, 3:332.
81. Hooper, *Letters*, 3:342.
82. Hooper, *Letters*, 3:342.
83. Hooper, *Letters*, 3:346.
84. Hooper, *Letters*, 3:347.
85. Hooper, *Letters*, 3:374.
86. Hooper, *Letters*, 3:382.
87. Hooper, *Letters*, 3:385.
88. Hooper, *Letters*, 3:387, 506.
89. Hooper, *Letters*, 3:402.
90. Hooper, *Letters*, 3:530, 585–86, 977.
91. Gardner, "Clive Staples Lewis, 1898–1963," 426.
92. Gardner, "Clive Staples Lewis, 1898–1963," 426–27.
93. George Sayer, *Jack: C. S. Lewis and His Times* (New York: Harper & Row, 1988), 197.
94. C. S. Lewis, *English Literature in the Sixteenth Century Excluding Drama*, Oxford History of English Literature (Oxford: Clarendon, 1954), 1.
95. Coghill, "The Approach to English," 59.
96. Coghill, "The Approach to English," 59–60.
97. A. N. Wilson, *C. S. Lewis: A Biography* (New York: Norton, 1990), 243.
98. John Wain, "A Great Clerke," in Como, *Remembering C. S. Lewis*, 160.
99. Wain, "A Great Clerke," 160.
100. Wain, "A Great Clerke," 162.
101. Sayer, *Jack*, 196.
102. Lewis, *English Literature in the Sixteenth Century*, 2.
103. Lewis, *English Literature in the Sixteenth Century*, 4–5.
104. Lewis, *English Literature in the Sixteenth Century*, 18.
105. Lewis, *English Literature in the Sixteenth Century*, 21.
106. Lewis, *English Literature in the Sixteenth Century*, 21.
107. Lewis, *English Literature in the Sixteenth Century*, 21.
108. Lewis, *English Literature in the Sixteenth Century*, 32ff.
109. Lewis, *English Literature in the Sixteenth Century*, 33–34.
110. Humphrey Carpenter, *The Inklings: C. S. Lewis, J. R. R. Tolkien, Charles Williams, and Their Friends* (Boston: Houghton Mifflin, 1979), 265.
111. Hooper, *Letters*, 2:798–801, 1036–39; 3:539.
112. Hooper, *Letters*, 2:646.
113. Hooper, *Letters*, 2:647.
114. Hooper, *Letters*, 2:816.
115. Lewis, *English Literature in the Sixteenth Century*, 44.
116. Hooper, *Letters*, 3:578.
117. Hooper, *Letters*, 3:1107n253.
118. One observer referred to this sudden surge in interest in the Puritans as a "minor industry." See John F. H. New, *Anglican and Puritan: The*

Basis of Their Opposition, 1558–1640 (Stanford, CA: Stanford University Press, 1964); Patrick Collinson, *The Elizabethan Puritans* (London: Jonathan Cape, 1967); H. C. Porter, *Puritanism in Tudor England* (London: Macmillan, 1970); Paul S. Seaver, *The Puritan Lectureships* (Stanford, CA: Stanford University Press, 1970); Leonard J. Trinterud, *Elizabethan Puritanism* (New York: Oxford University Press, 1971); Peter Toon, *Puritans and English Calvinism* (Swengel, PA: Reiner, 1973); R. T. Kendall, *Calvin and English Calvinism to 1649* (Oxford: Oxford University Press, 1979); and many, many more.

Chapter 5: The New Freedom
1. Walter Hooper, ed., *The Collected Letters of C. S. Lewis*, vol. 3 (New York: HarperSanFrancisco, 2007), 66.
2. Hooper, *Letters*, 3:45.
3. Hooper, *Letters*, 3:108.
4. Hooper, *Letters*, 3:108.
5. Hooper, *Letters*, 3:99.
6. Hooper, *Letters*, 3:28.
7. Hooper, *Letters*, 3:28.
8. Hooper, *Letters*, 3:31.
9. Hooper, *Letters*, 3:47.
10. Hooper, *Letters*, 3:37–38.
11. Hooper, *Letters*, 3:39.
12. Hooper, *Letters*, 3:39.
13. Hooper, *Letters*, 3:47.
14. Hooper, *Letters*, 3:54.
15. Hooper, *Letters*, 3:78.
16. Hooper, *Letters*, 3:90.
17. Hooper, *Letters*, 3:90n19.
18. Hooper, *Letters*, 3:90, 94.
19. Hooper, *Letters*, 3:102, 115.
20. Hooper, *Letters*, 3:122.
21. Hooper, *Letters*, 3:130.
22. Hooper, *Letters*, 3:110.
23. Hooper, *Letters*, 3:123.
24. Hooper, *Letters*, 3:123, 151–52.
25. Hooper, *Letters*, 3:123.
26. Hooper, *Letters*, 3:151–52.
27. Hooper, *Letters*, 3:152.
28. Hooper, *Letters*, 3:171.
29. Hooper, *Letters*, 3:173.
30. Hooper, *Letters*, 3:175.
31. Hooper, *Letters*, 3:179.
32. Hooper, *Letters*, 3:185n83.
33. Hooper, *Letters*, 3:186.

34. Hooper, *Letters*, 3:187.
35. Hooper, *Letters*, 3:188.
36. Hooper, *Letters*, 3:188.
37. Hooper, *Letters*, 3:189.
38. Hooper, *Letters*, 3:187n86.
39. Hooper, *Letters*, 3:188.
40. Hooper, *Letters*, 3:308–9.
41. Don W. King, *The Letters of Ruth Pitter: Silent Music* (Newark, DE: University of Delaware Press, 2014), 188.
42. King, *Letters of Pitter*, 198.
43. King, *Letters of Pitter*, 203.
44. Hooper, *Letters*, 3:65.
45. Hooper, *Letters*, 3:79, 117.
46. Hooper, *Letters*, 3:95.
47. King, *Letters of Pitter*, 211.
48. Hooper, *Letters*, 3:130.
49. King, *Letters of Pitter*, 214.
50. Hooper, *Letters*, 3:182n73.
51. Hooper, *Letters*, 3:182–83.
52. King, *Letters of Pitter*, 220.
53. Hooper, *Letters*, 3:225.
54. Hooper, *Letters*, 3:236–37, 238–40.
55. Hooper, *Letters*, 3:268.
56. Hooper, *Letters*, 3:268.
57. Hooper, *Letters*, 3:269.
58. Hooper, *Letters*, 3:267.
59. Hooper, *Letters*, 3:271.
60. Clyde S. Kilby and Marjorie Lamp Mead, *Brothers and Friends: The Diaries of Major Warren Hamilton Lewis* (New York: Harper & Row, 1982), 244.
61. Hooper, *Letters*, 3:222.
62. Joy Gresham, "The Longest Way Round," in *These Found the Way*, ed. David Wesley Soper (Philadelphia: Westminster Press, 1951), 15. In addition to this testimony of her conversion, which provides details of her early life, several important volumes offer a detailed look at her. Lyle W. Dorsett was at work on his biography of Davidman when he became director of the Marion E. Wade Center at Wheaton College. See Dorsett, *And God Came In* (New York: Macmillan, 1983). Don W. King has produced several important volumes on Davidman, including *Out of My Bone: The Letters of Joy Davidman* (Grand Rapids, MI: Eerdmans, 2009); *Yet One More Spring: A Critical Study of Joy Davidman* (Grand Rapids, MI: Eerdmans, 2015); and the edited Joy Davidman, *A Naked Tree: Love Sonnets to C. S. Lewis and Other Poems* (Grand Rapids, MI: Eerdmans, 2015). Several fictional treatments of the relationship between Davidman and Lewis have appeared over the years, including

Brian Sibley, *C. S. Lewis through the Shadowlands: The Story of His Life with Joy Davidman* (Old Tappan, NJ: Revell, 1985) and Patti Callahan, *Becoming Mrs. Lewis* (Nashville: Thomas Nelson, 2018). Norman Stone directed a film version of Sibley's book for BBC Wales in 1985 starring Joss Ackland and Claire Bloom. William Nicholson adapted the film to the stage in 1989 with runs in London and New York, for which Nigel Hawthorne won a Tony Award as best actor for his portrayal of Lewis. Richard Attenborough directed a second film based on Nicholson's script in 1993, starring Anthony Hopkins as Lewis and Debra Winger as Davidman. More recently, a new biography has been written by Abigail Santamaria, *Joy: Poet, Seeker, and the Woman Who Captivated C. S. Lewis*.

63. Gresham, "The Longest Way Round," 23.
64. King, *Out of My Bone*, 100.
65. Dorsett, *And God Came In*, 62; King, *Out of My Bone*, 105.
66. King, *Out of My Bone*, 109.
67. King, *Out of My Bone*, 118.
68. King, *Out of My Bone*, 122.
69. King, *Out of My Bone*, 105.
70. King, *Out of My Bone*, 106.
71. Dorsett, *And God Came In*, 75.
72. Dorsett, *And God Came In*, 76–77.
73. Dorsett, *And God Came In*, 87.
74. Douglas H. Gresham, *Lenten Lands: My Childhood with Joy Davidman and C. S. Lewis* (New York: Macmillan, 1988), 16.
75. Joy mentioned the sexual orientation in letters to Bill Gresham dated October 18 and 24, 1952. Joy Davidman Papers, folder 6 (letters Aug.–Oct. 1952), the Marion E. Wade Center, Wheaton College, Wheaton, IL.
76. George Sayer, who met her, recalled her name as Phyllis Williams, the name by which Lyle Dorsett also identified her. Douglas Gresham, however, remembered her name as Haring, which Don King has accepted. See Sayer, *Jack: C. S. Lewis and His Times* (New York: Harper & Row, 1988), 214; Dorsett, *And God Came In*, 85; Gresham, *Lenten Lands*, 61; King, *Out of My Bone*, 131. The deciding evidence is the forwarding address Joy gave when she returned to England in 1952: c/o Haring, 64 Belsize Park Gardens, London N.W.3. See King, *Out of My Bone*, 159.
77. Joy Gresham to Bill Gresham, August 20, 1952, Joy Davidman Papers, folder 6.
78. Joy Gresham to Bill Gresham, August 29, 1952, Joy Davidman Papers, folder 6. See also November 8 and 14, 1952, folder 7 (letters Nov.–Dec. 1952), the Marion E. Wade Center, Wheaton College, Wheaton, IL.
79. Joy Gresham to Bill Gresham, August 29, 1952, September 13, 1952, Joy Davidman Papers, folder 6; November 8, 1952, Joy Davidman Papers, folder 7.

80. Joy Gresham to Bill Gresham, September 1, 1952, Joy Davidman Papers, folder 6.

81. Joy Gresham to Bill Gresham, October 29, 1952, Joy Davidman Papers, folder 6.

82. Joy Gresham to Bill Gresham, September 13, 1952, Joy Davidman Papers, folder 6.

83. Hooper, *Letters*, 3:228; King, *Out of My Bone*, 131.

84. Sayer, *Jack*, 214.

85. Sayer, *Jack*, 214.

86. Sayer, *Jack*, 215.

87. Joy Gresham to Bill Gresham, October 4, 1952, Joy Davidman Papers, folder 6.

88. Hooper, *Letters*, 3:228.

89. Joy described her visit to Worcester and Edinburgh in a letter to Bill Gresham, September 30, 1952, Joy Davidman Papers, folder 6.

90. Joy Gresham to Bill Gresham, October 15, 1952, Joy Davidman Papers, folder 6.

91. Sayer, *Jack*, 215.

92. Joy Gresham to Bill Gresham, October 18 and 24, 1952, Joy Davidman Papers, folder 6.

93. Joy Gresham to Bill Gresham, October 29, 1952, Joy Davidman Papers, folder 6.

94. Joy Gresham to Bill Gresham, November 3, 1952, Joy Davidman Papers, folder 7.

95. Joy Gresham to Bill Gresham, November 3, 1952, Joy Davidman Papers, folder 7.

96. Joy Gresham to Bill Gresham, October 29, 1952, Joy Davidman Papers, folder 6.

97. Joy Gresham to Bill Gresham, November 8 and 14, 1952, Joy Davidman Papers, folder 7.

98. Joy Gresham to Bill Gresham, November 23, 1952, Joy Davidman Papers, folder 7.

99. Joy Gresham to Bill Gresham, December 1, 1952, Joy Davidman Papers, folder 7.

100. Joy Gresham to Bill Gresham, November 17, 1952, Joy Davidman Papers, folder 7.

101. Hooper, *Letters*, 3:260–61.

102. King, *Out of My Bone*, 132.

103. King, *Out of My Bone*, 140.

104. Kilby and Mead, *Brothers and Friends*, 244–45.

105. Joy Gresham to Bill Gresham, December 1, 1952, Joy Davidman Papers, folder 7.

106. King, *Out of My Bone*, 138–39.

107. King, *Out of My Bone*, 133–36.

108. King, *Out of My Bone*, 137.

109. King, *Out of My Bone*, 140.
110. King, *Out of My Bone*, 140.
111. King, *Letters of Pitter*, 226.
112. Hooper, *Letters*, 3:274.
113. Hooper, *Letters*, 3:273.
114. Don W. King, *Hunting the Unicorn: A Critical Biography of Ruth Pitter* (Kent, OH: Kent State University Press, 2008), 106; King, *Letters of Pitter*, 236.
115. King, *Hunting the Unicorn*, 162.
116. King, *Hunting the Unicorn*, 173.
117. King, *Hunting the Unicorn*, 172.
118. King, *Letters of Pitter*, 236.
119. Hooper, *Letters*, 3:327–28.
120. Hooper, *Letters*, 3:328.
121. King, *Letters of Pitter*, 240.
122. King, *Letters of Pitter*, 243.
123. Though Gresham and Lewis began corresponding in 1950, we do not have a surviving letter until a letter from Lewis on December 22, 1953, in which he addressed her as Joy. See Hooper, *Letters*, 3:390.
124. King, *Letters of Pitter*, 248.
125. Hooper, *Letters*, 3:488.
126. Hooper, *Letters*, 3:403.
127. Hooper, *Letters*, 3:405.
128. Hooper, *Letters*, 3:417.
129. King, *Letters of Pitter*, 247.
130. Hooper, *Letters*, 3:367–68.
131. Gresham, *Lenten Lands*, 22, 24.
132. Hooper, *Letters*, 3:1672.
133. King, *Out of My Bone*, 140.
134. King, *Out of My Bone*, 143–48, 157–58.
135. King, *Out of My Bone*, 141.
136. King, *Out of My Bone*, 141–42.
137. King, *Out of My Bone*, 151.
138. King, *Out of My Bone*, 149.
139. King, *Out of My Bone*, 153.
140. King, *Out of My Bone*, 157.
141. King, *Out of My Bone*, 158–59.
142. King, *Out of My Bone*, 159. Each of her letters to Bill Gresham had a different street number for the Avoca House, including 10 and 43 before settling in at 14.
143. King, *Out of My Bone*, 161.
144. King, *Out of My Bone*, 163.
145. King, *Out of My Bone*, 165.
146. Hooper, *Letters*, 3:388, 390, 394.
147. Hooper, *Letters*, 3:389, 390.

148. Hooper, *Letters*, 3:395.
149. Hooper, *Letters*, 3:390.
150. Hooper, *Letters*, 3:79, 169, 238, 394.
151. Hooper, *Letters*, 3:394.
152. Hooper, *Letters*, 3:287.
153. Hooper, *Letters*, 3:507.
154. Hooper, *Letters*, 3:521.
155. Hooper, *Letters*, 3:297, 299, 302, 305, 308, 309.
156. King, *Out of My Bone*, 166.
157. King, *Out of My Bone*, 166.
158. King, *Out of My Bone*, 169.
159. King, *Out of My Bone*, 164, 169, 178–79, 183, 209, 223.
160. King, *Out of My Bone*, 292–93.
161. Hooper, *Letters*, 3:410–11.
162. King, *Out of My Bone*, 172, 177, 179, 205.
163. King, *Out of My Bone*, 179.
164. King, *Out of My Bone*, 186.
165. King, *Out of My Bone*, 185–86.
166. King, *Out of My Bone*, 188.
167. King, *Out of My Bone*, 188–89.
168. Hooper, *Letters*, 3:450.
169. Hooper, *Letters*, 3:450.
170. Angela Thirkell (1890–1961) was a granddaughter of the Pre-Raphaelite painter Edward Burne-Jones, a cousin of Rudyard Kipling, and a goddaughter of J. M. Barrie. A prolific writer, she wrote popular novels from the 1930s through the 1950s.
171. King, *Out of My Bone*, 190–92.
172. King, *Out of My Bone*, 193.
173. King, *Out of My Bone*, 192.
174. King, *Out of My Bone*, 194.
175. King, *Out of My Bone*, 202.
176. King, *Out of My Bone*, 211.
177. Hooper, *Letters*, 3:461.
178. Sayer, *Jack*, 211.
179. King, *Letters of Pitter*, 262n33.
180. King, *Out of My Bone*, 209, 210.
181. Hooper, *Letters*, 3:499.
182. Hooper, *Letters*, 3:502.
183. King, *Out of My Bone*, 211.
184. King, *Out of My Bone*, 212.
185. King, *Out of My Bone*, 212.
186. King, *Out of My Bone*, 212; Hooper, *Letters*, 3:503.
187. King, *Out of My Bone*, 214.
188. King, *Out of My Bone*, 235.
189. King, *Out of My Bone*, 217–18, 220, 221.

190. King, *Out of My Bone*, 222.
191. King, *Out of My Bone*, 222.
192. King, *Out of My Bone*, 224.
193. King, *Out of My Bone*, 224.

Chapter 6: Journey to Cambridge

1. Walter Hooper, ed., *The Collected Letters of C. S. Lewis*, vol. 3 (New York: HarperSanFrancisco, 2007), 469. Hooper cites the records of Cambridge University for this information. See *Cambridge University Record* 84, no. 19 (1954): 663, and 84, no. 30 (1954): 986.
2. Hooper, *Letters*, 3:469–70.
3. Hooper, *Letters*, 3:1732.
4. Hooper, *Letters*, 3:469–70.
5. Hooper, *Letters*, 3:470.
6. Hooper, *Letters*, 3:470.
7. Hooper, *Letters*, 3:474.
8. Hooper, *Letters*, 3:475.
9. Hooper, *Letters*, 3:474.
10. Hooper, *Letters*, 3:480.
11. Hooper, *Letters*, 3:476.
12. Hooper, *Letters*, 3:480.
13. Hooper, *Letters*, 3:481.
14. Helen Gardner, "Clive Staples Lewis, 1898–1963," *The Proceedings of the British Academy* 51 (1966): 427–28.
15. Hooper, *Letters*, 3:483.
16. Hooper, *Letters*, 3:484.
17. Hooper, *Letters*, 3:529. I am indebted to Barbara Reynolds, who attended the lecture, for telling me where it took place.
18. W. H. Lewis, ed., *Letters of C. S. Lewis* (London: Bles, 1966), 22.
19. Barbara Reynolds, ed., *The Letters of Dorothy L. Sayers*, vol. 4, *1951–1957: In the Midst of Life* (New York: St. Martin's, 2000), 179. Reynolds knew Sayers for eleven years before her death in 1957. A brilliant scholar of Italian literature, Reynolds completed the final volume of Sayers's translation of Dante's *Divine Comedy* when Sayers died. Reynolds would edit five volumes of the letters of Sayers and write a biography of her. In 1980, she became the founding editor of *SEVEN: An Anglo-American Literary Review* dedicated to the study of Dorothy L. Sayers, C. S. Lewis, J. R. R. Tolkien, George MacDonald, G. K. Chesterton, Charles Williams, and Owen Barfield. See Barbara Reynolds, *Dorothy L. Sayers: Her Life and Soul* (New York: St. Martin's, 1993), ix, 364.
20. Hooper, *Letters*, 3:579, 581–82. Lewis went to Broadcasting House, the London home of the BBC from which he had made his radio broadcasts during the war, on April 1, 1955, to record his inaugural lecture.
21. Reynolds, *Letters of Sayers*, 4:186.

22. C. S. Lewis, *De Descriptione Temporum: An Inaugural Lecture* (London: Cambridge University Press, 1955), 12–17.

23. Lewis, *De Descriptione Temporum*, 21.

24. Don W. King, ed., *Out of My Bone: The Letters of Joy Davidman* (Grand Rapids, MI: Eerdmans, 2009), 226.

25. King, *Out of My Bone*, 228.

26. King, *Out of My Bone*, 226.

27. Hooper, *Letters*, 3:556.

28. Hooper, *Letters*, 3:607.

29. Hooper, *Letters*, 3:598.

30. Reynolds, *Letters of Sayers*, 4:222–23.

31. Hooper, *Letters*, 3:535.

32. Clyde S. Kilby and Marjorie Lamp Mead, eds., *Brothers and Friends: The Diaries of Major Warren Hamilton Lewis* (New York: Harper & Row, 1982), 243.

33. Hooper, *Letters*, 3:545.

34. Hooper, *Letters*, 3:550.

35. King, *Out of My Bone*, 230.

36. King, *Out of My Bone*, 227–28.

37. King, *Out of My Bone*, 230.

38. King, *Out of My Bone*, 235.

39. Hooper, *Letters*, 3:591.

40. Hooper, *Letters*, 3:550; King, *Out of My Bone*, 238.

41. King, *Out of My Bone*, 238.

42. Hooper, *Letters*, 3:574. Lewis wrote to George Sayer on February 29, 1955, that it had been Warnie's worst year for prolonged debauches.

43. Hooper, *Letters*, 3:597.

44. Hooper, *Letters*, 3:568.

45. Hooper, *Letters*, 3:377–78.

46. Clifford Morris, "A Christian Gentleman," in *Remembering C. S. Lewis: Recollections of Those Who Knew Him*, ed. James T. Como, 3rd ed. (San Francisco: Ignatius, 2005), 319.

47. Hooper, *Letters*, 3:558.

48. Derek Brewer, "The Tutor: A Portrait," in Como, *Remembering C. S. Lewis*, 145.

49. Derek Brewer was fond of telling this story. See Brewer, "The Tutor," 145; Brewer, "C. S. Lewis: Sixty Years On," in *C. S. Lewis Remembered: Collected Reflections of Students, Friends and Colleagues*, ed. Harry Lee Poe and Rebecca Whitten Poe (Grand Rapids, MI: Zondervan, 2006), 69.

50. Hooper, *Letters*, 3:521, 541.

51. Hooper, *Letters*, 3:539.

52. Conversation with Emrys Jones during the C. S. Lewis Summer Institute, Oxford, July 18, 2002.

53. Richard W. Ladborough, "In Cambridge," in Como, *Remembering C. S. Lewis*, 191.
54. Ladborough, "In Cambridge," 191–92.
55. Ladborough, "In Cambridge," 192.
56. Ladborough, "In Cambridge," 195.
57. Brewer, "The Tutor," 135.
58. Walter Hooper, *C. S. Lewis: Companion and Guide* (New York: HarperSanFrancisco, 1996), 76.
59. Simon Barrington-Ward, foreword to Poe and Poe, *C. S. Lewis Remembered*, 19.
60. Barrington-Ward, foreword, 20.
61. Barrington-Ward, foreword, 20. George Watson repeats the same story (in "The Art of Disagreement," in Poe and Poe, *C. S. Lewis Remembered*, 84), but Watson was at St John's College and not Magdalene. He probably heard the story second-hand through English faculty gossip. By Watson's account, Lewis tutored Stevens for only one term, but that seems unlikely. One does not usually master Anglo-Saxon in one term.
62. Barrington-Ward, foreword, 18.
63. Hooper, *Letters*, 3:555.
64. Ladborough, "In Cambridge," 194.
65. Ladborough, "In Cambridge," 197–98.
66. Hooper, *Letters*, 3:601.
67. Hooper, *Letters*, 3:615.
68. Barrington-Ward, foreword, 19.
69. Hooper, *Letters*, 3:197.
70. Ladborough, "In Cambridge," 194–95.
71. Watson, "The Art of Disagreement," 79. Watson was an old man, long since retired when I first met him in 2004. He still had his notebooks from Lewis's lectures. Politically and critically a conservative, he had no interest in religion.
72. Barrington-Ward, foreword, 18.
73. Barrington-Ward, foreword, 21.
74. Barrington-Ward, foreword, 22.
75. Barrington-Ward, foreword, 22.
76. C. S. Lewis, *Surprised by Joy* (London: Bles, 1955), 224.
77. Watson, "The Art of Disagreement," 79–80.
78. John Lawlor, *C. S. Lewis: Memories and Reflections* (Dallas: Spence, 1998), 42.
79. Watson, "The Art of Disagreement," 81.
80. Ladborough, "In Cambridge," 193.
81. Ladborough, "In Cambridge," 193.
82. George Sayer, *Jack: C. S. Lewis and His Times* (New York: Harper & Row, 1988), 219.
83. Watson, "The Art of Disagreement," 80–81.

84. Alastair Fowler, "C. S. Lewis: Supervisor," in Poe and Poe, *C. S. Lewis Remembered*, 99.

85. Ladborough, "In Cambridge," 195.

86. Hooper, *Letters*, 3:599.

87. Hooper, *Letters*, 3:624, 633, 654, 662, 731, 734, 756, 779.

88. Hooper, *Letters*, 3:711, 753.

89. Lawlor, *C. S. Lewis*, 27.

90. Watson, "The Art of Disagreement," 84.

91. C. S. Lewis, "Christianity and Culture," in *Christian Reflections* (Grand Rapids, MI: Eerdmans, 1967), 13.

92. Lewis, "Christianity and Culture," 28. This is the position Lewis advocated in "Christianity and Literature," which was published in *Theology* (May 1940) and included in *Christian Reflections*.

93. Hooper, *Letters*, 3:1731.

94. C. S. Lewis, *A Preface to Paradise Lost* (London: Oxford University Press, 1942), 130.

95. Hooper, *Letters*, 3:774.

96. Hooper, *Letters*, 3:775. Lewis here paraphrases 1 Kings 19:18.

97. Hooper, *Letters*, 3:802.

98. Hooper, *Letters*, 3:1233.

99. Hooper, *Letters*, 3:1341.

100. Brewer, "C. S. Lewis," in Poe and Poe, *C. S. Lewis Remembered*, 61.

101. Hooper, *Letters*, 3:1359–60n107.

102. Hooper, *Letters*, 3:1360.

103. Hooper, *Letters*, 3:1371.

104. Hooper, *Letters*, 3:1379.

105. Hooper, *Letters*, 3:1469n150.

106. John Wain, *Sprightly Running* (London: Macmillan, 1962), 174.

107. Wain, *Sprightly Running*, 174.

108. Wain, *Sprightly Running*, 176.

109. Watson, "The Art of Disagreement," 84.

110. Watson, "The Art of Disagreement," 84.

111. Brewer, "The Tutor," 132.

112. Hooper, *Letters*, 3:680.

113. Hooper, *Letters*, 3:793.

114. Hooper, *Letters*, 3:657.

115. Hooper, *Letters*, 3:739.

116. C. S. Lewis, "Christian Apologetics," in *God in the Dock: Essays on Theology and Ethics*, ed. Walter Hooper (Grand Rapids, MI: Eerdmans, 1970), 93.

117. J. A. W. Bennett, "'Grete Clerk,'" in *Light on C. S. Lewis*, ed. Jocelyn Gibb (London: Bles, 1965), 45.

118. Humphrey Carpenter, ed., *The Letters of J. R. R. Tolkien* (London: Allen & Unwin, 1981), 302.

119. Carpenter, *Letters of Tolkien*, 302. *BHŪ here is a Sanskrit word roughly meaning "being" or "existence."

120. Carpenter, *Letters of Tolkien*, 302.

121. C. S. Lewis, *The Discarded Image: An Introduction to Medieval and Renaissance Literature* (London: Cambridge University Press, 1964), 7.

122. C. S. Lewis, *Spenser's Images of Life*, ed. Alastair Fowler (London: Cambridge University Press, 1967), 2. Though Fowler edited Lewis's notes and fleshed them out to make the book, this passage comes directly from Lewis's hand. The frontispiece to the book includes a photograph of the page on which Lewis made these notes.

123. Lewis, *Spenser's Images of Life*, 3.

124. Lewis, *Spenser's Images of Life*, 20.

125. Lewis, *Spenser's Images of Life*, 20.

126. Lewis, *Spenser's Images of Life*, 78.

127. Lewis, *Spenser's Images of Life*, 104.

128. Lewis, *Spenser's Images of Life*, 19.

129. Walter Hooper, ed., *The Collected Letters of C. S. Lewis*, vol. 1 (New York: HarperSanFrancisco, 2004), 268.

130. Walter Hooper, ed., *All My Road before Me: The Diary of C. S. Lewis, 1922–1927* (New York: Harcourt Brace Jovanovich, 1991), 30.

131. Hooper, *All My Road before Me*, 142.

132. Hooper, *Letters*, 3:590.

133. King, *Out of My Bone*, 241.

134. Hooper, *Letters*, 3:129.

135. Hooper, *Letters*, 3:585.

136. Hooper, *Letters*, 3:651.

137. Hooper, *Letters*, 3:593–96.

138. King, *Out of My Bone*, 242.

139. Hooper, *Letters*, 3:590.

140. Hooper, *Letters*, 3:503.

141. Hooper, *Letters*, 3:716.

142. Hooper, *Letters*, 3:601.

143. Hooper, *Letters*, 3:611.

144. Hooper, *Letters*, 3:620, 630–31.

145. King, *Out of My Bone*, 248, 251.

146. King, *Out of My Bone*, 253.

147. King, *Out of My Bone*, 246, 254.

148. King, *Out of My Bone*, 254.

149. King, *Out of My Bone*, 245.

150. King, *Out of My Bone*, 252–53.

151. King, *Out of My Bone*, 621.

152. Walter Hooper, ed., *The Collected Letters of C. S. Lewis*, vol. 2 (New York: HarperSanFrancisco, 2004), 368.

153. Hooper, *Letters*, 3:615.

154. Hooper, *Letters*, 3:641.

155. Sayer, *Jack*, 211–12.
156. Hooper, *Letters*, 3:641.
157. Hooper, *Letters*, 3:618.
158. Hooper, *Letters*, 3:633.
159. Hooper, *Letters*, 3:643.
160. King, *Out of My Bone*, 256–57.
161. Hooper, *Lewis*, 3:642.

Chapter 7: Jack and Joy

  1. Don W. King, ed., *Out of My Bone: The Letters of Joy Davidman* (Grand Rapids, MI: Eerdmans, 2009), 258.
  2. King, *Out of My Bone*, 279.
  3. Walter Hooper, ed., *The Collected Letters of C. S. Lewis*, vol. 3 (New York: HarperSanFrancisco, 2007), 642, 644.
  4. King, *Out of My Bone*, 260.
  5. Hooper, *Letters*, 3:669.
  6. George Sayer, *Jack: C. S. Lewis and His Times* (New York: Harper & Row, 1988), 221.
  7. Hooper, *Letters*, 3:645.
  8. C. S. Lewis, *Mere Christianity* (New York: Macmillan, 1952), 87.
  9. Humphrey Carpenter, ed., *The Letters of J. R. R. Tolkien* (London: Allen & Unwin, 1981), 60–62.
10. Alister McGrath has pointed out this diversity of opinion. See McGrath, *C. S. Lewis: A Life* (Carol Stream, IL: Tyndale, 2013), 330.
11. Lyle W. Dorsett, *And God Came In* (New York: Macmillan, 1983), 112.
12. Joy Davidman, *A Naked Tree: Love Sonnets to C. S. Lewis and Other Poems*, ed. Don W. King (Grand Rapids, MI: Eerdmans, 2015), 267–307. Some of these sonnets ae clearly written to Lewis, but some are dated much earlier than her conversion to Christianity and appear to have been "reassigned" to Lewis.
13. McGrath, *C. S. Lewis*, 331.
14. Douglas H. Gresham, *Lenten Lands: My Childhood with Joy Davidman and C. S. Lewis* (New York: Macmillan, 1988), 63.
15. King, *Out of My Bone*, 240, 259.
16. King, *Out of My Bone*, 265.
17. King, *Out of My Bone*, 269.
18. King, *Out of My Bone*, 250, 267, 269, 295.
19. McGrath, *C. S. Lewis*, 329.
20. King, *Out of My Bone*, 299.
21. King, *Out of My Bone*, 247.
22. King, *Out of My Bone*, 248.
23. King, *Out of My Bone*, 286.
24. Hooper, *Letters*, 3:742.
25. Hooper, *Letters*, 3:630.
26. Carpenter, *Letters of Tolkien*, 130.
27. King, *Out of My Bone*, 283n13.

28. King, *Out of my Bone*, 288.
29. McGrath, *C. S. Lewis*, 329. Lyle Dorsett suggested that Joy "entrapped" Lewis into paying the rent for the Headington house, but he neglected to provide any evidence for the suggestion. See Dorsett, *And God Came In*, 113. A. N. Wilson implied that Joy latched onto Lewis because he was generous with his money. See Wilson, *C. S. Lewis: A Biography* (New York: Norton, 1990), 249–50.
30. Clyde S. Kilby and Marjorie Lamp Mead, *Brothers and Friends: The Diaries of Major Warren Hamilton Lewis* (New York: Harper & Row, 1982), 245.
31. Kilby and Mead, *Brothers and Friends*, 247.
32. King, *Out of My Bone*, 260–62.
33. King, *Out of My Bone*, 262.
34. King, *Out of My Bone*, 282.
35. King, *Out of My Bone*, 272.
36. King, *Out of My Bone*, 272.
37. King, *Out of My Bone*, 266.
38. King, *Out of My Bone*, 271.
39. King, *Out of My Bone*, 279.
40. King, *Out of My Bone*, 269.
41. King, *Out of My Bone*, 270.
42. King, *Out of My Bone*, 271.
43. Hooper, *Letters*, 3:633.
44. Don W. King, *Hunting the Unicorn: A Critical Biography of Ruth Pitter* (Kent, OH: Kent State University Press, 2008), 197, quoting from the February 14, 1975, letter from Walter Hooper to Ruth Pitter in the uncatalogued Ruth Pitter Papers in the Bodleian Library.
45. David Cecil, "Oxford's Magic Circle," *Books and Bookmen* 24, no. 4 (1979): 12.
46. King, *Out of My Bone*, 266, 278, 280.
47. Richard W. Ladborough, "In Cambridge," in *Remembering C. S. Lewis: Recollections of Those Who Knew Him*, ed. James T. Como, 3rd ed. (San Francisco: Ignatius, 2005), 197.
48. Hooper, *Letters*, 3:716.
49. C. S. Lewis, "Sir Walter Scott," in *They Asked for a Paper* (London: Bles, 1962), 94.
50. C. S. Lewis, *Studies in Words* (London: Cambridge University Press, 1960), 133–64.
51. Lewis, "Sir Walter Scott," 103.
52. Hooper, *Letters*, 3:716, 720.
53. Hooper, *Letters*, 3:563–64, 1657.
54. McGrath, *C. S. Lewis*, 326.
55. Joy Gresham to Bill Gresham, November 23, 1952, and December 1, 1952, Joy Davidman Papers, folder 7 (letters Nov.–Dec. 1952), the Marion E. Wade Center, Wheaton College, Wheaton, IL. Lewis recommended the

literary agency of Brandt and Brandt in New York to Dr. Warfield Firor upon Joy's advice in April 1958. See Hooper, *Letters*, 3:934.

56. Don W. King, *The Letters of Ruth Pitter: Silent Music* (Newark, DE: University of Delaware Press, 2014), 283.

57. King, *Out of My Bone*, 261.

58. King, *Out of My Bone*, 276.

59. King, *Out of My Bone*, 285.

60. King, *Out of My Bone*, 290.

61. King, *Letters of Pitter*, 284.

62. King, *Out of My Bone*, 285, 287–88.

63. W. H. Lewis, ed., *Letters of C. S. Lewis* (London: Bles, 1966), 24.

64. Hooper, *Letters*, 3:1282.

65. This section describes physical complaints of Lewis. It is intended not as a diagnosis but only as a catalog of symptoms that would explain Dr. Havard's warnings to Lewis beginning in the late 1940s. It is important to stress that little could be done for Lewis other than diet in the 1950s, before so many of the drugs we take for granted had been developed. I am grateful to several medical professionals who reviewed this section, including physicians, physician assistants, and nurses. They were particularly concerned with heart-related issues. My thanks go to Chelsea Schlegel, Brad Wyly, Thomas Boulden, Russell Kilpatrick, Carla Sanderson, and Tracey Maynor.

66. Sayer, *Jack*, 244.

67. Alastair Fowler, "C. S. Lewis: Supervisor," in *C. S. Lewis Remembered: Collected Reflections of Students, Friends and Colleagues*, ed. Harry Lee Poe and Rebecca Whitten Poe (Grand Rapids, MI: Zondervan, 2006), 112.

68. Sayer, *Jack*, 249.

69. C. S. Lewis, *Of Other Worlds*, ed. Walter Hooper (London: Bles, 1966), v.

70. Sayer, *Jack*, 207–9; Ladborough, "In Cambridge," 195, 198; Roger Lancelyn Green and Walter Hooper, *C. S. Lewis: A Biography* (New York: Harcourt Brace Jovanovich, 1974), 303.

71. Sayer, *Jack*, 208.

72. Ladborough, "In Cambridge," 194.

73. Ladborough, "In Cambridge," 194.

74. Sayer, *Jack*, 207.

75. George Sayer, "Jack on Holiday," in Como, *Remembering C. S. Lewis*, 336.

76. Hooper, *Letters*, 3:817.

77. Nevill Coghill, "The Approach to English," in *Light on C. S. Lewis*, ed. Jocelyn Gibb (London: Bles, 1965), 57.

78. John Lawlor, *C. S. Lewis: Memories and Reflections* (Dallas: Spence, 1998), 29.

79. Walter Hooper, ed., *The Collected Letters of C. S. Lewis*, vol. 2 (New York: HarperSanFrancisco, 2004), 290.

80. Sayer, *Jack*, 208; Hooper, *Letters*, 2:812.
81. Ladborough, "In Cambridge," 196.
82. Coghill, "The Approach to English," 57.
83. *C. S. Lewis: Speaker and Teacher* (Grand Rapids, MI: Zondervan, 1971), 134.
84. Hooper, *Letters*, 3:666. See also 3:762.
85. Hooper, *Letters*, 3:521.
86. Hooper, *Letters*, 3:620.
87. Hooper, *Letters*, 3:817.
88. Lawlor, *C. S. Lewis*, 44.
89. Lawlor, *C. S. Lewis*, 44.
90. Hooper, *Letters*, 3:586–87.
91. Hooper, *Letters*, 3:639.
92. Hooper, *Letters*, 3:695.
93. Hooper, *Letters*, 3:749, 751, 772.
94. Hooper, *Letters*, 3:759.
95. Hooper, *Letters*, 3:756, 767.
96. Hooper, *Letters*, 3:769n216.
97. Hooper, *Letters*, 3:700n23. For more information about this prestigious award, see King, *Letters of Pitter*, 268, 270, 272, 273, 275, 278, 279–80. See also King, *Hunting the Unicorn*, 214–19.
98. King, *Letters of Pitter*, 297n59.
99. Hooper, *Letters*, 3:771.
100. Hooper, *Letters*, 3:771.
101. Hooper, *Letters*, 3:781–83.
102. Hooper, *Letters*, 3:797.
103. Hooper, *Letters*, 3:797.
104. Hooper, *Letters*, 3:786.
105. Hooper, *Letters*, 3:788.
106. McGrath, *C. S. Lewis*, 332; Kilby and Mead, *Brothers and Friends*, 245.
107. Sayer, *Jack*, 221.
108. King, *Out of My Bone*, 297–98; Hooper, *Letters*, 3:797–98.
109. King, *Out of My Bone*, 295.
110. King, *Out of My Bone*, 298.
111. Hooper, *Letters*, 3:798.
112. King, *Out of My Bone*, 300.
113. Hooper, *Letters*, 3:801.
114. Hooper, *Letters*, 3:805.
115. Teletype article dated October 26, 1956, JSS/Keystone 100/664248, Keystone Press of New York, in the private collection of Harry Lee Poe.
116. Hooper, *Letters*, 3:812.
117. Hooper, *Letters*, 3:817.
118. King, *Out of My Bone*, 299.
119. King, *Out of My Bone*, 302.
120. Hooper, *Letters*, 3:818.

121. Hooper, *Letters*, 3:819.
122. Hooper, *Letters*, 3:820–21.
123. King, *Out of My Bone*, 299.
124. Hooper, *Letters*, 3:841; Sayer, *Jack*, 224.
125. Hooper, *Letters*, 3:826.
126. King, *Out of My Bone*, 305–6.
127. Hooper, *Letters*, 3:832.
128. King, *Out of My Bone*, 307.
129. King, *Out of My Bone*, 308.
130. King, *Out of My Bone*, 309.
131. Hooper, *Letters*, 3:825; Sayer, *Jack*, 224.
132. Hooper, *Letters*, 3:820.
133. King, *Out of My Bone*, 283, 285, 290.
134. King, *Out of My Bone*, 211, 258, 275, 293.
135. King, *Out of My Bone*, 185.
136. King, *Out of My Bone*, 280.
137. King, *Out of My Bone*, 225, 229, 256.
138. King, *Out of My Bone*, 226.
139. King, *Out of My Bone*, 283.
140. King, *Out of My Bone*, 285.
141. King, *Out of My Bone*, 347.
142. King, *Out of My Bone*, 350.
143. Hooper, *Letters*, 3:867, 906.
144. Douglas H. Gresham, *Lenten Lands: My Childhood with Joy David-man and C. S. Lewis* (New York: Macmillan, 1988), 59.
145. King, *Out of My Bone*, 241.
146. Douglas Gresham related these anecdotes in an interview with Don King at the International C. S. Lewis Symposium sponsored by the Presbyterian Heritage Center, Montreat, NC, November 2019 which may be viewed at www.youtube.com.
147. Hooper, *Letters*, 3:429.
148. Bide told this story at the meeting of the Oxford C. S. Lewis Society on January 24, 1995, and it is published as Peter Bide, "Marrying C. S. Lewis," in *C. S. Lewis and His Circle: Essays and Memoirs from the Oxford C. S. Lewis Society*, ed. Roger White, Judith White, and Brendan N. Wolfe (New York: Oxford University Press, 2015), 187–91. Lewis gave an abbreviated account in a letter to Dorothy L. Sayers on June 25, 1957. See Hooper, *Letters*, 3:861.
149. Kilby and Mead, *Brothers and Friends*, 245.
150. Kilby and Mead, *Brothers and Friends*, 246.

Chapter 8: Married Life

1. Clyde S. Kilby and Marjorie Lamp Mead, *Brothers and Friends: The Diaries of Major Warren Hamilton Lewis* (New York: Harper & Row, 1982), 246.

2. Walter Hooper, ed., *The Collected Letters of C. S. Lewis*, vol. 3 (New York: HarperSanFrancisco, 2007), 842.
3. Hooper, *Letters*, 3:843.
4. Don W. King has included the text of Bill's letter to Joy and a second letter to Jack, both written on April 2, 1957. See King, ed., *Out of My Bone: The Letters of Joy Davidman* (Grand Rapids, MI: Eerdmans, 2009), 310–13.
5. Hooper, *Letters*, 3:843.
6. Hooper, *Letters*, 3:844.
7. Hooper, *Letters*, 3:844.
8. Hooper, *Letters*, 3:845.
9. King, *Out of My Bone*, 314.
10. King, *Out of My Bone*, 312.
11. King, *Out of My Bone*, 315.
12. King, *Out of My Bone*, 316.
13. King, *Out of My Bone*, 317.
14. Hooper, *Letters*, 3:847.
15. King, *Out of My Bone*, 318, 319, 320; Hooper, *Letters*, 3:859–60.
16. Hooper, *Letters*, 3:858.
17. Hooper, *Letters*, 3:862.
18. Hooper, *Letters*, 3:867, 878.
19. Hooper, *Letters*, 3:855, 867, 934.
20. Hooper, *Letters*, 3:874, 875, 905.
21. Hooper, *Letters*, 3:878.
22. Hooper, *Letters*, 3:895, 897, 900, 901, 902.
23. Hooper, *Letters*, 3:902, 907.
24. Hooper, *Letters*, 3:867, 878, 884, 903.
25. Hooper, *Letters*, 3:859, 901.
26. King, *Out of My Bone*, 324; Hooper, *Letters*, 3:894.
27. Hooper, *Letters*, 3:864.
28. King, *Out of My Bone*, 322.
29. King, *Out of My Bone*, 325.
30. King, *Out of My Bone*, 326; Hooper, *Letters*, 3:926.
31. King, *Out of My Bone*, 329–30.
32. King, *Out of My Bone*, 330.
33. King, *Out of My Bone*, 333, 335, 336.
34. I have heard Douglas Gresham tell this story several times in Oxford and on the *Sea Cloud II* in the Irish Sea.
35. King, *Out of My Bone*, 330.
36. Several examples survive. See King, *Out of My Bone*, 332–36.
37. King, *Out of My Bone*, 337.
38. King, *Out of My Bone*, 332.
39. Hooper, *Letters*, 3:963.
40. King, *Out of My Bone*, 333.

41. Peter Bayley, "From Master to Colleague," in *Remembering C. S. Lewis: Recollections of Those Who Knew Him*, ed. James T. Como, 3rd ed. (San Francisco: Ignatius, 2005), 176.
42. Nevill Coghill, "The Approach to English," in *Light on C. S. Lewis*, ed. Jocelyn Gibb (London: Bles, 1965), 63. See also Bayley, "From Master to Colleague," 176.
43. Coghill, "The Approach to English," 63.
44. King, *Out of My Bone*, 321.
45. Hooper, *Letters*, 3:890.
46. Hooper, *Letters*, 3:900.
47. C. S. Lewis, *Reflections on the Psalms* (London: Bles, 1958), 1–2.
48. Lewis, *Reflections on the Psalms*, 3.
49. Lewis, *Reflections on the Psalms*, 3.
50. Lewis, *Reflections on the Psalms*, 4–5.
51. Lewis, *Reflections on the Psalms*, 6.
52. Lewis, *Reflections on the Psalms*, 6.
53. Lewis, *Reflections on the Psalms*, 7.
54. Hooper, *Letters*, 3:941nn57–58.
55. Walter Hooper, ed., *The Collected Letters of C. S. Lewis*, vol. 1 (New York: HarperSanFrancisco, 2004), 970.
56. Hooper, *Letters*, 3:864.
57. Hooper, *Letters*, 3:861.
58. Hooper, *Letters*, 3:884.
59. Hooper, *Letters*, 3:538.
60. Hooper, *Letters*, 3:428–29.
61. Hooper, *Letters*, 3:413.
62. Hooper, *Letters*, 3:964–65. Lewis appears to have joined the Athenaeum Club in the mid-1950s, when money became more available to him. The club was founded and continues to exist for an intellectual elite that has boasted several score of Nobel laureates.
63. King, *Out of My Bone*, 341.
64. King, *Out of My Bone*, 341.
65. King, *Out of My Bone*, 342.
66. Hooper, *Letters*, 3:1035.
67. Hooper, *Letters*, 3:1037.
68. Hooper, *Letters*, 3:1062.
69. Hooper, *Letters*, 3:1077.
70. Hooper, *Letters*, 3:1091. See also the front dust jacket flap of C. S. Lewis, *The Four Loves* (London: Bles, 1960).
71. Hooper, *Letters*, 3:1112.
72. Hooper, *Letters*, 3:1142n36.
73. King, *Out of My Bone*, 342.
74. George Sayer, *Jack: C. S. Lewis and His Times* (New York: Harper & Row, 1988), 237.

75. "Reinforcing the Spiritual Outreach of the Church: A Series of Ten Radio Talks on Love by Dr. C. S. Lewis" (Atlanta, GA: The Episcopal Radio-TV Foundation, 1959). The pamphlets are all single-sheet trifolds.
76. Lewis, *The Four Loves*, 17.
77. Lewis, *The Four Loves*, 43.
78. Lewis, *The Four Loves*, 93.
79. Lewis, *The Four Loves*, 77, 85.
80. Lewis, *The Four Loves*, 73–74.
81. Lewis, *The Four Loves*, 95.
82. Lewis, *The Four Loves*, 127–28.
83. Lewis, *The Four Loves*, 145–47.
84. Hooper, *Letters*, 3:925.
85. Hooper, *Letters*, 3:931.
86. Hooper, *Letters*, 3:960, 963.
87. Hooper, *Letters*, 3:967.
88. King, *Out of My Bone*, 339; Hooper, *Letters*, 3:949.
89. King, *Out of My Bone*, 332, 339.
90. King, *Out of My Bone*, 340.
91. Hooper, *Letters*, 3:1000, 1001, 1029, 1041.
92. Sayer, *Jack*, 228.
93. Sayer, *Jack*, 229.
94. Hooper, *Letters*, 3:968.
95. Hooper, *Letters*, 3:969.
96. Hooper, *Letters*, 3:993.
97. Hooper, *Letters*, 3:1010.
98. Richard W. Ladborough, "In Cambridge," in Como, *Remembering C. S. Lewis*, 193.
99. Hooper, *Letters*, 3:1010, 1016, 1017, 1018, 1019, 1020.
100. Hooper, *Letters*, 3:1022.
101. Hooper, *Letters*, 3:983.
102. A. N. Wilson, *C. S. Lewis: A Biography* (New York: Norton, 1990), 273.
103. Humphrey Carpenter, ed., *The Letters of J. R. R. Tolkien* (London: Allen & Unwin, 1981), 341, 349.
104. Carpenter, *Letters of Tolkien*, 341.
105. Carpenter, *Letters of Tolkien*, 256.
106. Sayer took the occasion, when he addressed the Oxford C. S. Lewis Society in 1990, to take exception to Wilson's newly published biography. See George Sayer, "Recollections of C. S. Lewis," in *C. S. Lewis and His Circle: Essays and Memoirs from the Oxford C. S. Lewis Society*, ed. Roger White, Judith Wolfe, and Brendan N. Wolfe (New York: Oxford University Press, 2015), 175–78.
107. Hooper, *Letters*, 3:971.
108. Hooper, *Letters*, 3:975n161.
109. Hooper, *Letters*, 3:976.

110. C. S. Lewis, "Rejoinder to Dr. Pittinger," in *God in the Dock: Essays on Theology and Ethics*, ed. Walter Hooper (Grand Rapids, MI: Eerdmans, 1970), 181–82.

111. Lewis, "Rejoinder to Dr. Pittinger," 183.

112. Hooper, *Letters*, 3:985n193.

113. Hooper, *Letters*, 3:988–89.

114. Hooper, *Letters*, 3:1015.

115. King, *Out of My Bone*, 345.

116. Mathew's account is recorded in Roger Lancelyn Green and Walter Hooper, *C. S. Lewis: A Biography* (New York: Harcourt Brace Jovanovich, 1974), 223–24.

117. King, *Out of My Bone*, 348.

118. King, *Out of My Bone*, 350.

119. Hooper, *Letters*, 3:1059.

120. Francis Warner, "Lewis' Involvement in the Revision of the Psalter," in *C. S. Lewis and the Church*, ed. Judith Wolfe and B. N. Wolfe (Edinburgh: T&T Clark, 2013), 53–55.

121. Warner, "Revision of the Psalter," 55.

122. Warner, "Revision of the Psalter," 54.

123. Hooper, *Letters*, 3:1048.

124. Hooper, *Letters*, 3:1041.

125. Hooper, *Letters*, 3:1051–53.

126. Hooper, *Letters*, 3:1050.

127. Hooper, *Letters*, 3:1033.

128. Hooper, *Letters*, 3:1038.

129. Hooper, *Letters*, 3:511, 584, 735, 745, 747, 799, 850, 888, 941, 981, 1041, 1142, 1253, 1413.

130. Hooper, *Letters*, 3:574.

131. Hooper, *Letters*, 3:724, 964, 1169.

132. King, *Out of My Bone*, 350.

133. King, *Out of My Bone*, 350.

134. King, *Out of My Bone*, 350.

135. Wilson, *C. S. Lewis*, 266.

136. Hooper, *Letters*, 3:765.

137. Hooper, *Letters*, 3:804.

138. Hooper, *Letters*, 3:927.

139. Hooper, *Letters*, 3:1048–49.

140. Hooper, *Letters*, 3:1087.

141. Hooper, *Letters*, 3:1111.

142. Kilby and Mead, *Brothers and Friends*, 276.

143. Kilby and Mead, *Brothers and Friends*, 279–80.

144. Walter Hooper gave the year as 1976, but the production actually appeared in 1979. See Hooper, *Letters*, 3:1111–12n263; IMDb, https://www.imdb.com, accessed February 3, 2021. In my C. S. Lewis collection, I have a clipping of the *TV Guide* advertisement for the production

with the date 1979. This TV production was my introduction to C. S. Lewis. I had never heard of The Chronicles of Narnia until I entered The Southern Baptist Theological Seminary in 1975. I did not care for the animation, but the story fascinated me. It also had a powerful effect on children. My friend Pete Parks was working his way through seminary as an orderly at Norton's Children's Hospital in Louisville. The children on his ward watched the program together, and when Aslan was killed by the White Witch, they were terribly upset and said: "That's not fair! He never did anything!"

145. Hooper, *Letters*, 3:1048, 1062, 1063, 1064, 1065.
146. Hooper, *Letters*, 3:1062.
147. Hooper, *Letters*, 3:1063.
148. Hooper, *Letters*, 3:1092, 1097, 1098, 1101, 1105, 1116.
149. Hooper, *Letters*, 3:1092.
150. Hooper, *Letters*, 3:1097, 1105.
151. Hooper, *Letters*, 3:1101.
152. Hooper, *Letters*, 3:1106. Lewis repeated this image to Vera Gebbert, 3:1123.
153. Hooper, *Letters*, 3:1116.
154. Hooper, *Letters*, 3:1162.
155. George Watson, "The Art of Disagreement," in *C. S. Lewis Remembered: Collected Reflections of Students, Friends and Colleagues*, ed. Harry Lee Poe and Rebecca Whitten Poe (Grand Rapids, MI: Zondervan, 2006), 86.
156. Hooper, *Letters*, 3:1101.
157. Hooper, *Letters*, 3:1139.
158. Hooper, *Letters*, 3:1134.
159. Walter Hooper, "What about Mrs. Boshell?," in Poe and Poe, *C. S. Lewis Remembered*, 46. Hooper repeated this story often, and it may also be found in "It All Began with a Picture," in White, Wolfe, and Wolfe, *C. S. Lewis and His Circle*, 158.
160. Green and Hooper, *C. S. Lewis*, 271. This biography includes a transcription of Green's diary entries for the trip to Greece.
161. Green and Hooper, *C. S. Lewis*, 272.
162. Green and Hooper, *C. S. Lewis*, 272.
163. Hooper, *Letters*, 3:1154.
164. Green and Hooper, *C. S. Lewis*, 272–73.
165. Hooper, *Letters*, 3:1147.
166. Green and Hooper, *C. S. Lewis*, 273–75.
167. Hooper, *Letters*, 3:1153.
168. Hooper, *Letters*, 3:1102.
169. Hooper, *Letters*, 3:1161.
170. Hooper, *Letters*, 3:1161.
171. Hooper, *Letters*, 3:1162.
172. Kilby and Mead, *Brothers and Friends*, 248; Hooper, *Letters*, 3:1153.

173. Kilby and Mead, *Brothers and Friends*, 248–49.
174. Kilby and Mead, *Brothers and Friends*, 248–50; Hooper, *Letters*, 3:1171.

Chapter 9: Life without Joy

1. Clyde S. Kilby and Marjorie Lamp Mead, *Brothers and Friends: The Diaries of Major Warren Hamilton Lewis* (New York: Harper & Row, 1982), 250.
2. Kilby and Mead, *Brothers and Friends*, 250–51.
3. Walter Hooper, ed., *The Collected Letters of C. S. Lewis*, vol. 2 (New York: HarperSanFrancisco, 2004), 358.
4. Walter Hooper, ed., *The Collected Letters of C. S. Lewis*, vol. 3 (New York: HarperSanFrancisco, 2007), 1171.
5. Hooper, *Letters*, 3:1174.
6. Hooper, *Letters*, 3:1175.
7. Hooper, *Letters*, 3:1177.
8. Hooper, *Letters*, 3:1182.
9. Hooper, *Letters*, 3:1184.
10. Hooper, *Letters*, 3:1185.
11. Hooper, *Letters*, 3:1179, 1180.
12. Hooper, *Letters*, 3:1180.
13. Roger Lancelyn Green and Walter Hooper, *C. S. Lewis: A Biography* (New York: Harcourt Brace Jovanovich, 1974), 277.
14. Hooper, *Letters*, 3:1182.
15. Hooper, *Letters*, 3:1460.
16. Hooper, *Letters*, 3:1187.
17. A. N. Wilson received this information from Monteith. See Wilson, *C. S. Lewis: A Biography* (New York: Norton, 1990), 285, 321n6.
18. Hooper, *Letters*, 3:1201.
19. Walter Hooper, "A Bibliography of the Writings of C. S. Lewis, Revised and Enlarged," in *Remembering C. S. Lewis: Recollections of Those Who Knew Him*, ed. James T. Como, 3rd ed. (San Francisco: Ignatius, 2005), 400.
20. C. S. Lewis, *The Problem of Pain* (London: Centenary, 1940), vii–viii.
21. C. S. Lewis, *A Grief Observed* (London: Faber and Faber, 1961), 7.
22. Hooper, *Letters*, 3:1174.
23. Lewis, *The Problem of Pain*, 3.
24. Lewis, *A Grief Observed*, 9.
25. Lewis, *A Grief Observed*, 9–10.
26. Lewis, *A Grief Observed*, 11.
27. Lewis, *A Grief Observed*, 18–19.
28. Lewis, *A Grief Observed*, 21–22.
29. Lewis, *A Grief Observed*, 25.
30. Hooper, *Letters*, 3:1175.
31. Lewis, *A Grief Observed*, 29 (emphasis added).

32. Lewis, *A Grief Observed*, 37, 38.
33. Lewis, *A Grief Observed*, 41.
34. Lewis, *A Grief Observed*, 42.
35. Lewis, *A Grief Observed*, 42.
36. Lewis, *A Grief Observed*, 43.
37. Hooper, *Letters*, 3:1188. I first met Douglas Gresham and heard him speak at the 1998 C. S. Lewis Summer Institute in Oxford. We were together again three or four times when I served as program director of the C. S. Lewis Summer Institute between 1999 and 2006, and for a week on a tall ship in the Irish Sea in 2004. Douglas has his mother's straightforward way of speaking his mind, but also her deep faith. He does not suffer fools gladly, as my mother used to say. He is very intelligent, though like many of his peers, he was not a slave to his studies in his youth. For many decades, he has devoted himself to safeguarding Lewis's legacy. In the past, he has often "rubbed people the wrong way." In 2019, we shared the platform with several other major Lewis scholars at the largest Lewis conference ever staged, which was sponsored by the Presbyterian Heritage Center and held in Montreat, North Carolina. What struck me most about Douglas was how kind and generous he was to the hundreds of people who wanted to meet him, and how gentle and considerate his comments were on the platform, compared with the Doug Gresham I had first heard speak twenty years before. I could only reflect on the wonder of sanctification within a Christian life. His mother would have been so proud—as she always was of young Douglas—of the man he became.
38. Lewis, *A Grief Observed*, 47.
39. Hooper, *Letters*, 3:1188, 1199.
40. Hooper, *Letters*, 3:1185.
41. Hooper, *Letters*, 3:1210.
42. Hooper, *Letters*, 3:1004.
43. Hooper, *Letters*, 3:1191, 1192–94, 1195–96, 1197–98.
44. Hooper, *Letters*, 3:1243.
45. Hooper, *Letters*, 3:1192.
46. Hooper, *Letters*, 3:1202.
47. Hooper, *Letters*, 3:1203, 1208.
48. Hooper, *Letters*, 3:1229.
49. Hooper, *Letters*, 3:1285.
50. Walter Hooper, ed., *The Collected Letters of C. S. Lewis*, vol. 1 (New York: HarperSanFrancisco, 2004), 161.
51. Hooper, *Letters*, 1:190.
52. Hooper, *Letters*, 1:246.
53. C. S. Lewis, *A Preface to Paradise Lost* (London: Oxford University Press, 1942), 9.
54. Hooper, *Letters*, 3:1371–72. Boileau was a French critic during the age of Louis XIV who established the principles of taste that governed neoclassicism.

55. C. S. Lewis, *An Experiment in Criticism* (London: Cambridge University Press, 1961), 2.

56. Lewis, *An Experiment in Criticism*, 2–3.

57. Lewis, *An Experiment in Criticism*, 3.

58. Lewis, *An Experiment in Criticism*, 3.

59. C. S. Lewis, Kingsley Amis, and Brian Aldiss, "The Establishment Must Rot and Die . . . ," in *C. S. Lewis Remembered: Collected Reflections of Students, Friends and Colleagues*, ed. Harry Lee Poe and Rebecca Whitten Poe (Grand Rapids, MI: Zondervan, 2006), 238.

60. Lewis, *An Experiment in Criticism*, 4.

61. Humphrey Carpenter, ed., *The Letters of J. R. R. Tolkien* (London: Allen & Unwin, 1981), 249.

62. Carpenter, *Letters of Tolkien*, 214, 377.

63. Carpenter, *Letters of Tolkien*, 377, 349.

64. Holly Ordway, *Tolkien's Modern Reading: Middle-earth beyond the Middle Ages* (Park Ridge, IL: Word on Fire Academic, 2021), 295–305. Ordway has listed in the appendix the authors and their books that we have clear evidence of Tolkien having read.

65. Carpenter, *Letters of Tolkien*, 39.

66. Carpenter, *Letters of Tolkien*, 55, 172, 201.

67. Robert E. Havard, "Philia: Jack at Ease," in Como, *Remembering C. S. Lewis*, 352.

68. C. S. Lewis, *The Discarded Image: An Introduction to Medieval and Renaissance Literature* (London: Cambridge University Press, 1964), 7.

69. Hooper, *Letters*, 3:1214.

70. Hooper, *Letters*, 3:1221.

71. Hooper, *Letters*, 3:1222.

72. Hooper, *Letters*, 3:1228.

73. Hooper, *Letters*, 3:1251.

74. Alister McGrath, *C. S. Lewis: A Life* (Carol Stream, IL: Tyndale, 2013), 352.

75. Hooper, *Letters*, 3:1037.

76. Hooper, *Letters*, 3:1062.

77. Hooper, *Letters*, 3:1132.

78. Hooper, *Letters*, 3:1247.

79. Hooper, *Letters*, 3:1254–56.

80. Hooper, *Letters*, 3:1272.

81. Hooper, *Letters*, 3:1275.

82. Hooper, *Letters*, 3:1319.

83. Hooper, *Letters*, 3:1257–58.

84. Hooper, *Letters*, 3:1260.

85. Hooper, *Letters*, 3:1259.

86. Hooper, *Letters*, 3:1259.

87. Hooper, *Letters*, 3:1262, 1263, 1266–67, 1268.

88. Hooper, *Letters*, 3:1270. For an account of Morris's service over the years as Lewis's driver, see Clifford Morris, "A Christian Gentleman," in Como, *Remembering C. S. Lewis*, 317–30.
89. Hooper, *Letters*, 3:1277.
90. Hooper, *Letters*, 3:1277–78.
91. Hooper, *Letters*, 3:1281.
92. Hooper, *Letters*, 3:1281.
93. Hooper, *Letters*, 3:1282–83. The first time I spent the night in the Kilns, in 2000, I slept in this room, to which Lewis had moved.
94. Hooper, *Letters*, 3:1283–84.
95. Hooper, *Letters*, 3:1284.
96. Hooper, *Letters*, 3:1287.
97. Hooper, *Letters*, 3:1288, 1290.
98. Hooper, *Letters*, 3:1290, 1292.
99. Hooper, *Letters*, 3:1295–96.
100. Hooper, *Letters*, 3:1296.
101. Hooper, *Letters*, 3:1296–97.
102. Hooper, *Letters*, 3:1298.
103. Hooper, *Letters*, 3:1301.
104. Hooper, *Letters*, 3:1301–2.
105. Hooper, *Letters*, 3:1304.
106. Hooper, *Letters*, 3:1302, 1306, 1307.
107. Hooper, *Letters*, 3:1313, 1314.
108. Hooper, *Letters*, 3:1316.
109. Hooper, *Letters*, 3:1318.
110. Hooper, *Letters*, 3:1319.
111. Hooper, *Letters*, 3:1324.
112. Hooper, *Letters*, 3:1320, 1327.
113. Hooper, *Letters*, 3:1321.
114. Hooper, *Letters*, 3:1331. See also 3:1333–34.
115. Hooper, *Letters*, 3:1334.
116. Hooper, *Letters*, 3:1334.
117. Hooper, *Letters*, 3:1337.
118. Hooper, *Letters*, 3:1345.
119. Hooper, *Letters*, 3:1347. He mentioned the same matters to Arthur Greeves. See 3:1352.
120. Hooper, *Letters*, 3:1349.
121. Hooper, *Letters*, 3:1352, 1373.
122. Wilson, *C. S. Lewis*, 293–94.
123. Hooper, *Letters*, 3:1343.
124. Hooper, *Letters*, 3:1397–98.
125. Lewis, *The Discarded Image*, 11.
126. Lewis, *The Discarded Image*, 18.
127. Lewis, *The Discarded Image*, 112.
128. Lewis, *The Discarded Image*, 134.

129. Hooper, *Letters*, 3:1188.
130. Lewis, *The Discarded Image*, 215.
131. Hooper, *Letters*, 3:1354.
132. Hooper, *Letters*, 3:1361.
133. Hooper, *Letters*, 3:1362.
134. Hooper, *Letters*, 3:1369.
135. Hooper, *Letters*, 3:1369.
136. Hooper, *Letters*, 3:1384.
137. Hooper, *Letters*, 3:1363.
138. Hooper, *Letters*, 3:1365.
139. Hooper, *Letters*, 3:1363n112.
140. Hooper, *Letters*, 3:1365n118–19.
141. The essay was also published in C. S. Lewis, *Selected Literary Essays*, ed. Walter Hooper (London: Cambridge University Press, 1969), 146–53.
142. Hooper, *Letters*, 3:1370.
143. Hooper, *Letters*, 3:1372.
144. Hooper, *Letters*, 3:1373.
145. Hooper, *Letters*, 3:1370.
146. Hooper, *Letters*, 3:1378.
147. Hooper, *Letters*, 3:1379.
148. Hooper, *Letters*, 3:1382–83, 1383n149.
149. This letter is not included in Walter Hooper's *Collected Letters of C. S. Lewis*. The letter, which was in the possession of Christopher Tolkien, was loaned to A. N. Wilson, who included it—unfortunately without its date—in Wilson, *C. S. Lewis*, 294.
150. Wilson, *C. S. Lewis*, 294.
151. Ordway, *Tolkien's Modern Reading*, 12–14.
152. Wilson, *C. S. Lewis*, 294.
153. Hooper, *Letters*, 3:1404.
154. Hooper, *Letters*, 3:1410n28.
155. Hooper, *Letters*, 3:1408–9. Within a year of each other, both pubs closed. The Eagle and Child, after changing hands a number of times before becoming part of a national chain, was bought to become a hotel. A current plan calls for demolishing the rear portions, which had been added after 1963, where a multistory addition will provide rooms for guests. As of this writing, it is unclear if the old pub will reopen as it once was. As for the Lamb and Flag, the decline in business during the COVID pandemic of 2020–2021 resulted in great financial losses for its owner, St John's College. In the midst of the pandemic, St John's closed the pub indefinitely.
156. Hooper, *Letters*, 3:1422.
157. Hooper, *Letters*, 3:1407–8.
158. Hooper, *Letters*, 2:965. I have Van Deusen's copies of Lewis's books in my collection, including her copy of *Letters to Malcolm*.

159. Hooper, *Letters*, 3:276, 295, 307. Lewis wrote to Sister Penelope that he had to give up writing the book on prayer—"it was clearly not for me." See Hooper, *Letters*, 3:428; also 3:651.
160. Hooper, *Letters*, 3:1423.
161. Hooper, *Letters*, 3:1427.
162. C. S. Lewis, *Letters to Malcolm: Chiefly on Prayer* (London: Bles, 1963, 1964), 11.
163. Hooper, *Letters*, 3:276.
164. Lewis, *Letters to Malcolm*, 11.
165. Lewis did not dislike the services of the Book of Common Prayer, but he had a deep loathing of the hymns as a combination of bad poetry and bad music. See Hooper, *Letters*, 2:721–22, 740–41; 3:68, 434, 776. His distaste for hymns extended to church music in general. See Hooper, *Letters*, 3:461, 731.
166. Hooper, *Letters*, 3:1362.
167. Hooper, *Letters*, 3:1588.
168. Lewis, *Letters to Malcolm*, 11–13.
169. Hooper, *Letters*, 3:177–78.
170. Hooper, *Letters*, 3:1424.
171. Lewis, *Letters to Malcolm*, 14–17.
172. Hooper, *Letters*, 3:281.
173. Hooper, *Letters*, 3:295.
174. Shelburne donated her large collection of letters, which may also be found in Walter Hooper's *Collected Letters of C. S. Lewis* under her name, to Wheaton College, where they became a cornerstone of what would become the Marion E. Wade Center. See Clyde S. Kilby, *Letters to an American Lady* (Grand Rapids, MI: Eerdmans, 1967), 9.
175. Hooper, *Letters*, 3:720; Lewis, *Letters to Malcolm*, 19.
176. Lewis, *Letters to Malcolm*, 25.
177. Lewis, *Letters to Malcolm*, 53.
178. Lewis, *Letters to Malcolm*, 60.

Chapter 10: The Last Summer
1. Walter Hooper, ed., *The Collected Letters of C. S. Lewis*, vol. 3 (New York: HarperSanFrancisco, 2007), 1412–13.
2. Hooper, *Letters*, 3:1414.
3. Hooper, *Letters*, 3:1418.
4. Hooper, *Letters*, 3:1426.
5. Hooper, *Letters*, 3:1428.
6. Hooper, *Letters*, 3:1429.
7. Hooper, *Letters*, 3:1355.
8. James Dundas-Grant, "From an 'Outsider,'" in *Remembering C. S Lewis*, ed. James T. Como, 3rd ed. (San Francisco: Ignatius, 2005), 371, 373. Walter Hooper also mentioned people he met through Lewis, but he does not distinguish the ones he met at the Lamb and Flag from

those he met otherwise. See Roger Lancelyn Green and Walter Hooper, *C. S. Lewis: A Biography* (New York: Harcourt Brace Jovanovich, 1974), 299.

9. Hooper, *Letters*, 3:1429.
10. Green and Hooper, *C. S. Lewis*, 299.
11. Hooper, *Letters*, 3:1429.
12. Hooper, *Letters*, 3:1439.
13. Hooper, *Letters*, 3:1440.
14. Hooper, *Letters*, 3:1441.
15. Hooper, *Letters*, 3:1442.
16. Hooper, *Letters*, 3:1441.
17. Hooper, *Letters*, 3:1442.
18. Hooper, *Letters*, 3:1442.
19. Hooper, *Letters*, 3:1443, 1446.
20. Dundas-Grant, "From an 'Outsider,'" 372.
21. Douglas H. Gresham, *Lenten Lands: My Childhood with Joy Davidman and C. S. Lewis* (New York: Macmillan, 1988), 151–52.
22. Gresham, *Lenten Lands*, 152.
23. Walter Hooper, *Through Joy and Beyond: A Pictorial Biography of C. S. Lewis* (New York: Macmillan, 1982), 155.
24. George Sayer, *Jack: C. S. Lewis and His Times* (New York: Harper & Row, 1988), 247–48.
25. Sayer, *Jack*, 248.
26. Sayer, *Jack*, 249.
27. Hooper, *Letters*, 3:1446, 1448.
28. Sayer, *Jack*, 249.
29. Hooper, *Letters*, 3:1444–45.
30. Hooper mentioned the resignation in a letter Lewis instructed him to send to Mary Willis Shelburne on August 10. See Hooper, *Letters*, 3:1447–48.
31. Hooper, *Letters*, 3:1449–50.
32. Hooper, *Letters*, 3:1451.
33. Hooper, *Through Joy and Beyond*, 101
34. Hooper, *Through Joy and Beyond*, 101.
35. Hooper, *Letters*, 3:1055.
36. Hooper, *Through Joy and Beyond*, 101.
37. Roger Lancelyn Green and Walter Hooper, *C. S. Lewis: A Biography* (London: HarperCollins, 2002), 430, as cited by Colin Duriez, *The Oxford Inklings* (Oxford: Lion Hudson, 2015), 203.
38. Hooper, *Letters*, 3:1454.
39. Hooper, *Letters*, 3:1457, 1462, 1470.
40. Hooper, *Letters*, 3:1449, 1452, 1454, 1456, 1467.
41. Hooper, *Letters*, 3:1468, 1475, 1478.
42. Hooper, *Letters*, 3:1452, 1453, 1456, 1461, 1474.
43. Hooper, *Letters*, 3:1461.

44. Hooper, *Letters*, 3:1455, 1456, 1463, 1464, 1470, 1473.
45. Hooper, *Letters*, 3:1481.
46. Hooper, *Letters*, 3:1452, 1454, 1466, 1468, 1469, 1478.
47. Hooper, *Letters*, 3:1482, 1483.
48. Hooper, *Letters*, 3:1481.
49. Hooper, *Letters*, 3:1455.
50. Hooper, *Letters*, 3:1456.
51. Sayer, *Jack*, 250.
52. Sayer, *Jack*, 250–51.
53. Hooper, *Letters*, 3:1464–65.
54. C. S. Lewis, "We Have No 'Right to Happiness,'" *The Saturday Evening Post* 236, no. 45 (1963): 10, 12.
55. Richard W. Ladborough, "In Cambridge," in Como, *Remembering C. S. Lewis*, 199.
56. Sayer, *Jack*, 251.
57. W. H. Lewis, ed., *Letters of C. S. Lewis* (London: Bles, 1966), 24.
58. W. H. Lewis, *Letters*, 25.
59. W. H. Lewis, *Letters*, 25. Green and Hooper provide an expanded version of Major Lewis's account, probably from an earlier manuscript that had been edited down by the publisher of his memoir. See Green and Hooper, *C. S. Lewis*, 307.
60. Gresham, *Lenten Lands*, 142–44, 156–57.
61. Gresham, *Lenten Lands*, 150.
62. Gresham, *Lenten Lands*, 157.
63. Gresham, *Lenten Lands*, 157.
64. Hooper, *Letters*, 3:1465.
65. Alister McGrath, *C. S. Lewis: A Life* (Carol Stream, IL: Tyndale, 2013), 359. McGrath does not provide a source for this information.
66. Sayer, *Jack*, 251; Peter Bayley, "From Master to Colleague," in Como, *Remembering C. S. Lewis*, 176; Dundas-Grant, "From an 'Outsider,'" 373–74; Gresham, *Lenten Lands*, 158.
67. Sayer, *Jack*, 251.
68. Sayer, *Jack*, 252.
69. "Memoirs of the Lewis Family, 1850–1930," ed. Warren Hamilton Lewis (Marion E. Wade Center Collection, Wheaton College), 3:140–41, 199.

Index

For More on the Life of C. S. Lewis, See These Earlier Volumes by Harry Lee Poe

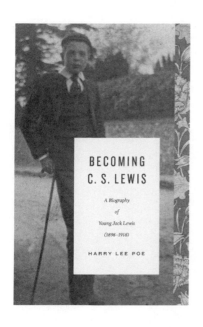

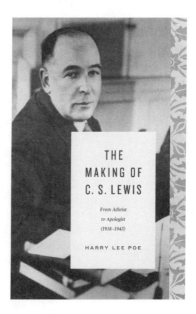

For more information, visit **crossway.org**.